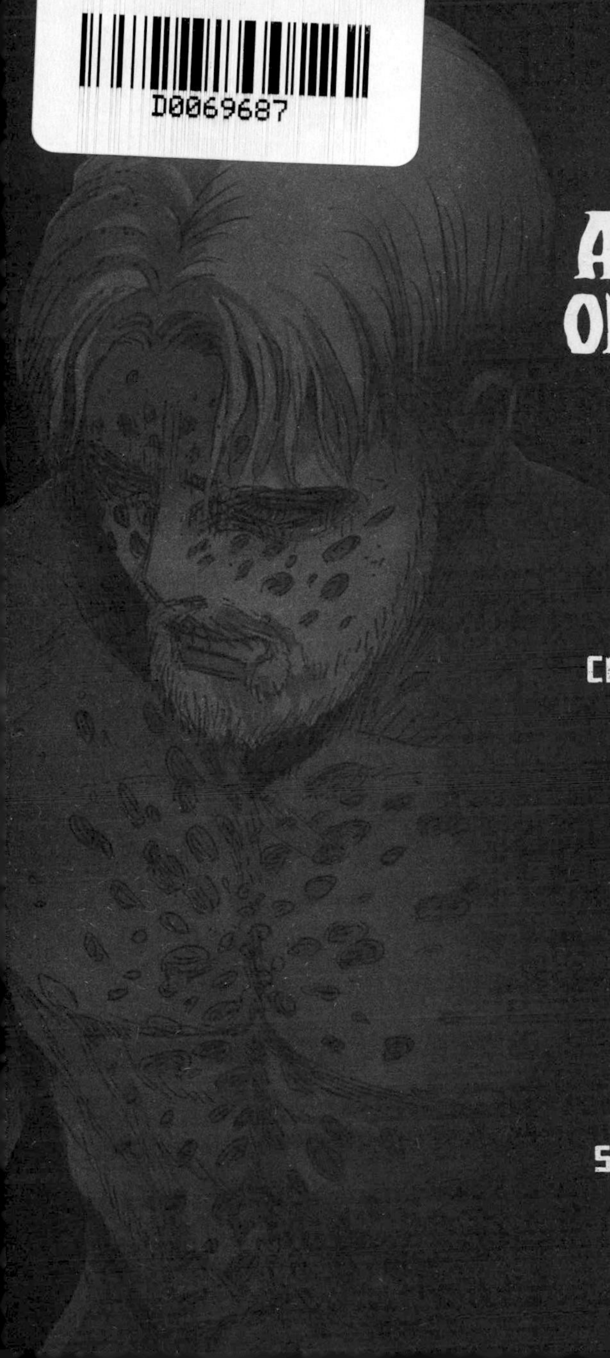

ATTACK ON TITAN 28

HAJIME ISAYAMA

THE CHARACTERS OF ATTACK ON TITAN

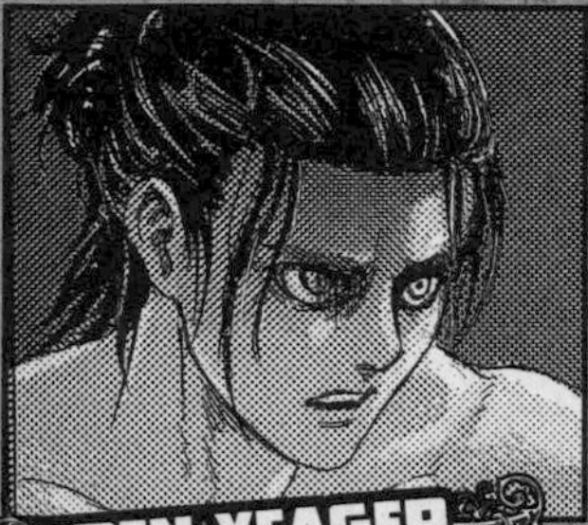

EREN YEAGER

FROM THE 104TH TRAINING CORPS; NOW IN THE SURVEY CORPS. HOLDS THE POWER OF THE ATTACK TITAN AND THE FOUNDING TITAN. BOLDLY INFILTRATED MARLEY ON HIS OWN.

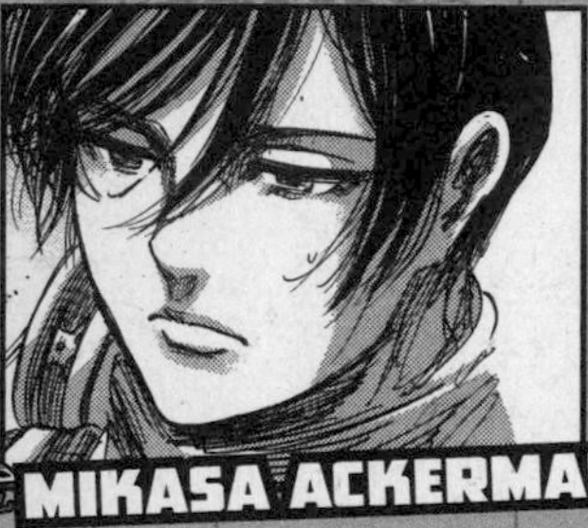

MIKASA ACKERMAN

FROM THE 104TH TRAINING CORPS; NOW IN THE SURVEY CORPS. SHE HAS SHOWN INCREDIBLE COMBAT ABILITIES EVER SINCE SHE WAS A RECRUIT. SHE SEES PROTECTING EREN AS HER MISSION.

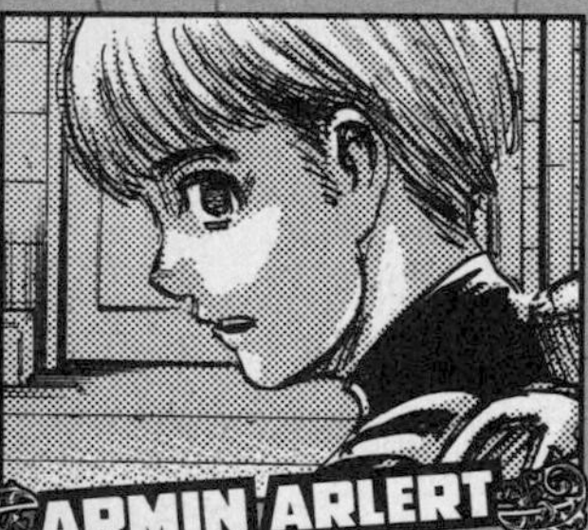

ARMIN ARLERT

FROM THE 104TH TRAINING CORPS; NOW IN THE SURVEY CORPS. HOLDS THE POWER OF THE COLOSSUS TITAN. HE HAS SAVED HIS COMRADES COUNTLESS TIMES WITH HIS SHARP INTELLECT AND BRAVERY.

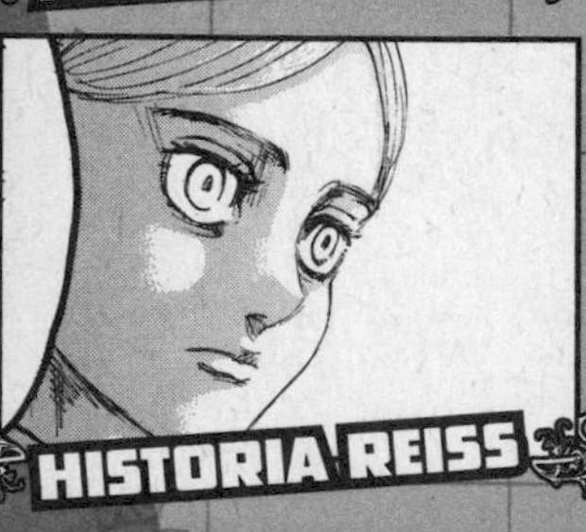

HISTORIA REISS

A DESCENDANT OF THE REISS FAMILY, THE TRUE ROYAL BLOODLINE, HISTORIA HAS NOW ASCENDED TO THE THRONE AS QUEEN. SHE ONCE BELONGED TO THE SURVEY CORPS UNDER THE NAME KRISTA LENZ.

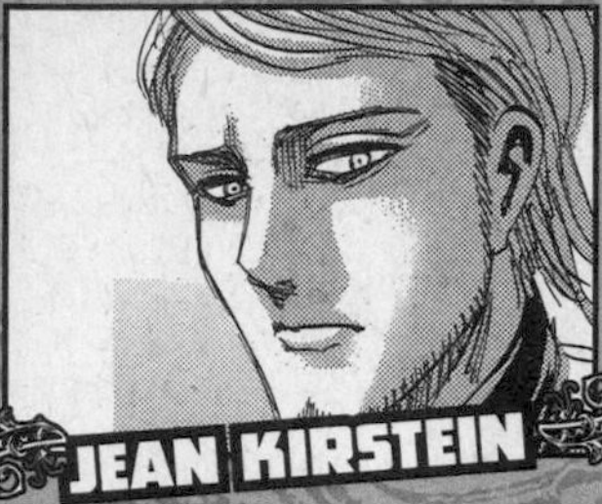

JEAN KIRSTEIN

FROM THE 104TH TRAINING CORPS; NOW IN THE SURVEY CORPS. ONCE KNOWN FOR HIS SARCASTIC PERSONALITY, HE HAS NOW GROWN INTO A LEADER FIGURE.

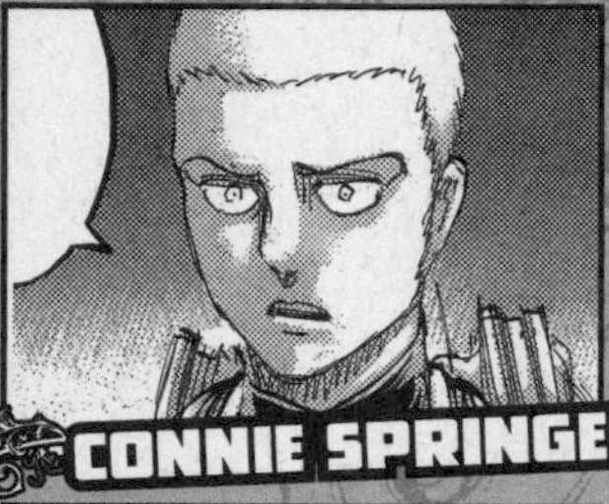

CONNIE SPRINGER

FROM THE 104TH TRAINING CORPS; NOW IN THE SURVEY CORPS. HE IS CHEERFUL IN PERSONALITY, BUT FINDS HIMSELF LOSING EVERYONE IMPORTANT TO HIM... ORIGINALLY FROM RAGAKO VILLAGE.

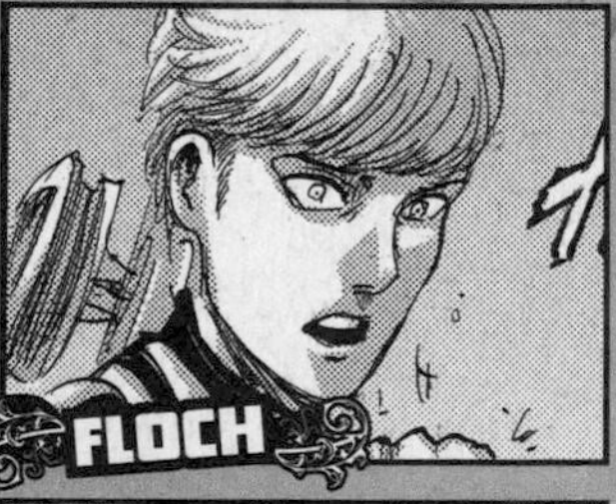

FLOCH

A MEMBER OF THE SURVEY CORPS. A SURVIVOR OF THE DECISIVE BATTLE FOR SHIGANSHINA DISTRICT, WHICH CLAIMED MANY LIVES, INCLUDING ERWIN'S.

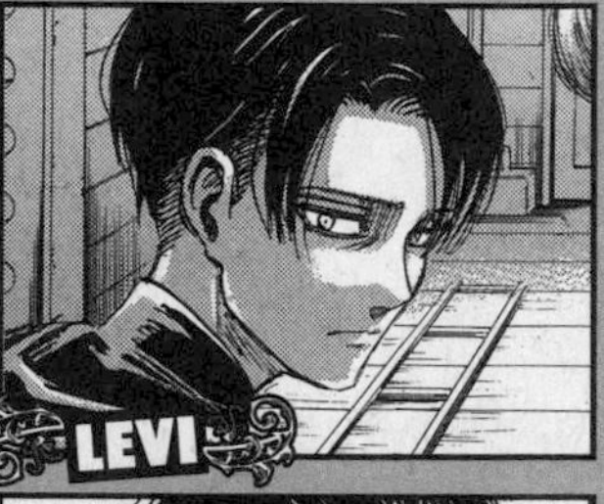

LEVI

A CAPTAIN IN THE SURVEY CORPS. KNOWN AS "HUMANITY'S STRONGEST SOLDIER." HE FIGHTS THROUGH HIS STRUGGLES IN ORDER TO CARRY ON HIS GOOD FRIEND ERWIN'S DYING WISHES.

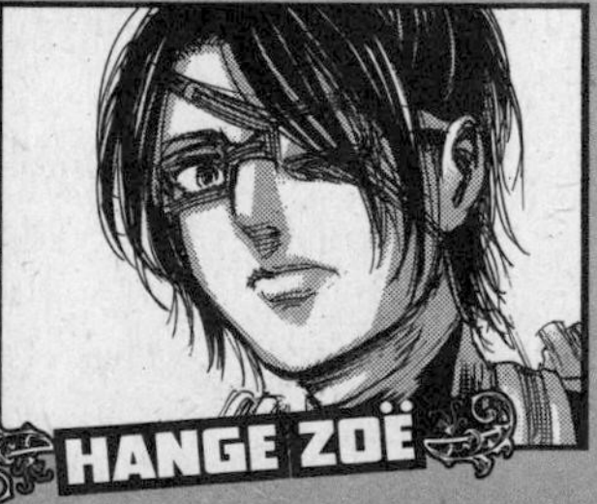

HANGE ZOË

COMMANDER OF THE SURVEY CORPS. DESPITE THE STRANGE WAY HANGE MAY ACT, THEIR KEEN POWERS OF OBSERVATION LED ERWIN TO NAME HANGE HIS SUCCESSOR.

THE NATION OF ELDIA [THE ISLAND OF PARADIS]

THE ELDIAN WARRIORS OF THE MARLEYAN ARMY

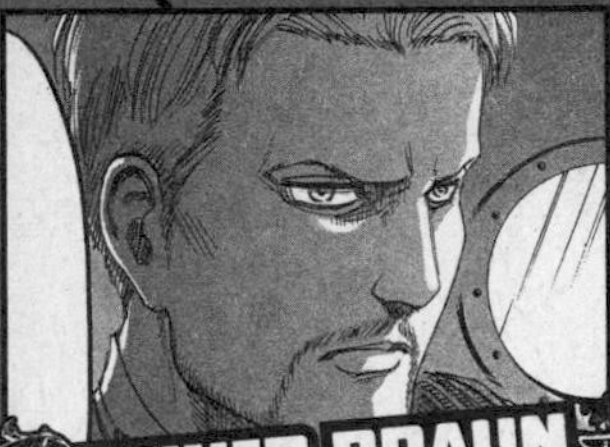

REINER BRAUN

HOLDS THE ARMORED TITAN WITHIN HIM. SINCE HE WAS THE ONLY ONE TO MAKE IT BACK FROM THE MISSION ON PARADIS, HE SUFFERS FROM A GUILTY CONSCIENCE.

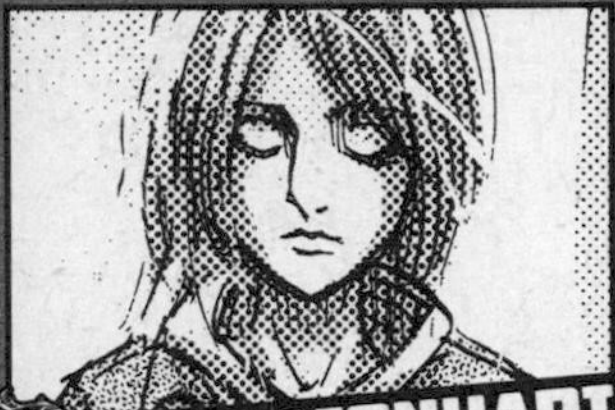

ANNIE LEONHART

HOLDS THE FEMALE TITAN WITHIN HER. A MEMBER OF THE 104TH. SHE HAS BEEN SLEEPING WITHIN A HARDENED CRYSTAL EVER SINCE HER TRUE IDENTITY WAS DISCOVERED.

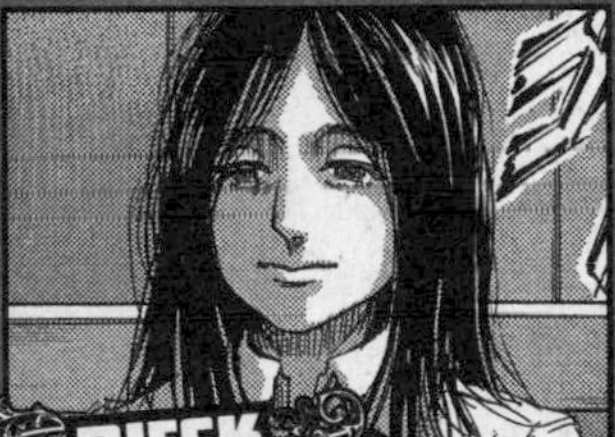

PIECK

HOLDS THE CART TITAN WITHIN HER, CARRYING THE PANZER UNIT ON THE BACK OF THE "CARTMAN" TO FIGHT. HIGHLY PERCEPTIVE.

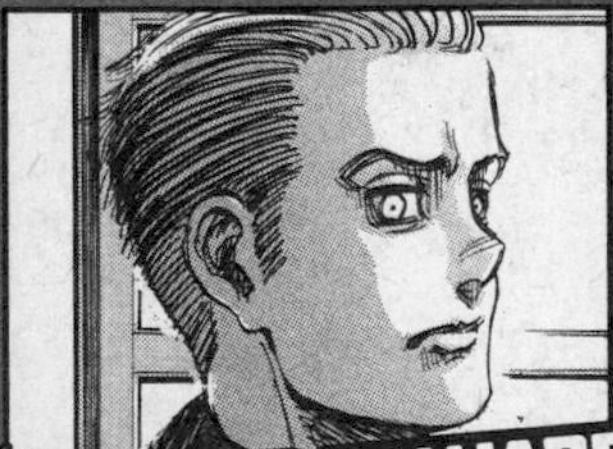

PORCO GALLIARD

HOLDS THE JAW TITAN WITHIN HIM. THERE IS STRIFE BETWEEN HIM AND REINER OVER BOTH THE INHERITANCE OF THE ARMORED TITAN AND THE DEATH OF HIS OLDER BROTHER, MARCEL.

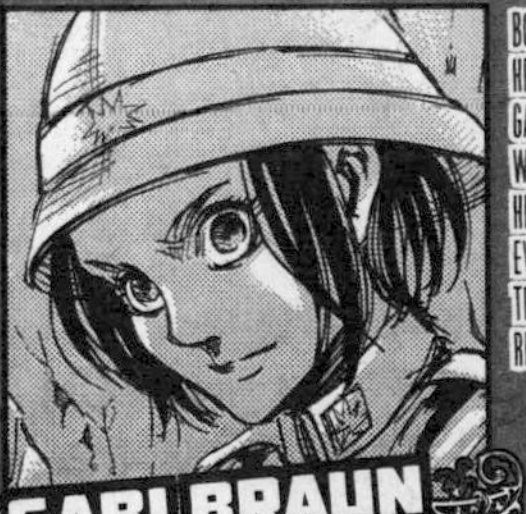

GABI BRAUN

BOLD DESPITE HER SMALL SIZE, GABI IS A DYNAMIC WARRIOR CANDIDATE. HER GOAL IS TO EVENTUALLY INHERIT THE ARMORED TITAN. REINER'S COUSIN.

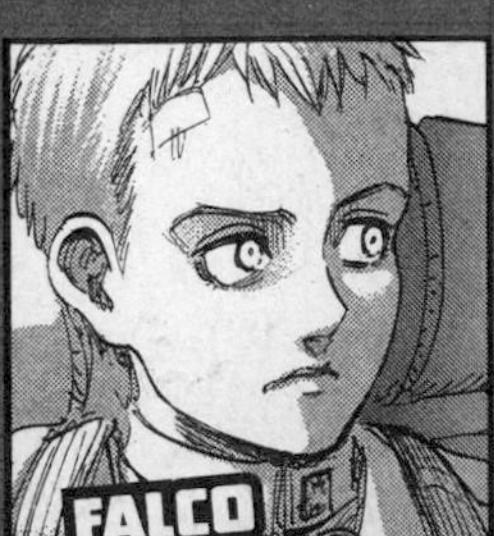

FALCO GRICE

A WARRIOR CANDIDATE HE HAS AFFECTION FOR GABI AND WANTS TO PROTECT HER. DURING EREN'S TIME INFILTRATING MARLEY FALCO COMES IN CONTACT WITH EREN WITHOUT REALIZING H TRUE IDENTITY.

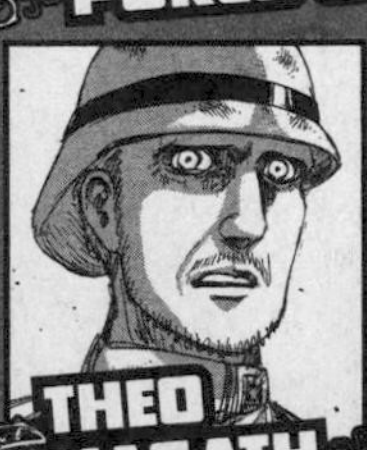

THEO MAGATH

LEADER OF THE WARRIOR UNIT. A MARLEYAN WHO LEADS A UNIT OF ELDIANS.

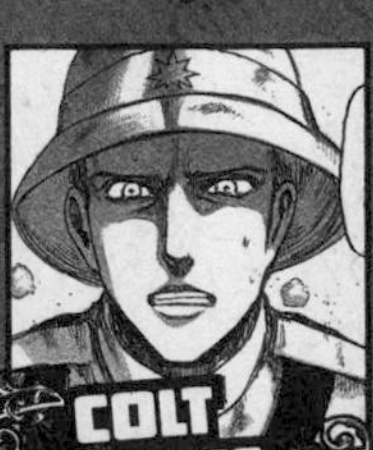

COLT GRICE

FALCO'S OLDER BROTHER. THE OLDEST OF THE WARRIOR CANDIDATES, AND, IN EFFECT, THEIR LEADER.

THE ANTI-MARLEYAN VOLUNTEERS

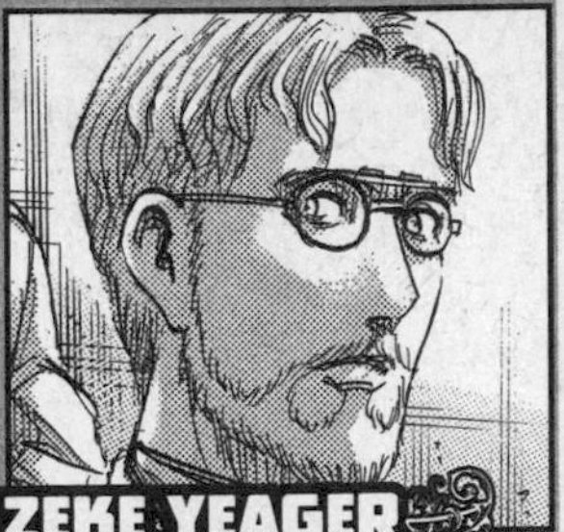

ZEKE YEAGER

HOLDS THE POWER OF THE BEAST TITAN. A LEADER OF THE WARRIORS, HE WAS ONCE KNOWN AS THE "WONDER CHILD." HIS MOTHER IS A DESCENDANT OF THE ROYAL BLOODLINE. HE IS ALSO EREN'S HALF-BROTHER.

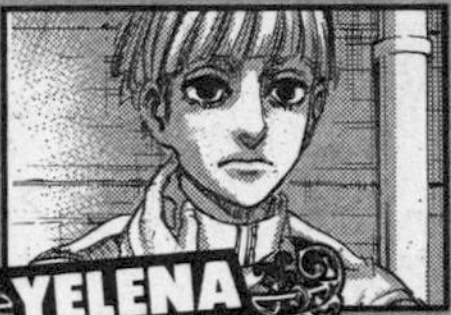

YELENA

YELENA COMMANDS THE VOLUNTEERS AND FOLLOWS ZEKE. SHE DRESSED AS A MAN DURING THE EXPEDITION TO MARLEY IN ORDER TO WORK IN SECRET.

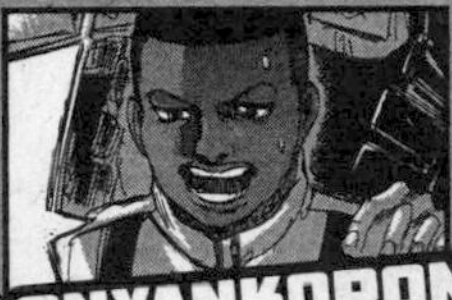

ONYANKOPON

AFTER TRAVELING TO PARADIS WITH YELENA, HE TELLS ITS INHABITANTS OF MARLEY'S ADVANCED CULTURE.

ATTACK on TITAN

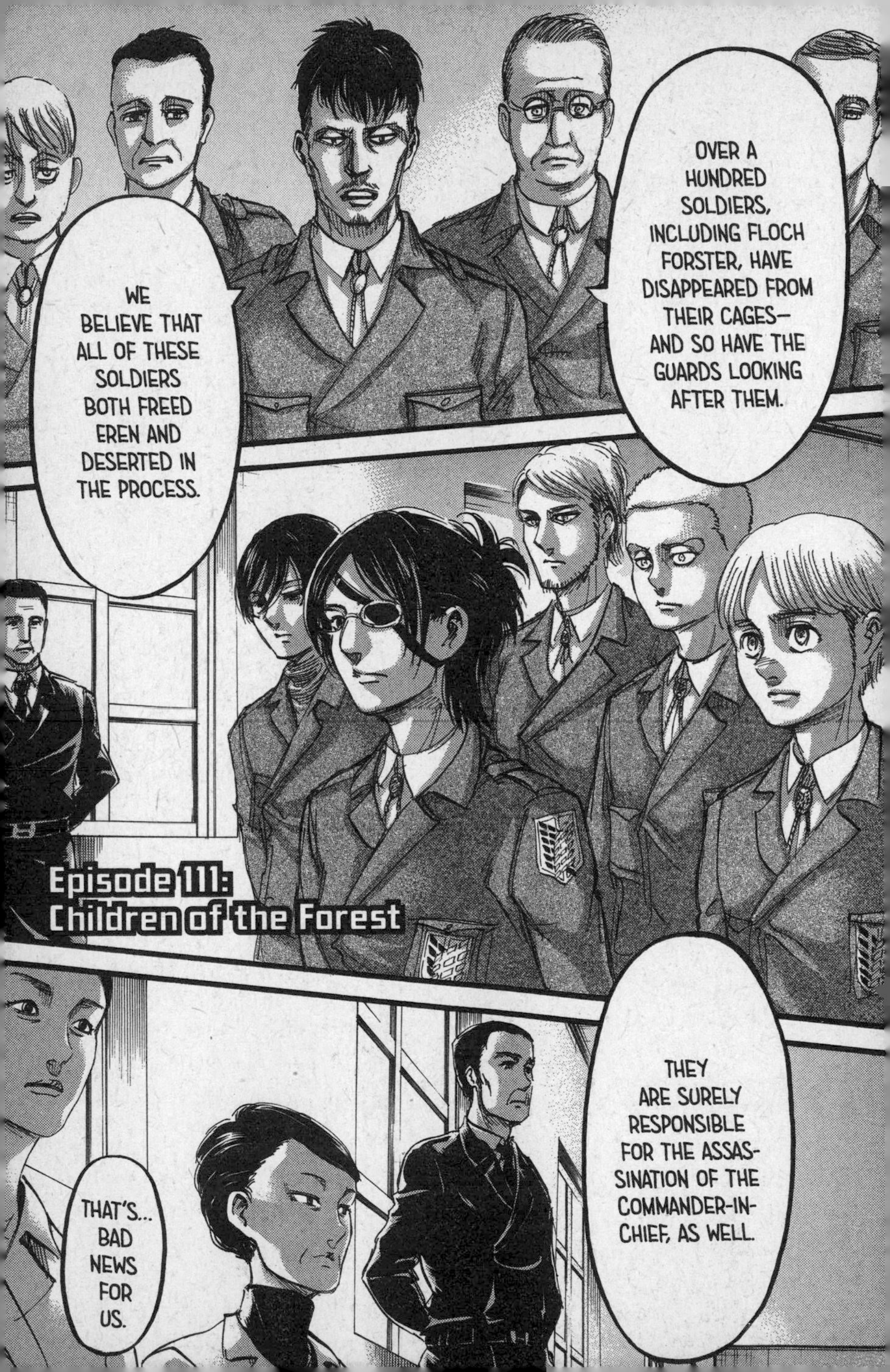
OVER A HUNDRED SOLDIERS, INCLUDING FLOCH FORSTER, HAVE DISAPPEARED FROM THEIR CAGES—AND SO HAVE THE GUARDS LOOKING AFTER THEM.
WE BELIEVE THAT ALL OF THESE SOLDIERS BOTH FREED EREN AND DESERTED IN THE PROCESS.
Episode 111: Children of the Forest
THEY ARE SURELY RESPONSIBLE FOR THE ASSAS-SINATION OF THE COMMANDER-IN-CHIEF, AS WELL.
THAT'S... BAD NEWS FOR US.

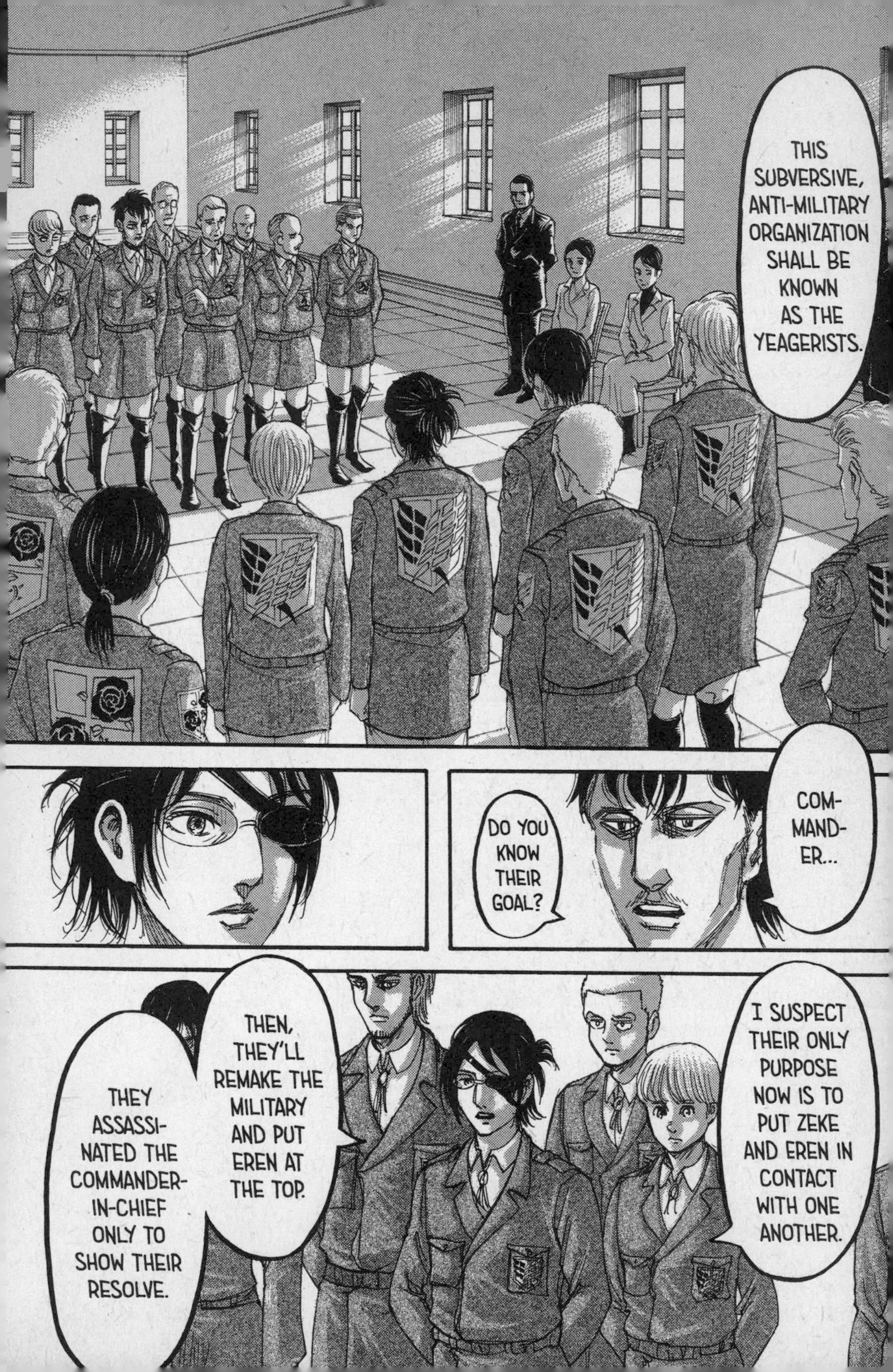
THIS SUBVERSIVE, ANTI-MILITARY ORGANIZATION SHALL BE KNOWN AS THE YEAGERISTS.
COM-MAND-ER...
DO YOU KNOW THEIR GOAL?
I SUSPECT THEIR ONLY PURPOSE NOW IS TO PUT ZEKE AND EREN IN CONTACT WITH ONE ANOTHER.
THEN, THEY'LL REMAKE THE MILITARY AND PUT EREN AT THE TOP.
THEY ASSASSI-NATED THE COMMANDER-IN-CHIEF ONLY TO SHOW THEIR RESOLVE.

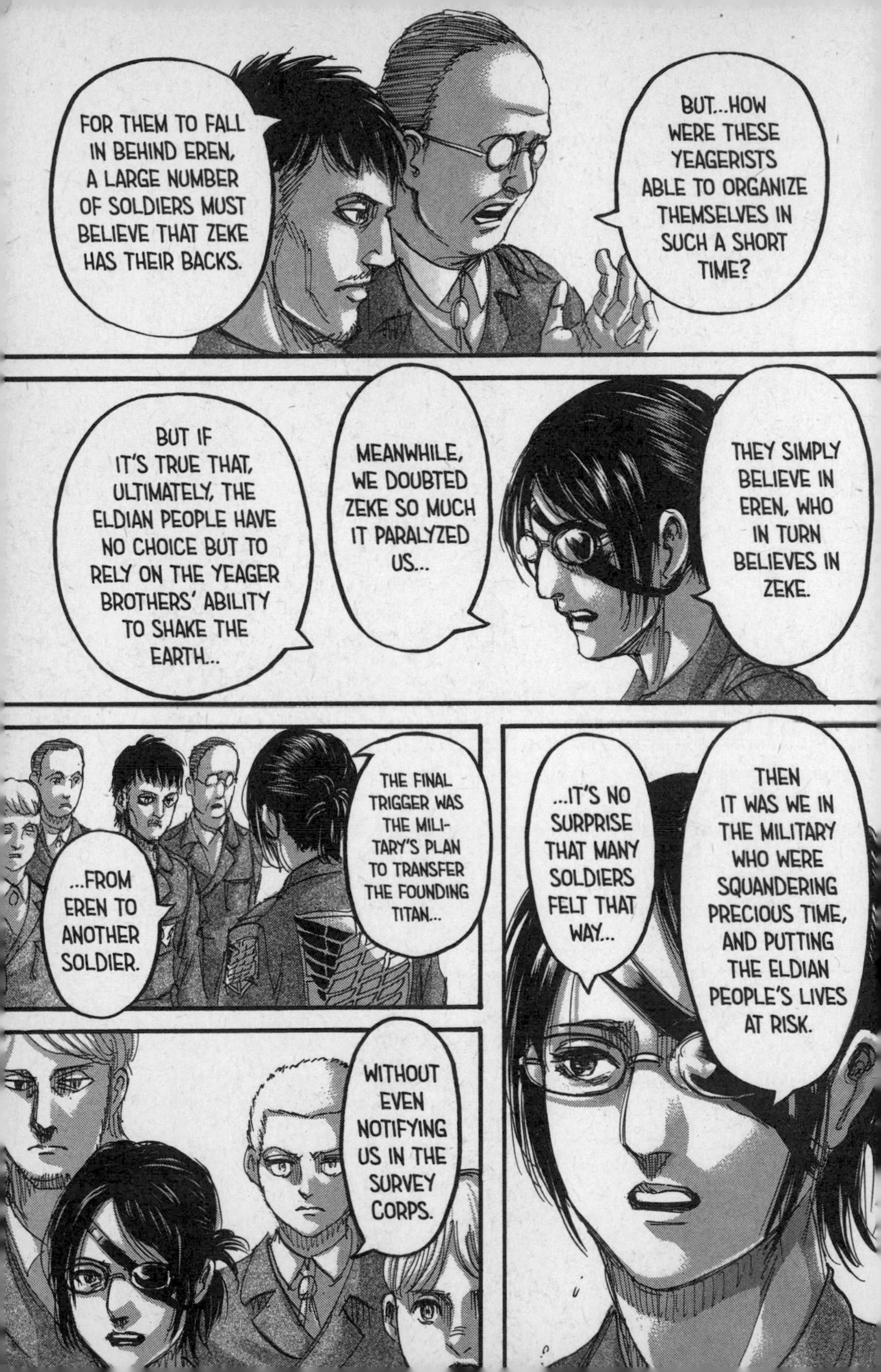
BUT...HOW WERE THESE YEAGERISTS ABLE TO ORGANIZE THEMSELVES IN SUCH A SHORT TIME?
FOR THEM TO FALL IN BEHIND EREN, A LARGE NUMBER OF SOLDIERS MUST BELIEVE THAT ZEKE HAS THEIR BACKS.
THEY SIMPLY BELIEVE IN EREN, WHO IN TURN BELIEVES IN ZEKE.
MEANWHILE, WE DOUBTED ZEKE SO MUCH IT PARALYZED US...
BUT IF IT'S TRUE THAT, ULTIMATELY, THE ELDIAN PEOPLE HAVE NO CHOICE BUT TO RELY ON THE YEAGER BROTHERS' ABILITY TO SHAKE THE EARTH...
...IT'S NO SURPRISE THAT MANY SOLDIERS FELT THAT WAY...
THEN IT WAS WE IN THE MILITARY WHO WERE SQUANDERING PRECIOUS TIME, AND PUTTING THE ELDIAN PEOPLE'S LIVES AT RISK.
THE FINAL TRIGGER WAS THE MILI- TARY'S PLAN TO TRANSFER THE FOUNDING TITAN...
...FROM EREN TO ANOTHER SOLDIER.
WITHOUT EVEN NOTIFYING US IN THE SURVEY CORPS.

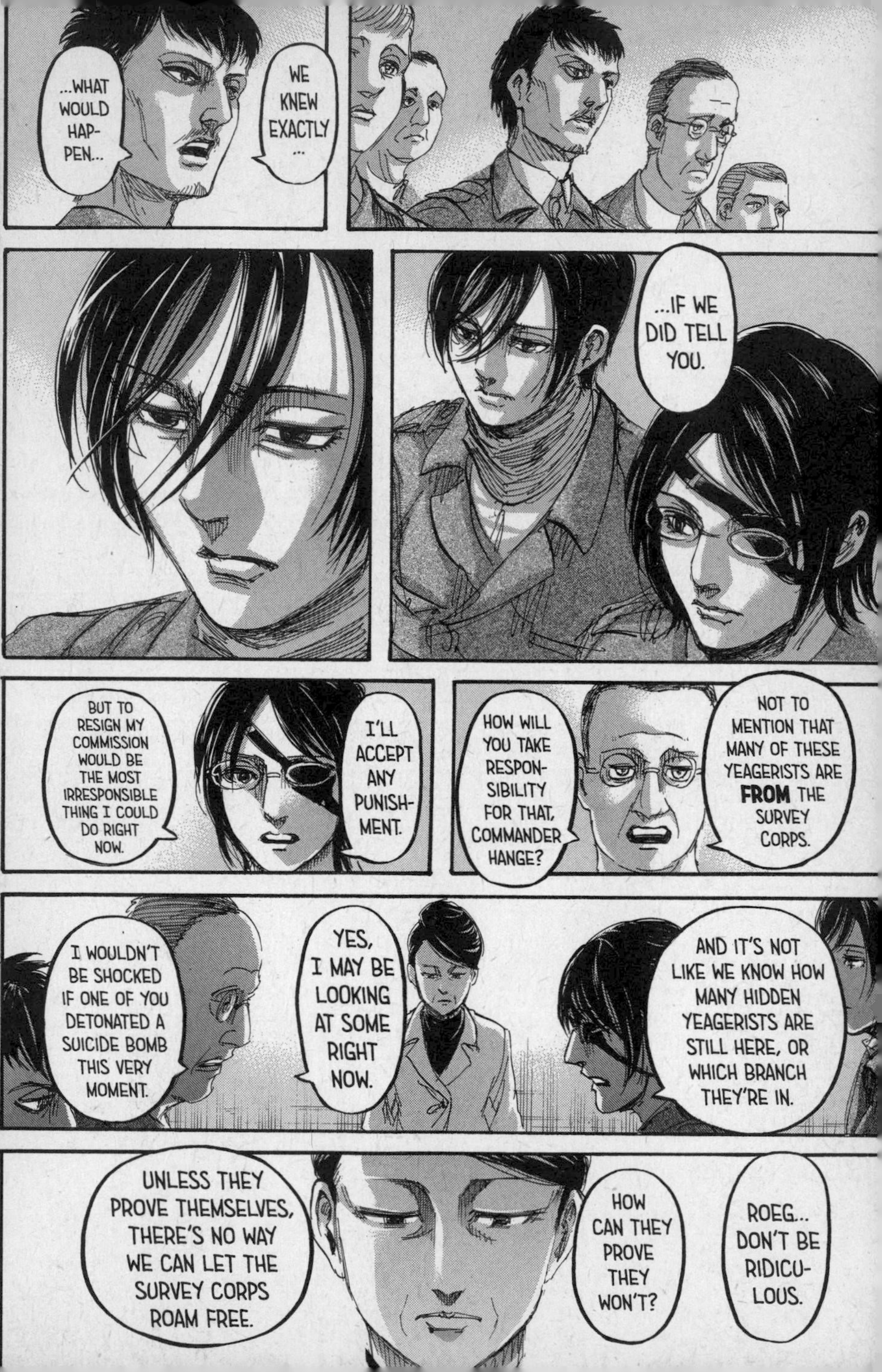
WE KNEW EXACTLY ...
...WHAT WOULD HAP- PEN...
...IF WE DID TELL YOU.
NOT TO MENTION THAT MANY OF THESE YEAGERISTS ARE **FROM** THE SURVEY CORPS.
HOW WILL YOU TAKE RESPON- SIBILITY FOR THAT, COMMANDER HANGE?
I'LL ACCEPT ANY PUNISH- MENT.
BUT TO RESIGN MY COMMISSION WOULD BE THE MOST IRRESPONSIBLE THING I COULD DO RIGHT NOW.
AND IT'S NOT LIKE WE KNOW HOW MANY HIDDEN YEAGERISTS ARE STILL HERE, OR WHICH BRANCH THEY'RE IN.
YES, I MAY BE LOOKING AT SOME RIGHT NOW.
I WOULDN'T BE SHOCKED IF ONE OF YOU DETONATED A SUICIDE BOMB THIS VERY MOMENT.
ROEG... DON'T BE RIDICU- LOUS.
HOW CAN THEY PROVE THEY WON'T?
UNLESS THEY PROVE THEMSELVES, THERE'S NO WAY WE CAN LET THE SURVEY CORPS ROAM FREE.

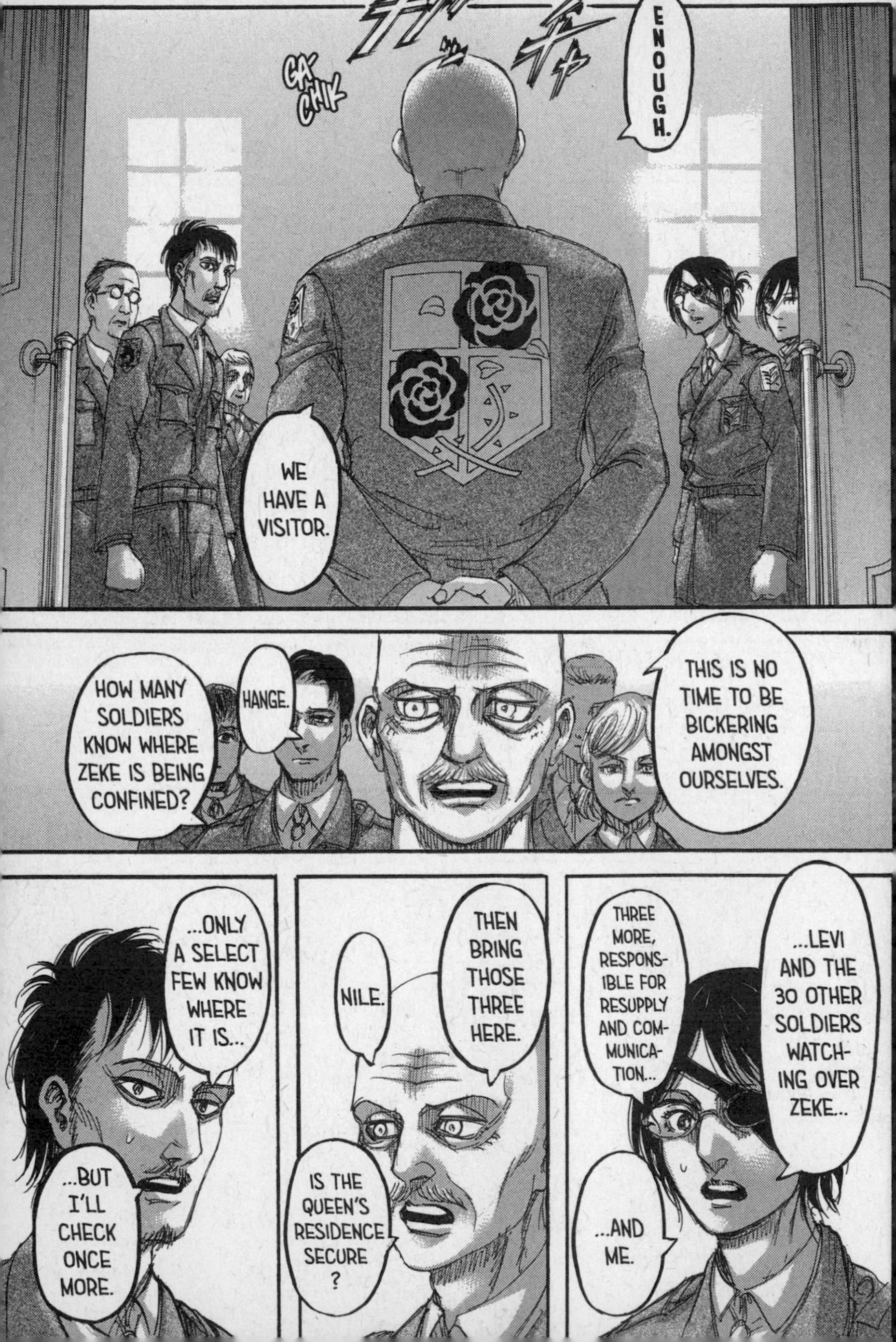
ENOUGH.
GA-CHIK
WE HAVE A VISITOR.
THIS IS NO TIME TO BE BICKERING AMONGST OURSELVES.
HANGE.
HOW MANY SOLDIERS KNOW WHERE ZEKE IS BEING CONFINED?
...LEVI AND THE 30 OTHER SOLDIERS WATCHING OVER ZEKE...
THREE MORE, RESPONSIBLE FOR RESUPPLY AND COMMUNICATION...
...AND ME.
THEN BRING THOSE THREE HERE.
NILE.
IS THE QUEEN'S RESIDENCE SECURE?
...ONLY A SELECT FEW KNOW WHERE IT IS...
...BUT I'LL CHECK ONCE MORE.

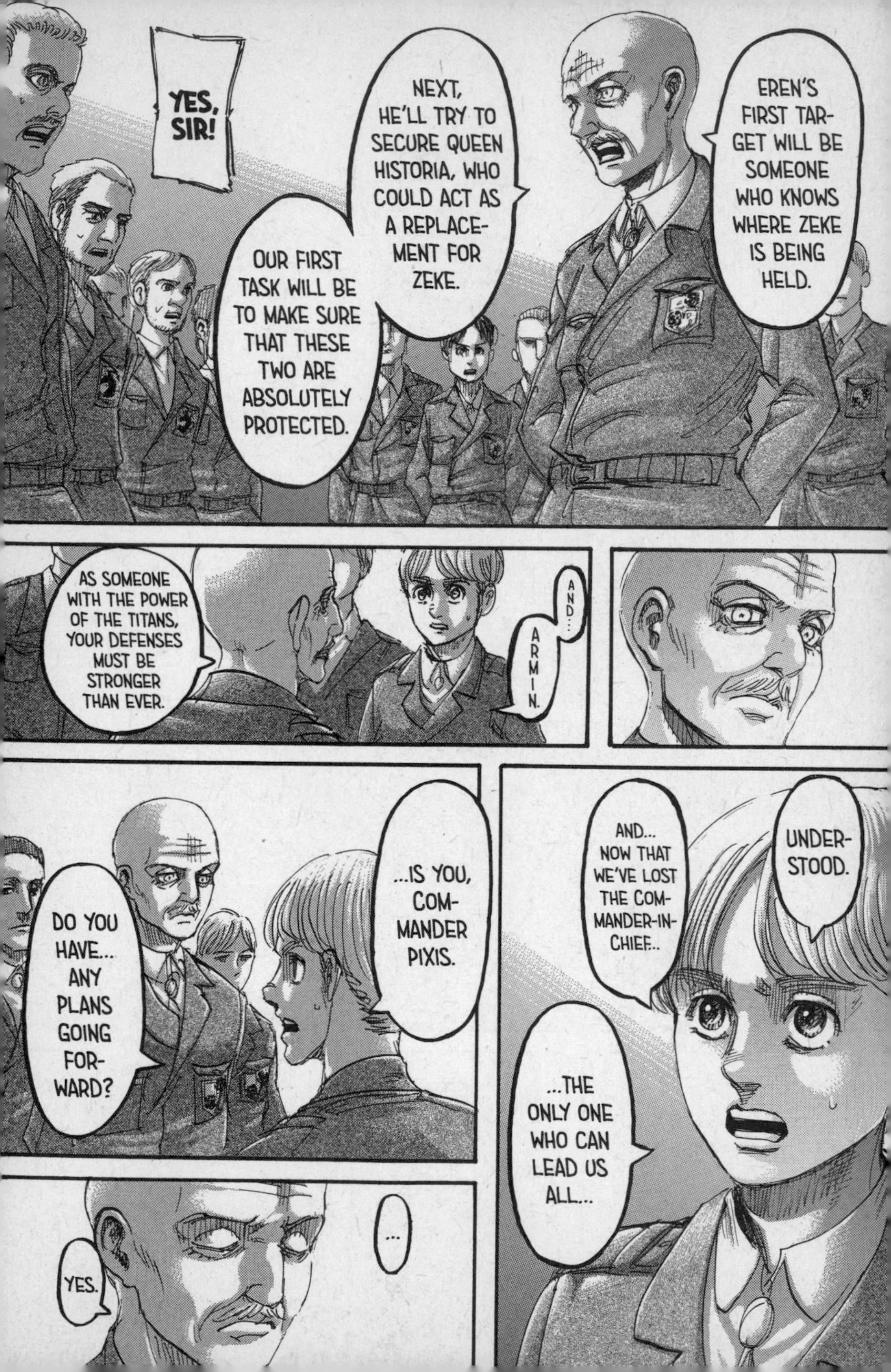
EREN'S FIRST TARGET WILL BE SOMEONE WHO KNOWS WHERE ZEKE IS BEING HELD.
NEXT, HE'LL TRY TO SECURE QUEEN HISTORIA, WHO COULD ACT AS A REPLACEMENT FOR ZEKE.
OUR FIRST TASK WILL BE TO MAKE SURE THAT THESE TWO ARE ABSOLUTELY PROTECTED.
YES, SIR!
AND... ARMIN.
AS SOMEONE WITH THE POWER OF THE TITANS, YOUR DEFENSES MUST BE STRONGER THAN EVER.
UNDERSTOOD.
AND... NOW THAT WE'VE LOST THE COMMANDER-IN-CHIEF..
...THE ONLY ONE WHO CAN LEAD US ALL...
...IS YOU, COMMANDER PIXIS.
DO YOU HAVE... ANY PLANS GOING FORWARD?
...
YES.

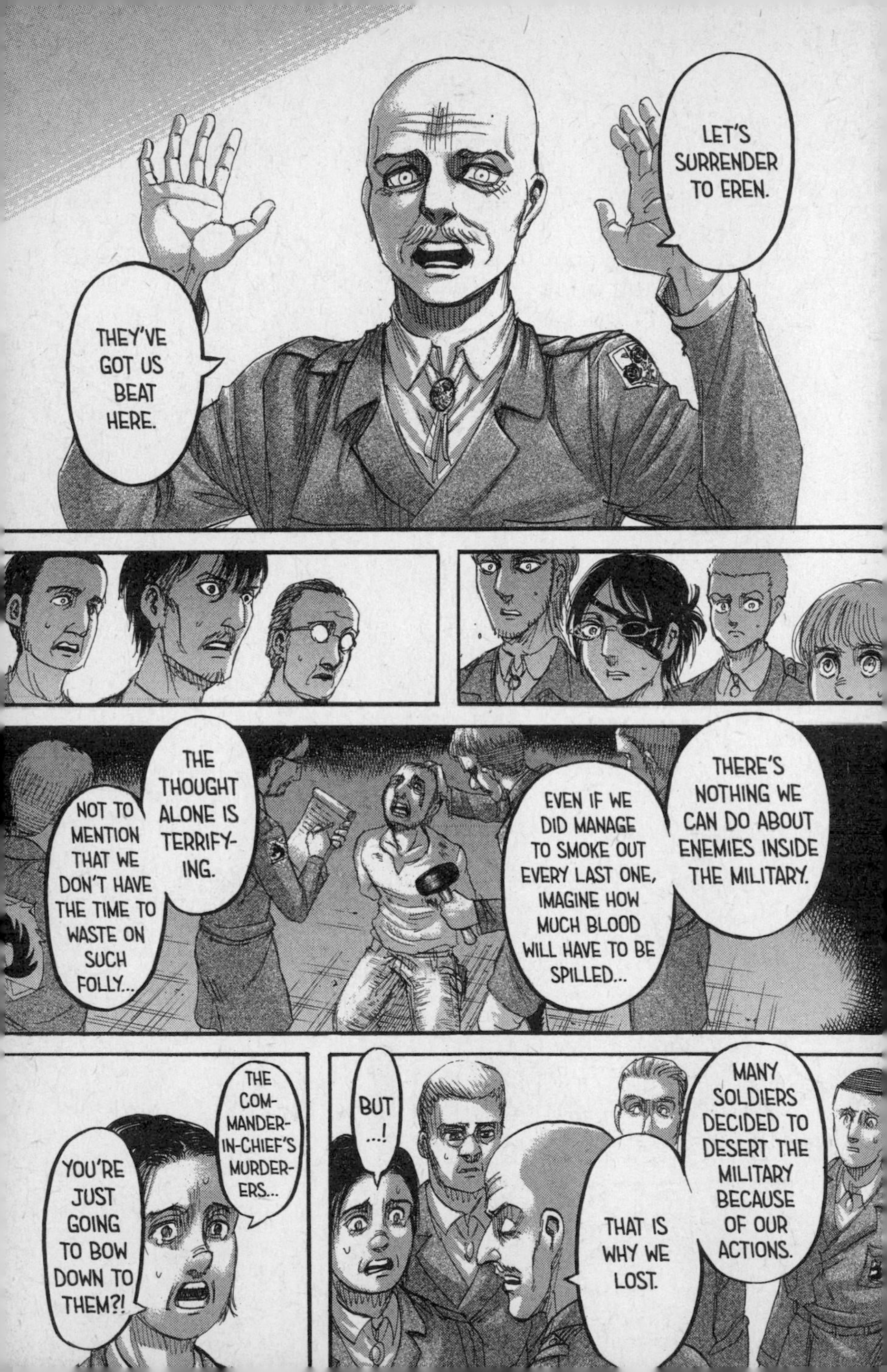
LET'S SURRENDER TO EREN.
THEY'VE GOT US BEAT HERE.
THERE'S NOTHING WE CAN DO ABOUT ENEMIES INSIDE THE MILITARY.
EVEN IF WE DID MANAGE TO SMOKE OUT EVERY LAST ONE, IMAGINE HOW MUCH BLOOD WILL HAVE TO BE SPILLED...
THE THOUGHT ALONE IS TERRIFY-ING.
NOT TO MENTION THAT WE DON'T HAVE THE TIME TO WASTE ON SUCH FOLLY...
MANY SOLDIERS DECIDED TO DESERT THE MILITARY BECAUSE OF OUR ACTIONS.
THAT IS WHY WE LOST.
BUT ...!
THE COM-MANDER-IN-CHIEF'S MURDER-ERS...
YOU'RE JUST GOING TO BOW DOWN TO THEM?!

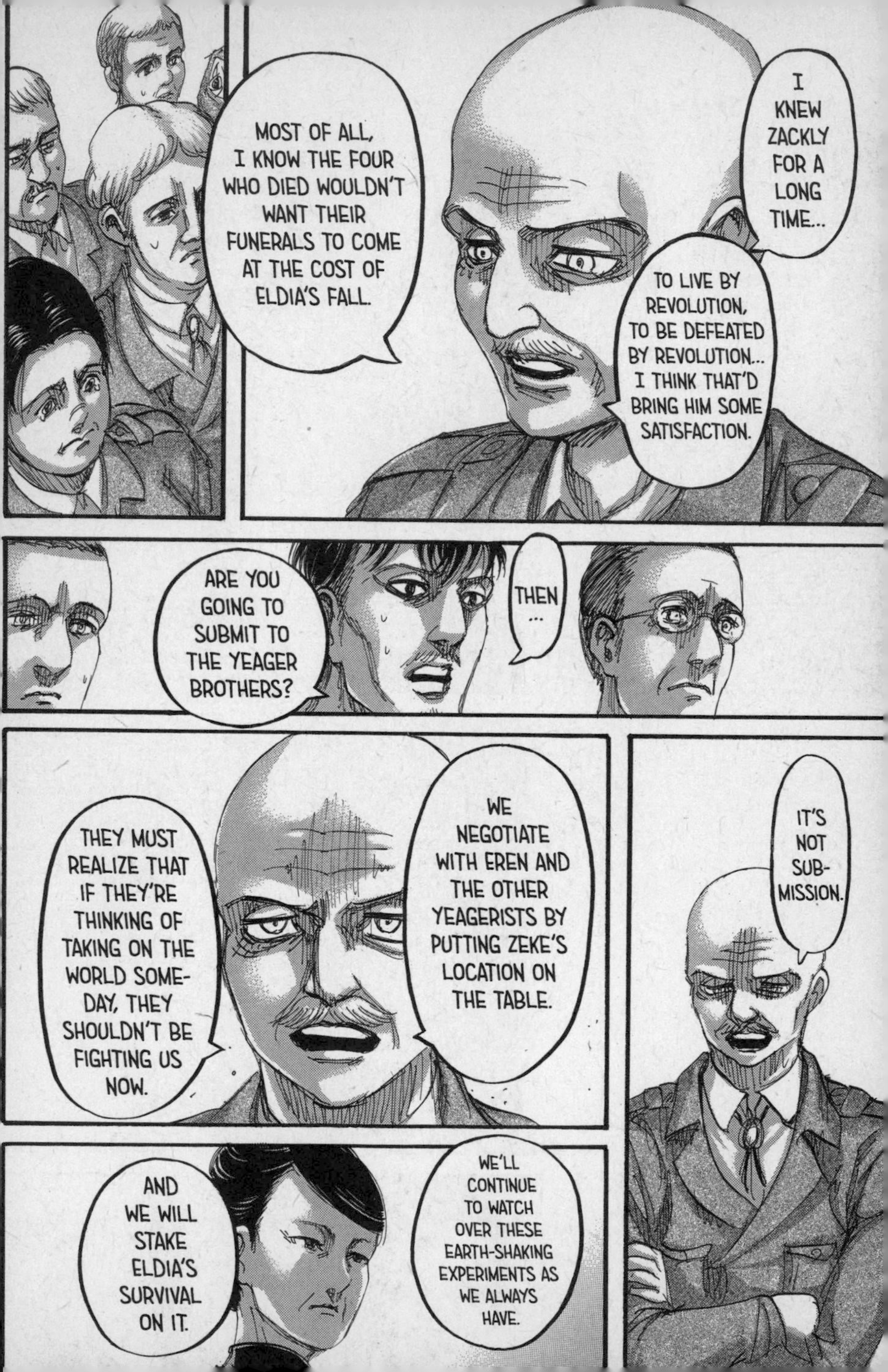

I KNEW ZACKLY FOR A LONG TIME...
TO LIVE BY REVOLUTION, TO BE DEFEATED BY REVOLUTION... I THINK THAT'D BRING HIM SOME SATISFACTION.
MOST OF ALL, I KNOW THE FOUR WHO DIED WOULDN'T WANT THEIR FUNERALS TO COME AT THE COST OF ELDIA'S FALL.
THEN...
ARE YOU GOING TO SUBMIT TO THE YEAGER BROTHERS?
IT'S NOT SUB-MISSION.
WE NEGOTIATE WITH EREN AND THE OTHER YEAGERISTS BY PUTTING ZEKE'S LOCATION ON THE TABLE.
THEY MUST REALIZE THAT IF THEY'RE THINKING OF TAKING ON THE WORLD SOME-DAY, THEY SHOULDN'T BE FIGHTING US NOW.
WE'LL CONTINUE TO WATCH OVER THESE EARTH-SHAKING EXPERIMENTS AS WE ALWAYS HAVE.
AND WE WILL STAKE ELDIA'S SURVIVAL ON IT.

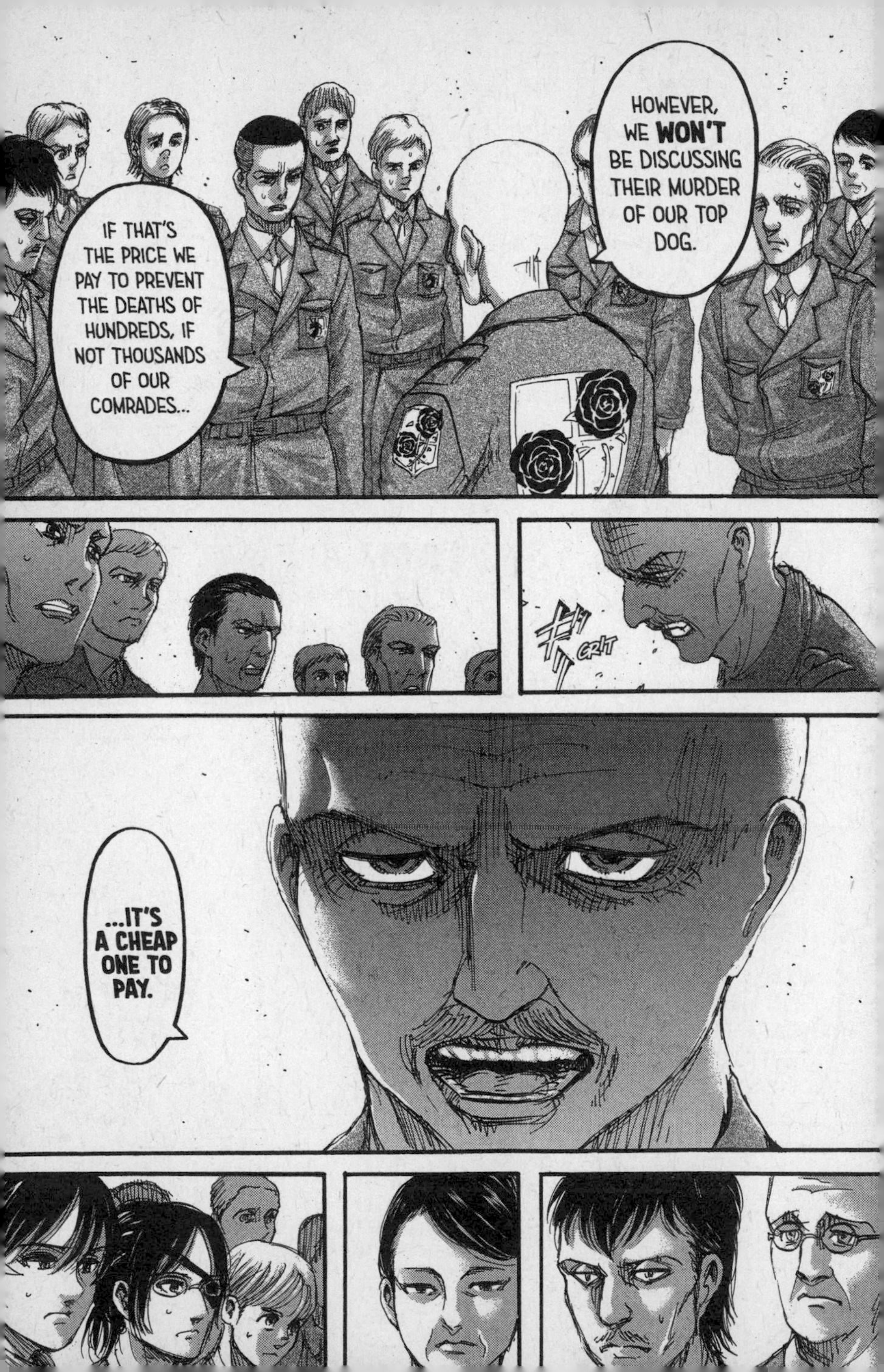
HOWEVER, WE **WON'T** BE DISCUSSING THEIR MURDER OF OUR TOP DOG.
IF THAT'S THE PRICE WE PAY TO PREVENT THE DEATHS OF HUNDREDS, IF NOT THOUSANDS OF OUR COMRADES...
CRIT
...IT'S A CHEAP ONE TO PAY.

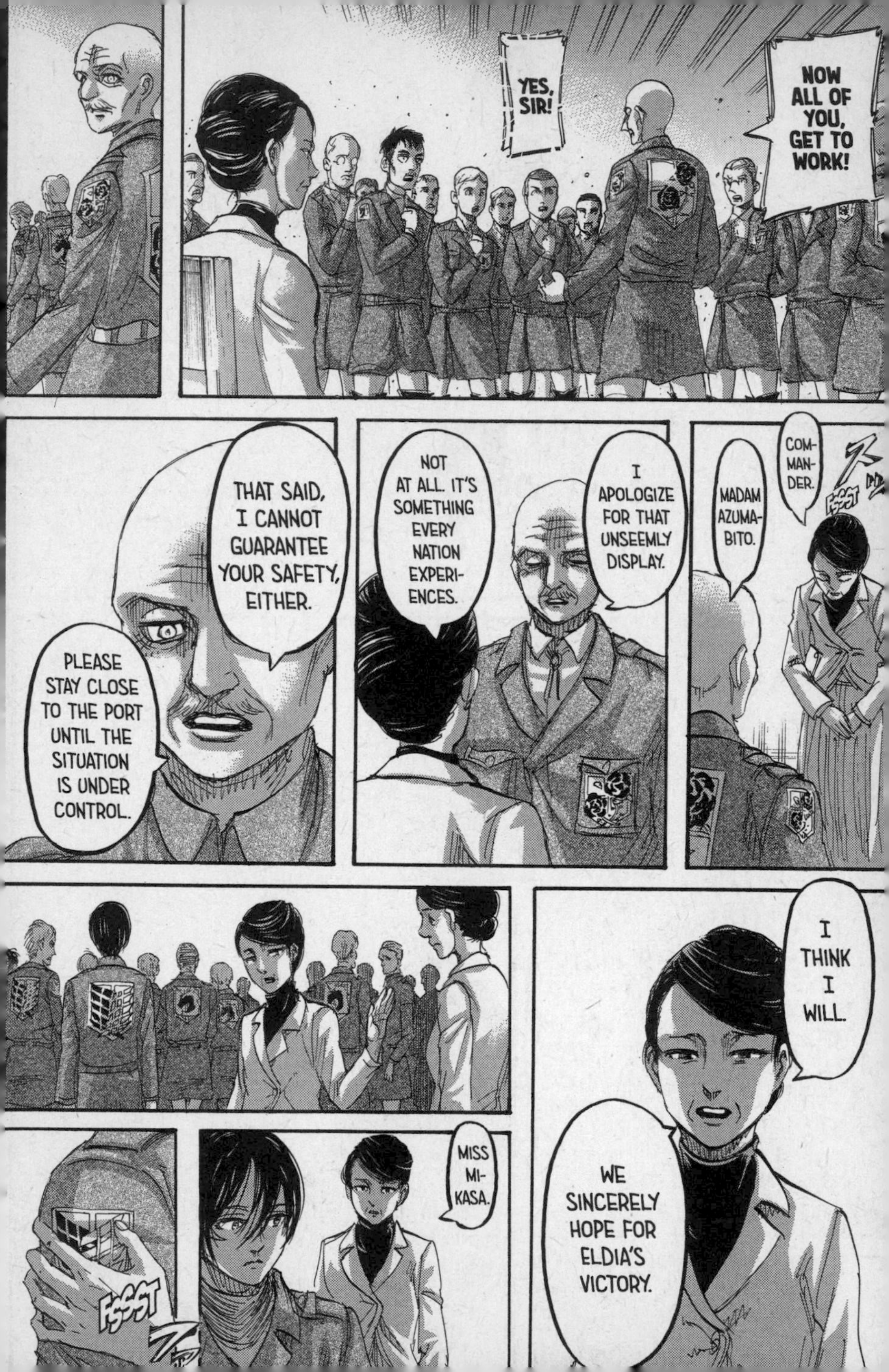
NOW ALL OF YOU, GET TO WORK!
YES, SIR!
COMMANDER.
FSSST
MADAM AZUMABITO.
I APOLOGIZE FOR THAT UNSEEMLY DISPLAY.
NOT AT ALL. IT'S SOMETHING EVERY NATION EXPERIENCES.
THAT SAID, I CANNOT GUARANTEE YOUR SAFETY, EITHER.
PLEASE STAY CLOSE TO THE PORT UNTIL THE SITUATION IS UNDER CONTROL.
I THINK I WILL.
WE SINCERELY HOPE FOR ELDIA'S VICTORY.
MISS MIKASA.
FSSST

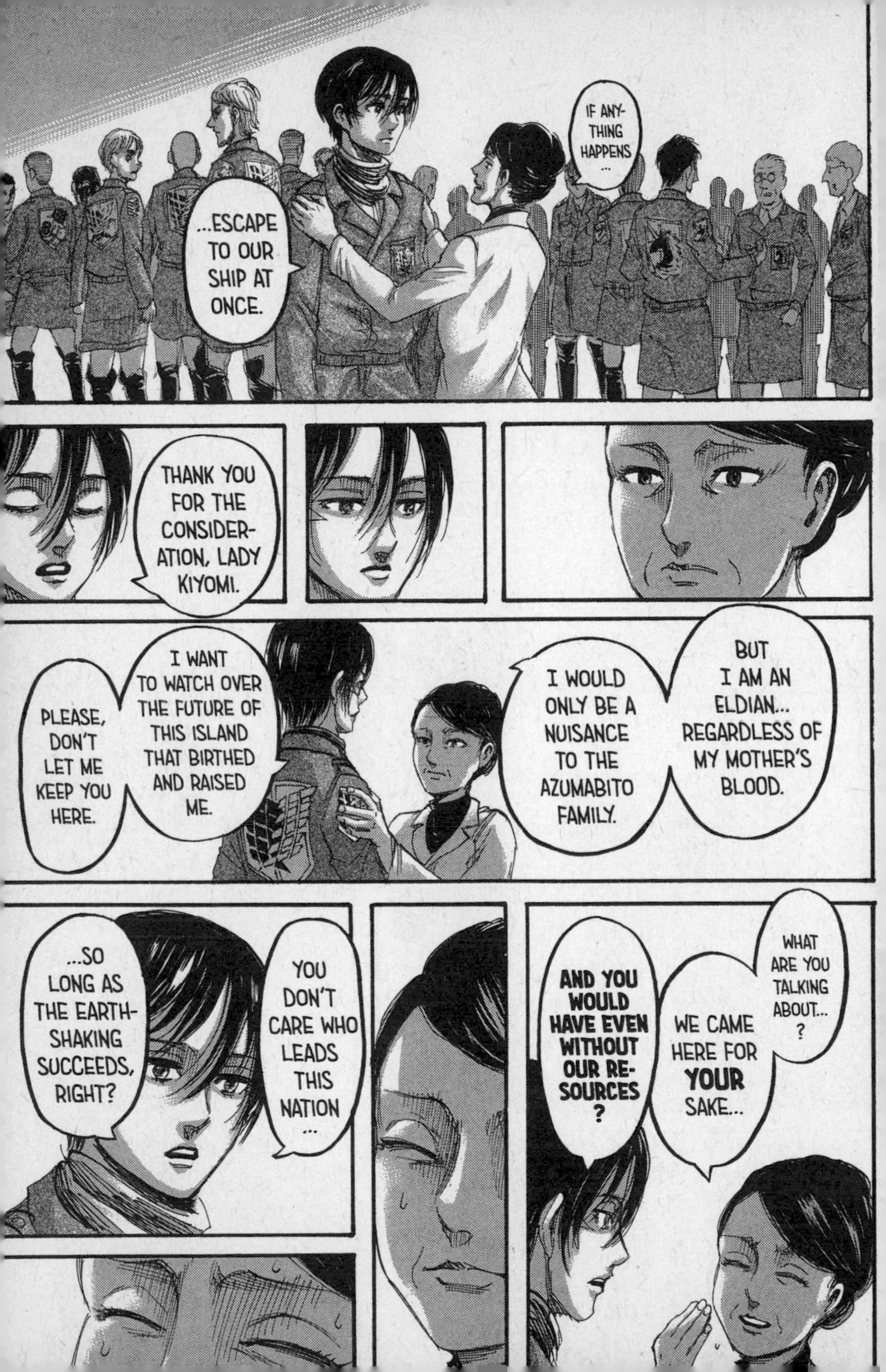
IF ANYTHING HAPPENS ...
...ESCAPE TO OUR SHIP AT ONCE.
THANK YOU FOR THE CONSIDERATION, LADY KIYOMI.
BUT I AM AN ELDIAN... REGARDLESS OF MY MOTHER'S BLOOD.
I WOULD ONLY BE A NUISANCE TO THE AZUMABITO FAMILY.
I WANT TO WATCH OVER THE FUTURE OF THIS ISLAND THAT BIRTHED AND RAISED ME.
PLEASE, DON'T LET ME KEEP YOU HERE.
WHAT ARE YOU TALKING ABOUT...?
WE CAME HERE FOR **YOUR** SAKE...
AND YOU WOULD HAVE EVEN WITHOUT OUR RESOURCES?
YOU DON'T CARE WHO LEADS THIS NATION...
...SO LONG AS THE EARTH-SHAKING SUCCEEDS, RIGHT?

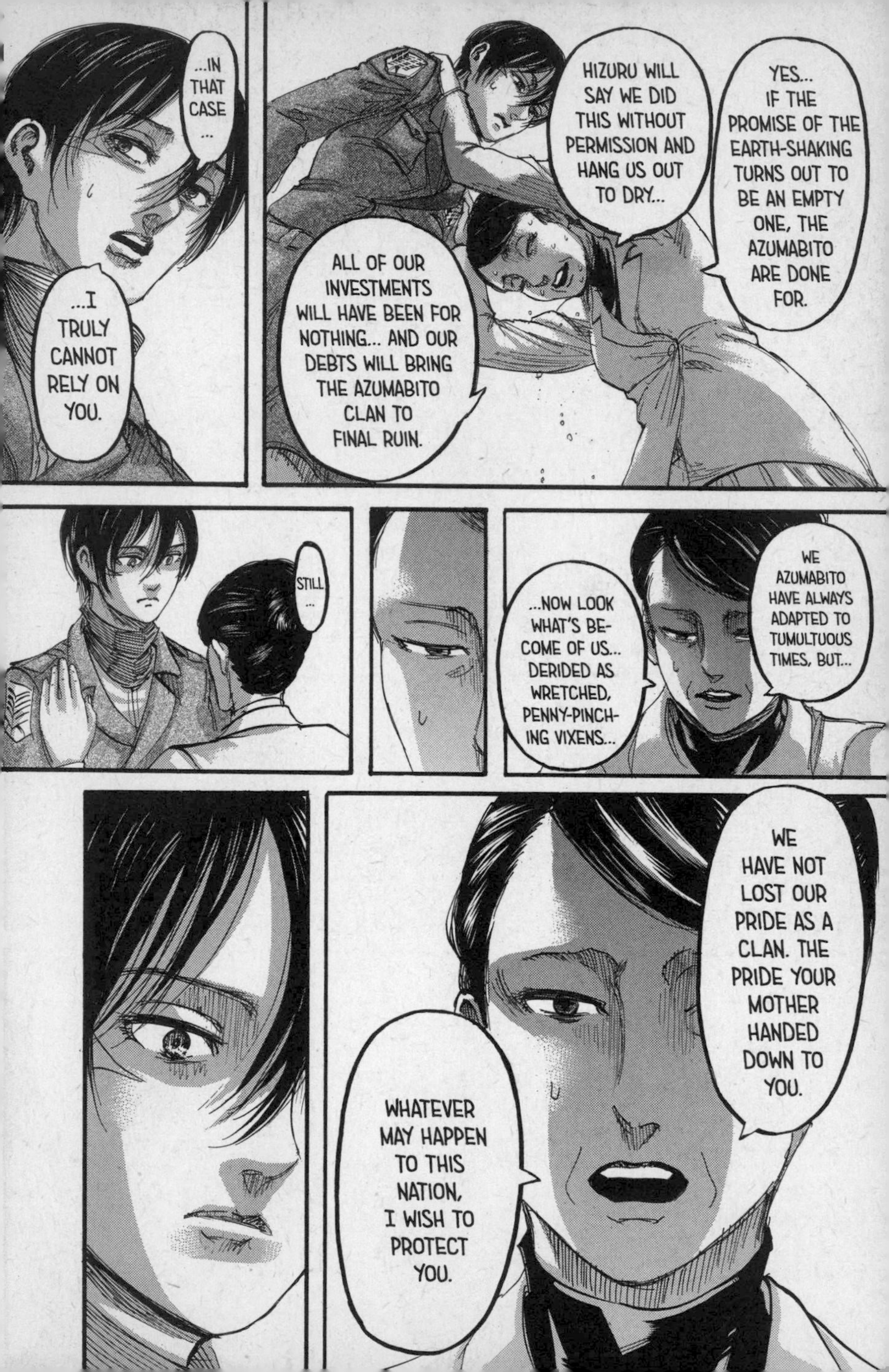
YES... IF THE PROMISE OF THE EARTH-SHAKING TURNS OUT TO BE AN EMPTY ONE, THE AZUMABITO ARE DONE FOR.
HIZURU WILL SAY WE DID THIS WITHOUT PERMISSION AND HANG US OUT TO DRY...
ALL OF OUR INVESTMENTS WILL HAVE BEEN FOR NOTHING... AND OUR DEBTS WILL BRING THE AZUMABITO CLAN TO FINAL RUIN.
...IN THAT CASE...
...I TRULY CANNOT RELY ON YOU.
WE AZUMABITO HAVE ALWAYS ADAPTED TO TUMULTUOUS TIMES, BUT...
...NOW LOOK WHAT'S BE-COME OF US... DERIDED AS WRETCHED, PENNY-PINCH-ING VIXENS...
STILL...
WE HAVE NOT LOST OUR PRIDE AS A CLAN. THE PRIDE YOUR MOTHER HANDED DOWN TO YOU.
WHATEVER MAY HAPPEN TO THIS NATION, I WISH TO PROTECT YOU.

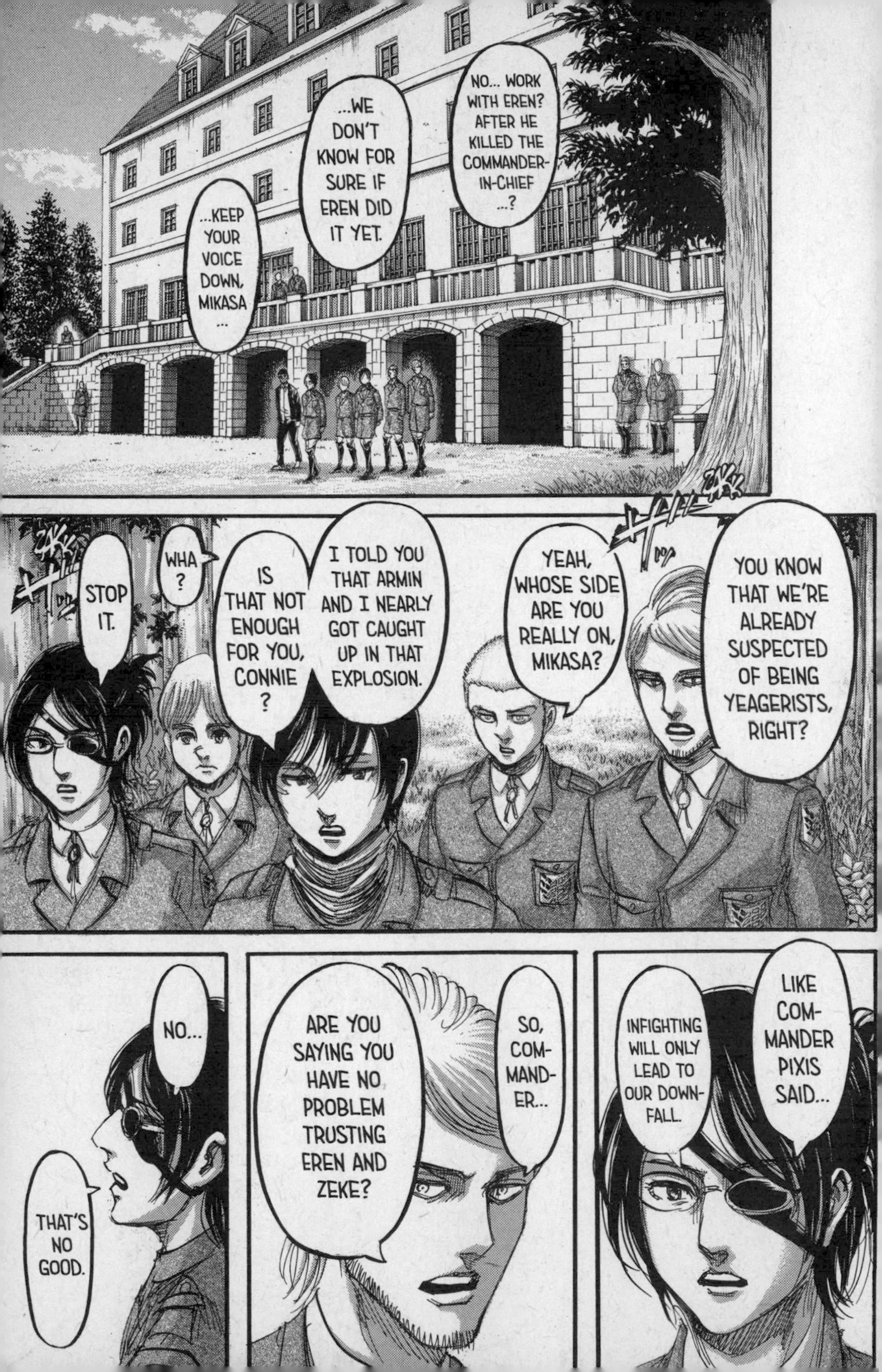
NO... WORK WITH EREN? AFTER HE KILLED THE COMMANDER-IN-CHIEF ...?
...WE DON'T KNOW FOR SURE IF EREN DID IT YET.
...KEEP YOUR VOICE DOWN, MIKASA ...
YOU KNOW THAT WE'RE ALREADY SUSPECTED OF BEING YEAGERISTS, RIGHT?
YEAH, WHOSE SIDE ARE YOU REALLY ON, MIKASA?
I TOLD YOU THAT ARMIN AND I NEARLY GOT CAUGHT UP IN THAT EXPLOSION.
IS THAT NOT ENOUGH FOR YOU, CONNIE ?
WHA ?
STOP IT.
LIKE COMMANDER PIXIS SAID...
INFIGHTING WILL ONLY LEAD TO OUR DOWNFALL.
SO, COMMANDER...
ARE YOU SAYING YOU HAVE NO PROBLEM TRUSTING EREN AND ZEKE?
NO...
THAT'S NO GOOD.

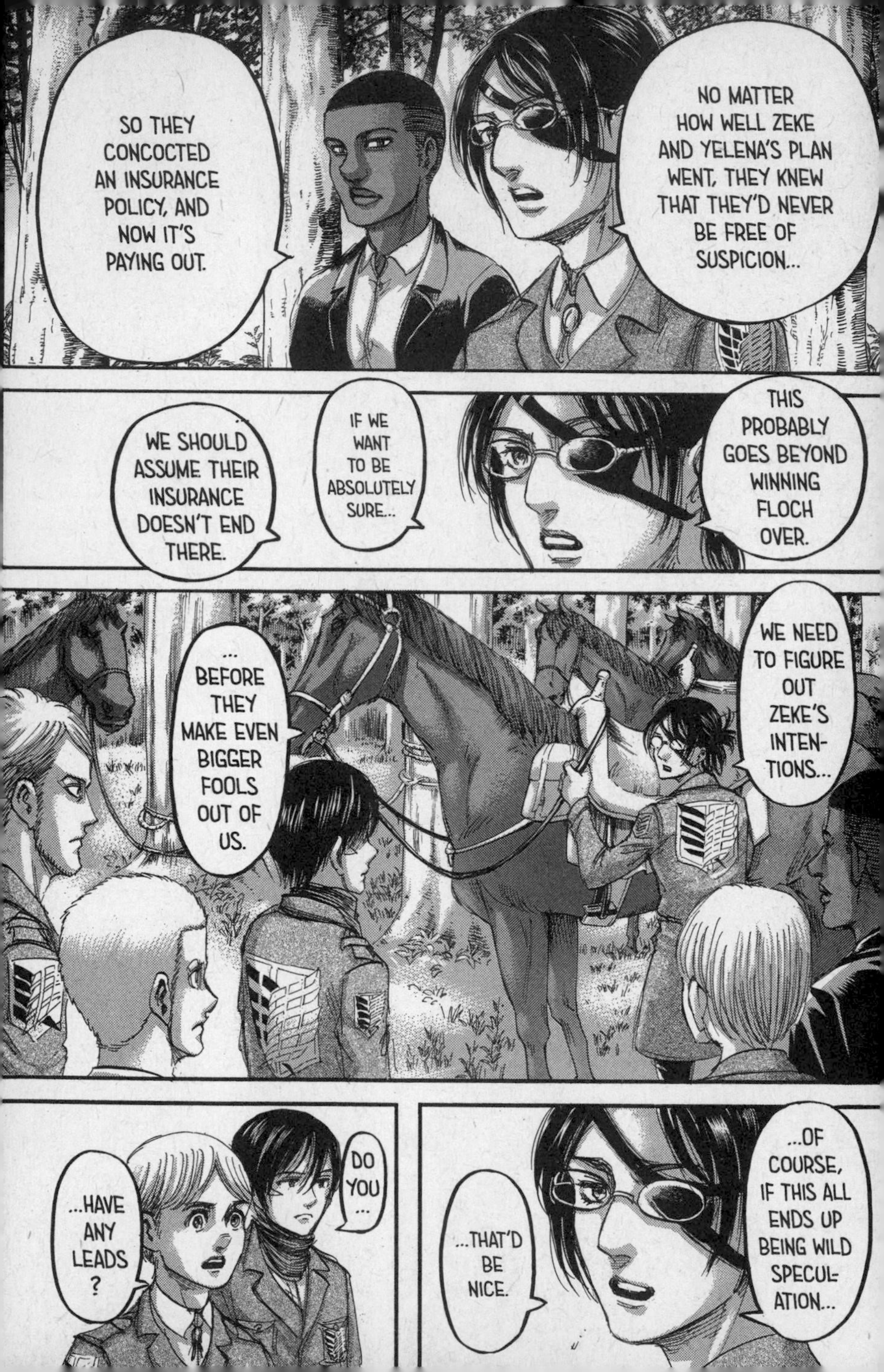
NO MATTER HOW WELL ZEKE AND YELENA'S PLAN WENT, THEY KNEW THAT THEY'D NEVER BE FREE OF SUSPICION...
SO THEY CONCOCTED AN INSURANCE POLICY, AND NOW IT'S PAYING OUT.
THIS PROBABLY GOES BEYOND WINNING FLOCH OVER.
IF WE WANT TO BE ABSOLUTELY SURE...
...WE SHOULD ASSUME THEIR INSURANCE DOESN'T END THERE.
WE NEED TO FIGURE OUT ZEKE'S INTEN-TIONS...
...BEFORE THEY MAKE EVEN BIGGER FOOLS OUT OF US.
...OF COURSE, IF THIS ALL ENDS UP BEING WILD SPECUL-ATION...
...THAT'D BE NICE.
DO YOU...
...HAVE ANY LEADS?

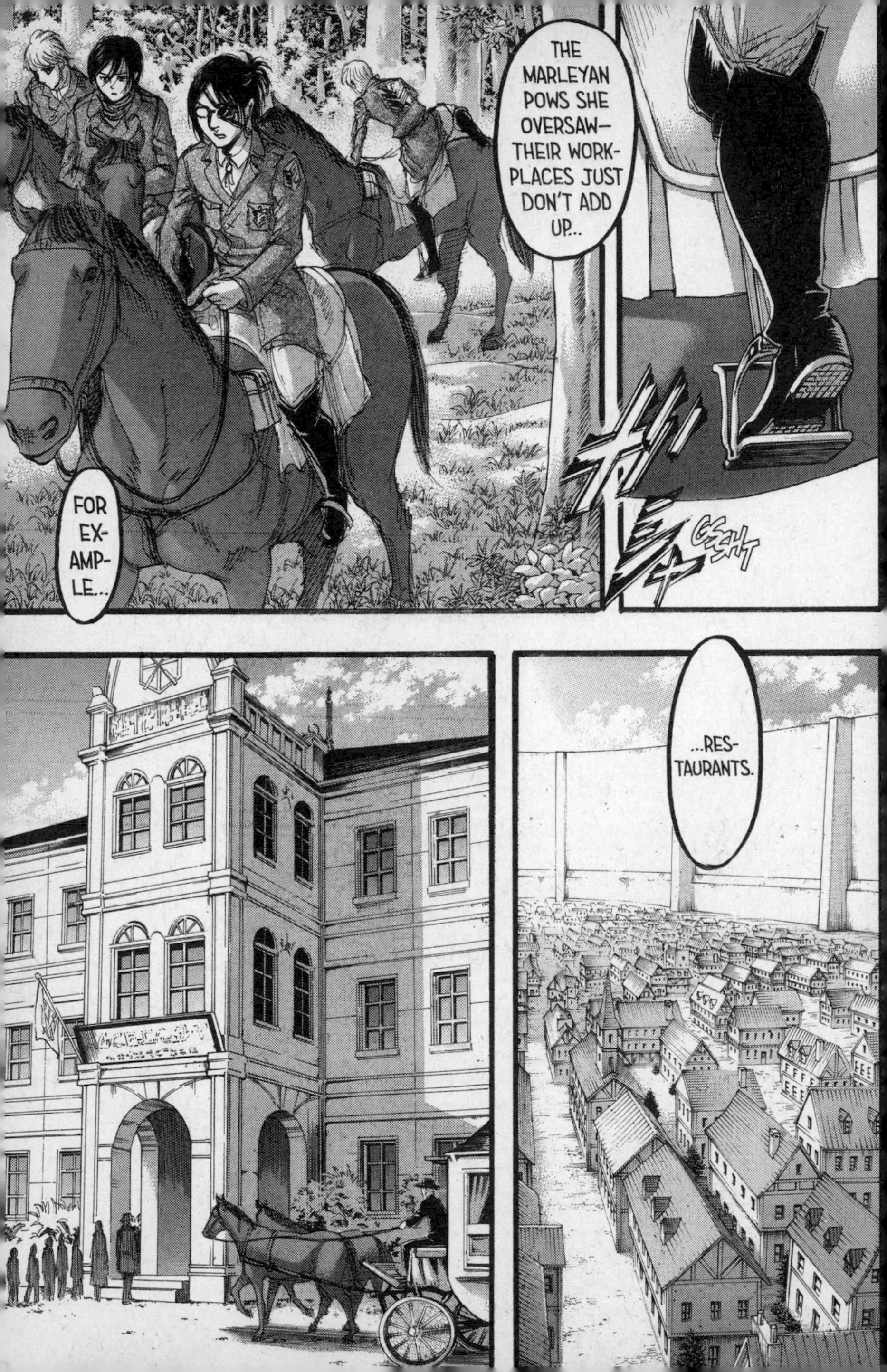
GSSHT
THE MARLEYAN POWS SHE OVERSAW—THEIR WORKPLACES JUST DON'T ADD UP...
FOR EXAMPLE...
...RESTAURANTS.

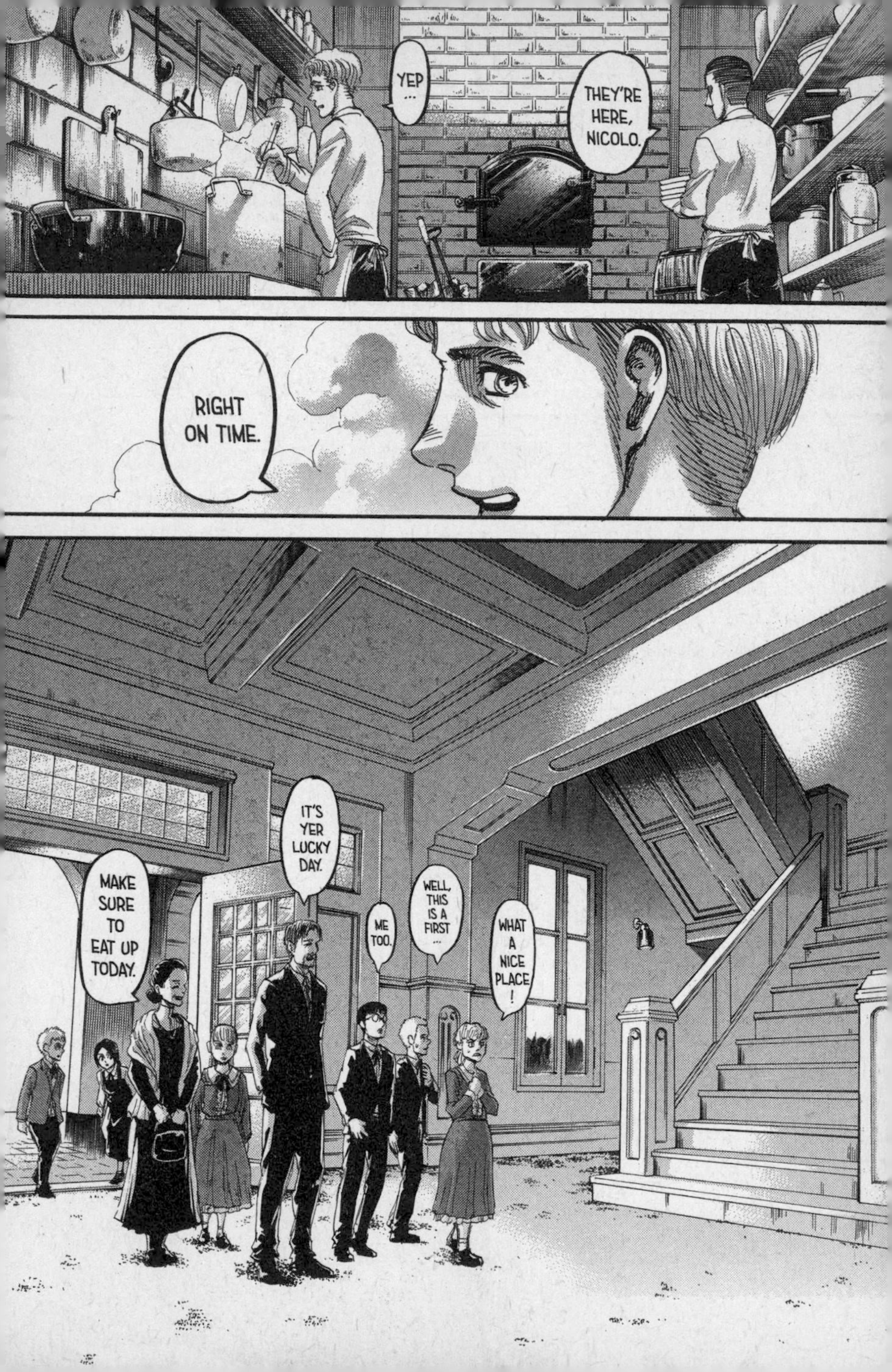
THEY'RE HERE, NICOLO.
YEP ...
RIGHT ON TIME.
WHAT A NICE PLACE!
WELL, THIS IS A FIRST ...
ME TOO.
IT'S YER LUCKY DAY.
MAKE SURE TO EAT UP TODAY.

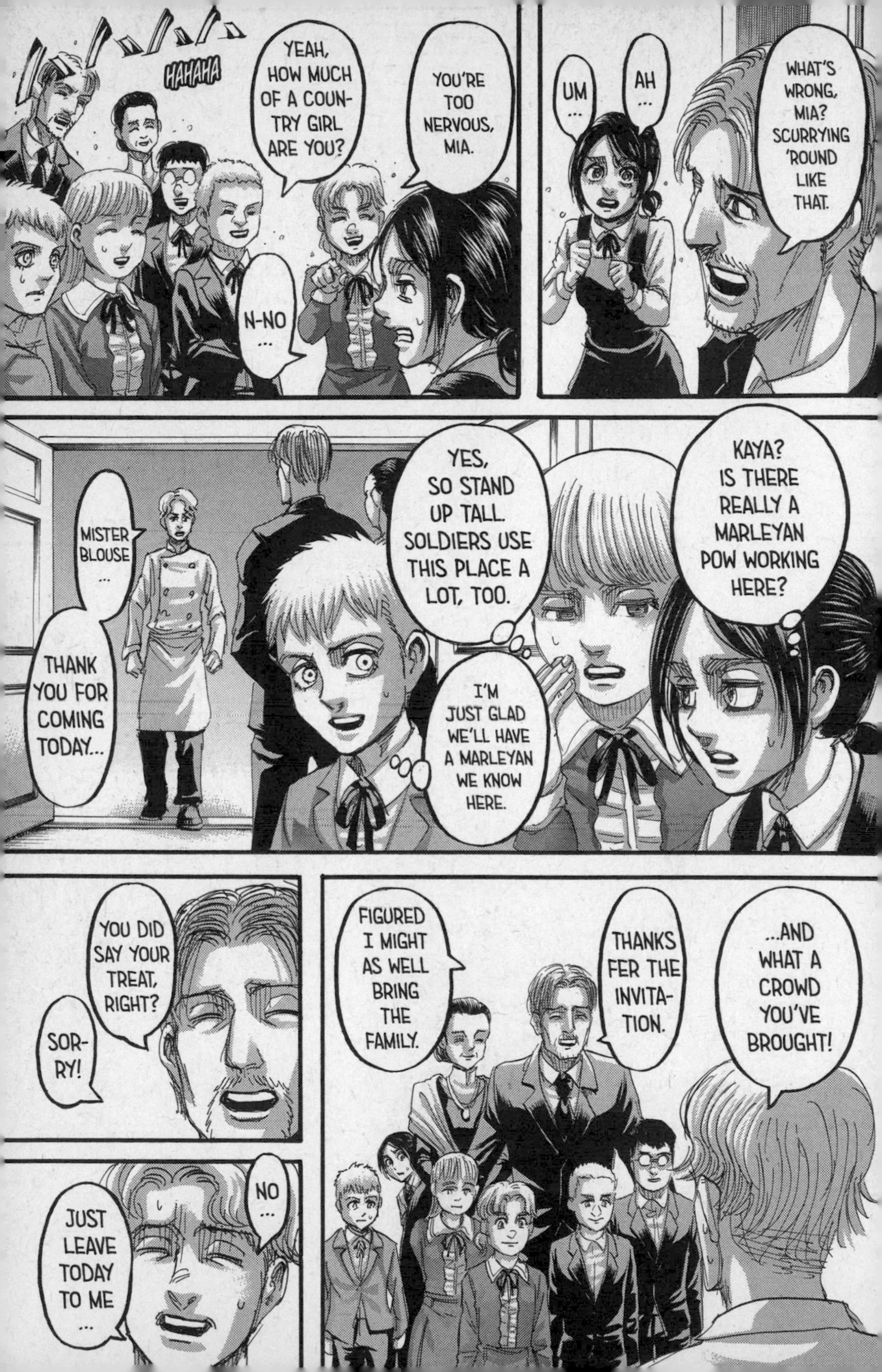
WHAT'S WRONG, MIA? SCURRYING 'ROUND LIKE THAT.
AH ...
UM ...
YOU'RE TOO NERVOUS, MIA.
YEAH, HOW MUCH OF A COUNTRY GIRL ARE YOU?
HAHAHA
N-NO ...
KAYA? IS THERE REALLY A MARLEYAN POW WORKING HERE?
YES, SO STAND UP TALL. SOLDIERS USE THIS PLACE A LOT, TOO.
I'M JUST GLAD WE'LL HAVE A MARLEYAN WE KNOW HERE.
MISTER BLOUSE ...
THANK YOU FOR COMING TODAY...
...AND WHAT A CROWD YOU'VE BROUGHT!
THANKS FER THE INVITATION.
FIGURED I MIGHT AS WELL BRING THE FAMILY.
YOU DID SAY YOUR TREAT, RIGHT?
SORRY!
NO ...
JUST LEAVE TODAY TO ME ...

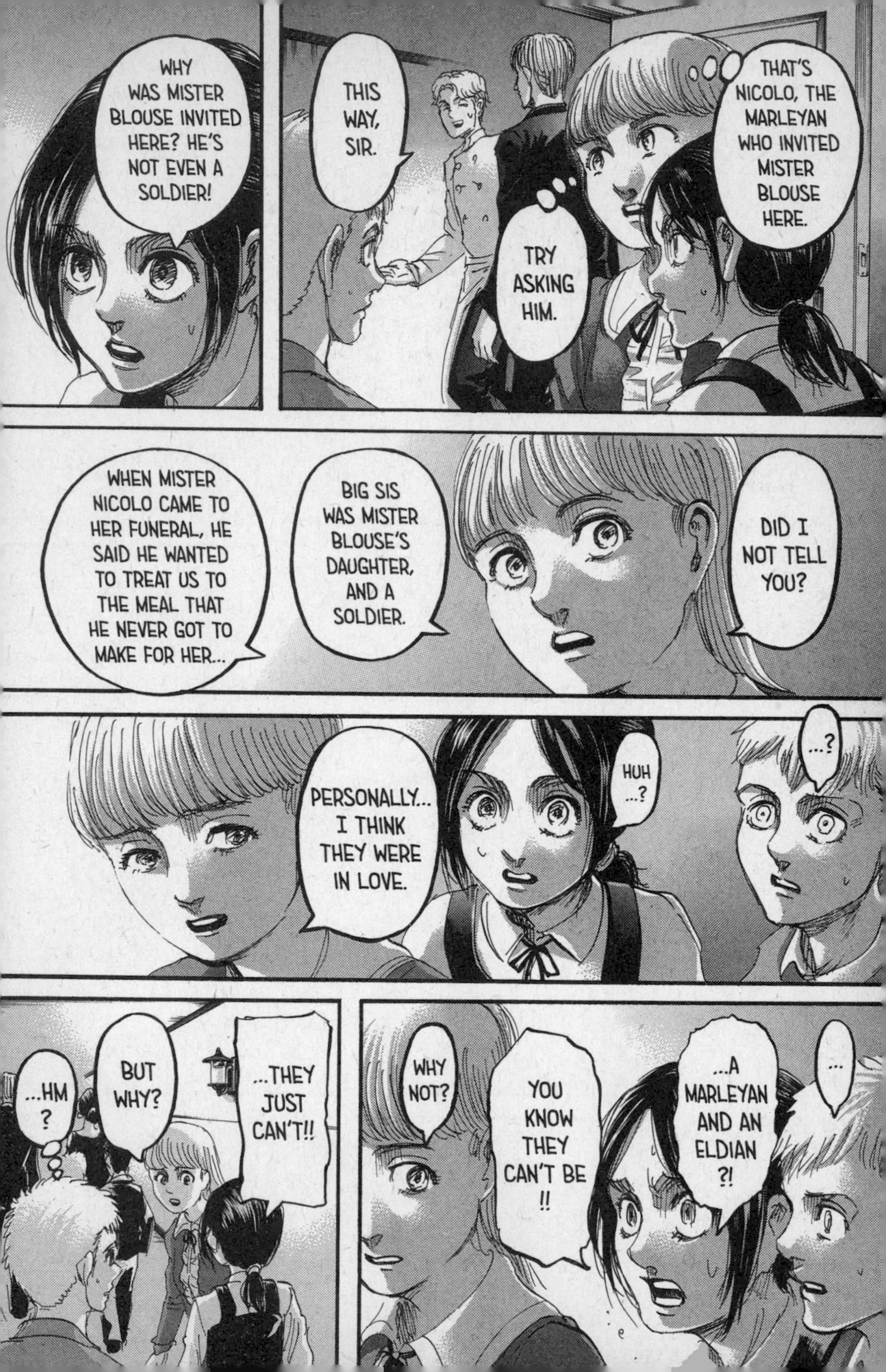
THAT'S NICOLO, THE MARLEYAN WHO INVITED MISTER BLOUSE HERE.
THIS WAY, SIR.
TRY ASKING HIM.
WHY WAS MISTER BLOUSE INVITED HERE? HE'S NOT EVEN A SOLDIER!
DID I NOT TELL YOU?
BIG SIS WAS MISTER BLOUSE'S DAUGHTER, AND A SOLDIER.
WHEN MISTER NICOLO CAME TO HER FUNERAL, HE SAID HE WANTED TO TREAT US TO THE MEAL THAT HE NEVER GOT TO MAKE FOR HER...
...?
HUH ...?
PERSONALLY... I THINK THEY WERE IN LOVE.
...
...A MARLEYAN AND AN ELDIAN ?!
YOU KNOW THEY CAN'T BE !!
WHY NOT?
...THEY JUST CAN'T!!
BUT WHY?
...HM ?

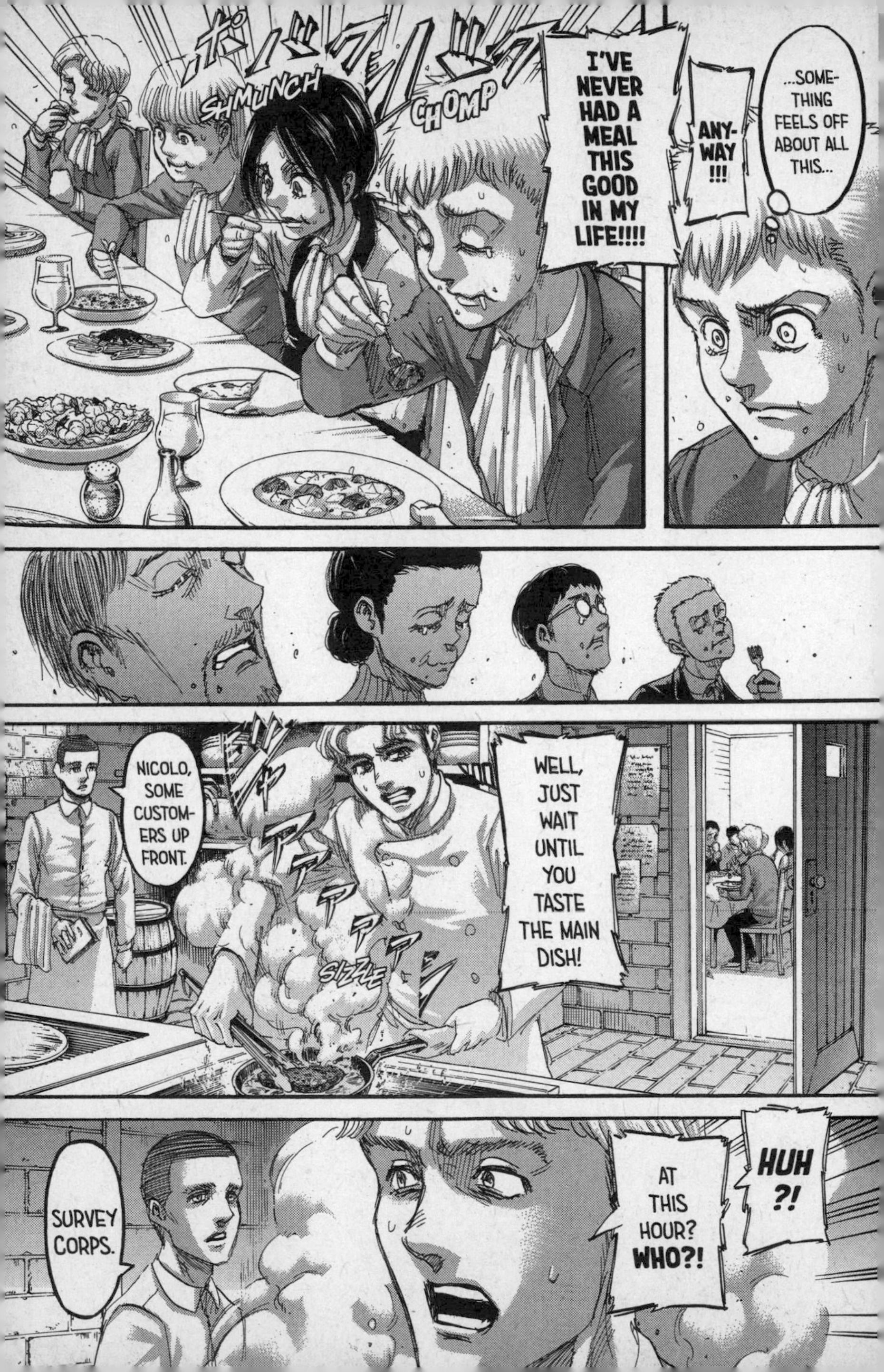

...SOME-THING FEELS OFF ABOUT ALL THIS...
ANY-WAY!!!
I'VE NEVER HAD A MEAL THIS GOOD IN MY LIFE!!!!
CHOMP
SHMUNCH
WELL, JUST WAIT UNTIL YOU TASTE THE MAIN DISH!
NICOLO, SOME CUSTOM-ERS UP FRONT.
SIZZLE
HUH?!
AT THIS HOUR? WHO?!
SURVEY CORPS.

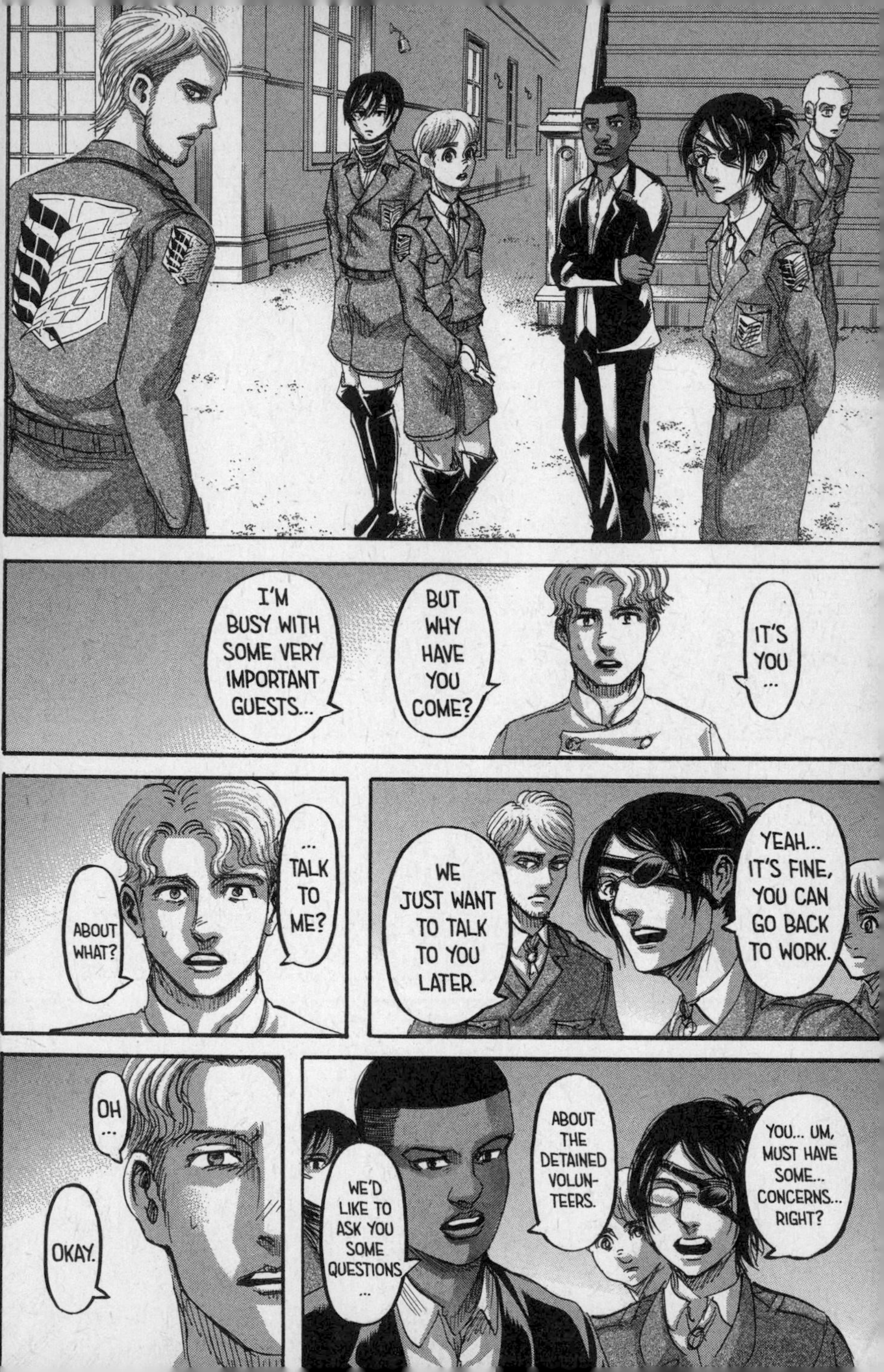
IT'S YOU ...
BUT WHY HAVE YOU COME?
I'M BUSY WITH SOME VERY IMPORTANT GUESTS...
YEAH... IT'S FINE, YOU CAN GO BACK TO WORK.
WE JUST WANT TO TALK TO YOU LATER.
... TALK TO ME?
ABOUT WHAT?
YOU... UM, MUST HAVE SOME... CONCERNS... RIGHT?
ABOUT THE DETAINED VOLUN-TEERS.
WE'D LIKE TO ASK YOU SOME QUESTIONS ...
OH ...
OKAY.

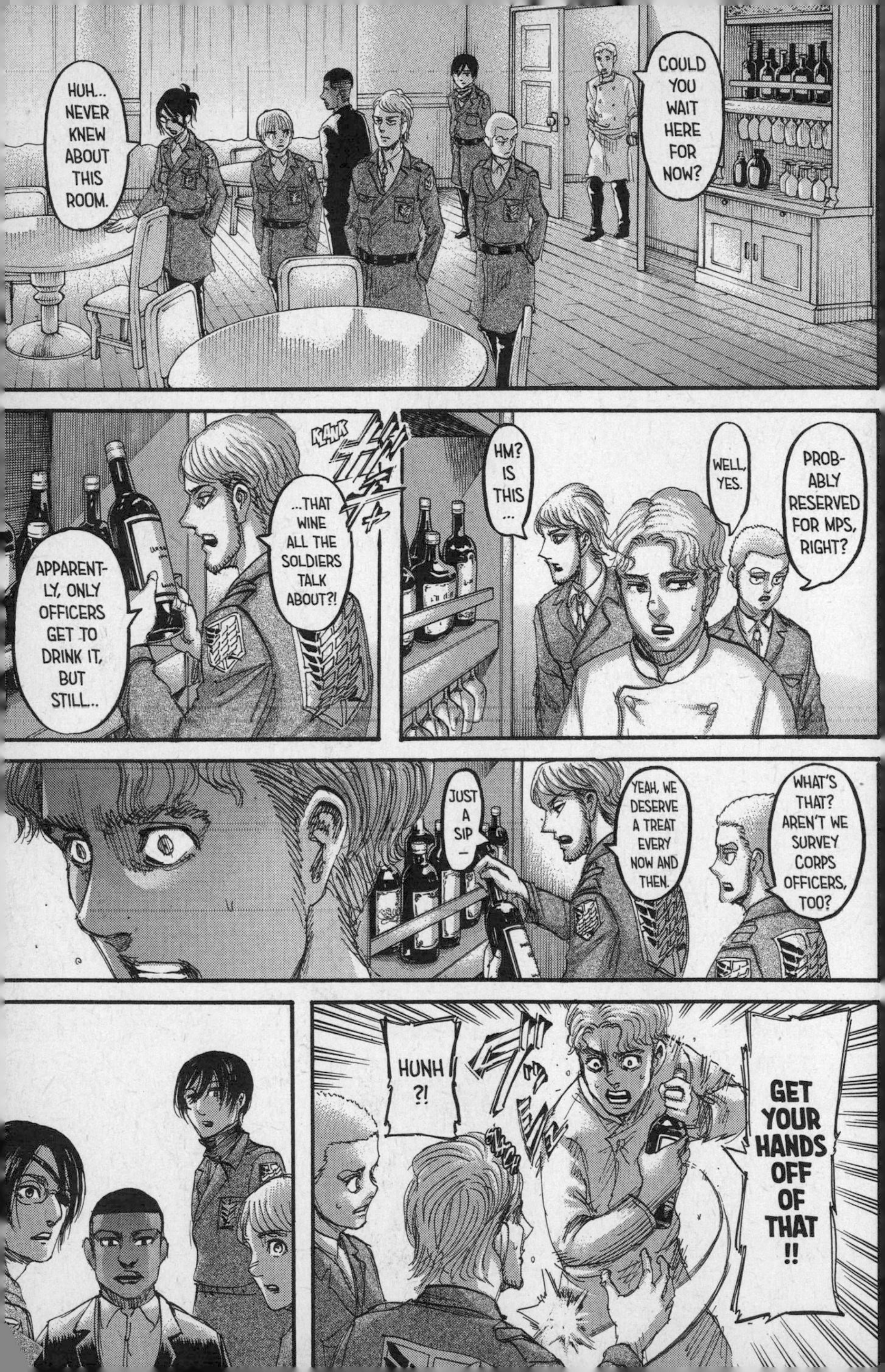
COULD YOU WAIT HERE FOR NOW?
HUH.. NEVER KNEW ABOUT THIS ROOM.
PROB-ABLY RESERVED FOR MPS, RIGHT?
WELL, YES.
HM? IS THIS ...
KLANK
...THAT WINE ALL THE SOLDIERS TALK ABOUT?!
APPARENT-LY, ONLY OFFICERS GET TO DRINK IT, BUT STILL..
WHAT'S THAT? AREN'T WE SURVEY CORPS OFFICERS, TOO?
YEAH, WE DESERVE A TREAT EVERY NOW AND THEN.
JUST A SIP —
GET YOUR HANDS OFF OF THAT !!
HUNH ?!

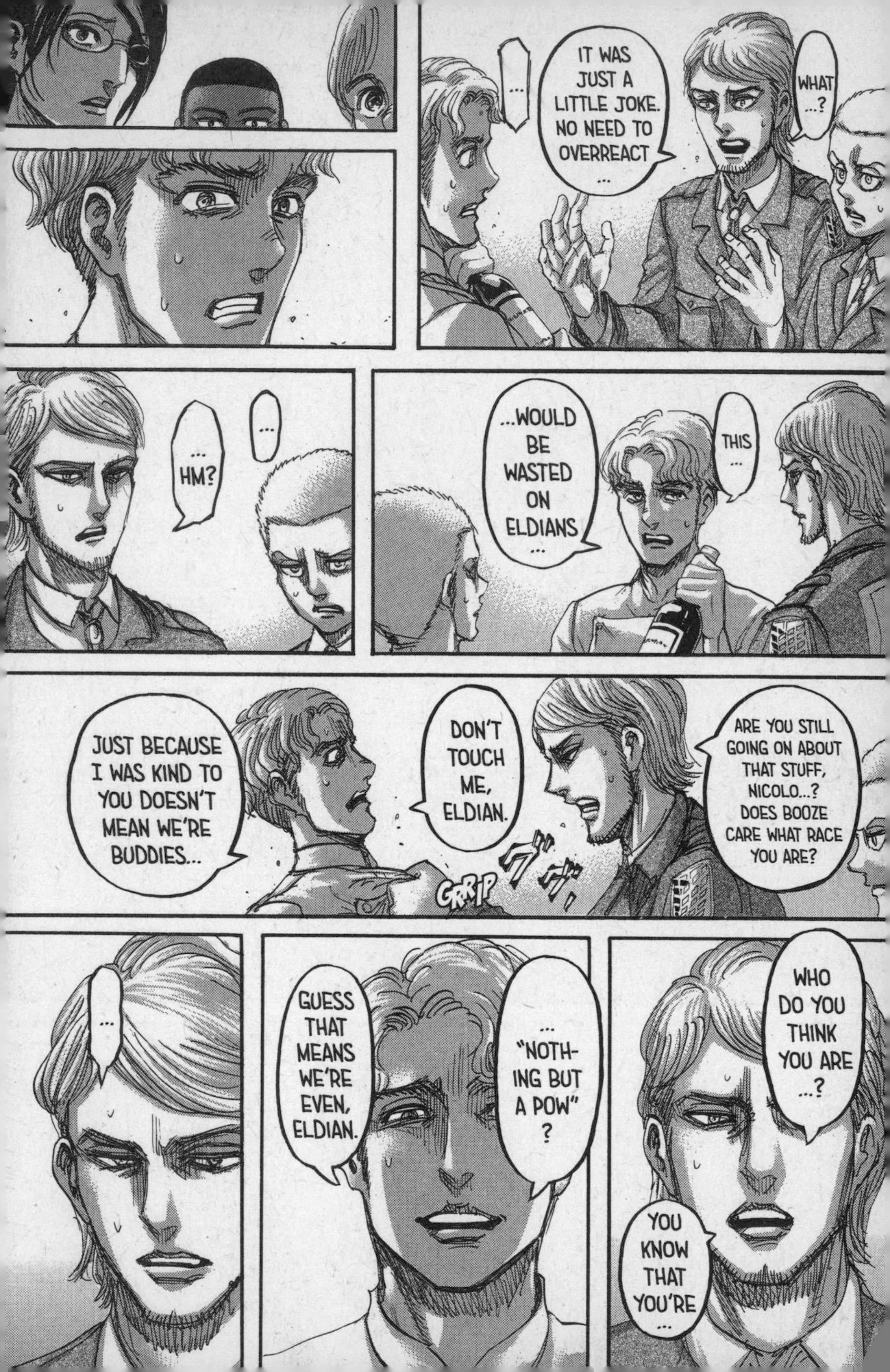
WHAT ...?
IT WAS JUST A LITTLE JOKE. NO NEED TO OVERREACT ...
...
THIS ...
...WOULD BE WASTED ON ELDIANS ...
...
... HM?
ARE YOU STILL GOING ON ABOUT THAT STUFF, NICOLO...? DOES BOOZE CARE WHAT RACE YOU ARE?
GRRIP
DON'T TOUCH ME, ELDIAN.
JUST BECAUSE I WAS KIND TO YOU DOESN'T MEAN WE'RE BUDDIES...
WHO DO YOU THINK YOU ARE ...?
YOU KNOW THAT YOU'RE ...
... "NOTHING BUT A POW" ?
GUESS THAT MEANS WE'RE EVEN, ELDIAN.
...

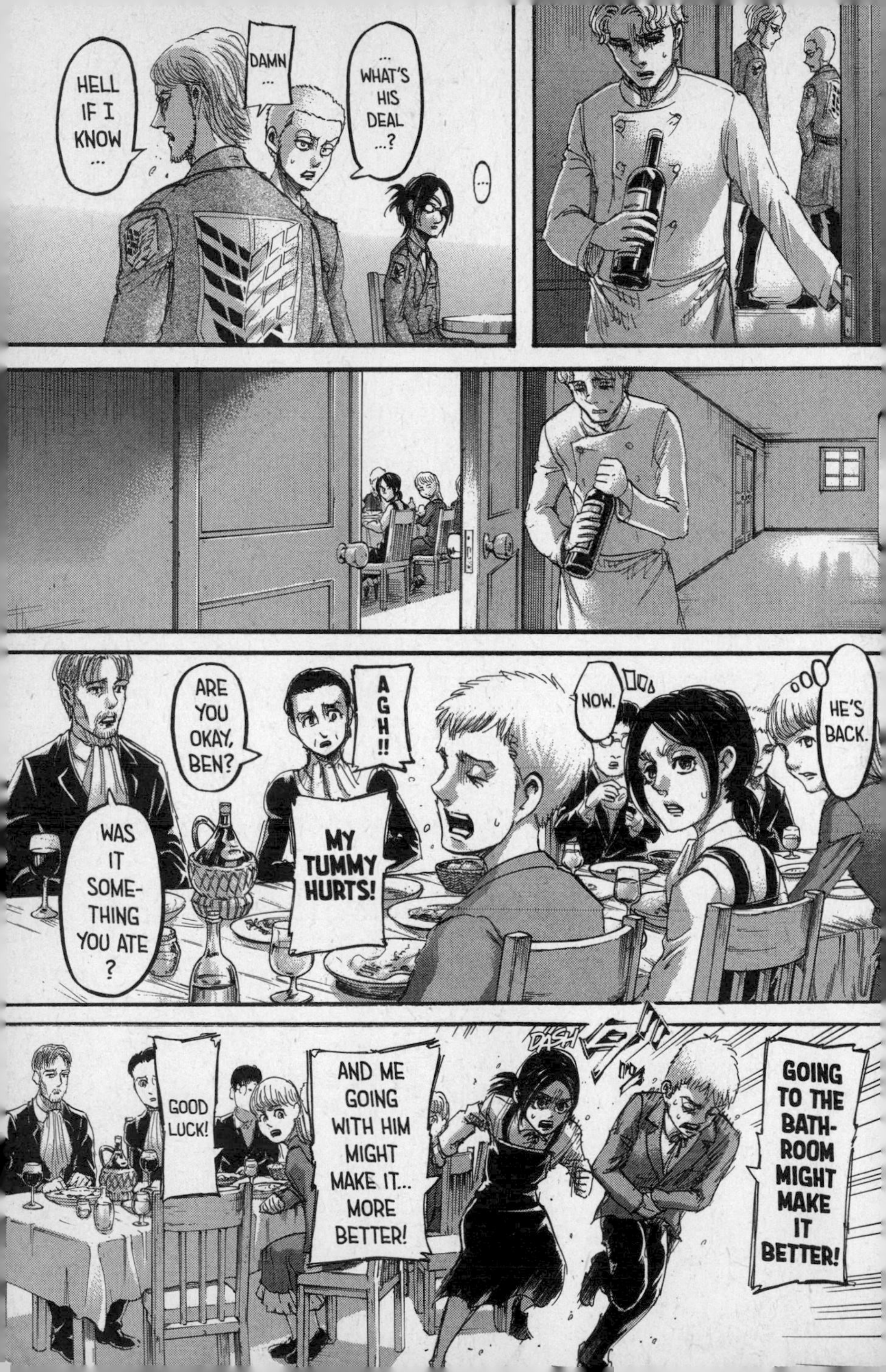
... WHAT'S HIS DEAL ...?
DAMN ...
HELL IF I KNOW ...
...
HE'S BACK.
NOW.
AGH!!
MY TUMMY HURTS!
ARE YOU OKAY, BEN?
WAS IT SOMETHING YOU ATE?
GOING TO THE BATHROOM MIGHT MAKE IT BETTER!
DASH
AND ME GOING WITH HIM MIGHT MAKE IT... MORE BETTER!
GOOD LUCK!

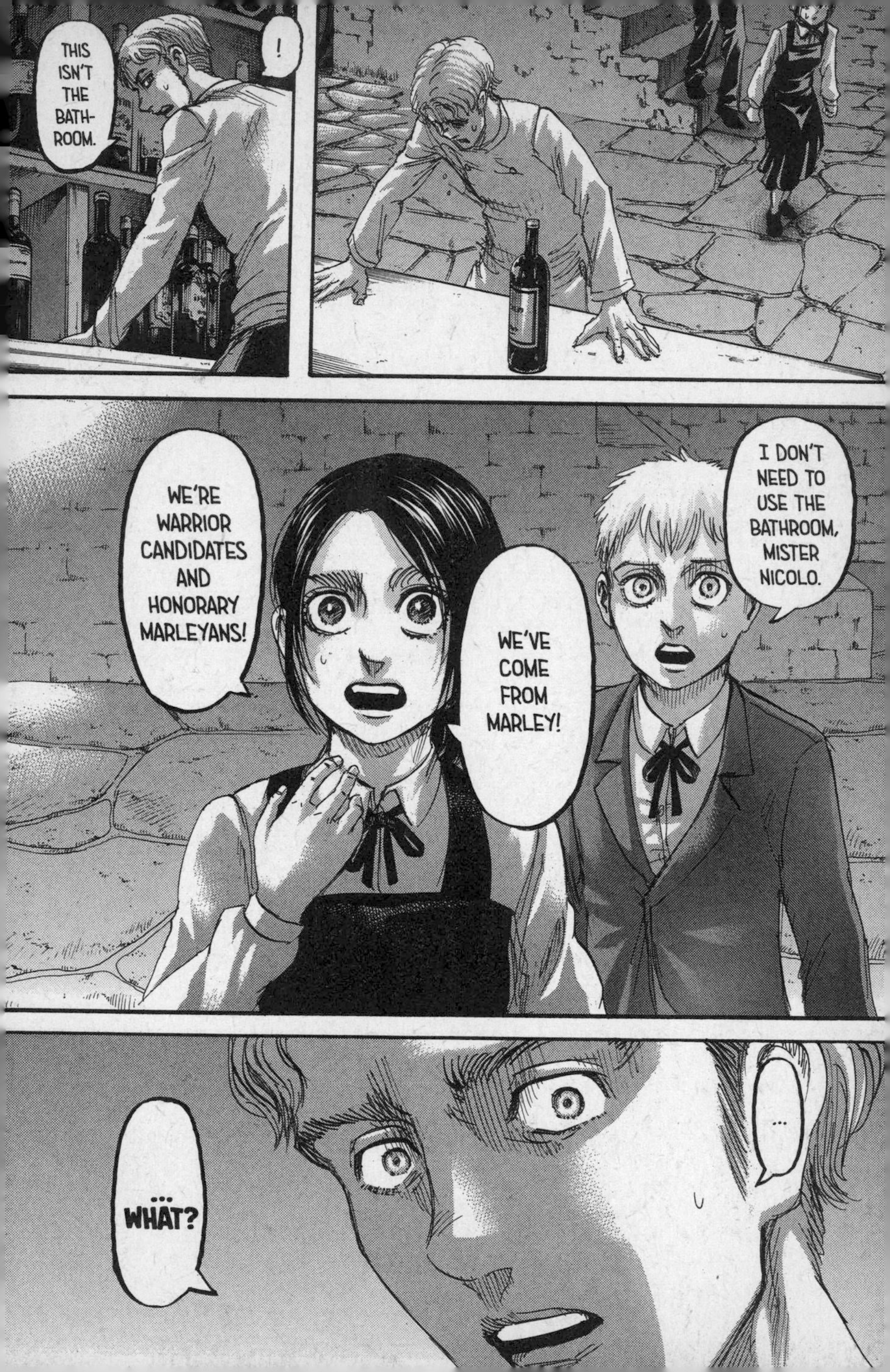
!
THIS ISN'T THE BATH-ROOM.
I DON'T NEED TO USE THE BATHROOM, MISTER NICOLO.
WE'RE WARRIOR CANDIDATES AND HONORARY MARLEYANS!
WE'VE COME FROM MARLEY!
...
... WHAT?

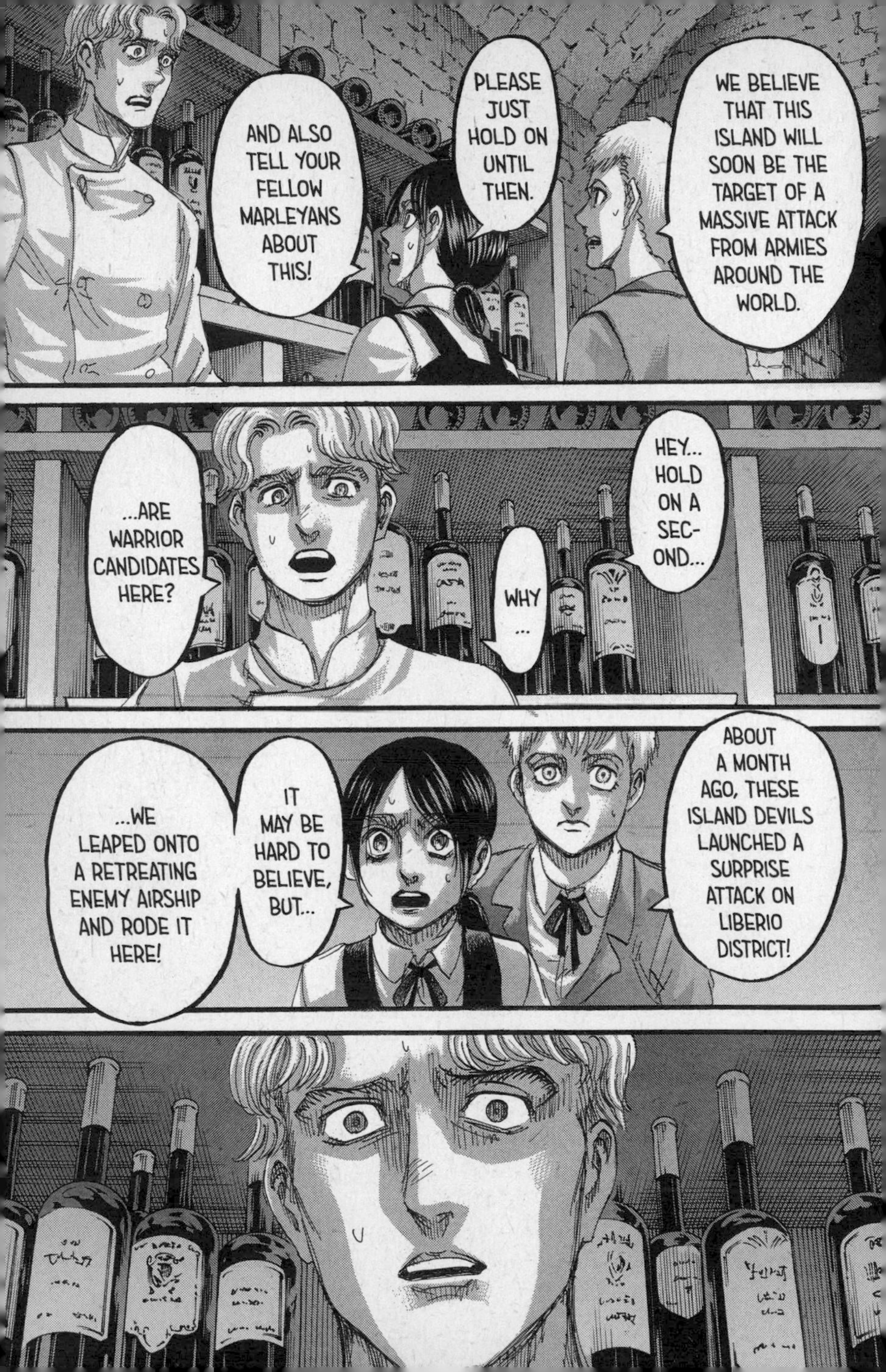
WE BELIEVE THAT THIS ISLAND WILL SOON BE THE TARGET OF A MASSIVE ATTACK FROM ARMIES AROUND THE WORLD.
PLEASE JUST HOLD ON UNTIL THEN.
AND ALSO TELL YOUR FELLOW MARLEYANS ABOUT THIS!
HEY... HOLD ON A SEC-OND...
WHY...
...ARE WARRIOR CANDIDATES HERE?
ABOUT A MONTH AGO, THESE ISLAND DEVILS LAUNCHED A SURPRISE ATTACK ON LIBERIO DISTRICT!
IT MAY BE HARD TO BELIEVE, BUT...
...WE LEAPED ONTO A RETREATING ENEMY AIRSHIP AND RODE IT HERE!

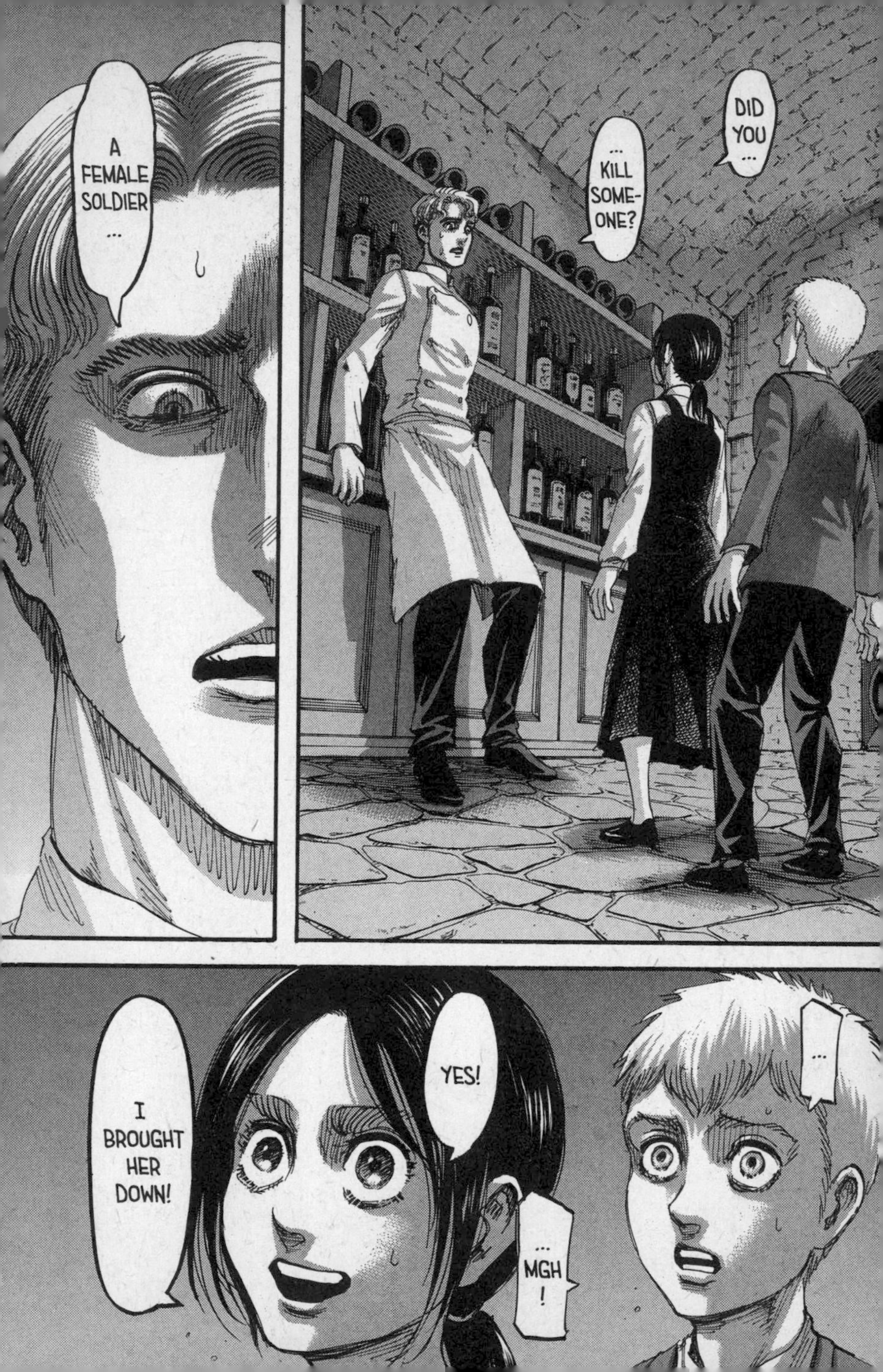
DID YOU ...
... KILL SOME-ONE?
A FEMALE SOLDIER ...
...
YES!
I BROUGHT HER DOWN!
... MGH !

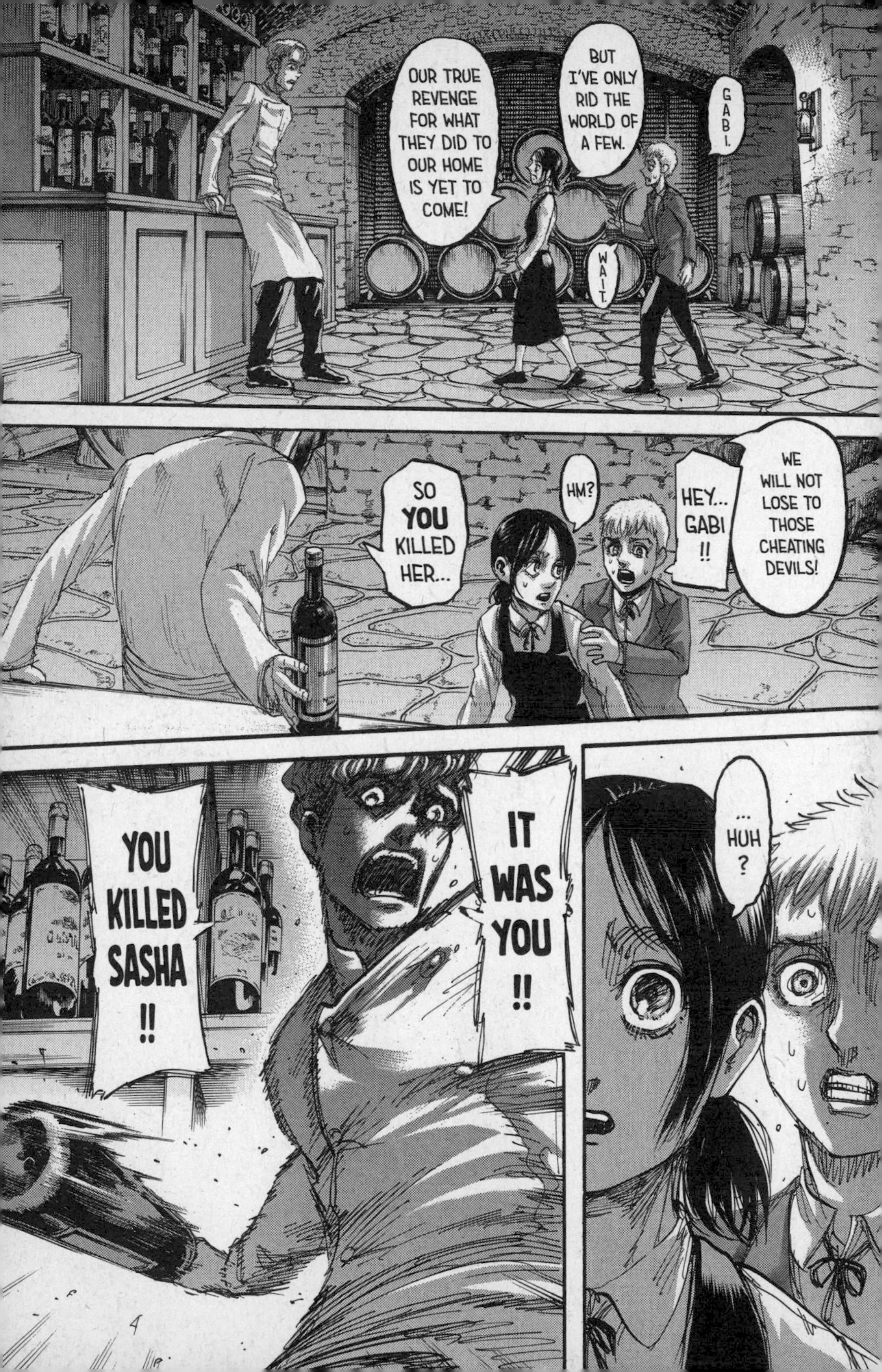
GABI.
BUT I'VE ONLY RID THE WORLD OF A FEW.
OUR TRUE REVENGE FOR WHAT THEY DID TO OUR HOME IS YET TO COME!
WAIT.
WE WILL NOT LOSE TO THOSE CHEATING DEVILS!
HEY... GABI!!
HM?
SO YOU KILLED HER...
...HUH?
IT WAS YOU!!
YOU KILLED SASHA!!

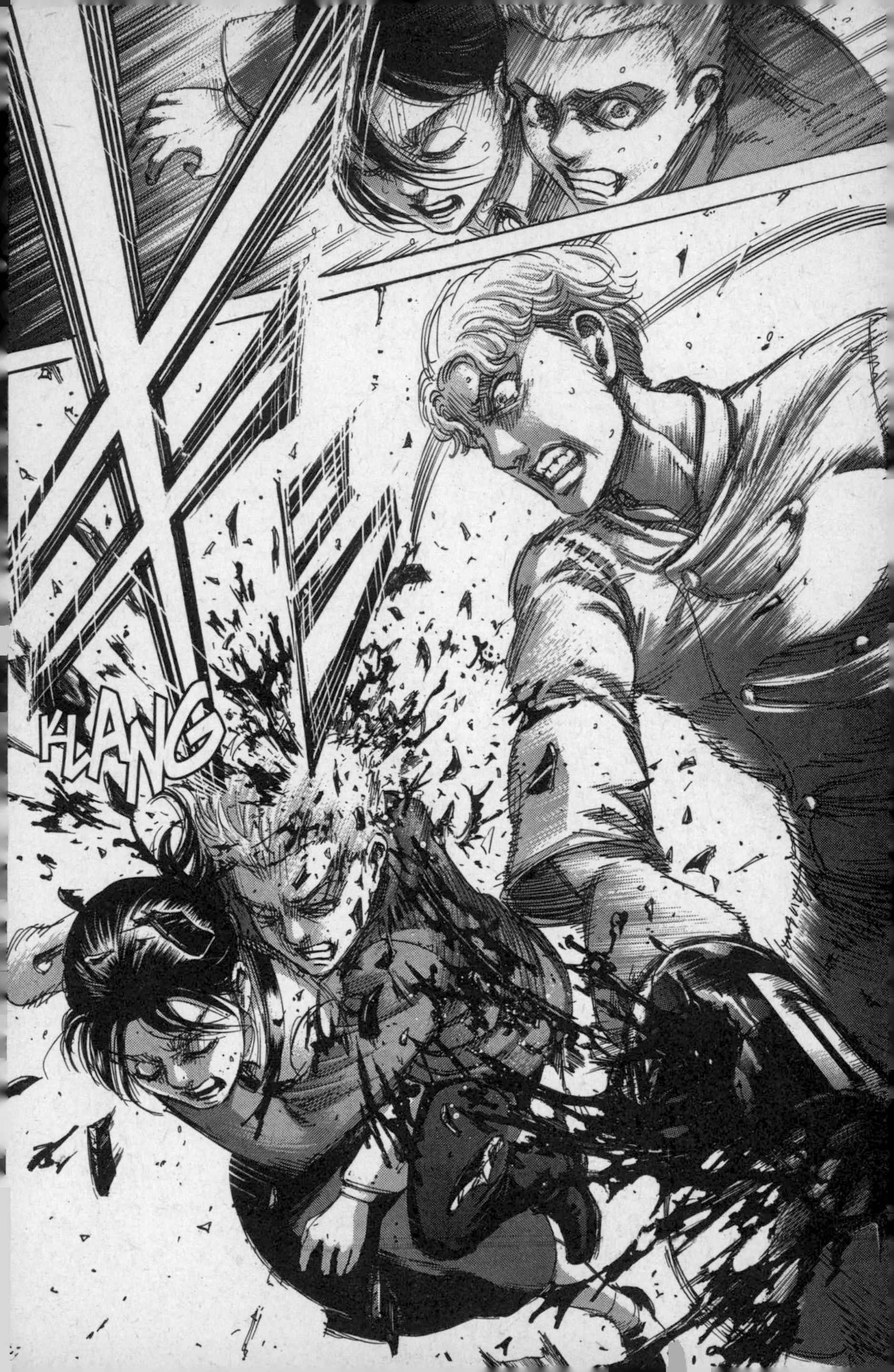
KLANG

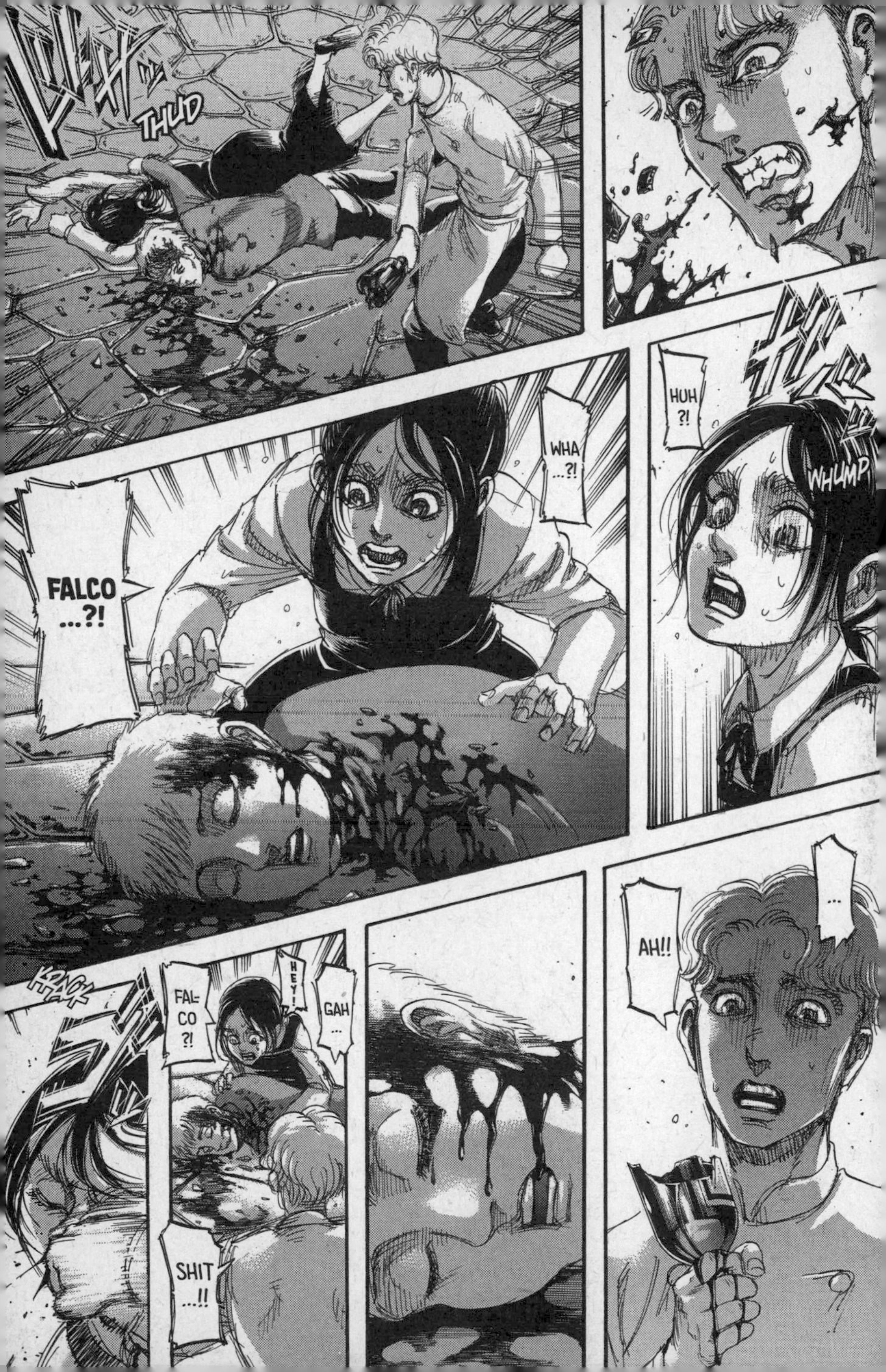
THUD
HUH ?!
WHUMP
WHA ...?!
FALCO ...?!
...
AH!!
HEY!
GAH ...
FAL-CO ?!
KRACK
SHIT ...!!

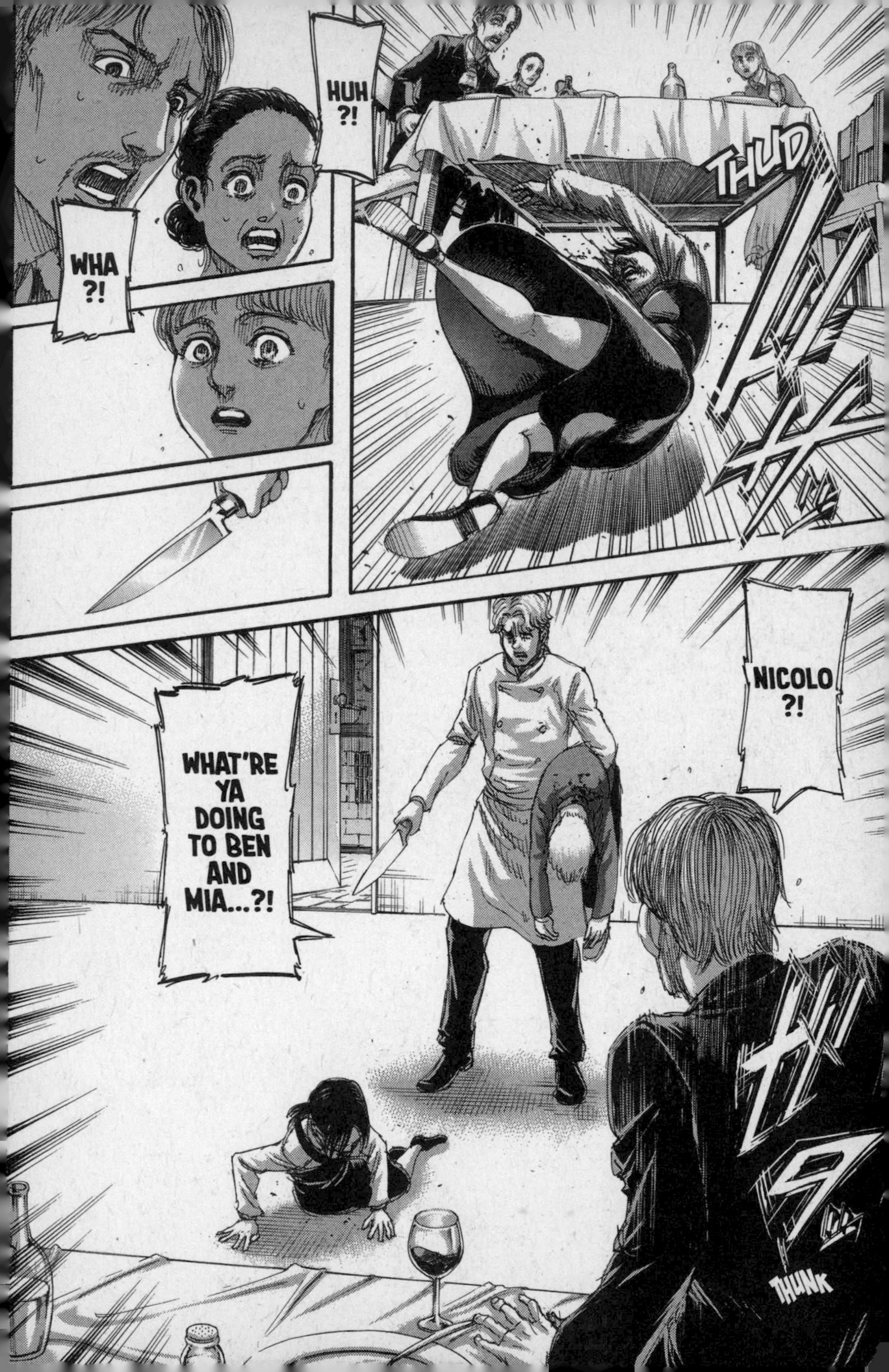
HUH ?!
THUD
WHA ?!
NICOLO ?!
WHAT'RE YA DOING TO BEN AND MIA...?!
THUNK

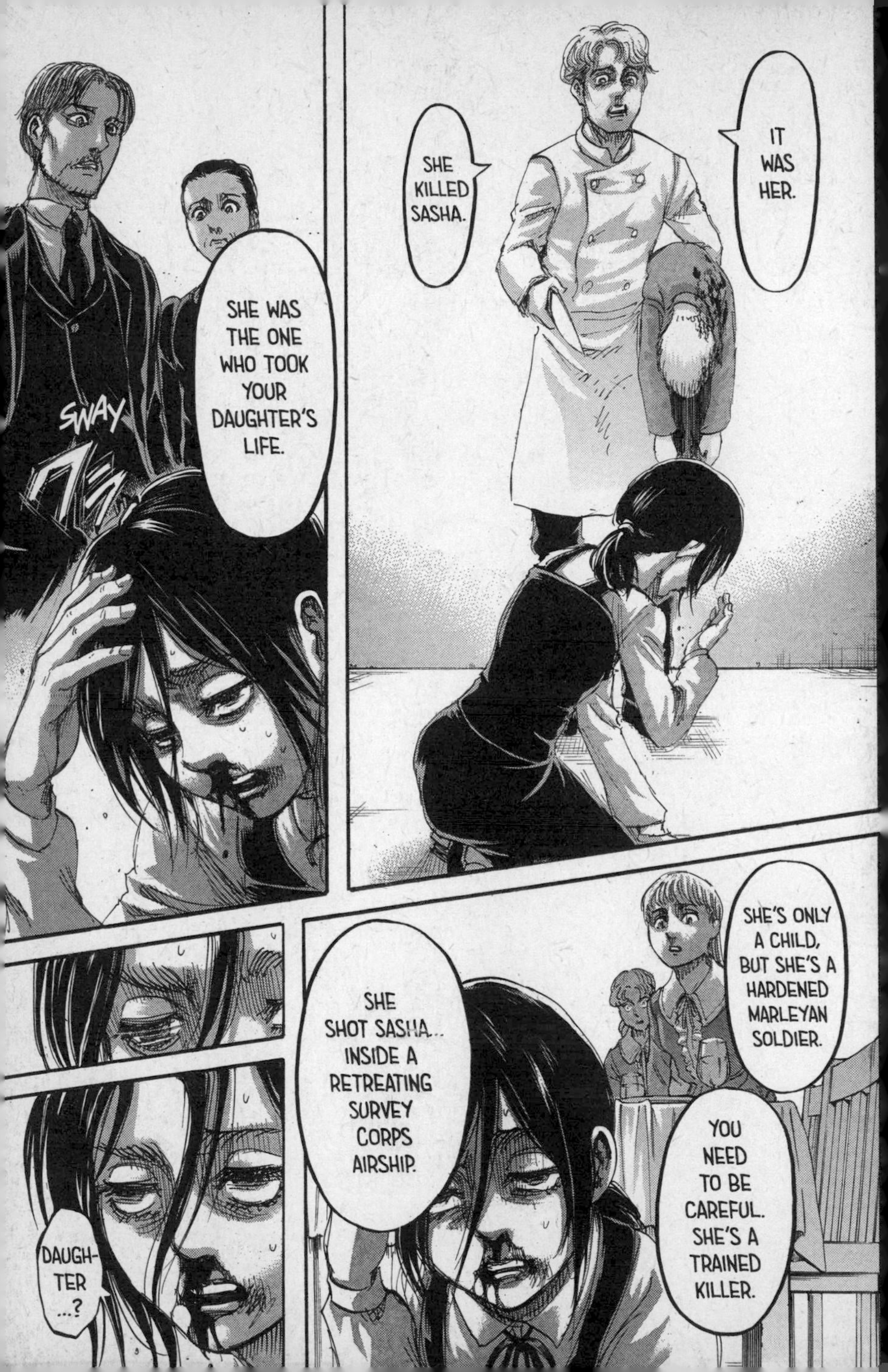
IT WAS HER.
SHE KILLED SASHA.
SHE WAS THE ONE WHO TOOK YOUR DAUGHTER'S LIFE.
SWAY
SHE'S ONLY A CHILD, BUT SHE'S A HARDENED MARLEYAN SOLDIER.
YOU NEED TO BE CAREFUL. SHE'S A TRAINED KILLER.
SHE SHOT SASHA... INSIDE A RETREATING SURVEY CORPS AIRSHIP.
DAUGHTER...?

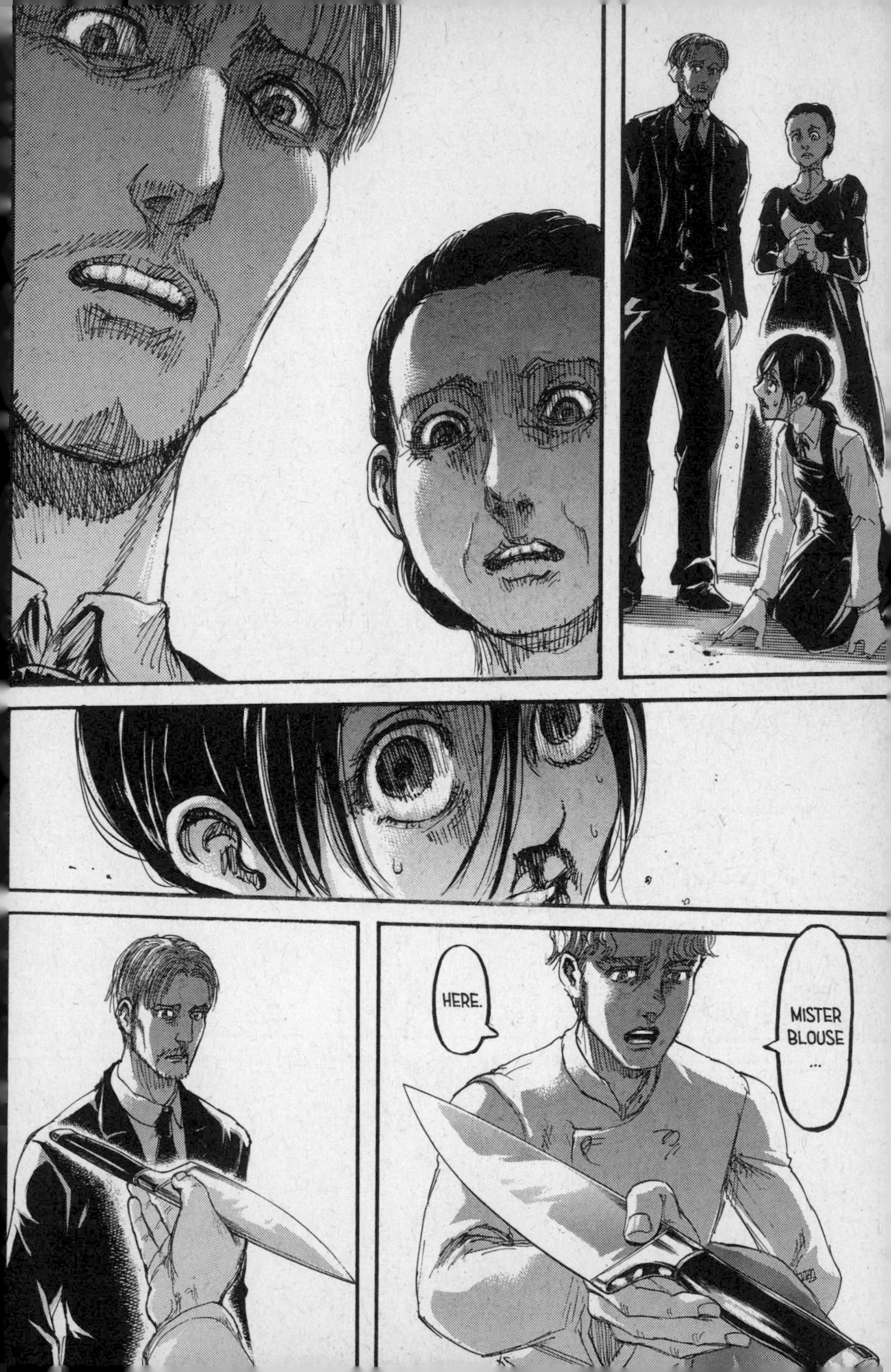
MISTER BLOUSE ...
HERE.

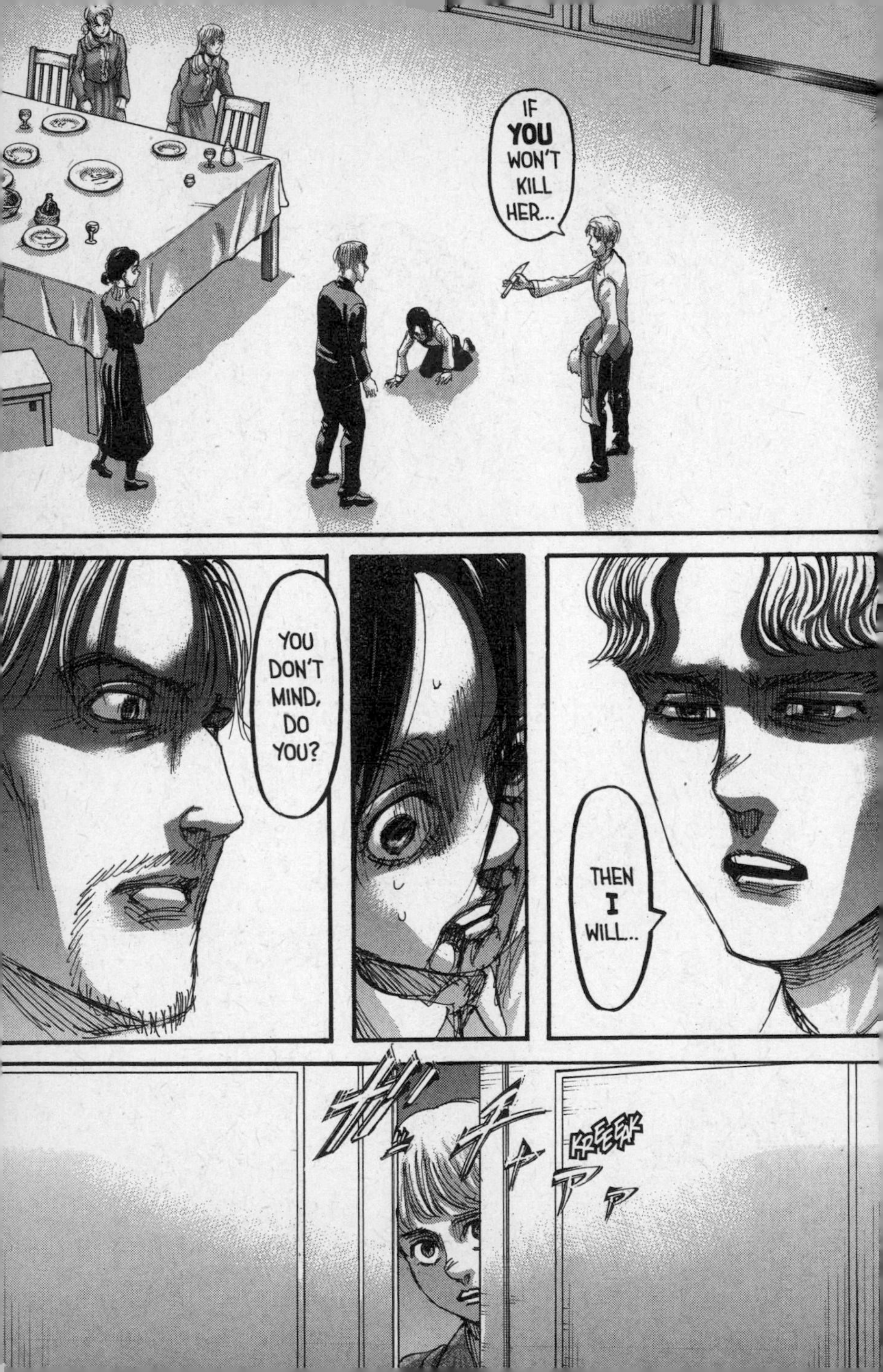

IF YOU WON'T KILL HER...
THEN I WILL...
YOU DON'T MIND, DO YOU?
KREEEAK

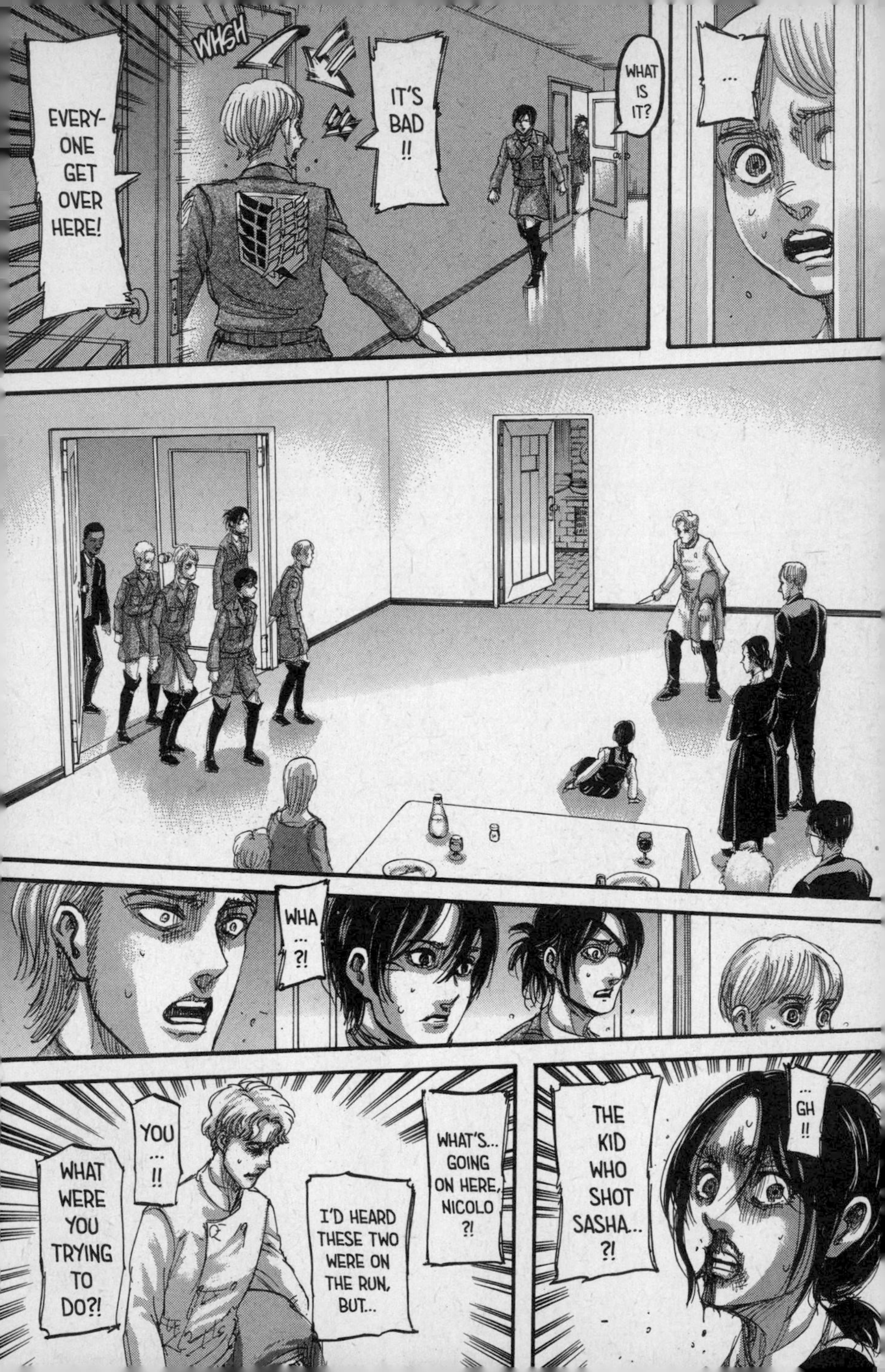
...
WHAT IS IT?
IT'S BAD!!
WHSH
EVERY-ONE GET OVER HERE!
WHA...?!
...GH!!
THE KID WHO SHOT SASHA...?!
WHAT'S... GOING ON HERE, NICOLO?!
I'D HEARD THESE TWO WERE ON THE RUN, BUT...
YOU...!!
WHAT WERE YOU TRYING TO DO?!

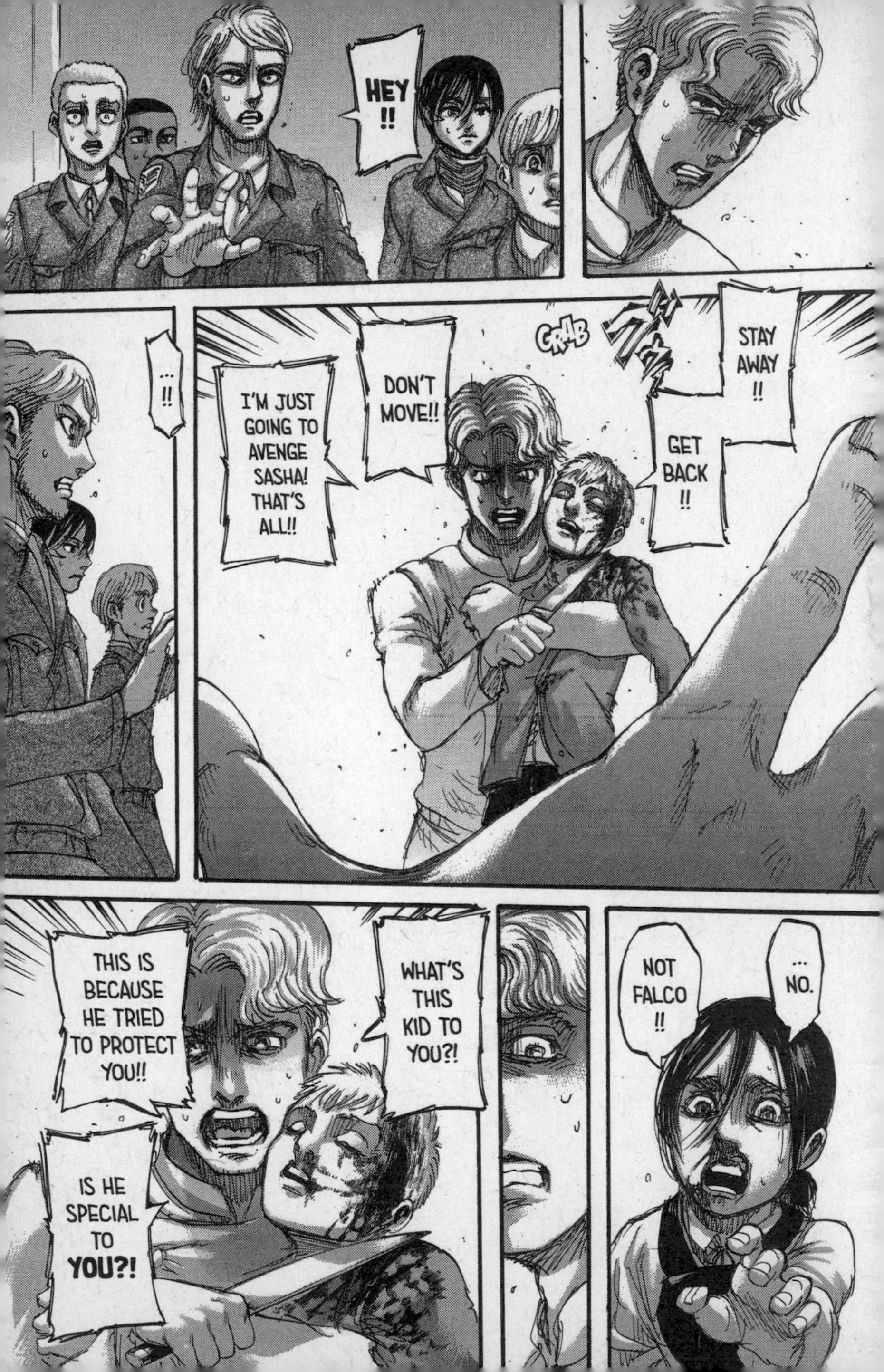
HEY !!
STAY AWAY !!
GET BACK !!
GRAB
DON'T MOVE!!
I'M JUST GOING TO AVENGE SASHA! THAT'S ALL!!
... !!
... NO.
NOT FALCO !!
WHAT'S THIS KID TO YOU?!
THIS IS BECAUSE HE TRIED TO PROTECT YOU!!
IS HE SPECIAL TO YOU?!

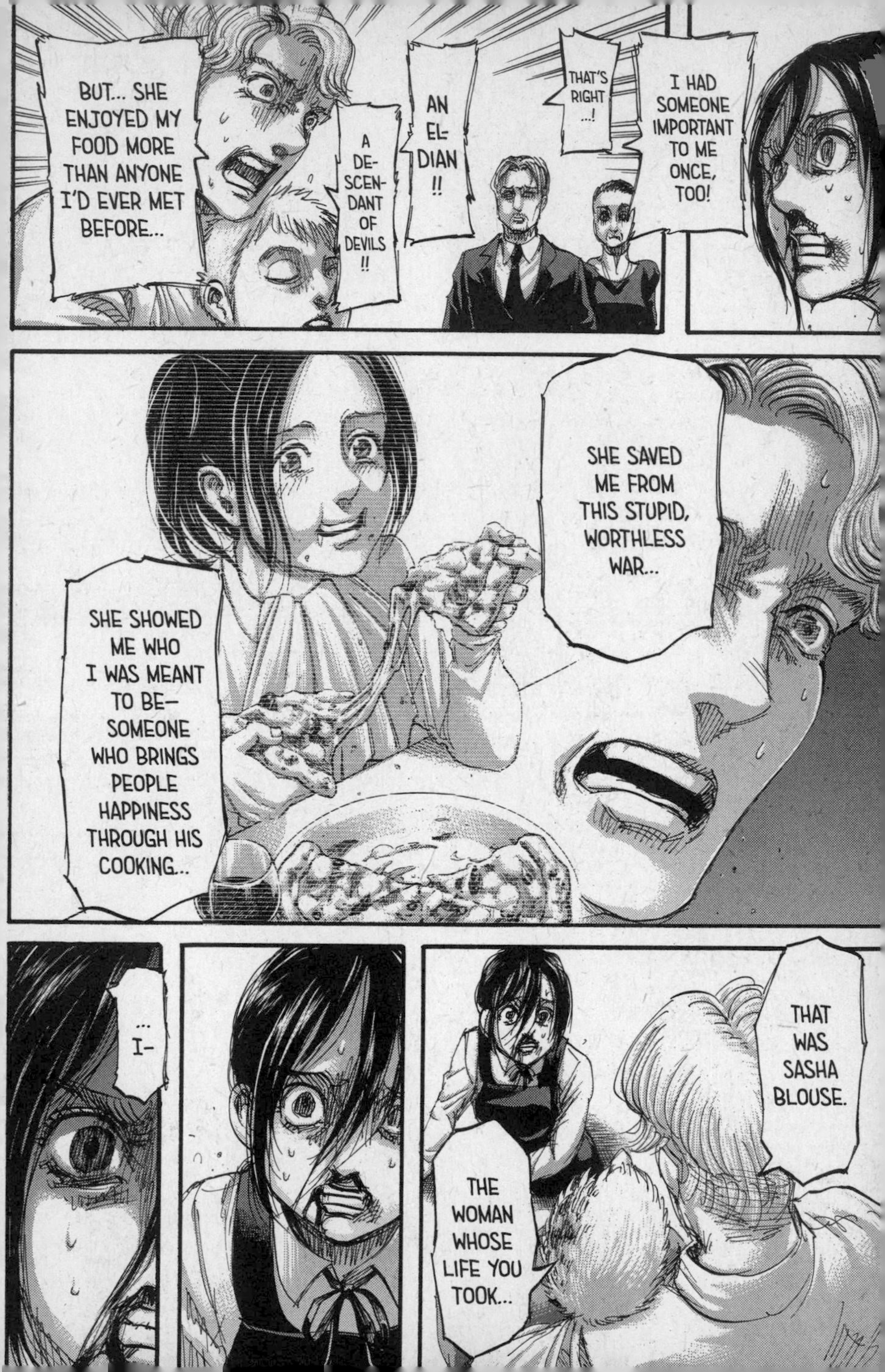
I HAD SOMEONE IMPORTANT TO ME ONCE, TOO!
THAT'S RIGHT ...!
AN EL-DIAN !!
A DE-SCEN-DANT OF DEVILS !!
BUT... SHE ENJOYED MY FOOD MORE THAN ANYONE I'D EVER MET BEFORE...
SHE SAVED ME FROM THIS STUPID, WORTHLESS WAR...
SHE SHOWED ME WHO I WAS MEANT TO BE—SOMEONE WHO BRINGS PEOPLE HAPPINESS THROUGH HIS COOKING...
THAT WAS SASHA BLOUSE.
THE WOMAN WHOSE LIFE YOU TOOK...
... I-

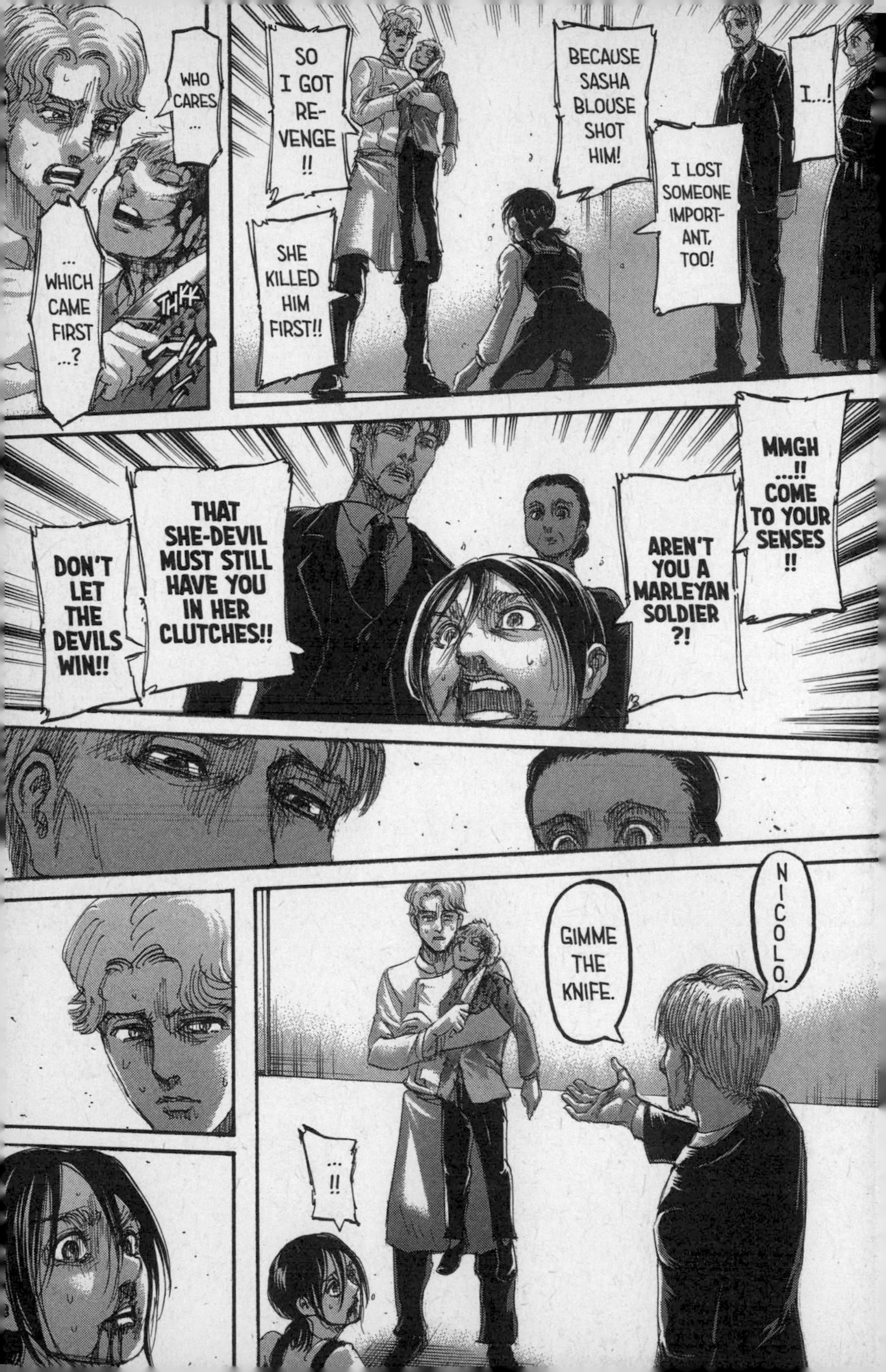
I...!
BECAUSE SASHA BLOUSE SHOT HIM!
I LOST SOMEONE IMPORTANT, TOO!
SO I GOT RE-VENGE!!
SHE KILLED HIM FIRST!!
WHO CARES...
...WHICH CAME FIRST...?
THKK
MMGH...!! COME TO YOUR SENSES!!
AREN'T YOU A MARLEYAN SOLDIER?!
THAT SHE-DEVIL MUST STILL HAVE YOU IN HER CLUTCHES!!
DON'T LET THE DEVILS WIN!!
NICOLO.
GIMME THE KNIFE.
...!!

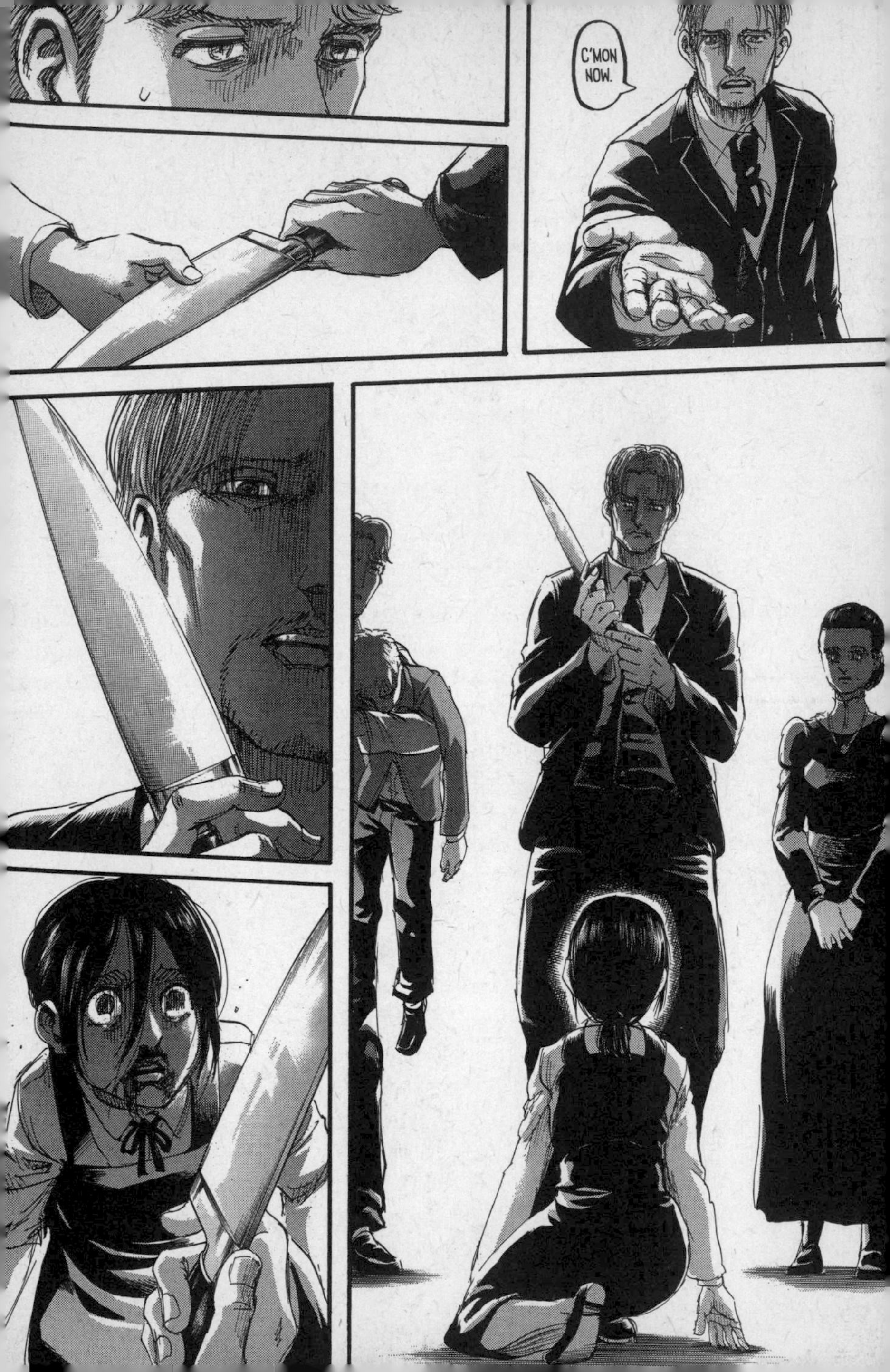
C'MON NOW.

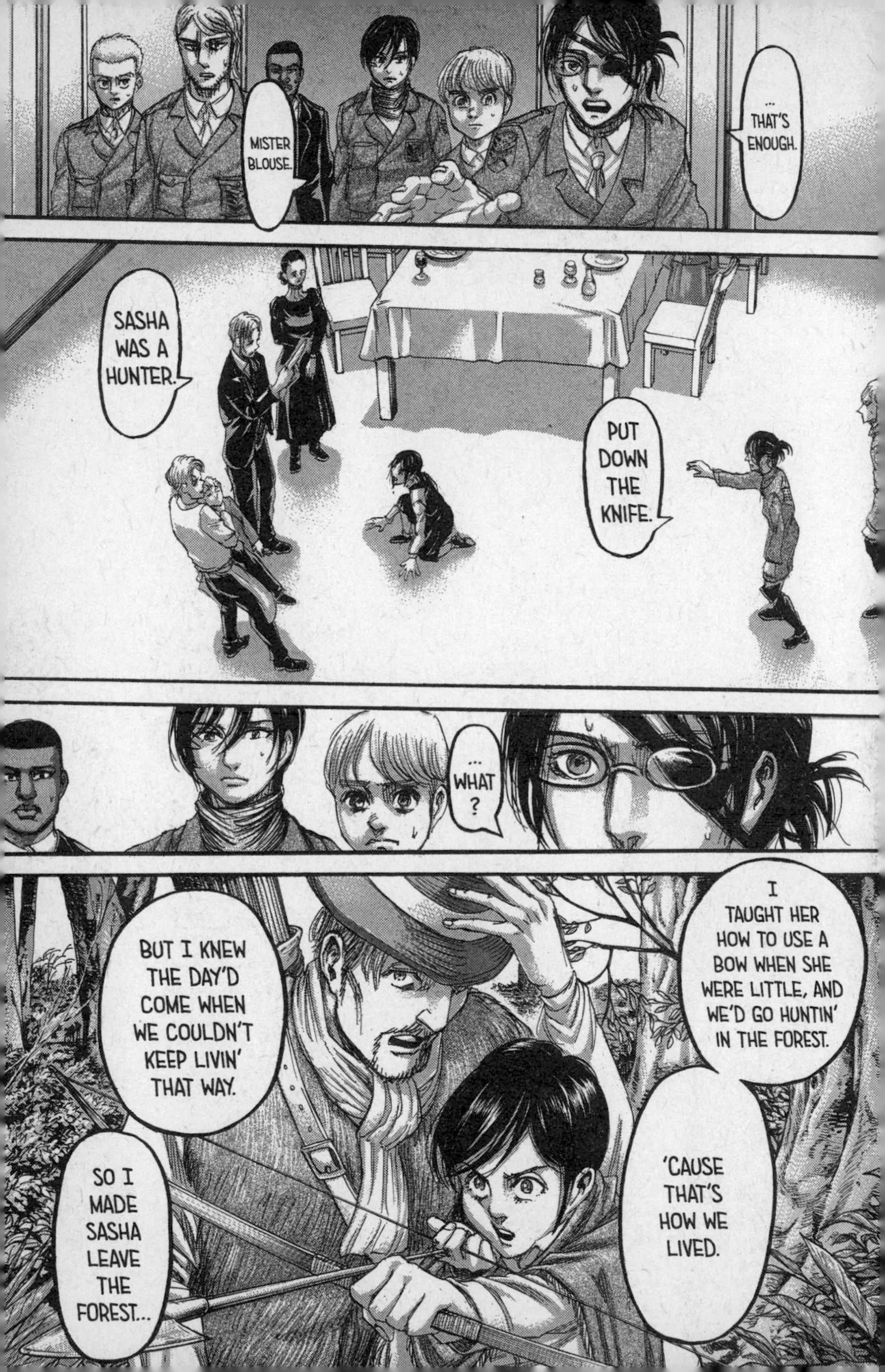
... THAT'S ENOUGH.
MISTER BLOUSE.
PUT DOWN THE KNIFE.
SASHA WAS A HUNTER.
... WHAT ?
I TAUGHT HER HOW TO USE A BOW WHEN SHE WERE LITTLE, AND WE'D GO HUNTIN' IN THE FOREST.
'CAUSE THAT'S HOW WE LIVED.
BUT I KNEW THE DAY'D COME WHEN WE COULDN'T KEEP LIVIN' THAT WAY.
SO I MADE SASHA LEAVE THE FOREST...

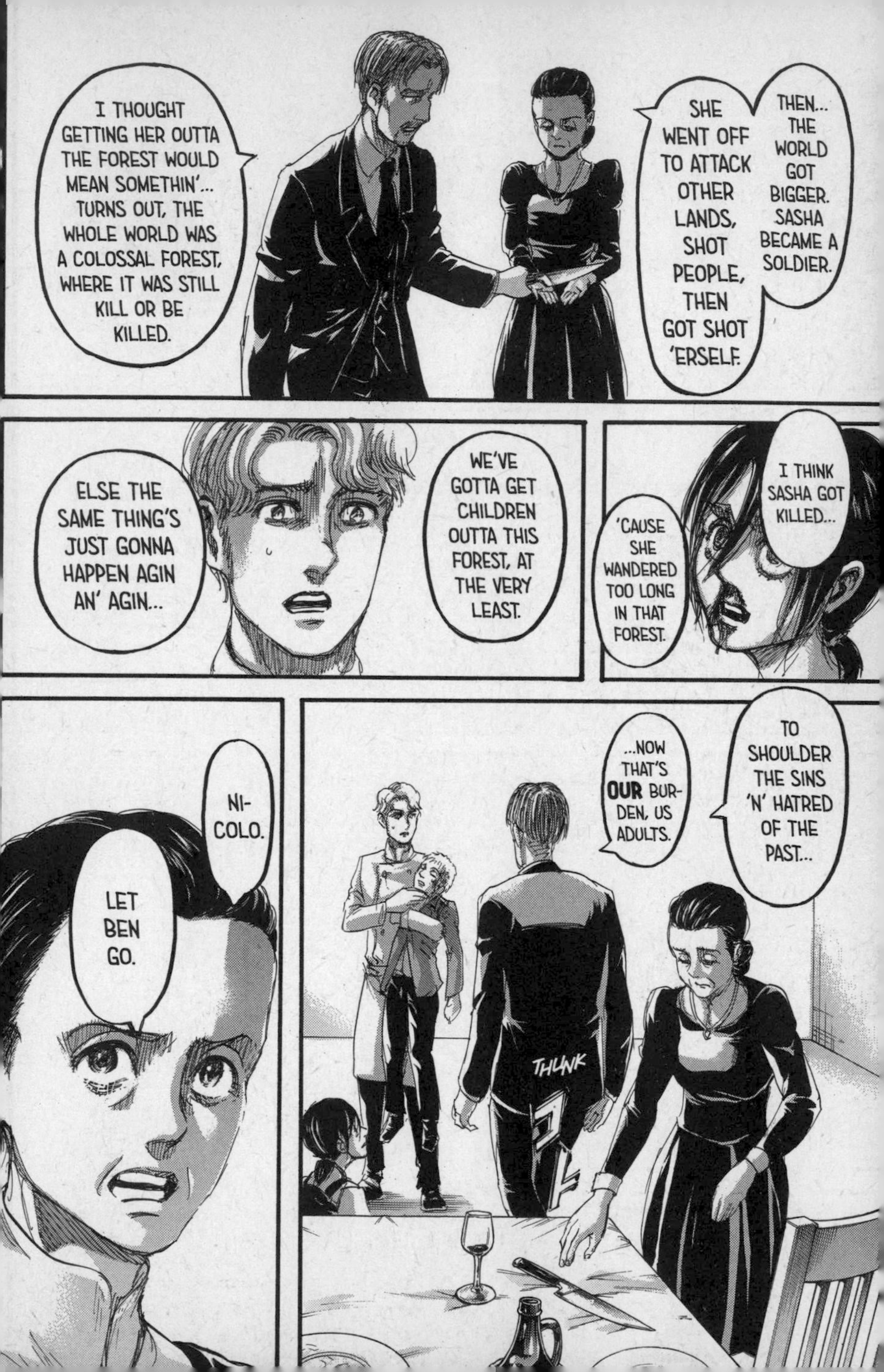
THEN... THE WORLD GOT BIGGER. SASHA BECAME A SOLDIER.
SHE WENT OFF TO ATTACK OTHER LANDS, SHOT PEOPLE, THEN GOT SHOT 'ERSELF.
I THOUGHT GETTING HER OUTTA THE FOREST WOULD MEAN SOMETHIN'... TURNS OUT, THE WHOLE WORLD WAS A COLOSSAL FOREST, WHERE IT WAS STILL KILL OR BE KILLED.
I THINK SASHA GOT KILLED...
'CAUSE SHE WANDERED TOO LONG IN THAT FOREST.
WE'VE GOTTA GET CHILDREN OUTTA THIS FOREST, AT THE VERY LEAST.
ELSE THE SAME THING'S JUST GONNA HAPPEN AGIN AN' AGIN...
TO SHOULDER THE SINS 'N' HATRED OF THE PAST...
...NOW THAT'S **OUR** BURDEN, US ADULTS.
THUNK
NI-COLO.
LET BEN GO.

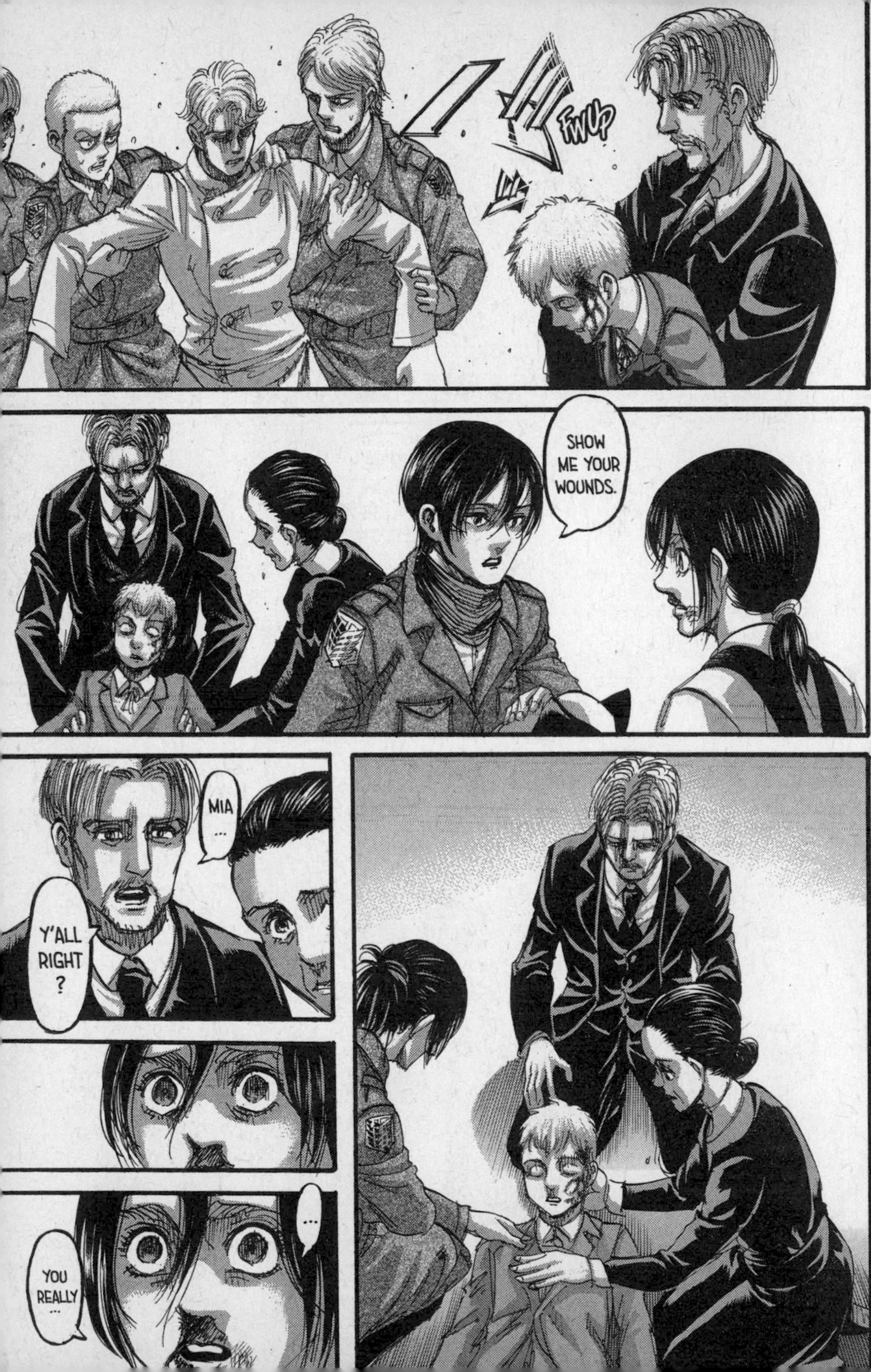
FWUP
SHOW ME YOUR WOUNDS.
MIA ...
Y'ALL RIGHT ?
...
YOU REALLY ...

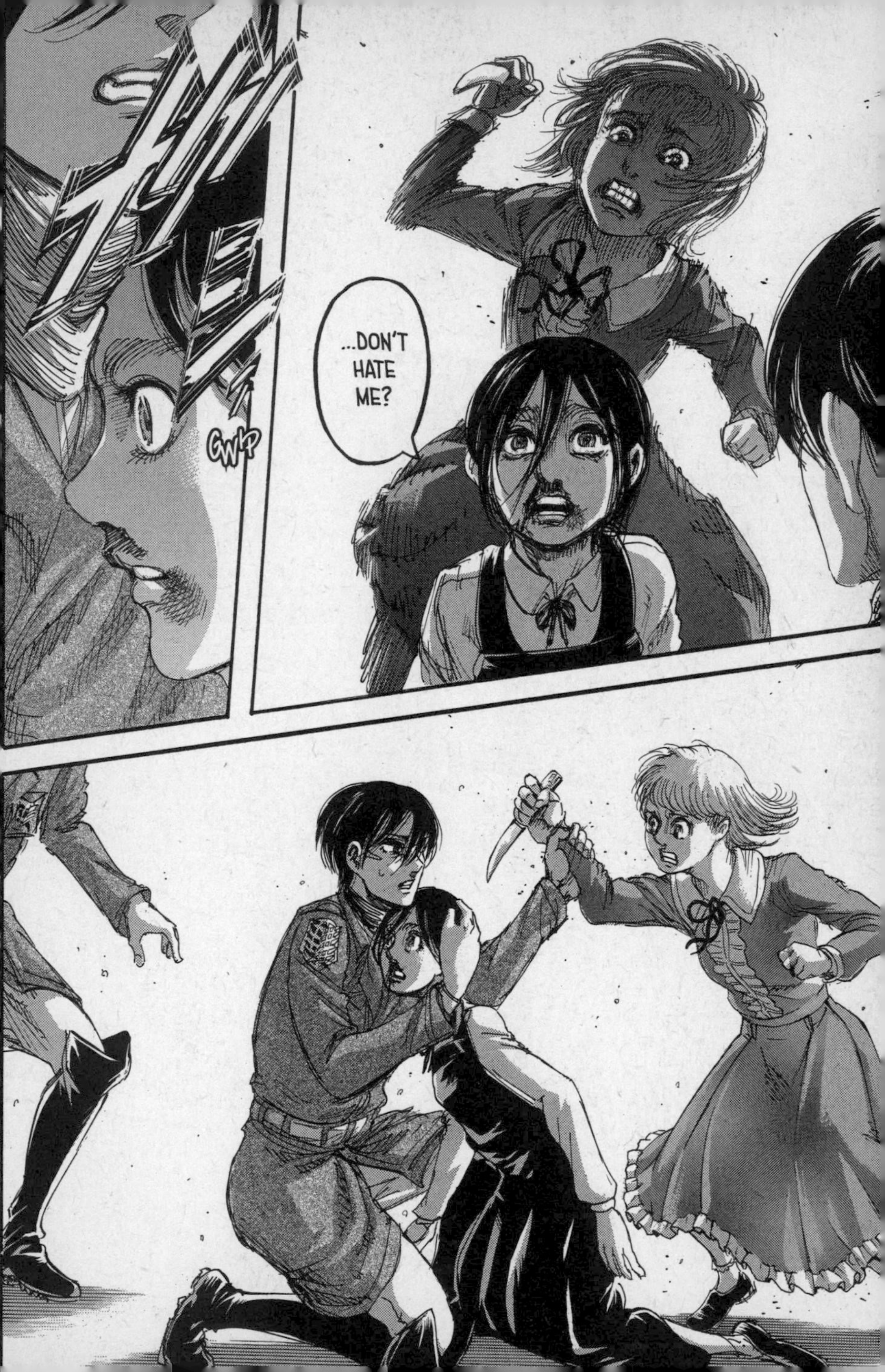
...DON'T HATE ME?
GWIP

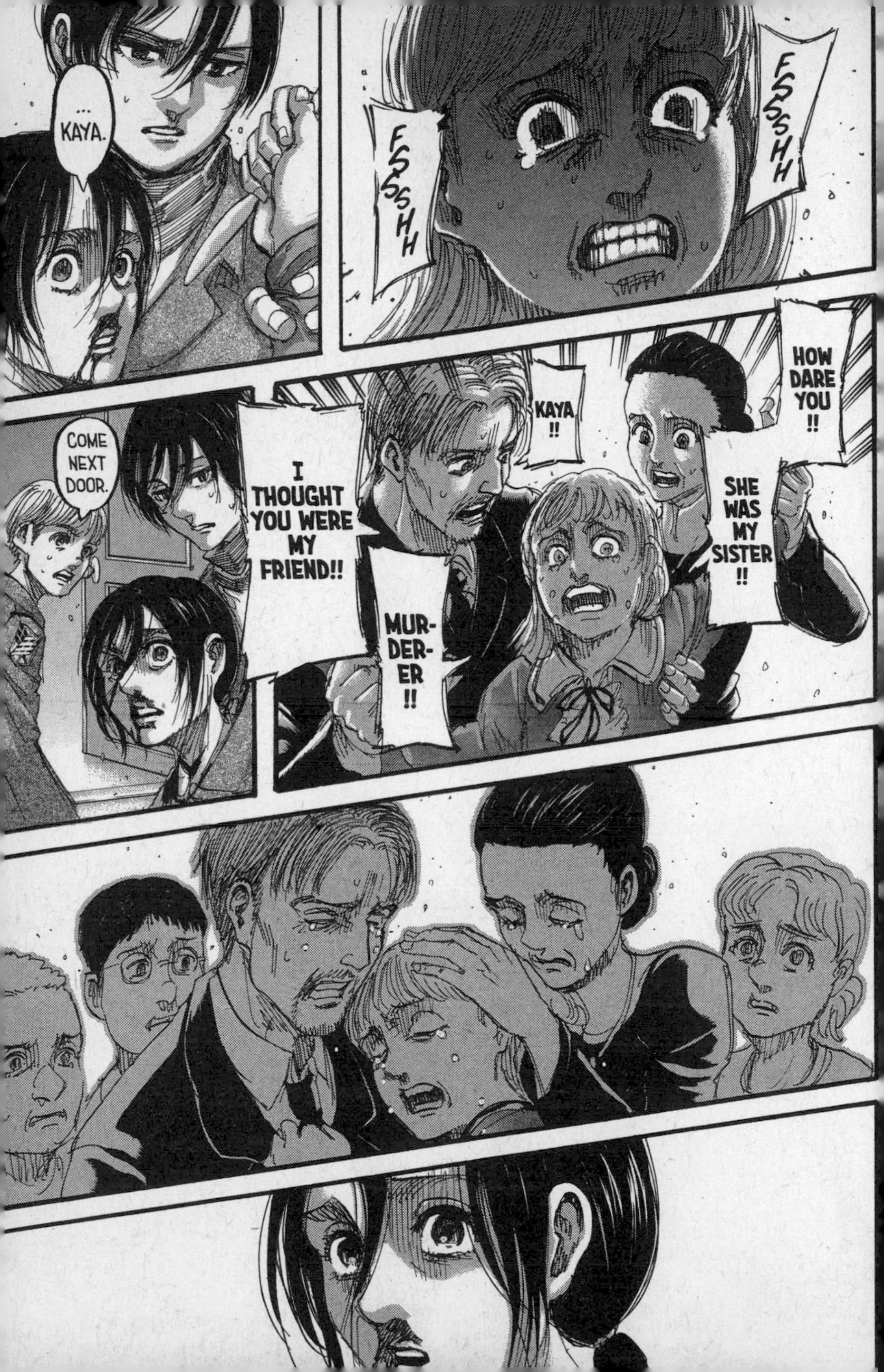
FSSSHH
FSSSHH
... KAYA.
HOW DARE YOU!!
KAYA!!
SHE WAS MY SISTER!!
I THOUGHT YOU WERE MY FRIEND!!
MUR-DER-ER!!
COME NEXT DOOR.

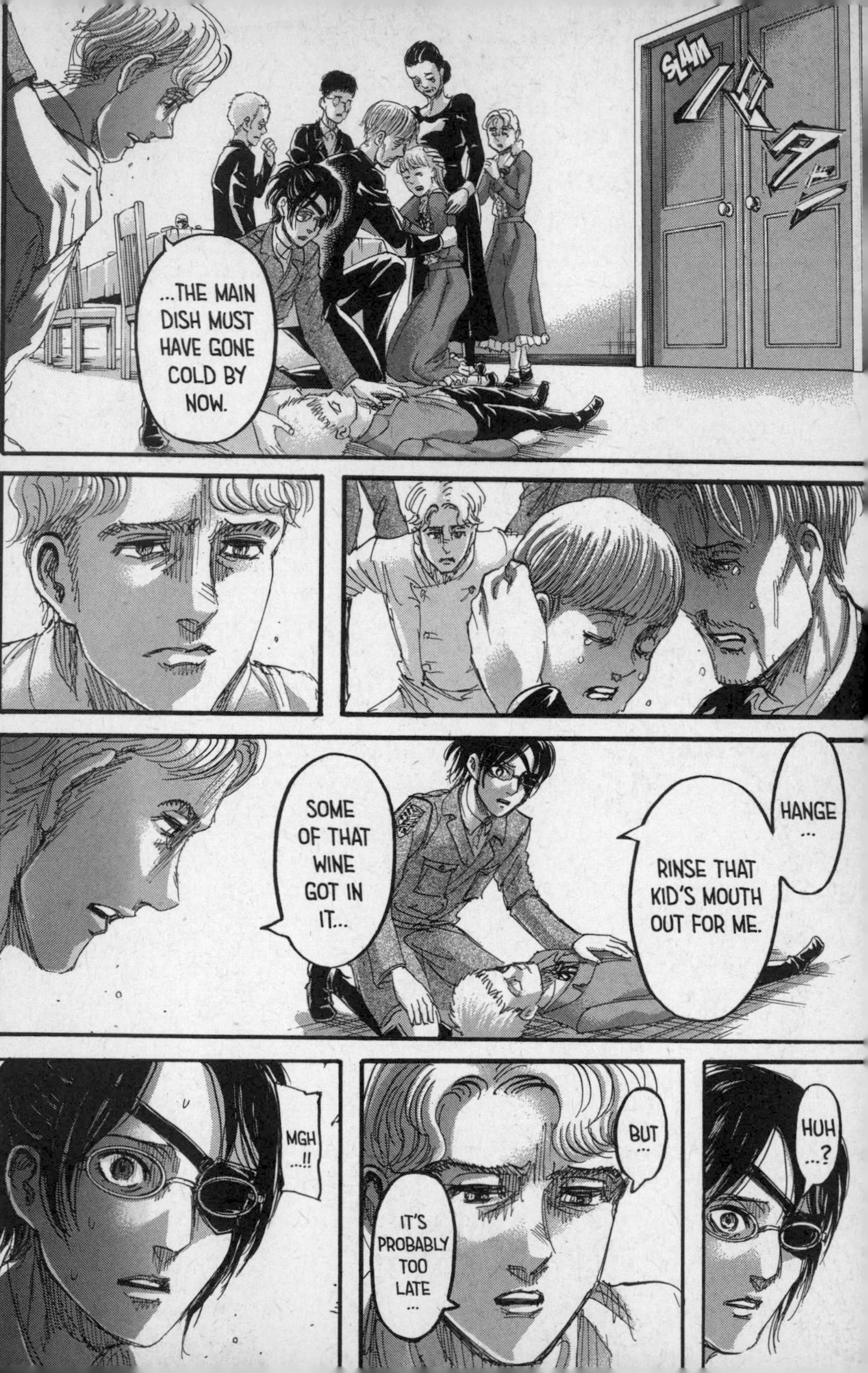
SLAM
...THE MAIN DISH MUST HAVE GONE COLD BY NOW.
HANGE ...
RINSE THAT KID'S MOUTH OUT FOR ME.
SOME OF THAT WINE GOT IN IT...
HUH ...?
BUT ...
IT'S PROBABLY TOO LATE ...
MGH ...!!

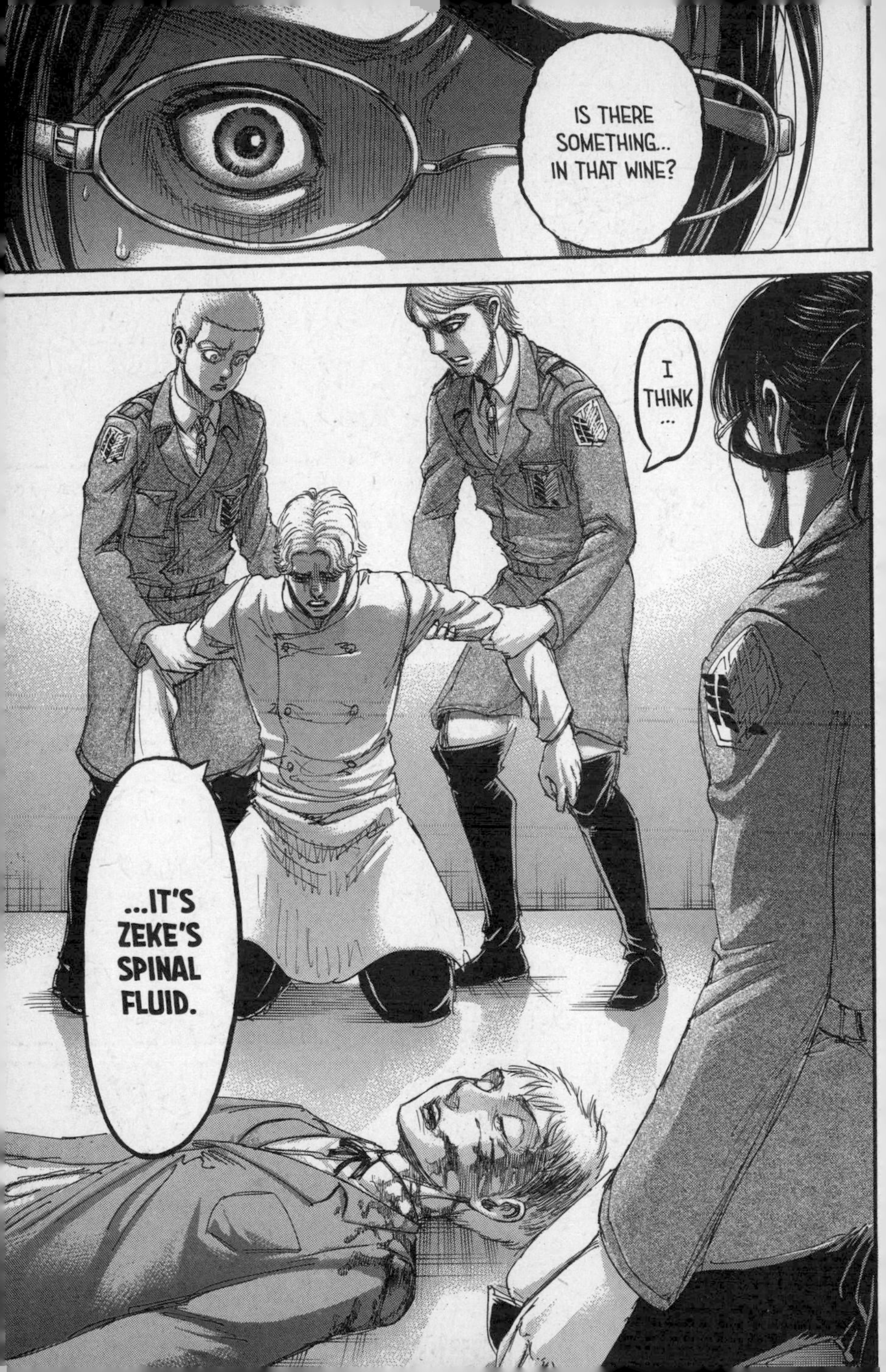
IS THERE SOMETHING... IN THAT WINE?
I THINK ...
...IT'S ZEKE'S SPINAL FLUID.

ATTACK on TITAN

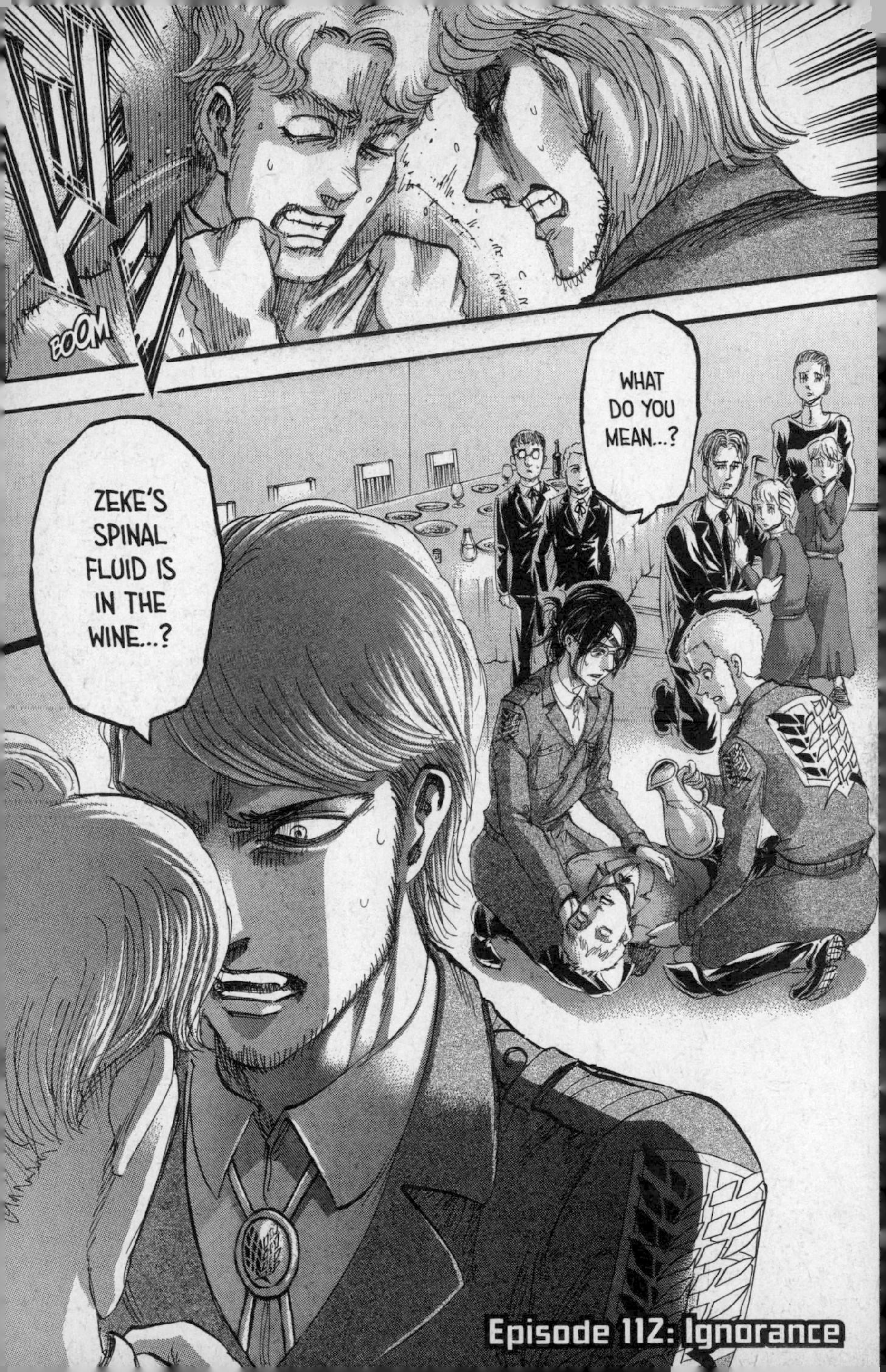
BOOM
WHAT DO YOU MEAN...?
ZEKE'S SPINAL FLUID IS IN THE WINE...?

Episode 112: Ignorance

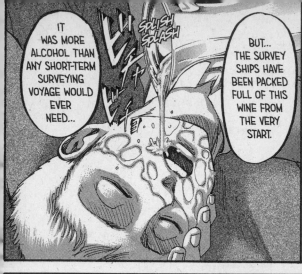

I DON'T HAVE PROOF ...
BUT... THE SURVEY SHIPS HAVE BEEN PACKED FULL OF THIS WINE FROM THE VERY START.
SPLISH SPLASH
IT WAS MORE ALCOHOL THAN ANY SHORT-TERM SURVEYING VOYAGE WOULD EVER NEED...
AND... JUST AS I STARTED TO SETTLE IN HERE AS THE CHEF...
AGAIN.
...I WAS TOLD TO SERVE IT TO THE MILITARY, STARTING WITH HIGH-RANKING OFFICERS.
WHO TOLD YOU?!
YELENA.
AS FAR AS I KNOW, SHE WAS ACTING ALONE.
I DON'T KNOW ABOUT THE OTHER VOLUN-TEERS.
I-I'VE NEVER HEARD OF THIS BEFORE, EITHER ...!

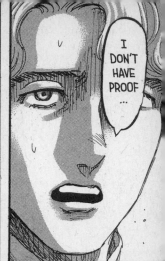

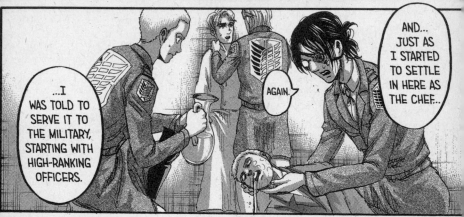

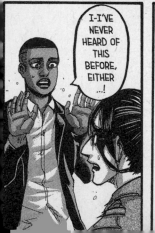

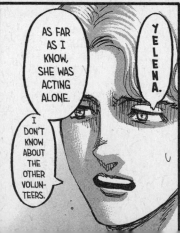

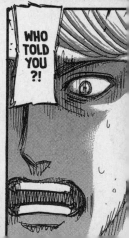

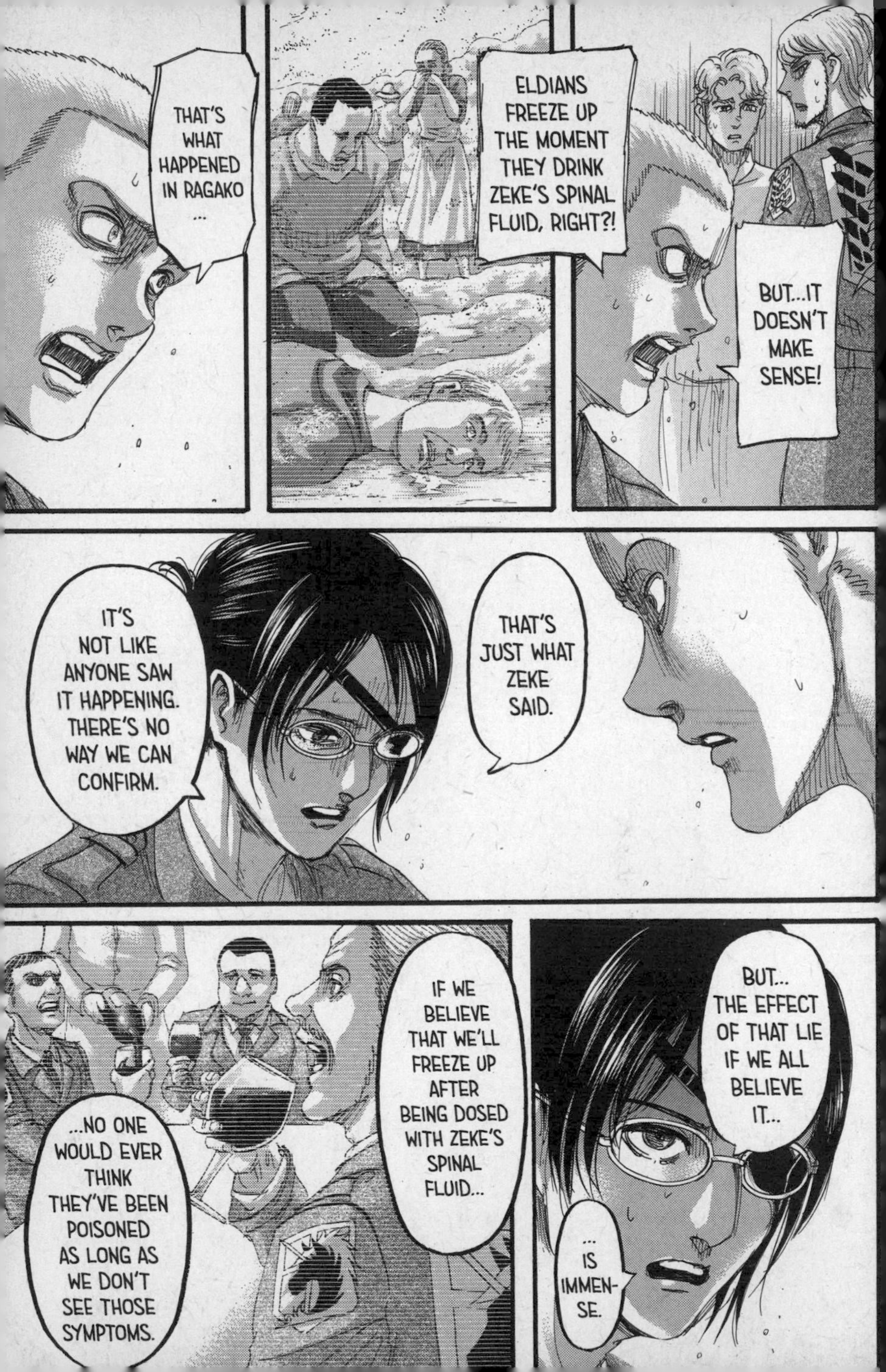
BUT...IT DOESN'T MAKE SENSE!
ELDIANS FREEZE UP THE MOMENT THEY DRINK ZEKE'S SPINAL FLUID, RIGHT?!
THAT'S WHAT HAPPENED IN RAGAKO ...
THAT'S JUST WHAT ZEKE SAID.
IT'S NOT LIKE ANYONE SAW IT HAPPENING. THERE'S NO WAY WE CAN CONFIRM.
BUT... THE EFFECT OF THAT LIE IF WE ALL BELIEVE IT...
... IS IMMEN-SE.
IF WE BELIEVE THAT WE'LL FREEZE UP AFTER BEING DOSED WITH ZEKE'S SPINAL FLUID...
...NO ONE WOULD EVER THINK THEY'VE BEEN POISONED AS LONG AS WE DON'T SEE THOSE SYMPTOMS.

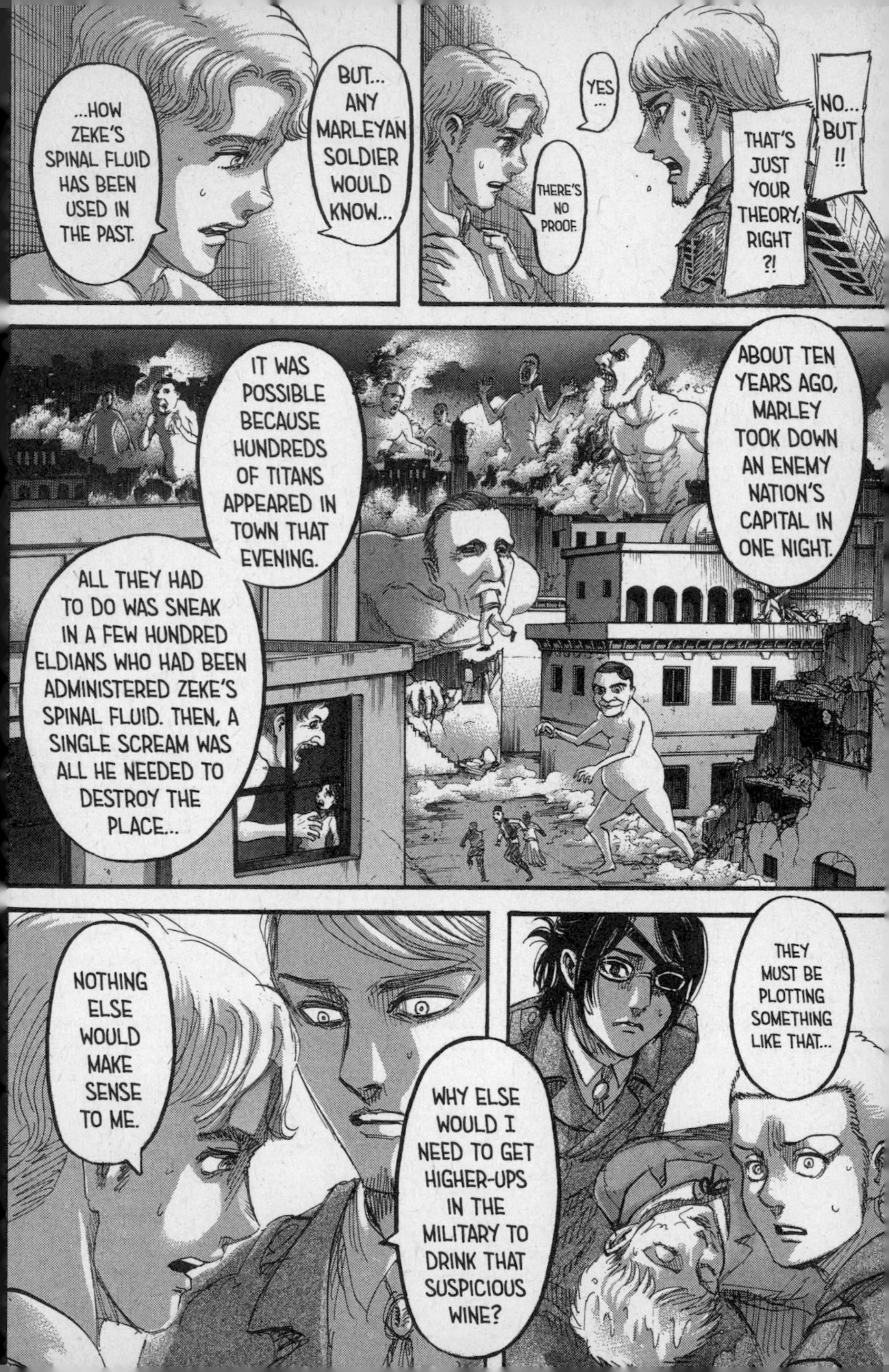
NO... BUT !!
THAT'S JUST YOUR THEORY, RIGHT ?!
YES ...
THERE'S NO PROOF.
BUT... ANY MARLEYAN SOLDIER WOULD KNOW...
...HOW ZEKE'S SPINAL FLUID HAS BEEN USED IN THE PAST.
ABOUT TEN YEARS AGO, MARLEY TOOK DOWN AN ENEMY NATION'S CAPITAL IN ONE NIGHT.
IT WAS POSSIBLE BECAUSE HUNDREDS OF TITANS APPEARED IN TOWN THAT EVENING.
ALL THEY HAD TO DO WAS SNEAK IN A FEW HUNDRED ELDIANS WHO HAD BEEN ADMINISTERED ZEKE'S SPINAL FLUID. THEN, A SINGLE SCREAM WAS ALL HE NEEDED TO DESTROY THE PLACE...
THEY MUST BE PLOTTING SOMETHING LIKE THAT...
WHY ELSE WOULD I NEED TO GET HIGHER-UPS IN THE MILITARY TO DRINK THAT SUSPICIOUS WINE?
NOTHING ELSE WOULD MAKE SENSE TO ME.

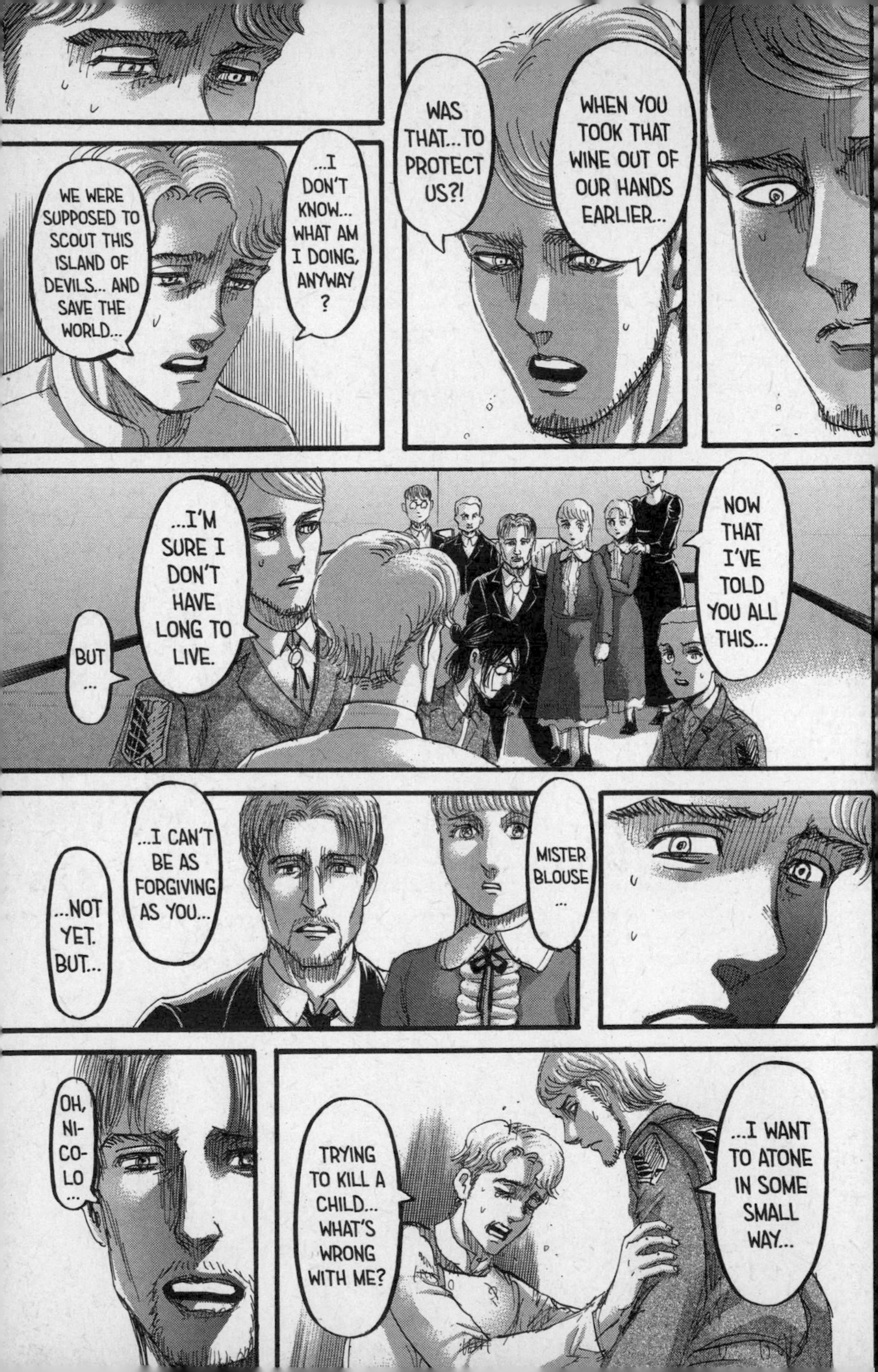
WHEN YOU TOOK THAT WINE OUT OF OUR HANDS EARLIER...
WAS THAT...TO PROTECT US?!
...I DON'T KNOW... WHAT AM I DOING, ANYWAY ?
WE WERE SUPPOSED TO SCOUT THIS ISLAND OF DEVILS... AND SAVE THE WORLD...
NOW THAT I'VE TOLD YOU ALL THIS...
...I'M SURE I DON'T HAVE LONG TO LIVE.
BUT ...
MISTER BLOUSE ...
...I CAN'T BE AS FORGIVING AS YOU...
...NOT YET. BUT...
...I WANT TO ATONE IN SOME SMALL WAY...
TRYING TO KILL A CHILD... WHAT'S WRONG WITH ME?
OH, NI-CO-LO ...

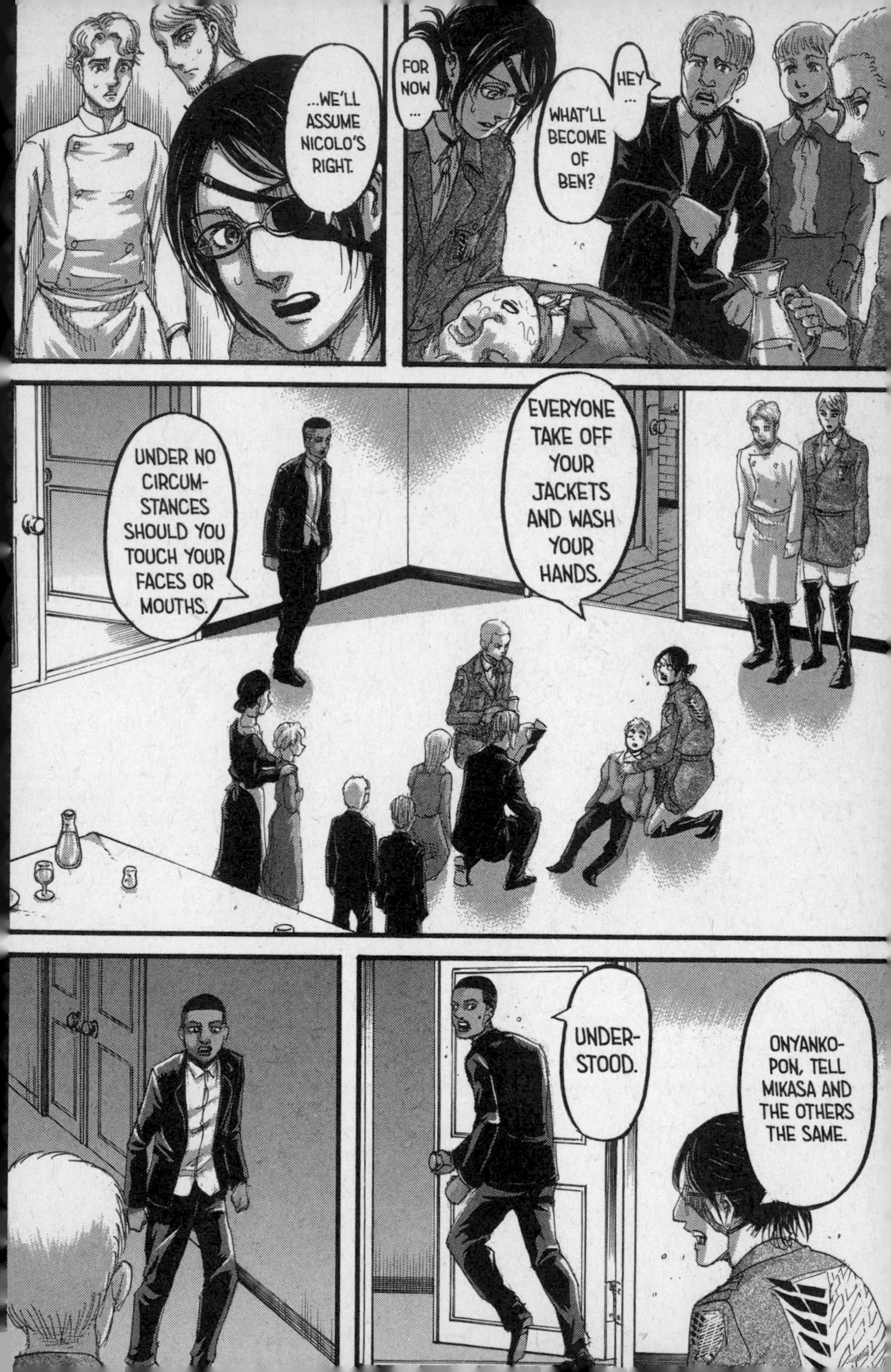
HEY ... WHAT'LL BECOME OF BEN?
FOR NOW ...
...WE'LL ASSUME NICOLO'S RIGHT.
EVERYONE TAKE OFF YOUR JACKETS AND WASH YOUR HANDS.
UNDER NO CIRCUM-STANCES SHOULD YOU TOUCH YOUR FACES OR MOUTHS.
ONYANKO-PON, TELL MIKASA AND THE OTHERS THE SAME.
UNDER-STOOD.

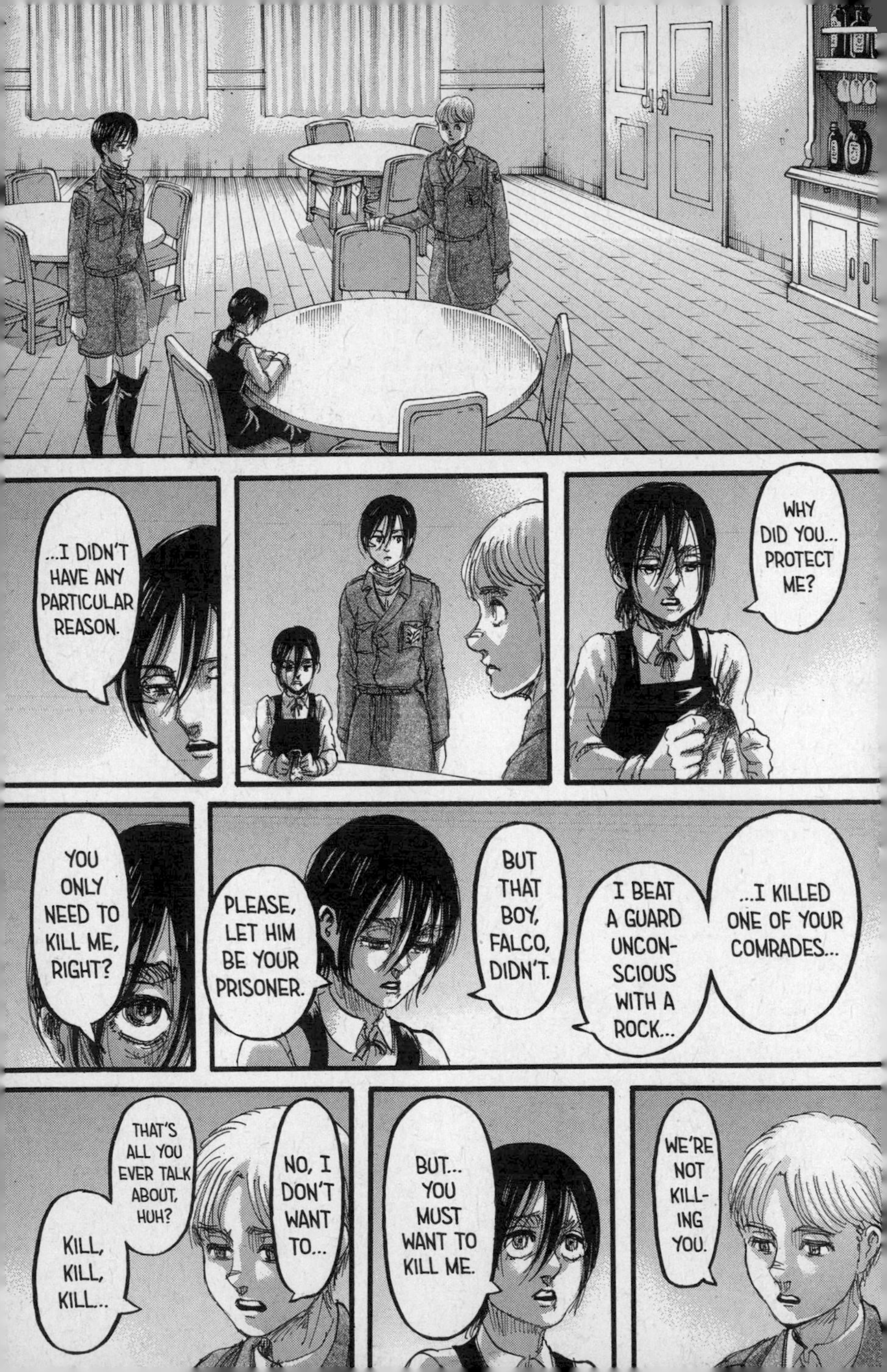

WHY DID YOU... PROTECT ME?
...I DIDN'T HAVE ANY PARTICULAR REASON.
...I KILLED ONE OF YOUR COMRADES...
I BEAT A GUARD UNCON-SCIOUS WITH A ROCK...
BUT THAT BOY, FALCO, DIDN'T.
PLEASE, LET HIM BE YOUR PRISONER.
YOU ONLY NEED TO KILL ME, RIGHT?
WE'RE NOT KILL-ING YOU.
BUT... YOU MUST WANT TO KILL ME.
NO, I DON'T WANT TO...
THAT'S ALL YOU EVER TALK ABOUT, HUH?
KILL, KILL, KILL...

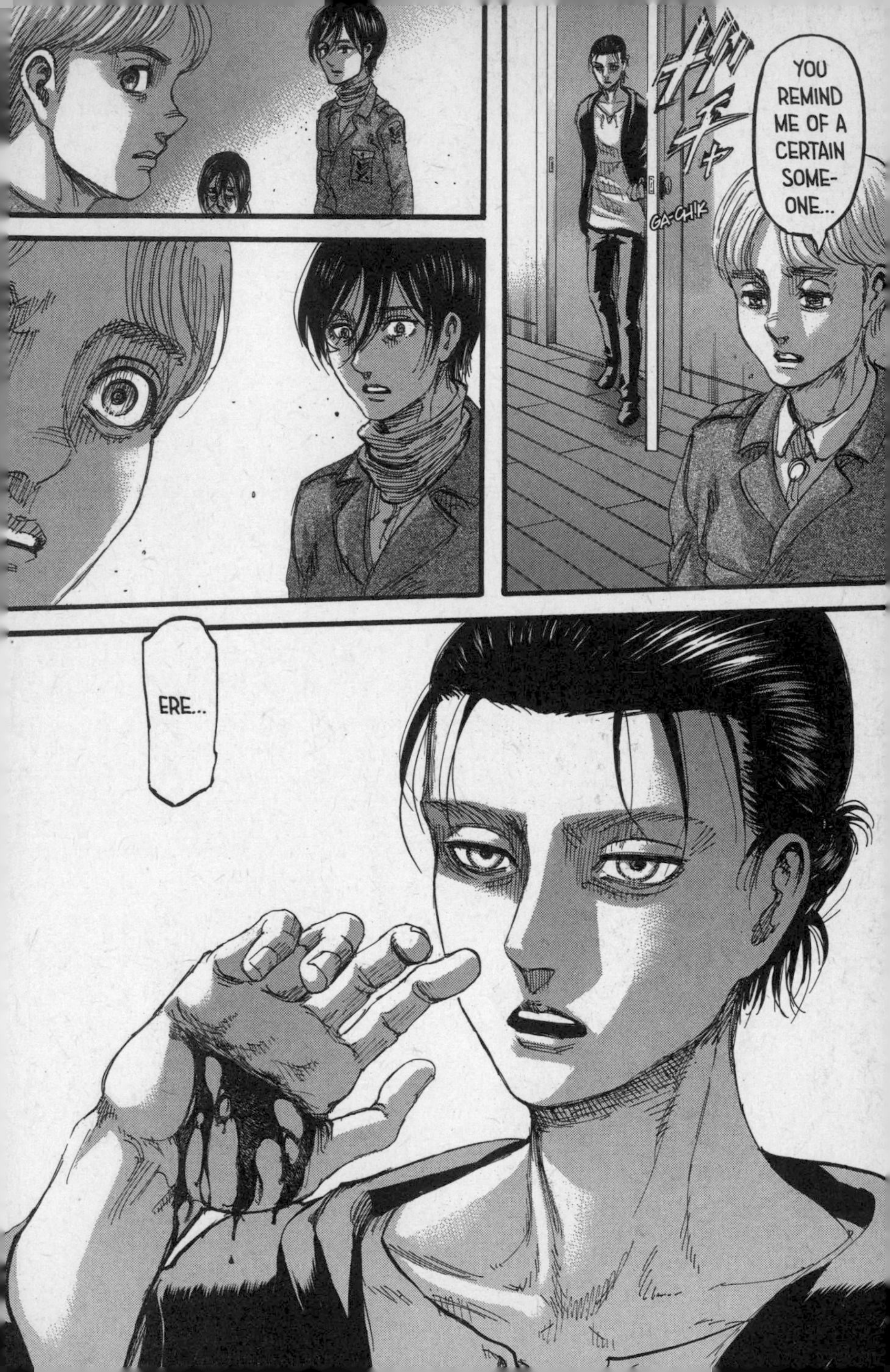
YOU REMIND ME OF A CERTAIN SOME-ONE...
GA-CHIK
ERE...

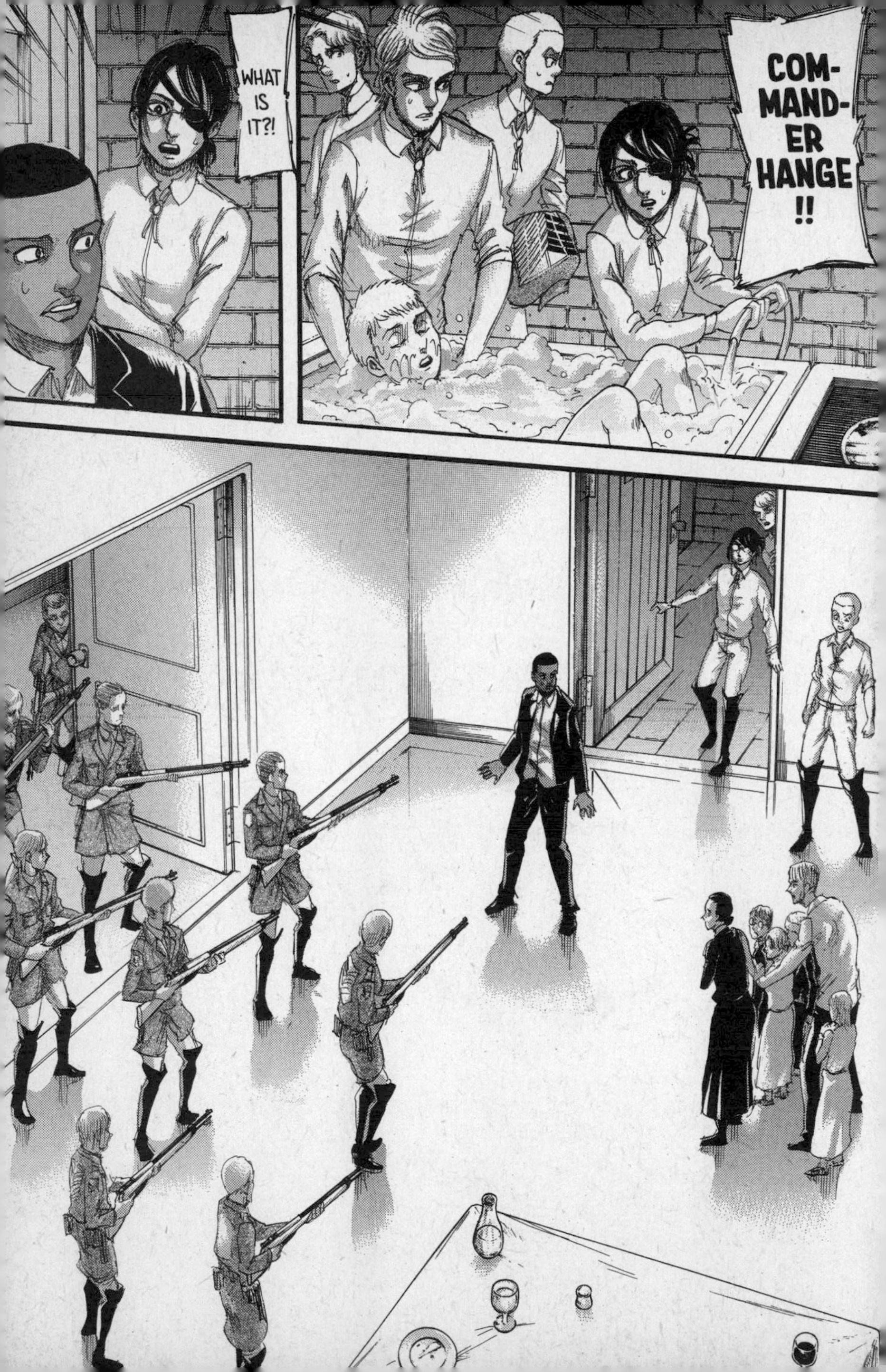
COM-MAND-ER HANGE !!
WHAT IS IT?!

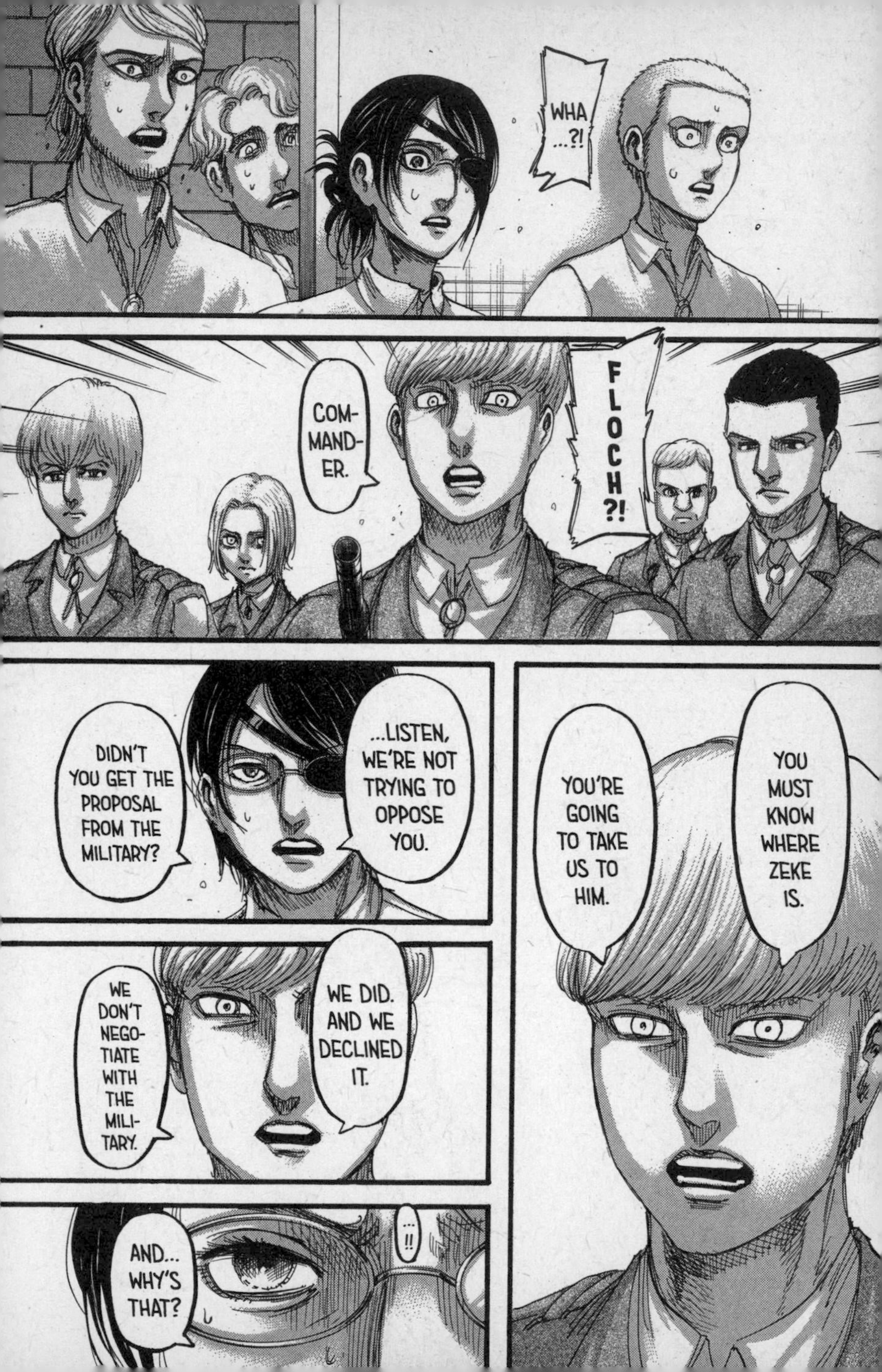
WHA...?!
FLOCH?!
COMMANDER.
YOU MUST KNOW WHERE ZEKE IS.
YOU'RE GOING TO TAKE US TO HIM.
...LISTEN, WE'RE NOT TRYING TO OPPOSE YOU.
DIDN'T YOU GET THE PROPOSAL FROM THE MILITARY?
WE DID. AND WE DECLINED IT.
WE DON'T NEGOTIATE WITH THE MILITARY.
...!!
AND... WHY'S THAT?

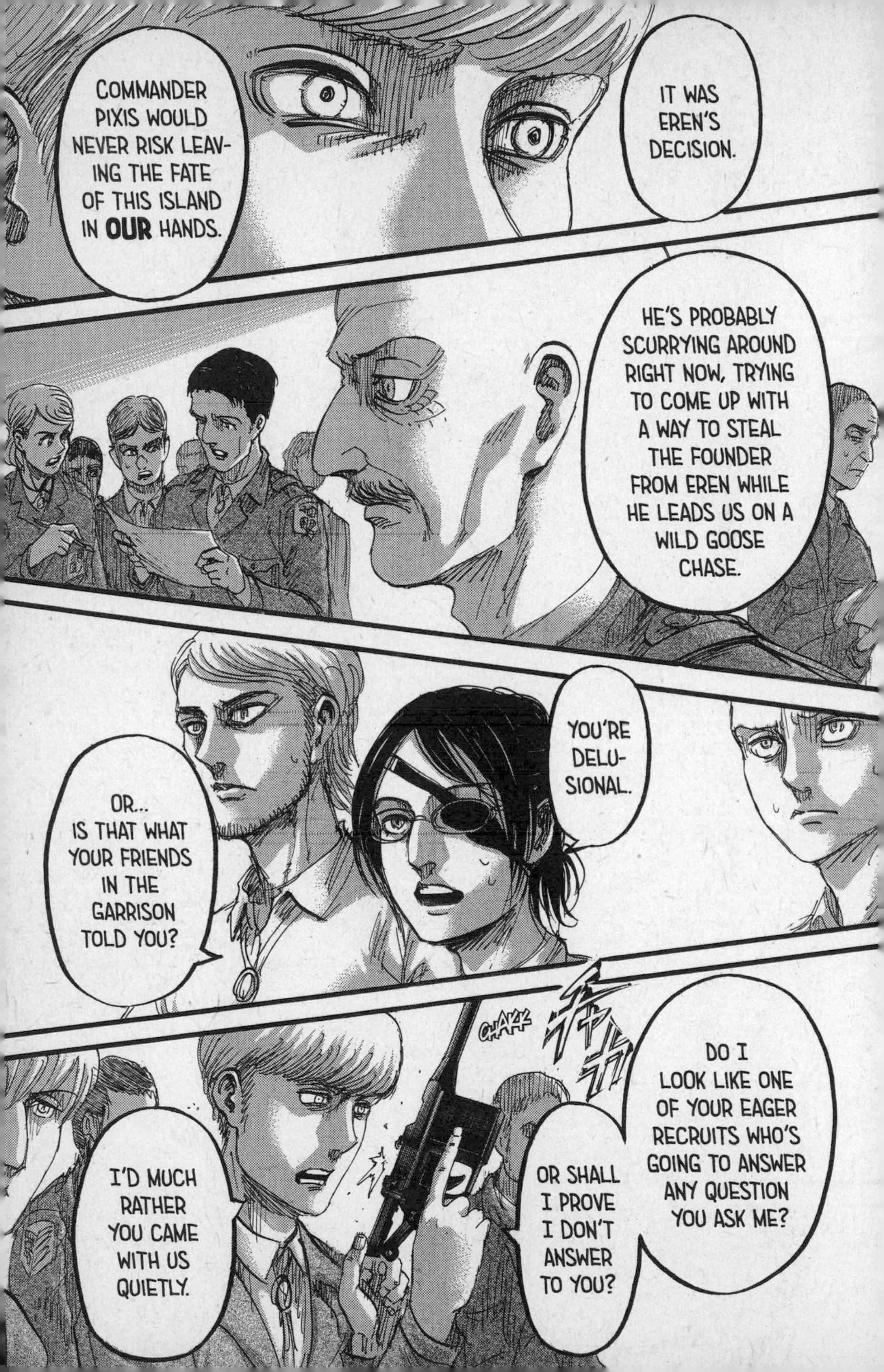
IT WAS EREN'S DECISION.
COMMANDER PIXIS WOULD NEVER RISK LEAV-ING THE FATE OF THIS ISLAND IN **OUR** HANDS.
HE'S PROBABLY SCURRYING AROUND RIGHT NOW, TRYING TO COME UP WITH A WAY TO STEAL THE FOUNDER FROM EREN WHILE HE LEADS US ON A WILD GOOSE CHASE.
YOU'RE DELU-SIONAL.
OR... IS THAT WHAT YOUR FRIENDS IN THE GARRISON TOLD YOU?
DO I LOOK LIKE ONE OF YOUR EAGER RECRUITS WHO'S GOING TO ANSWER ANY QUESTION YOU ASK ME?
CHAKK
OR SHALL I PROVE I DON'T ANSWER TO YOU?
I'D MUCH RATHER YOU CAME WITH US QUIETLY.

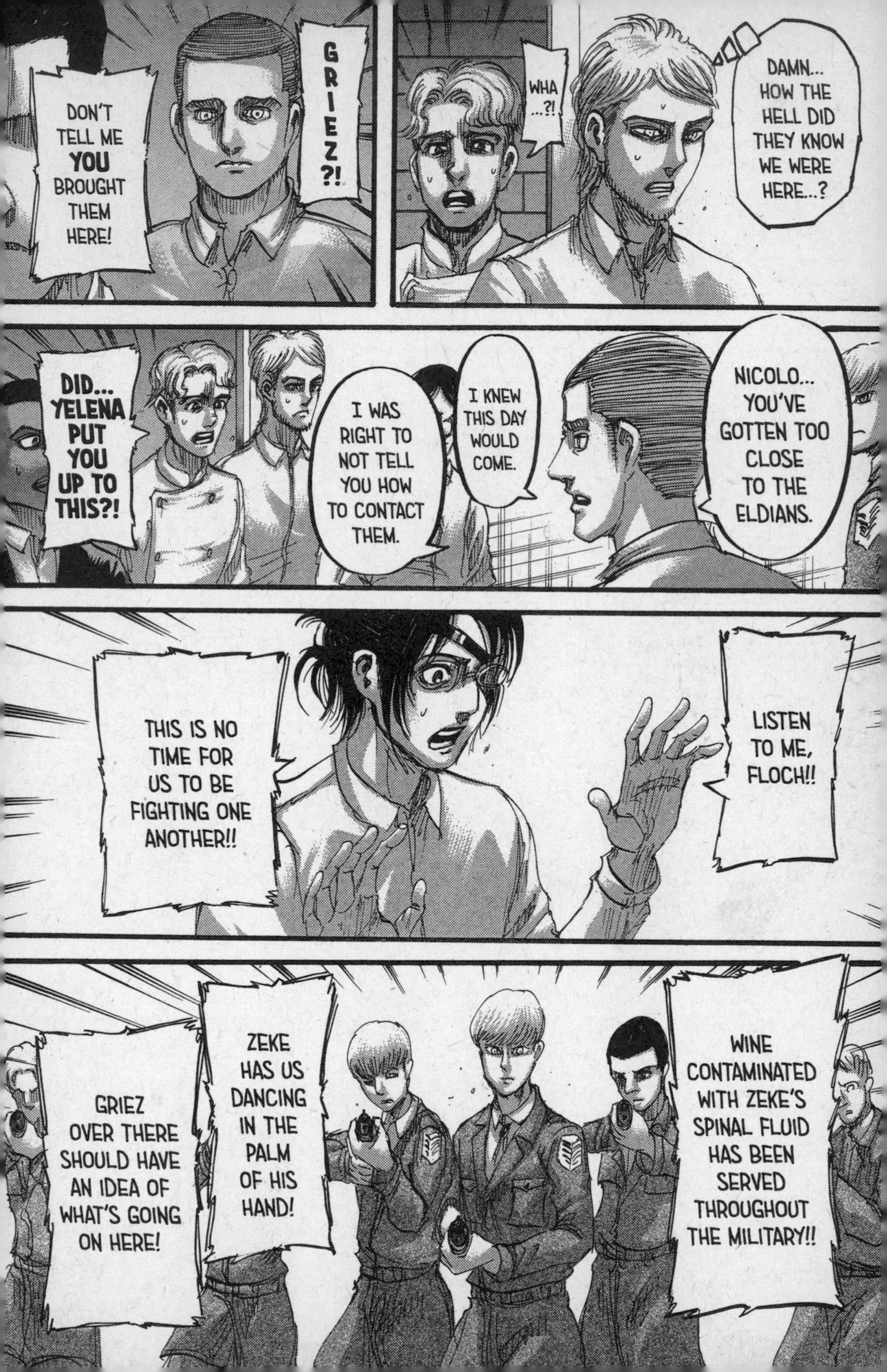
DAMN... HOW THE HELL DID THEY KNOW WE WERE HERE...?
WHA ...?!
GRIEZ ?!
DON'T TELL ME **YOU** BROUGHT THEM HERE!
NICOLO... YOU'VE GOTTEN TOO CLOSE TO THE ELDIANS.
I KNEW THIS DAY WOULD COME.
I WAS RIGHT TO NOT TELL YOU HOW TO CONTACT THEM.
DID... YELENA PUT YOU UP TO THIS?!
LISTEN TO ME, FLOCH!!
THIS IS NO TIME FOR US TO BE FIGHTING ONE ANOTHER!!
WINE CONTAMINATED WITH ZEKE'S SPINAL FLUID HAS BEEN SERVED THROUGHOUT THE MILITARY!!
ZEKE HAS US DANCING IN THE PALM OF HIS HAND!
GRIEZ OVER THERE SHOULD HAVE AN IDEA OF WHAT'S GOING ON HERE!

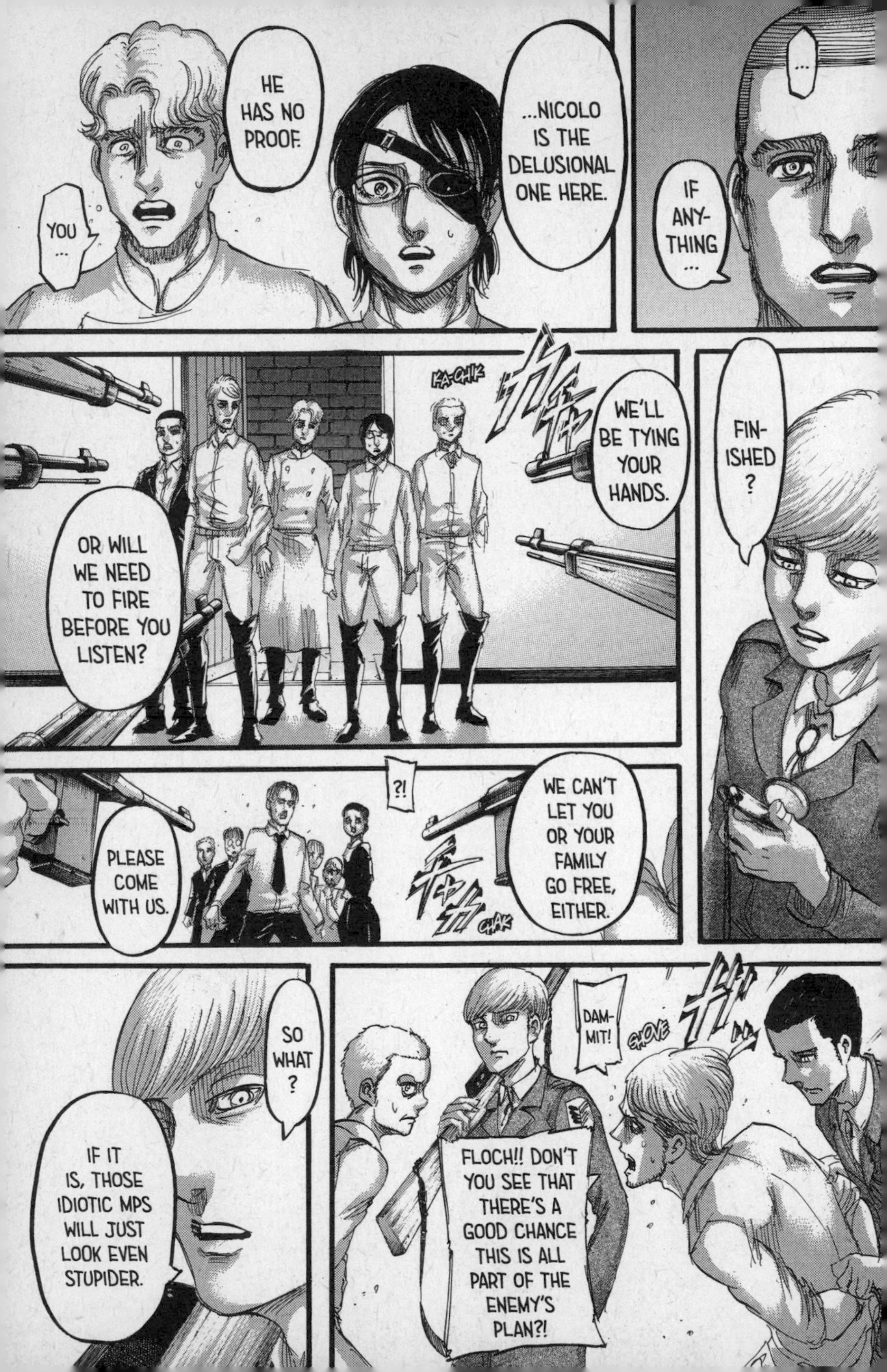
...
IF ANY-THING ...
...NICOLO IS THE DELUSIONAL ONE HERE.
HE HAS NO PROOF.
YOU ...
FIN-ISHED?
KA-CHIK
WE'LL BE TYING YOUR HANDS.
OR WILL WE NEED TO FIRE BEFORE YOU LISTEN?
WE CAN'T LET YOU OR YOUR FAMILY GO FREE, EITHER.
?!
CHAK
PLEASE COME WITH US.
DAM-MIT!
SHOVE
FLOCH!! DON'T YOU SEE THAT THERE'S A GOOD CHANCE THIS IS ALL PART OF THE ENEMY'S PLAN?!
SO WHAT?
IF IT IS, THOSE IDIOTIC MPS WILL JUST LOOK EVEN STUPIDER.

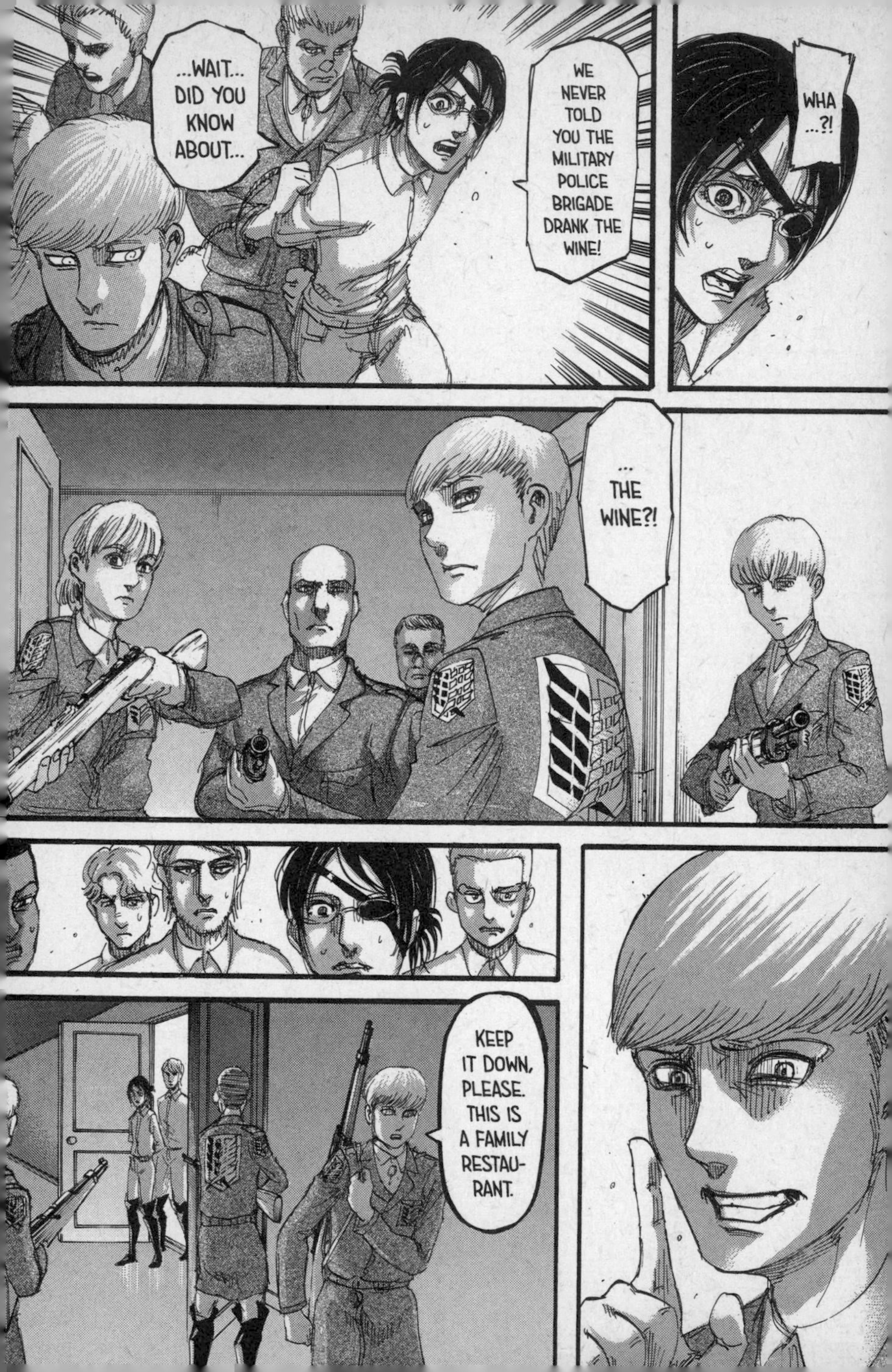
WHA ...?!
WE NEVER TOLD YOU THE MILITARY POLICE BRIGADE DRANK THE WINE!
...WAIT... DID YOU KNOW ABOUT...
... THE WINE?!
KEEP IT DOWN, PLEASE. THIS IS A FAMILY RESTAU- RANT.

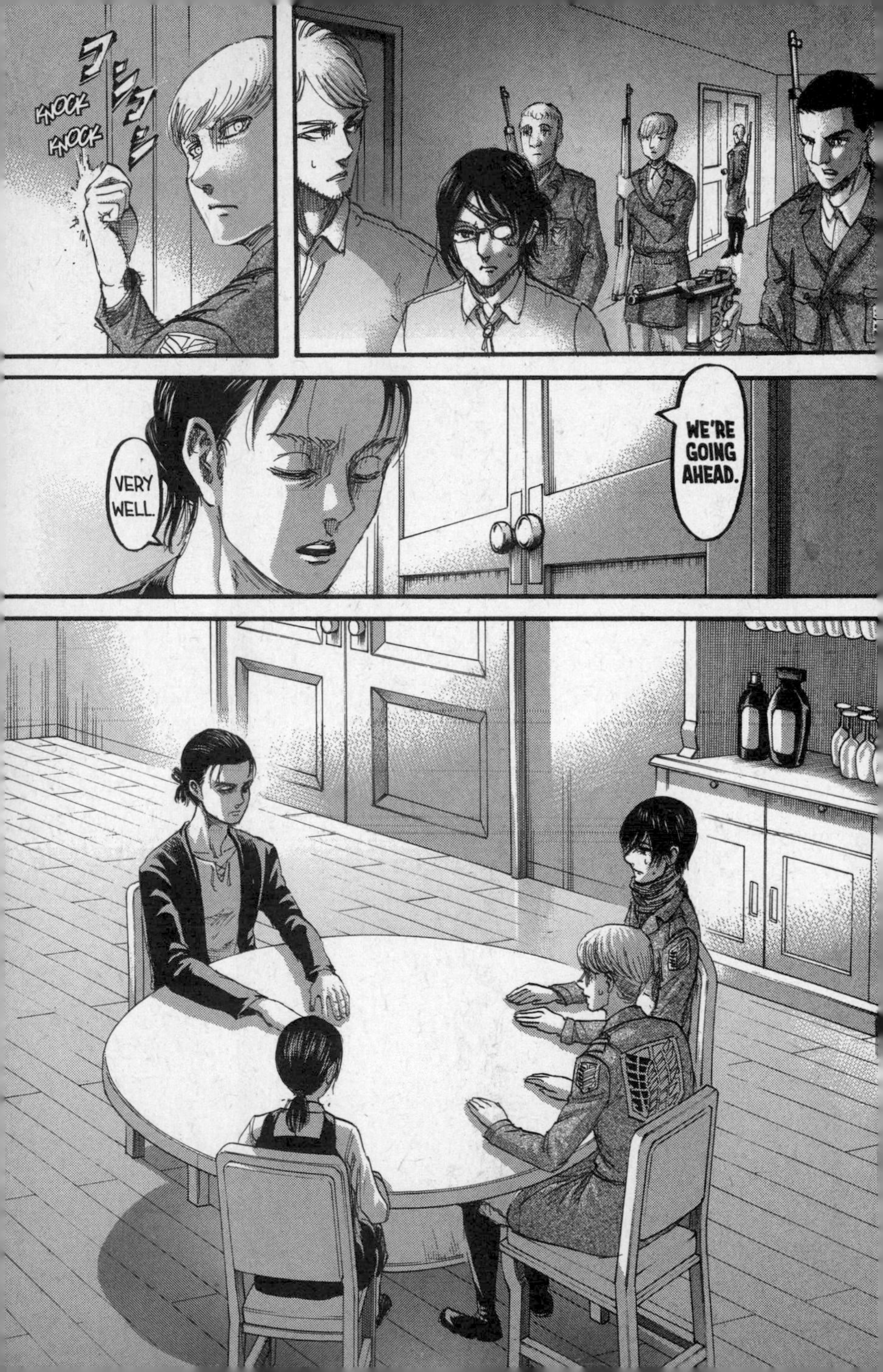
KNOCK KNOCK
WE'RE GOING AHEAD.
VERY WELL.

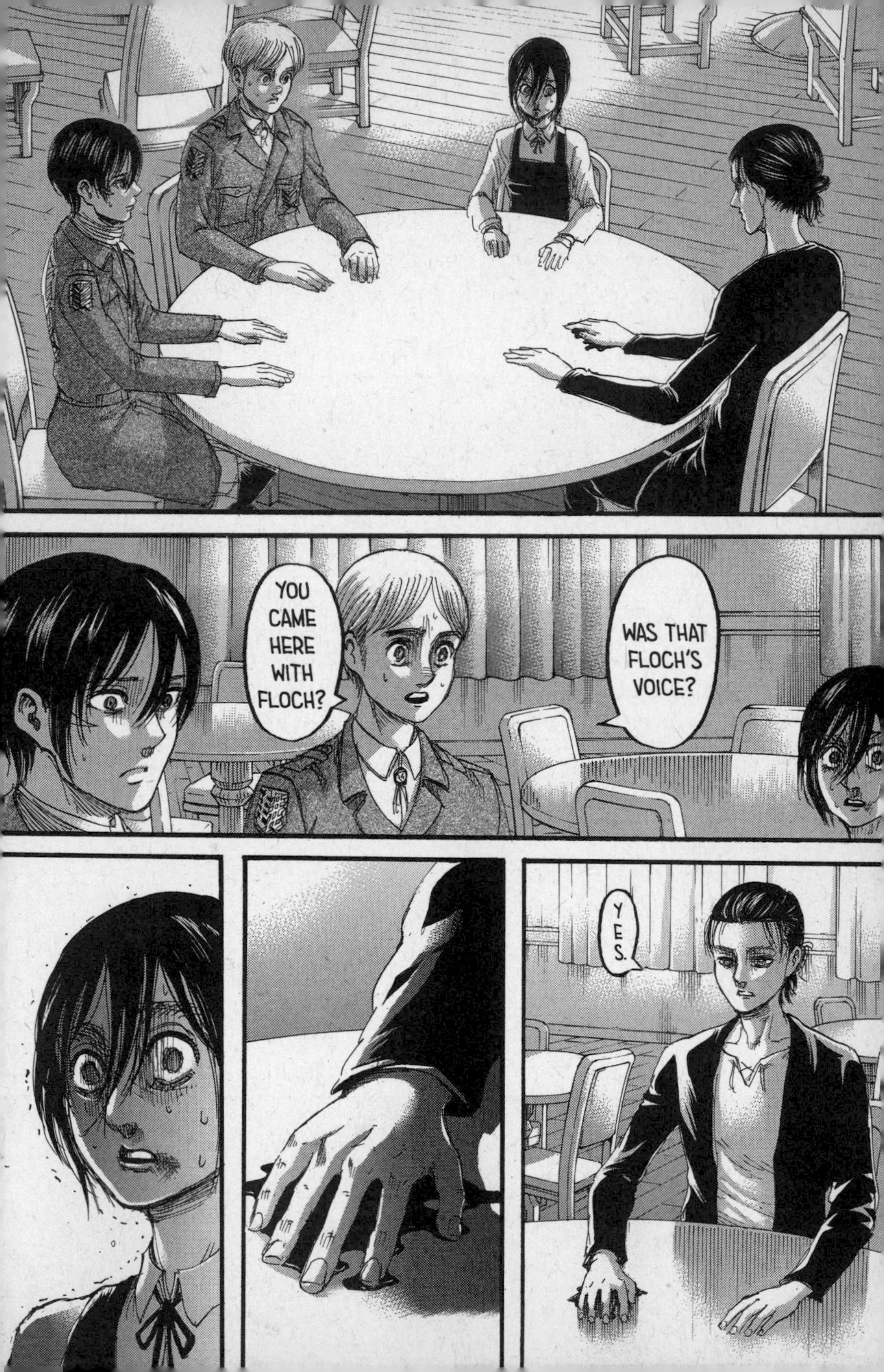
WAS THAT FLOCH'S VOICE?
YOU CAME HERE WITH FLOCH?
YES.

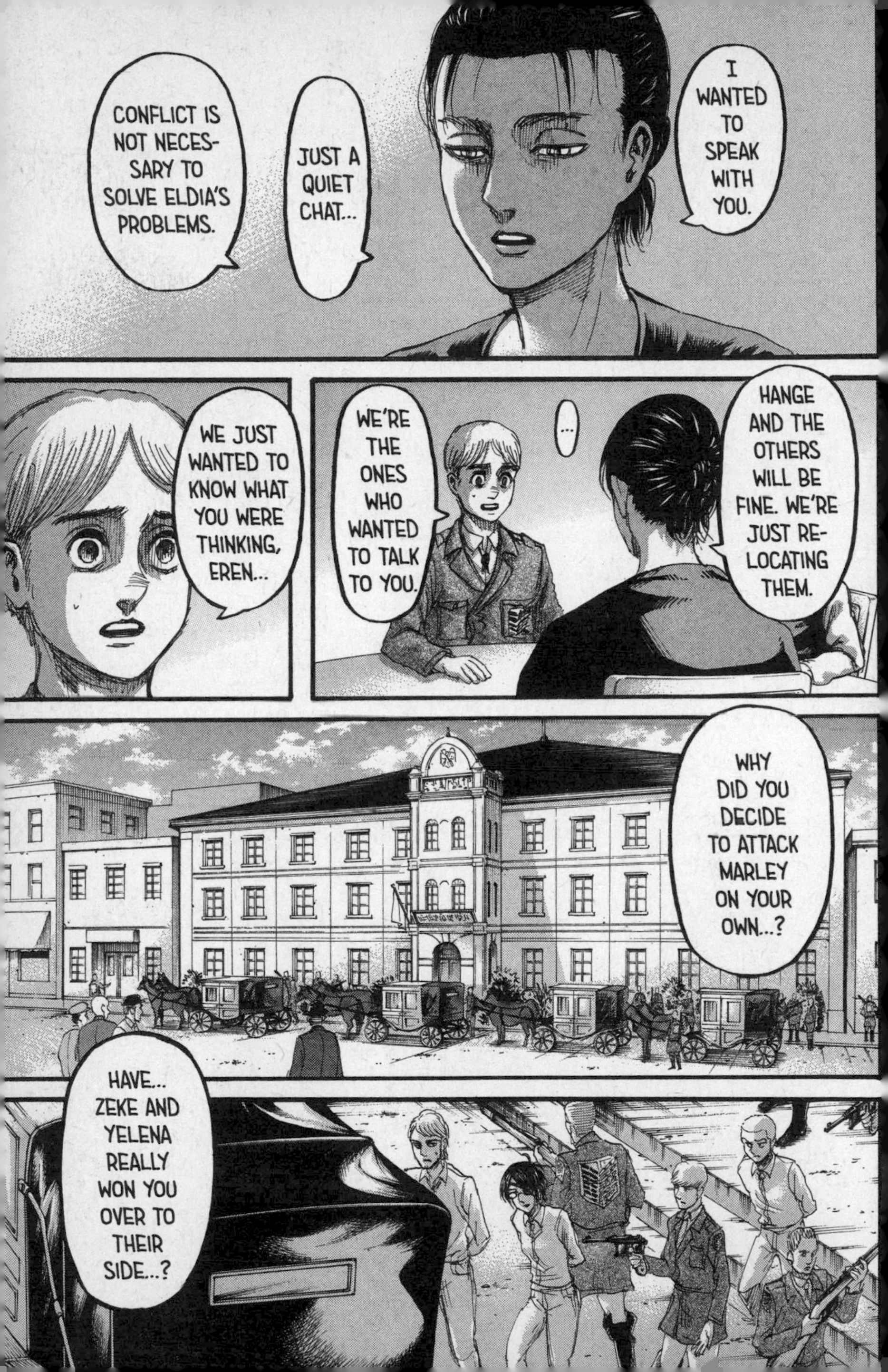
I WANTED TO SPEAK WITH YOU.
JUST A QUIET CHAT...
CONFLICT IS NOT NECESSARY TO SOLVE ELDIA'S PROBLEMS.
HANGE AND THE OTHERS WILL BE FINE. WE'RE JUST RELOCATING THEM.
...
WE'RE THE ONES WHO WANTED TO TALK TO YOU.
WE JUST WANTED TO KNOW WHAT YOU WERE THINKING, EREN...
WHY DID YOU DECIDE TO ATTACK MARLEY ON YOUR OWN...?
HAVE... ZEKE AND YELENA REALLY WON YOU OVER TO THEIR SIDE...?

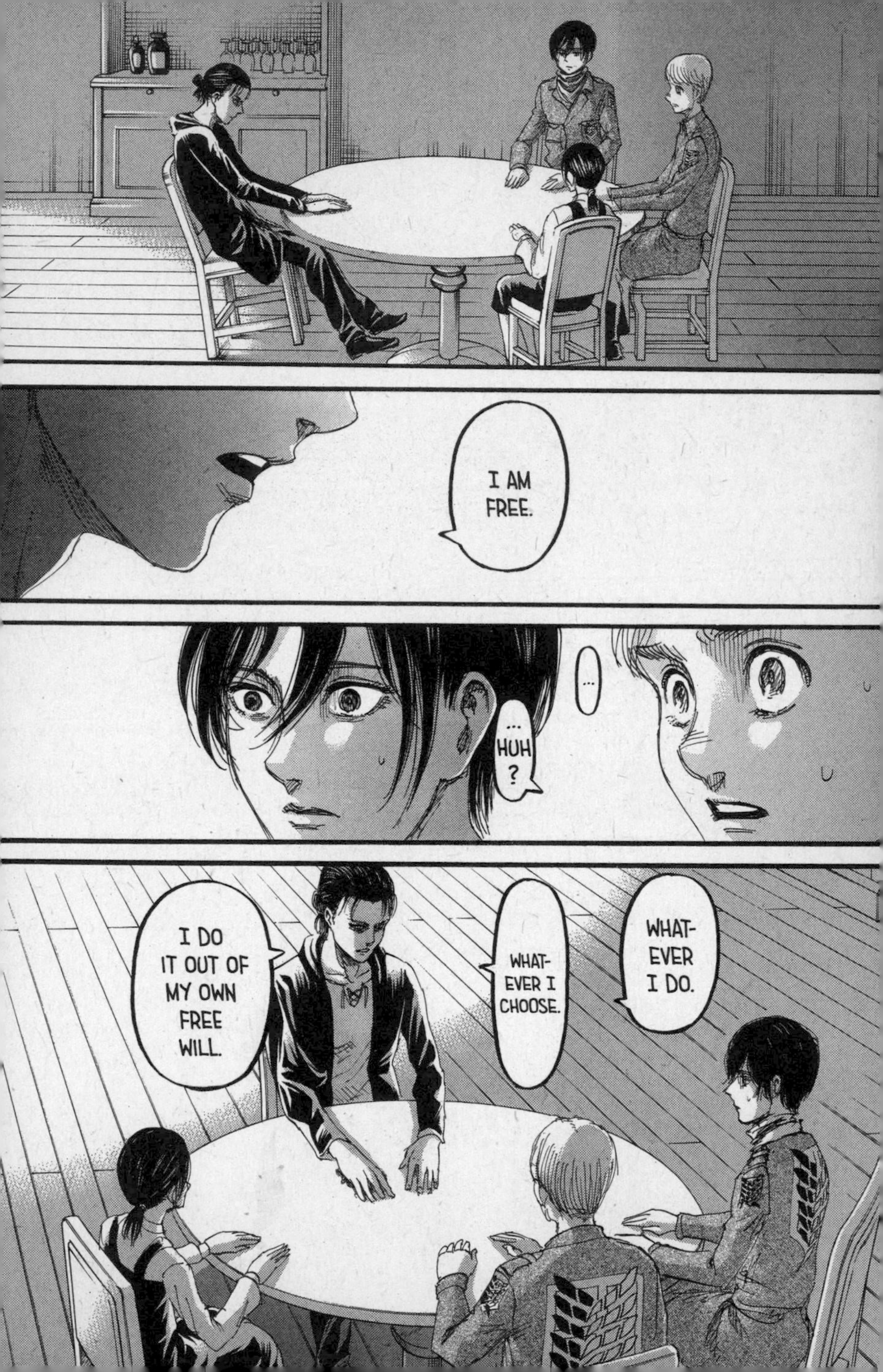
I AM FREE.
...
... HUH ?
WHAT-EVER I DO.
WHAT-EVER I CHOOSE.
I DO IT OUT OF MY OWN FREE WILL.

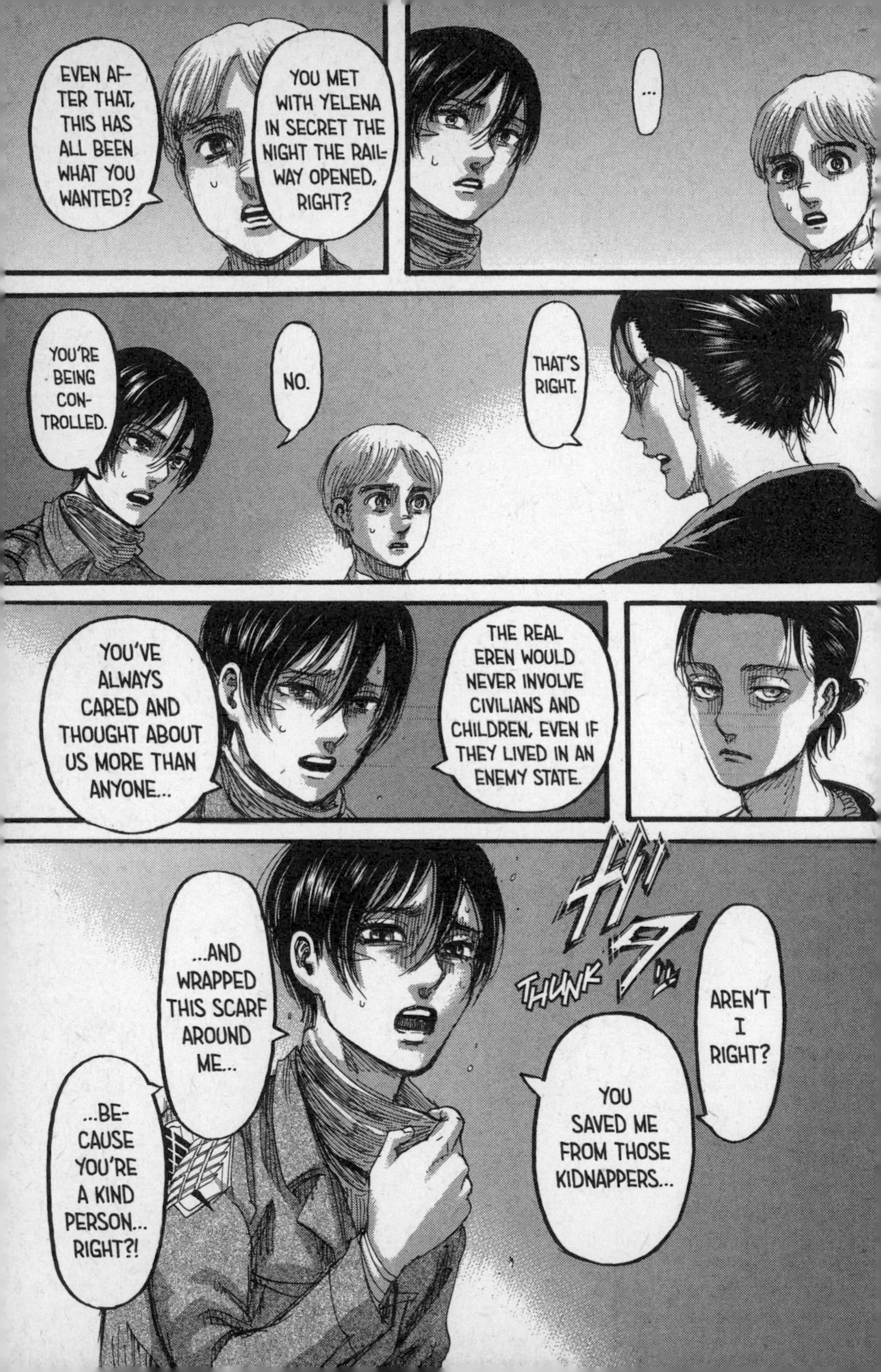
...
YOU MET WITH YELENA IN SECRET THE NIGHT THE RAILWAY OPENED, RIGHT?
EVEN AFTER THAT, THIS HAS ALL BEEN WHAT YOU WANTED?
THAT'S RIGHT.
NO.
YOU'RE BEING CONTROLLED.
THE REAL EREN WOULD NEVER INVOLVE CIVILIANS AND CHILDREN, EVEN IF THEY LIVED IN AN ENEMY STATE.
YOU'VE ALWAYS CARED AND THOUGHT ABOUT US MORE THAN ANYONE...
AREN'T I RIGHT?
THUNK
YOU SAVED ME FROM THOSE KIDNAPPERS...
...AND WRAPPED THIS SCARF AROUND ME...
...BECAUSE YOU'RE A KIND PERSON... RIGHT?!

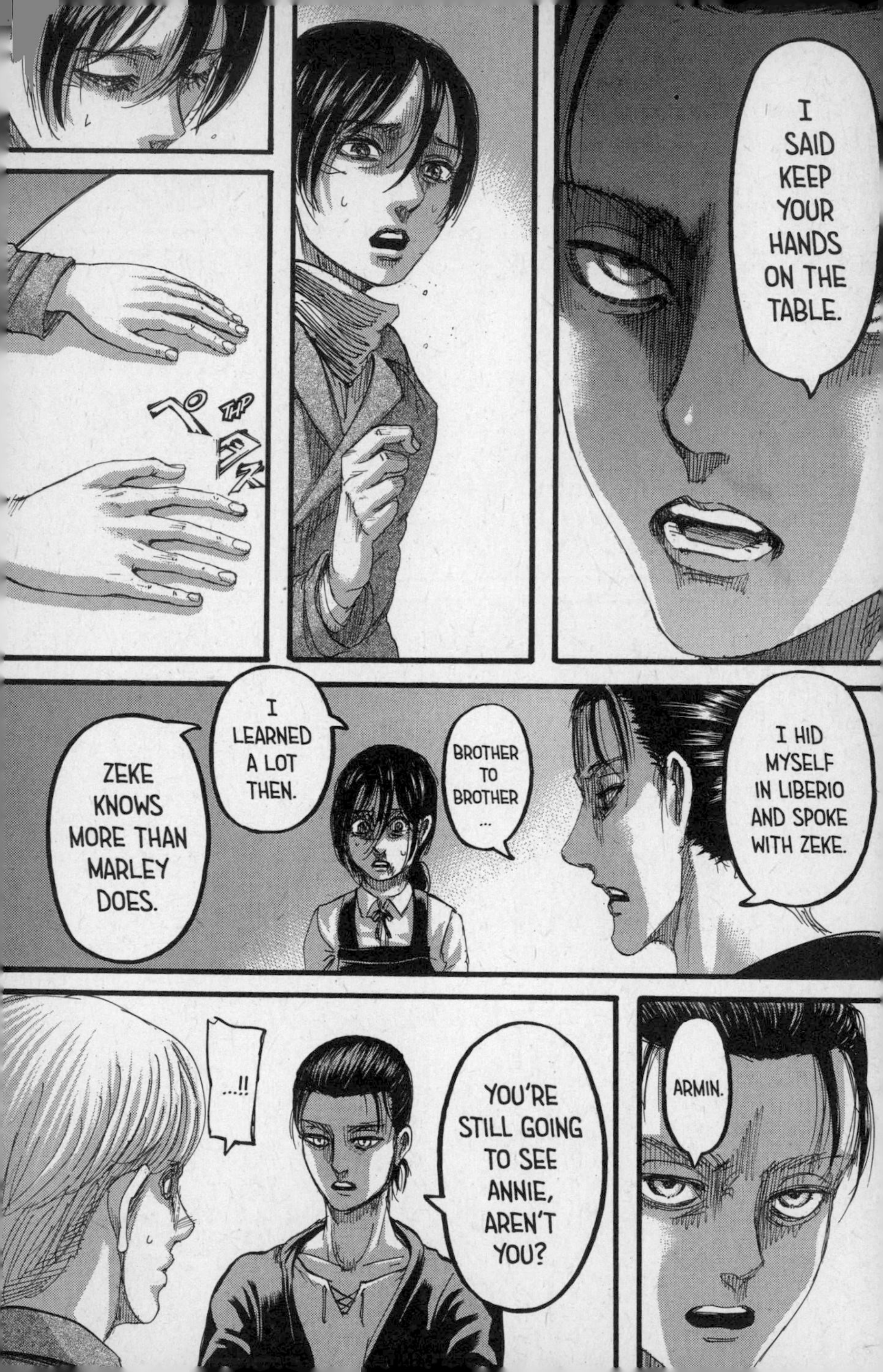
I SAID KEEP YOUR HANDS ON THE TABLE.
THP
I HID MYSELF IN LIBERIO AND SPOKE WITH ZEKE.
BROTHER TO BROTHER ...
I LEARNED A LOT THEN.
ZEKE KNOWS MORE THAN MARLEY DOES.
ARMIN.
YOU'RE STILL GOING TO SEE ANNIE, AREN'T YOU?
...!!

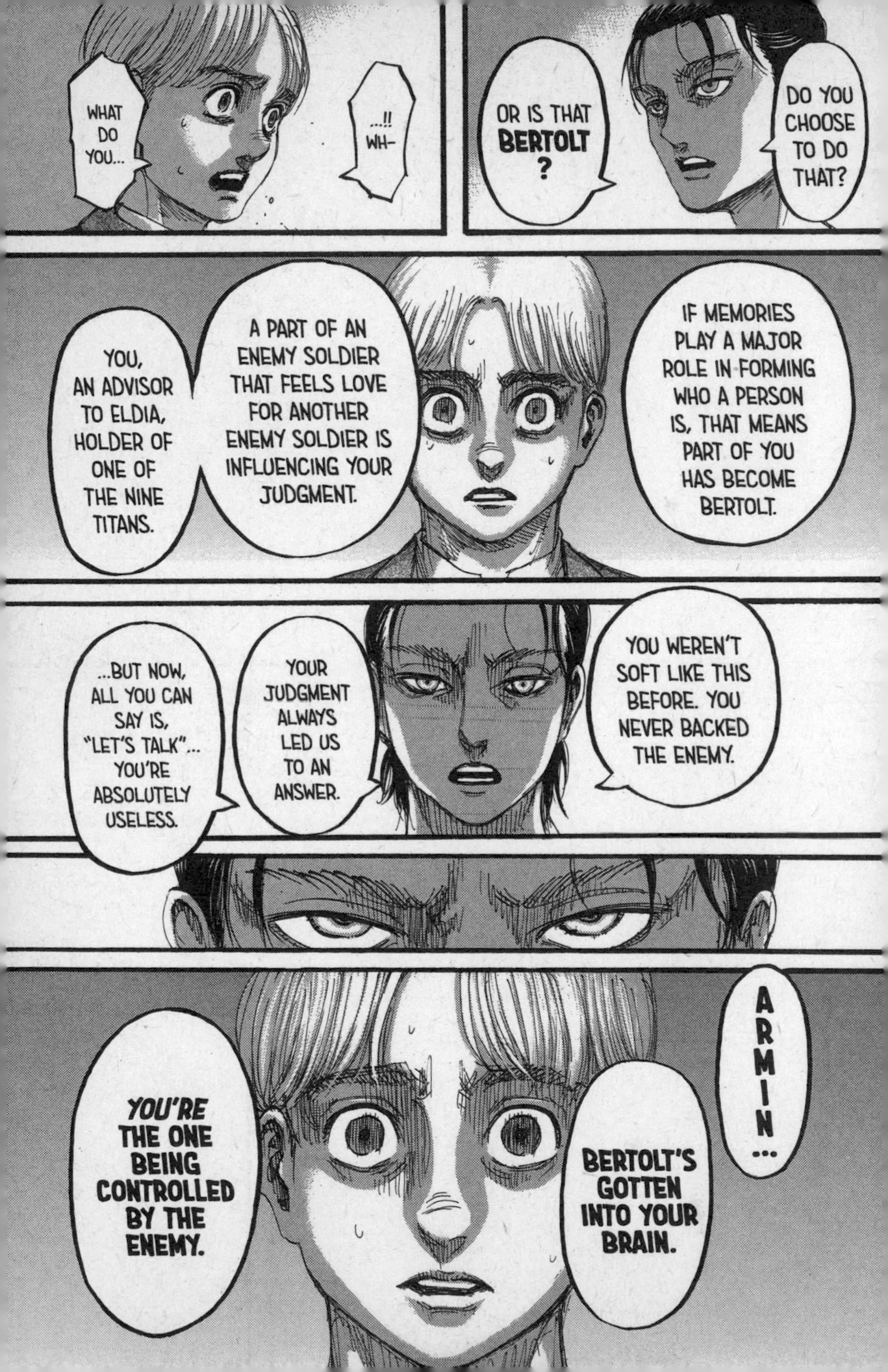
DO YOU CHOOSE TO DO THAT?
OR IS THAT **BERTOLT** ?
...!! WH-
WHAT DO YOU...
IF MEMORIES PLAY A MAJOR ROLE IN FORMING WHO A PERSON IS, THAT MEANS PART OF YOU HAS BECOME BERTOLT.
A PART OF AN ENEMY SOLDIER THAT FEELS LOVE FOR ANOTHER ENEMY SOLDIER IS INFLUENCING YOUR JUDGMENT.
YOU, AN ADVISOR TO ELDIA, HOLDER OF ONE OF THE NINE TITANS.
YOU WEREN'T SOFT LIKE THIS BEFORE. YOU NEVER BACKED THE ENEMY.
YOUR JUDGMENT ALWAYS LED US TO AN ANSWER.
...BUT NOW, ALL YOU CAN SAY IS, "LET'S TALK"... YOU'RE ABSOLUTELY USELESS.
ARMIN...
BERTOLT'S GOTTEN INTO YOUR BRAIN.
YOU'RE **THE ONE BEING CONTROLLED BY THE ENEMY.**

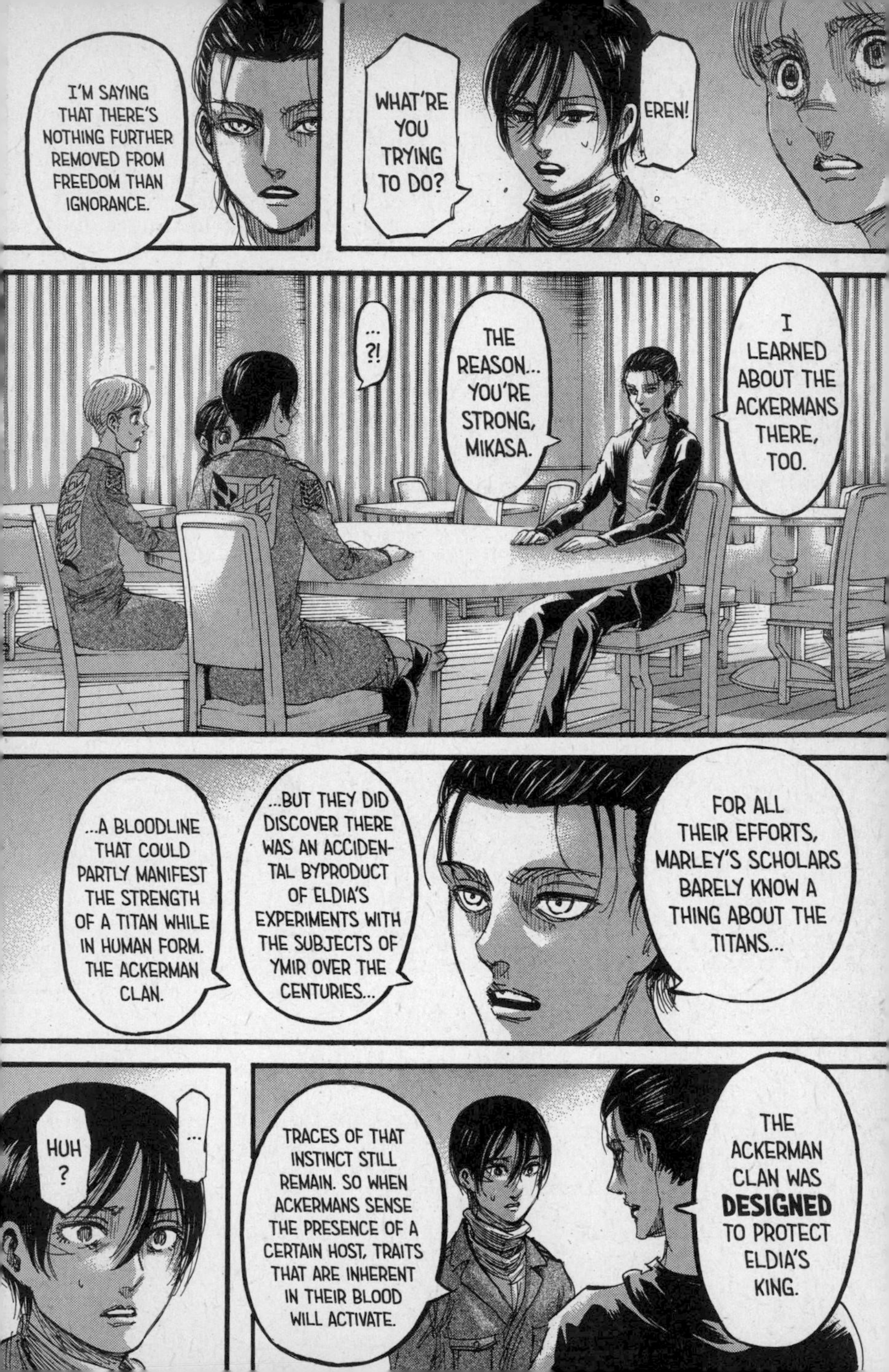
EREN!
WHAT'RE YOU TRYING TO DO?
I'M SAYING THAT THERE'S NOTHING FURTHER REMOVED FROM FREEDOM THAN IGNORANCE.
I LEARNED ABOUT THE ACKERMANS THERE, TOO.
THE REASON... YOU'RE STRONG, MIKASA.
...?!
FOR ALL THEIR EFFORTS, MARLEY'S SCHOLARS BARELY KNOW A THING ABOUT THE TITANS...
...BUT THEY DID DISCOVER THERE WAS AN ACCIDEN-TAL BYPRODUCT OF ELDIA'S EXPERIMENTS WITH THE SUBJECTS OF YMIR OVER THE CENTURIES...
...A BLOODLINE THAT COULD PARTLY MANIFEST THE STRENGTH OF A TITAN WHILE IN HUMAN FORM. THE ACKERMAN CLAN.
THE ACKERMAN CLAN WAS **DESIGNED** TO PROTECT ELDIA'S KING.
TRACES OF THAT INSTINCT STILL REMAIN. SO WHEN ACKERMANS SENSE THE PRESENCE OF A CERTAIN HOST, TRAITS THAT ARE INHERENT IN THEIR BLOOD WILL ACTIVATE.
...
HUH?

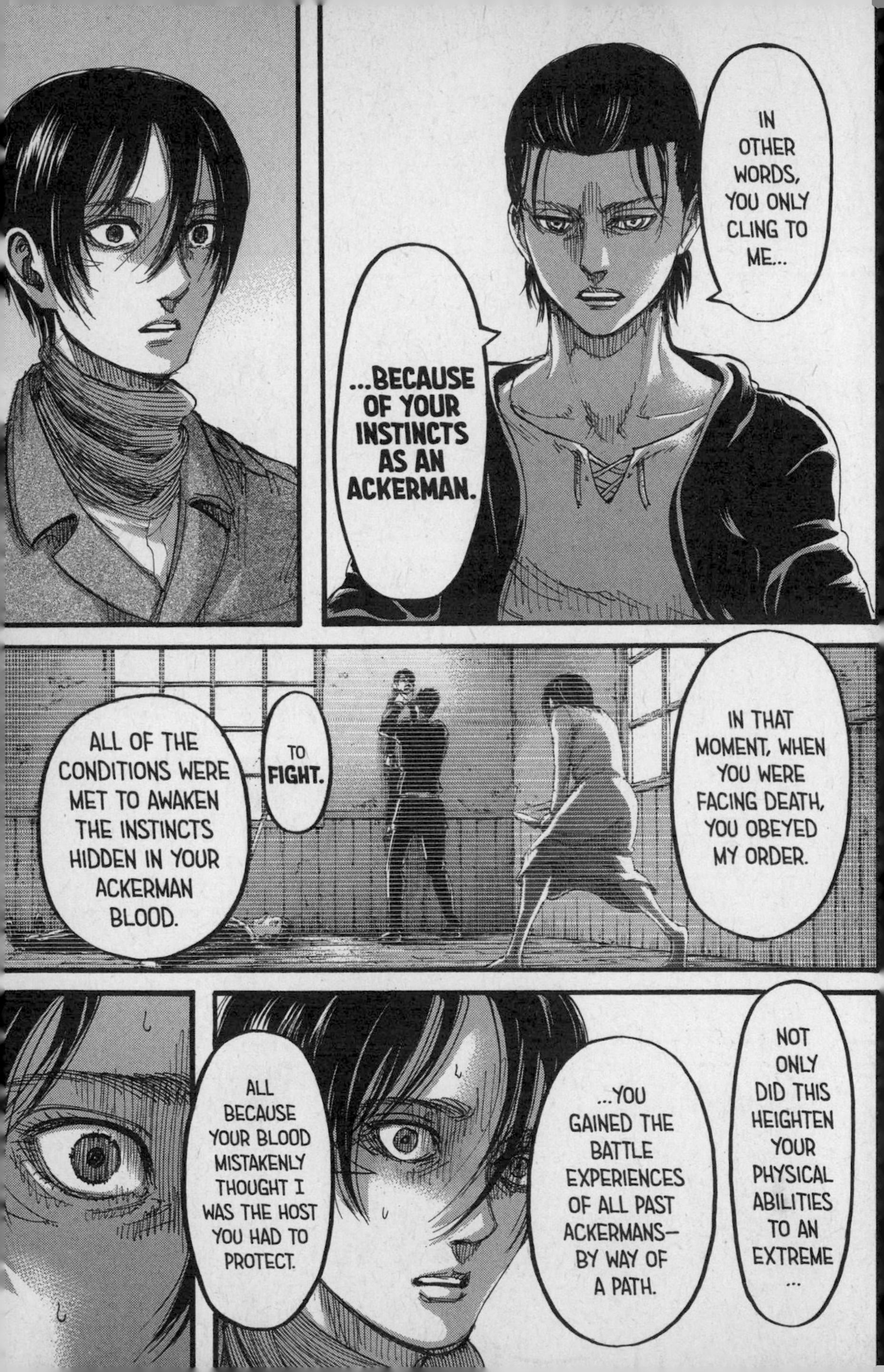
IN OTHER WORDS, YOU ONLY CLING TO ME...
...BECAUSE OF YOUR INSTINCTS AS AN ACKERMAN.
IN THAT MOMENT, WHEN YOU WERE FACING DEATH, YOU OBEYED MY ORDER.
TO FIGHT.
ALL OF THE CONDITIONS WERE MET TO AWAKEN THE INSTINCTS HIDDEN IN YOUR ACKERMAN BLOOD.
NOT ONLY DID THIS HEIGHTEN YOUR PHYSICAL ABILITIES TO AN EXTREME ...
...YOU GAINED THE BATTLE EXPERIENCES OF ALL PAST ACKERMANS— BY WAY OF A PATH.
ALL BECAUSE YOUR BLOOD MISTAKENLY THOUGHT I WAS THE HOST YOU HAD TO PROTECT.

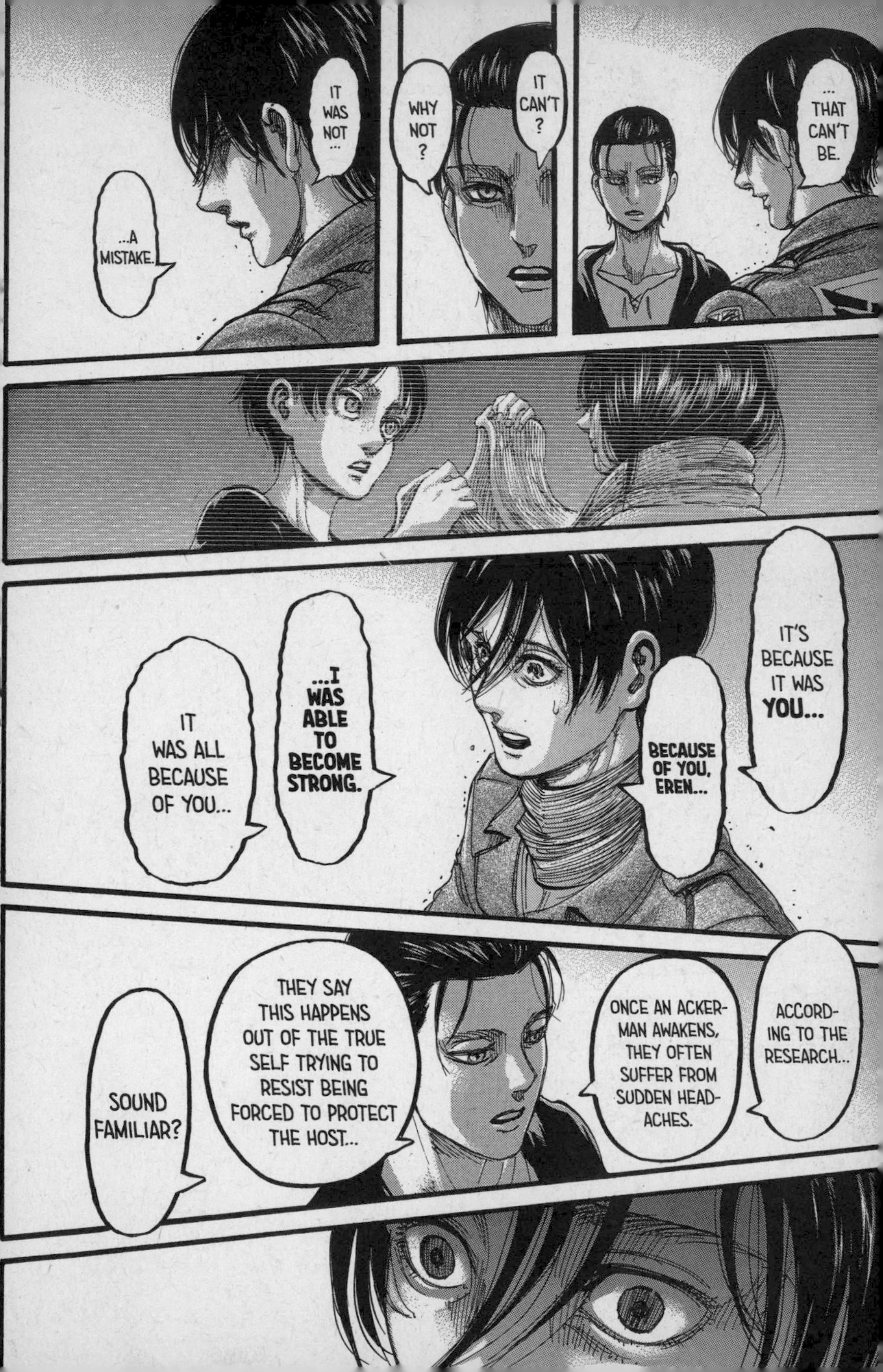
... THAT CAN'T BE.
IT CAN'T?
WHY NOT?
IT WAS NOT...
...A MISTAKE.
IT'S BECAUSE IT WAS **YOU...**
BECAUSE OF YOU, EREN...
...I WAS ABLE TO BECOME STRONG.
IT WAS ALL BECAUSE OF YOU...
ACCORDING TO THE RESEARCH...
ONCE AN ACKERMAN AWAKENS, THEY OFTEN SUFFER FROM SUDDEN HEADACHES.
THEY SAY THIS HAPPENS OUT OF THE TRUE SELF TRYING TO RESIST BEING FORCED TO PROTECT THE HOST...
SOUND FAMILIAR?

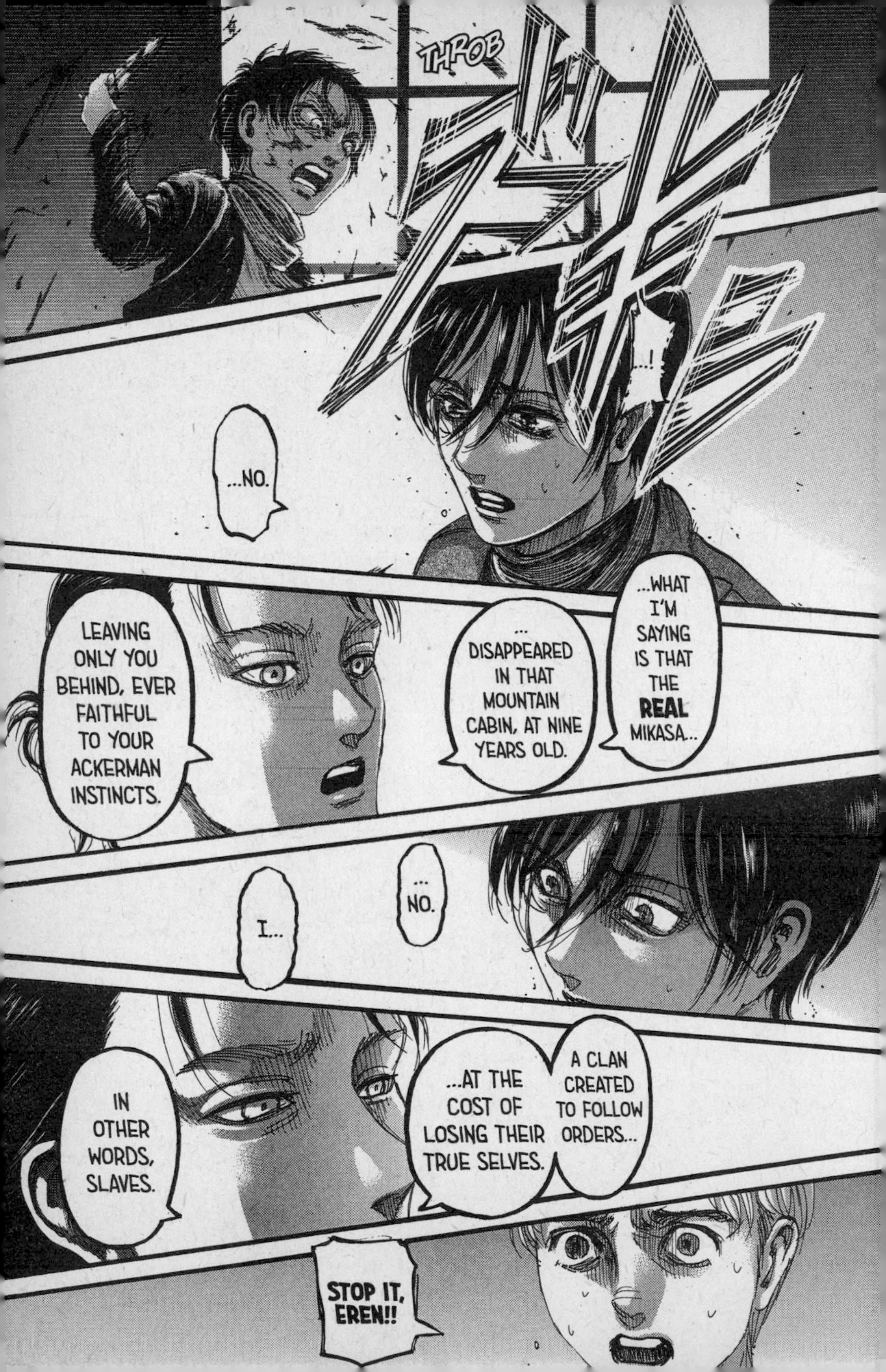
THROB
...NO.
...WHAT I'M SAYING IS THAT THE REAL MIKASA...
...DISAPPEARED IN THAT MOUNTAIN CABIN, AT NINE YEARS OLD.
LEAVING ONLY YOU BEHIND, EVER FAITHFUL TO YOUR ACKERMAN INSTINCTS.
... NO.
I...
A CLAN CREATED TO FOLLOW ORDERS...
...AT THE COST OF LOSING THEIR TRUE SELVES.
IN OTHER WORDS, SLAVES.
STOP IT, EREN!!

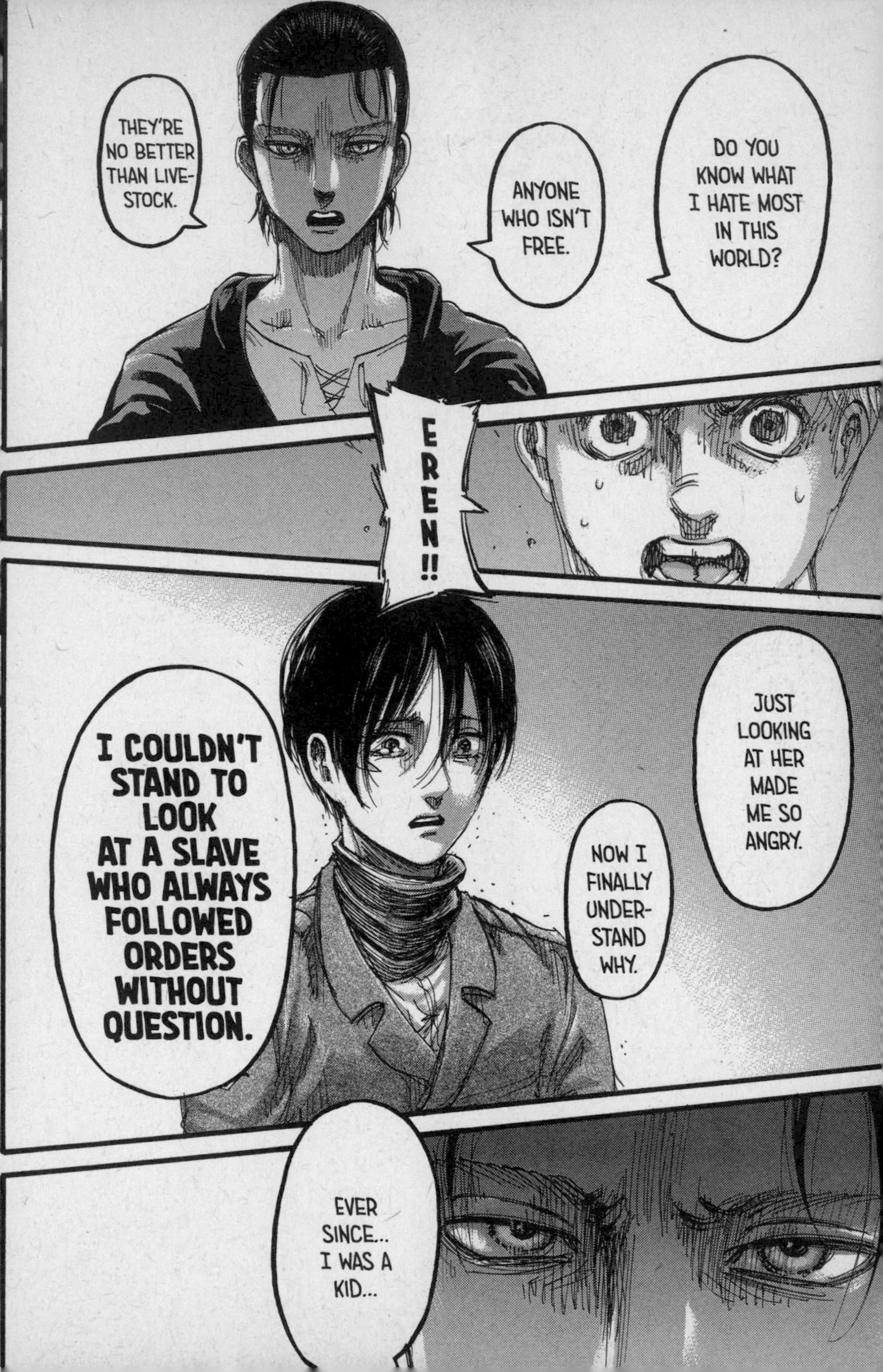
DO YOU KNOW WHAT I HATE MOST IN THIS WORLD?
ANYONE WHO ISN'T FREE.
THEY'RE NO BETTER THAN LIVE-STOCK.
EREN!!
JUST LOOKING AT HER MADE ME SO ANGRY.
NOW I FINALLY UNDER-STAND WHY.
I COULDN'T STAND TO LOOK AT A SLAVE WHO ALWAYS FOLLOWED ORDERS WITHOUT QUESTION.
EVER SINCE... I WAS A KID...

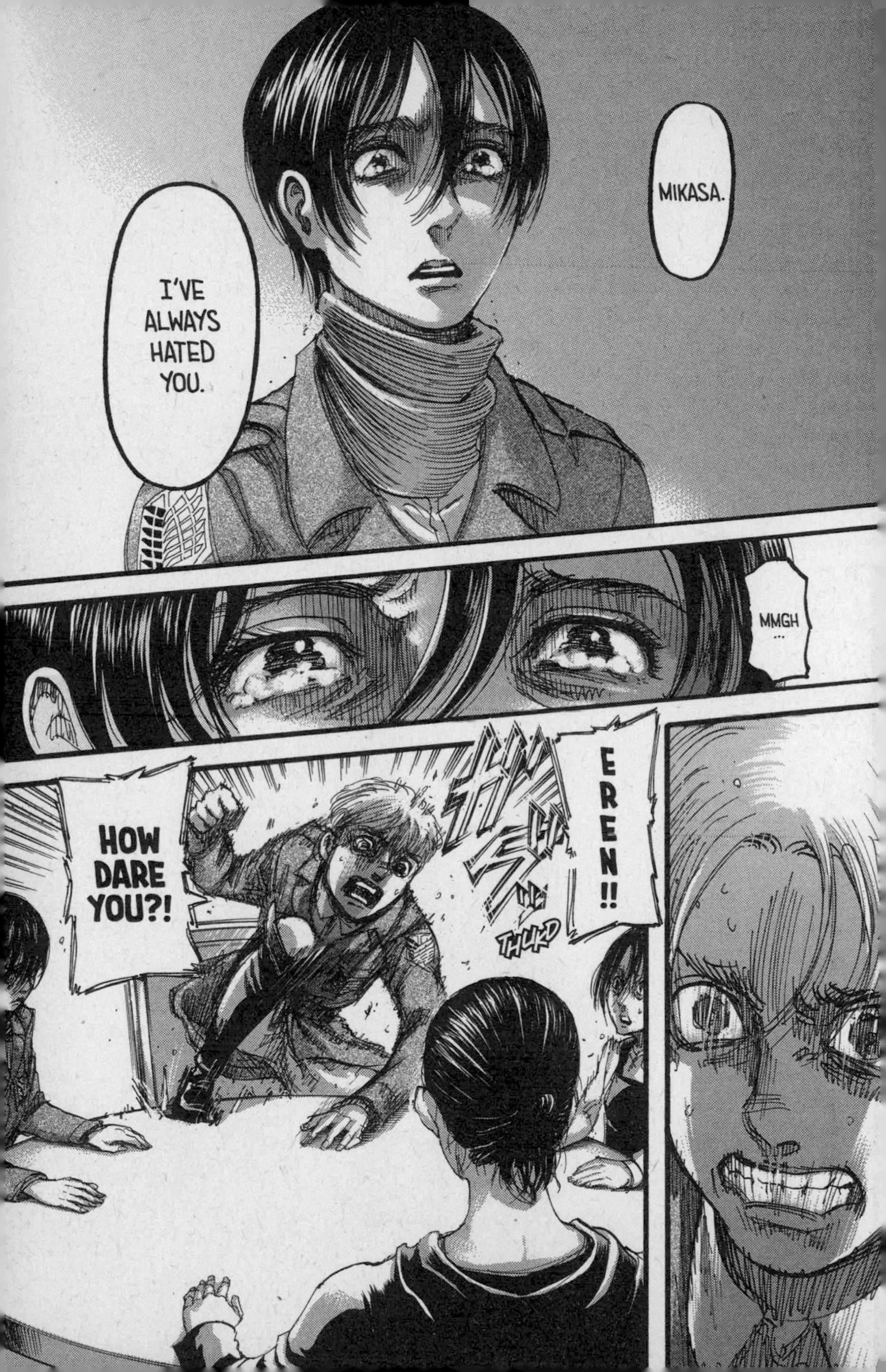
MIKASA.
I'VE ALWAYS HATED YOU.
MMGH ...
EREN!!
THUD
HOW DARE YOU?!

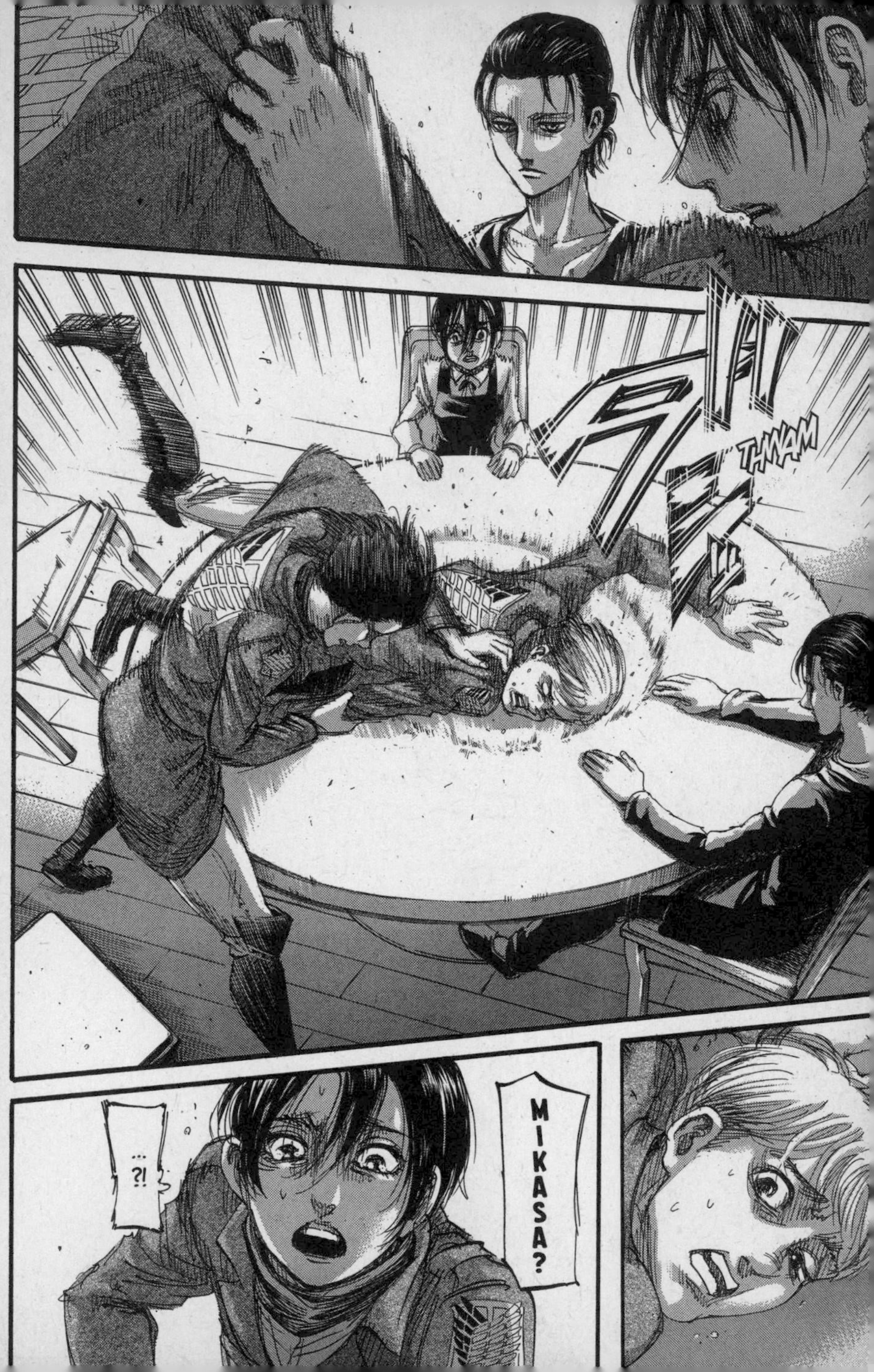
THWAM
MIKASA?
...?!

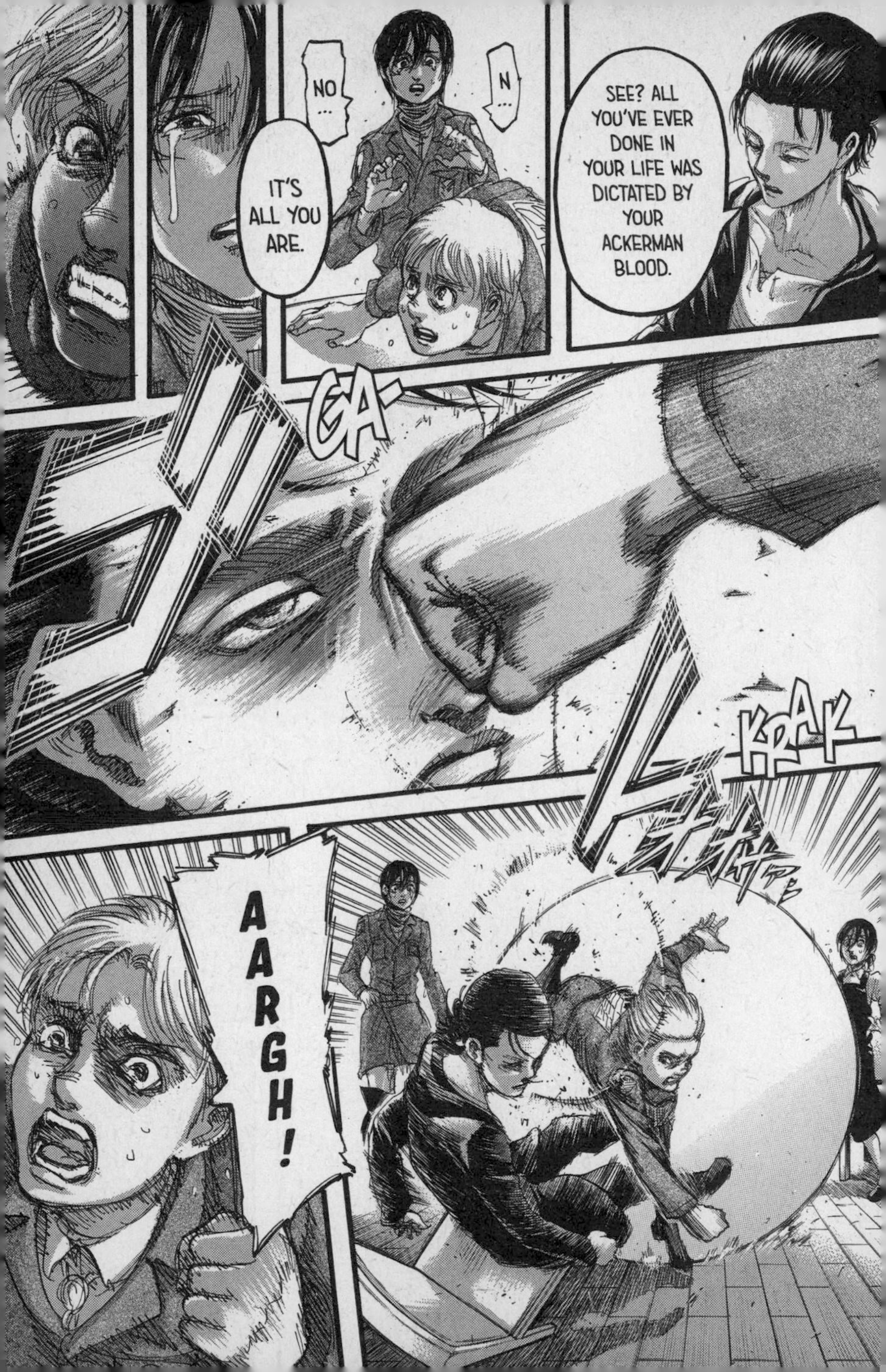
SEE? ALL YOU'VE EVER DONE IN YOUR LIFE WAS DICTATED BY YOUR ACKERMAN BLOOD.
N ...
NO ...
IT'S ALL YOU ARE.
GA-
KRAK
AARGH!

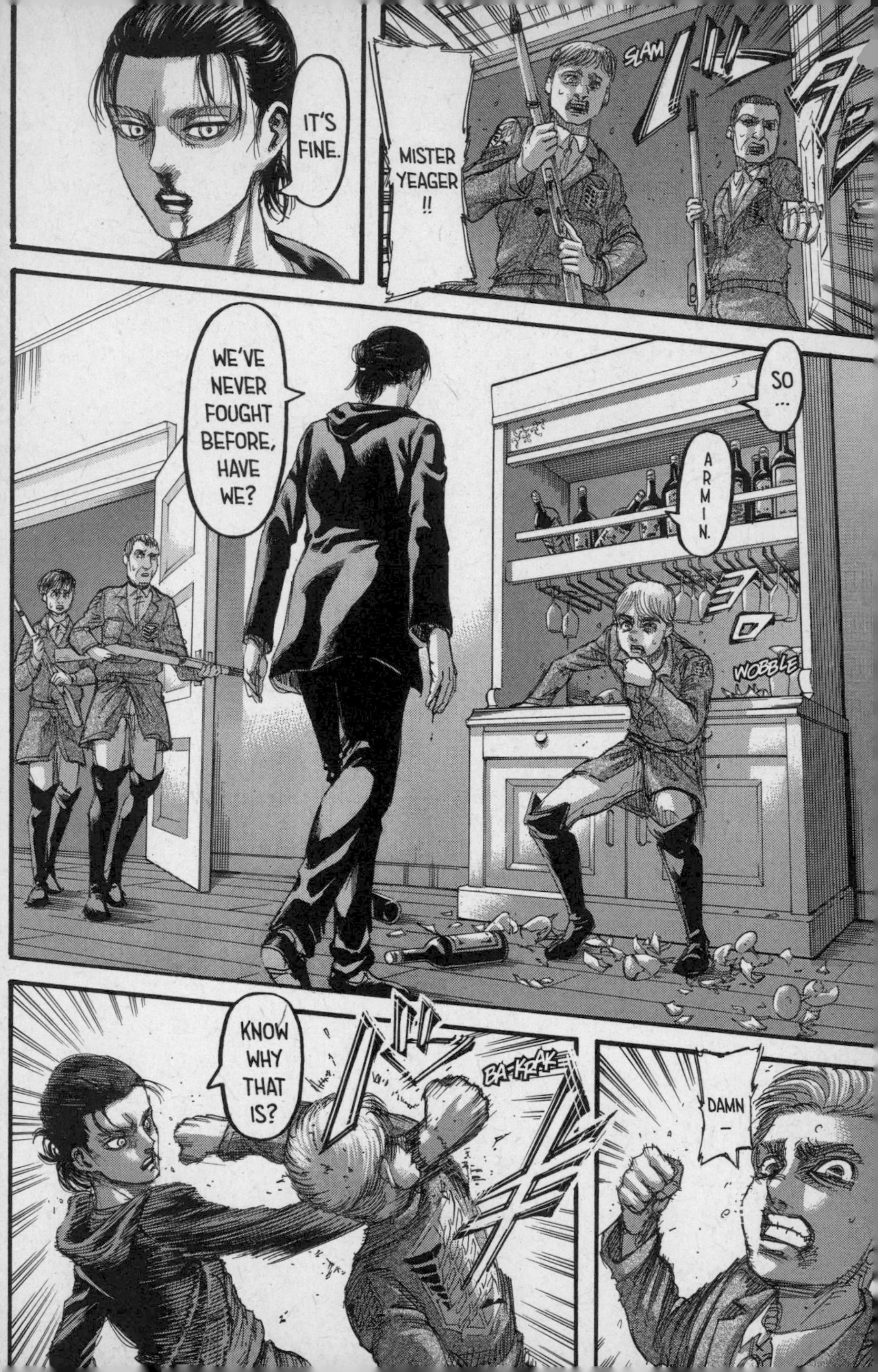
SLAM
MISTER YEAGER !!
IT'S FINE.
SO ...
ARMIN.
WE'VE NEVER FOUGHT BEFORE, HAVE WE?
WOBBLE
DAMN —
KNOW WHY THAT IS?
BA-KRAK

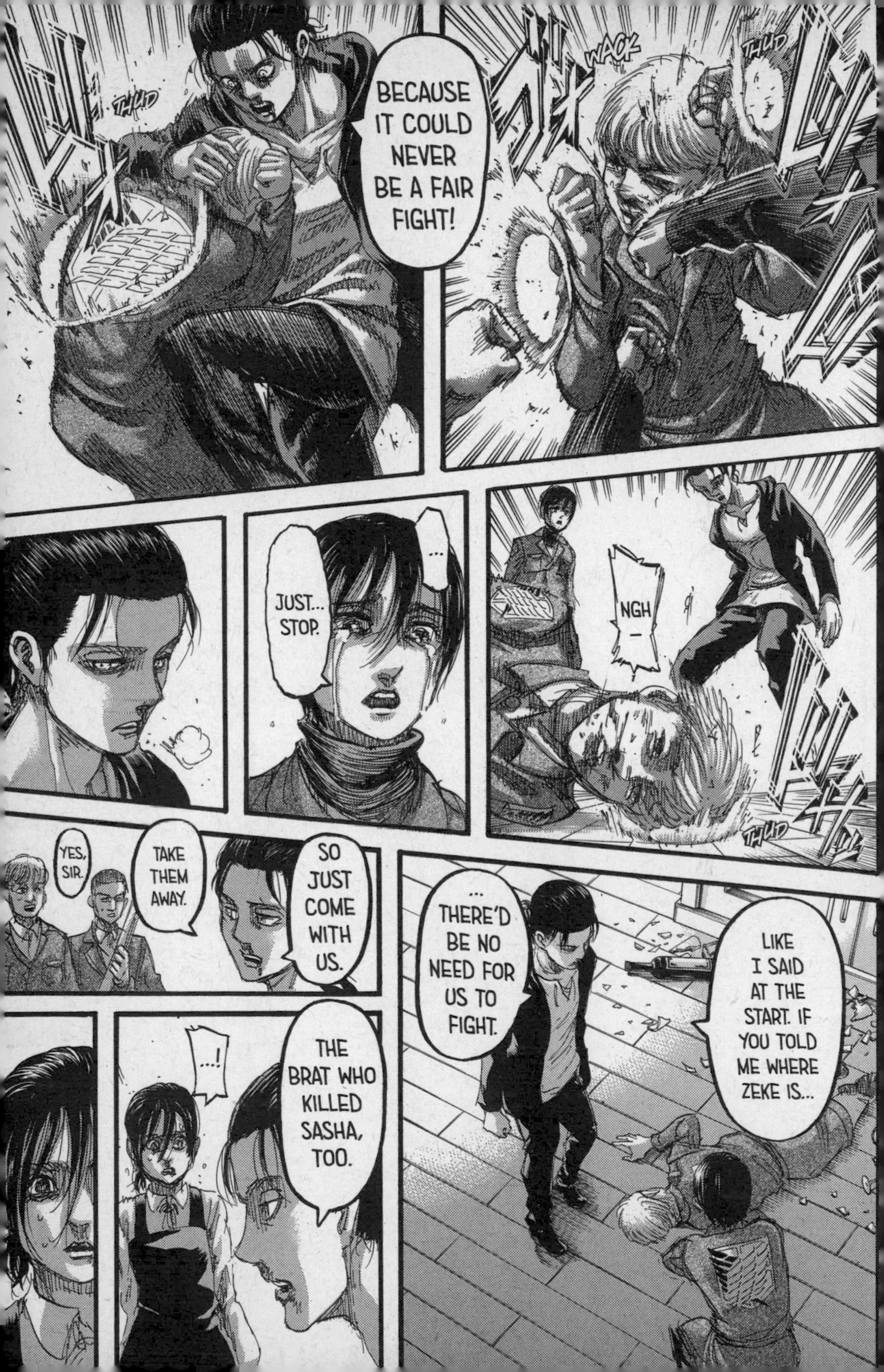
WACK
THUD
THUD
BECAUSE IT COULD NEVER BE A FAIR FIGHT!
NGH—
THUD
...
JUST... STOP.
LIKE I SAID AT THE START. IF YOU TOLD ME WHERE ZEKE IS...
... THERE'D BE NO NEED FOR US TO FIGHT.
SO JUST COME WITH US.
TAKE THEM AWAY.
YES, SIR.
THE BRAT WHO KILLED SASHA, TOO.
...!

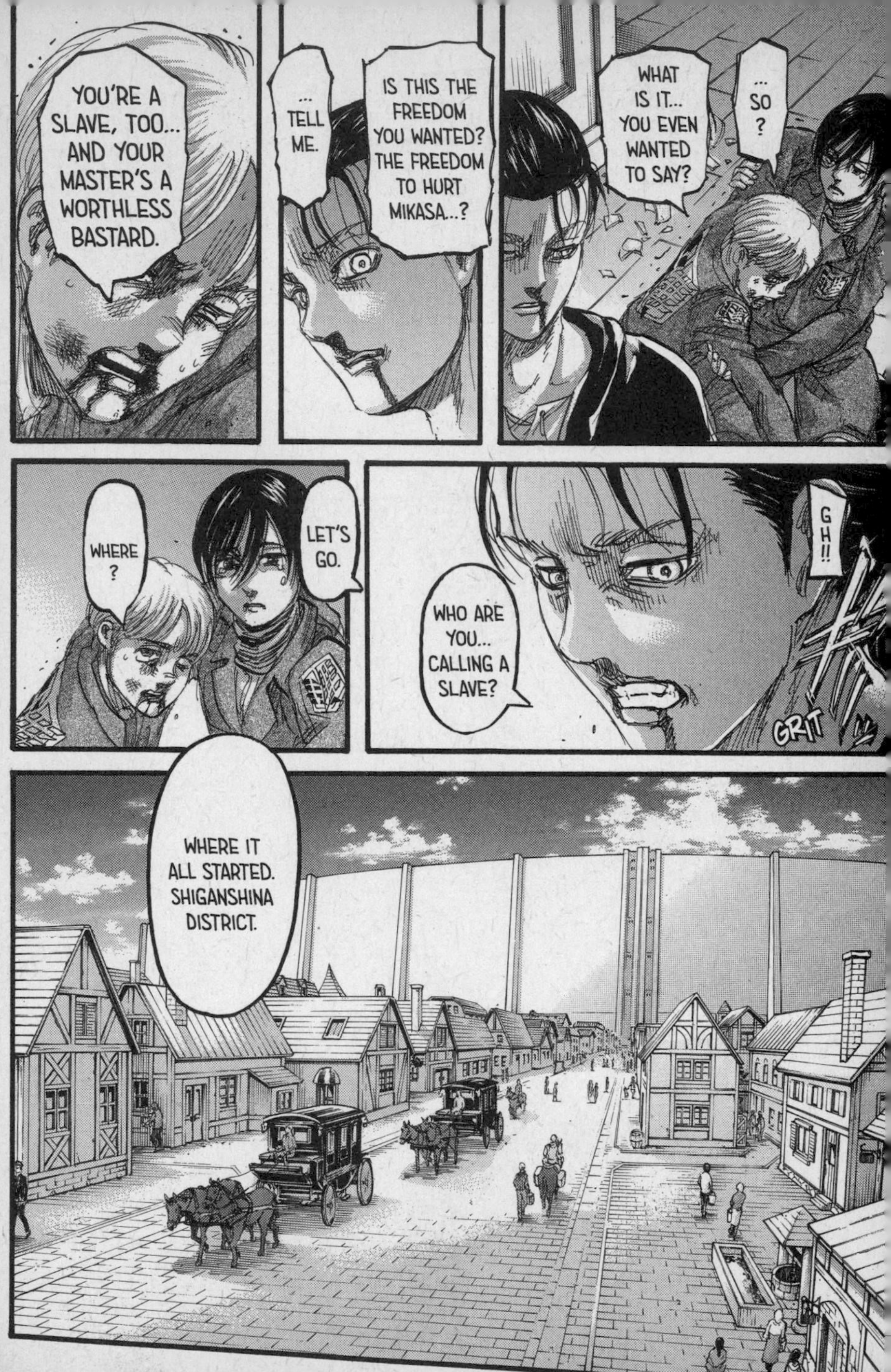
... SO ?
WHAT IS IT... YOU EVEN WANTED TO SAY?
IS THIS THE FREEDOM YOU WANTED? THE FREEDOM TO HURT MIKASA...?
... TELL ME.
YOU'RE A SLAVE, TOO... AND YOUR MASTER'S A WORTHLESS BASTARD.
GH!!
WHO ARE YOU... CALLING A SLAVE?
GRIT
LET'S GO.
WHERE ?
WHERE IT ALL STARTED. SHIGANSHINA DISTRICT.

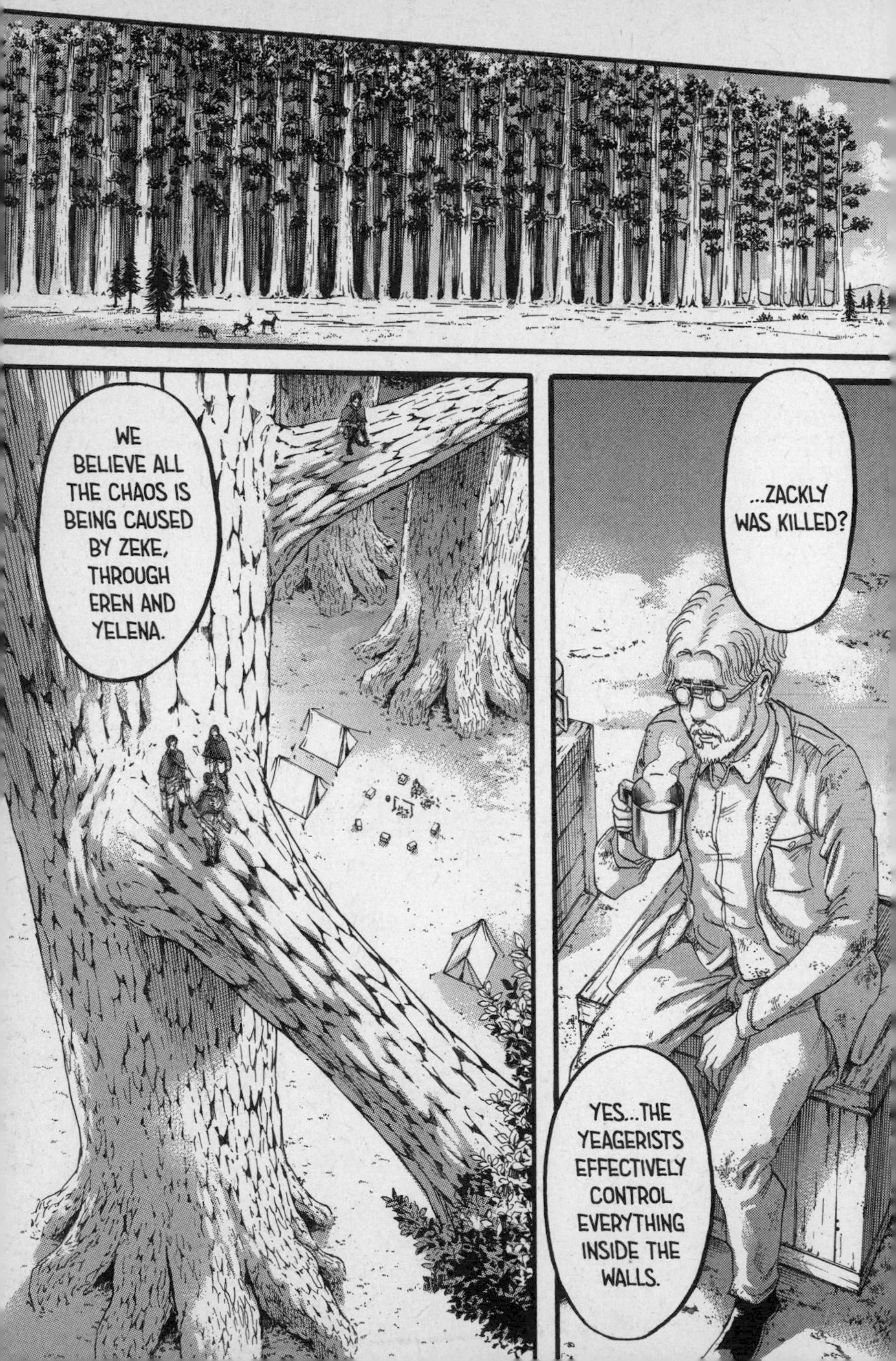
...ZACKLY WAS KILLED?
YES...THE YEAGERISTS EFFECTIVELY CONTROL EVERYTHING INSIDE THE WALLS.
WE BELIEVE ALL THE CHAOS IS BEING CAUSED BY ZEKE, THROUGH EREN AND YELENA.

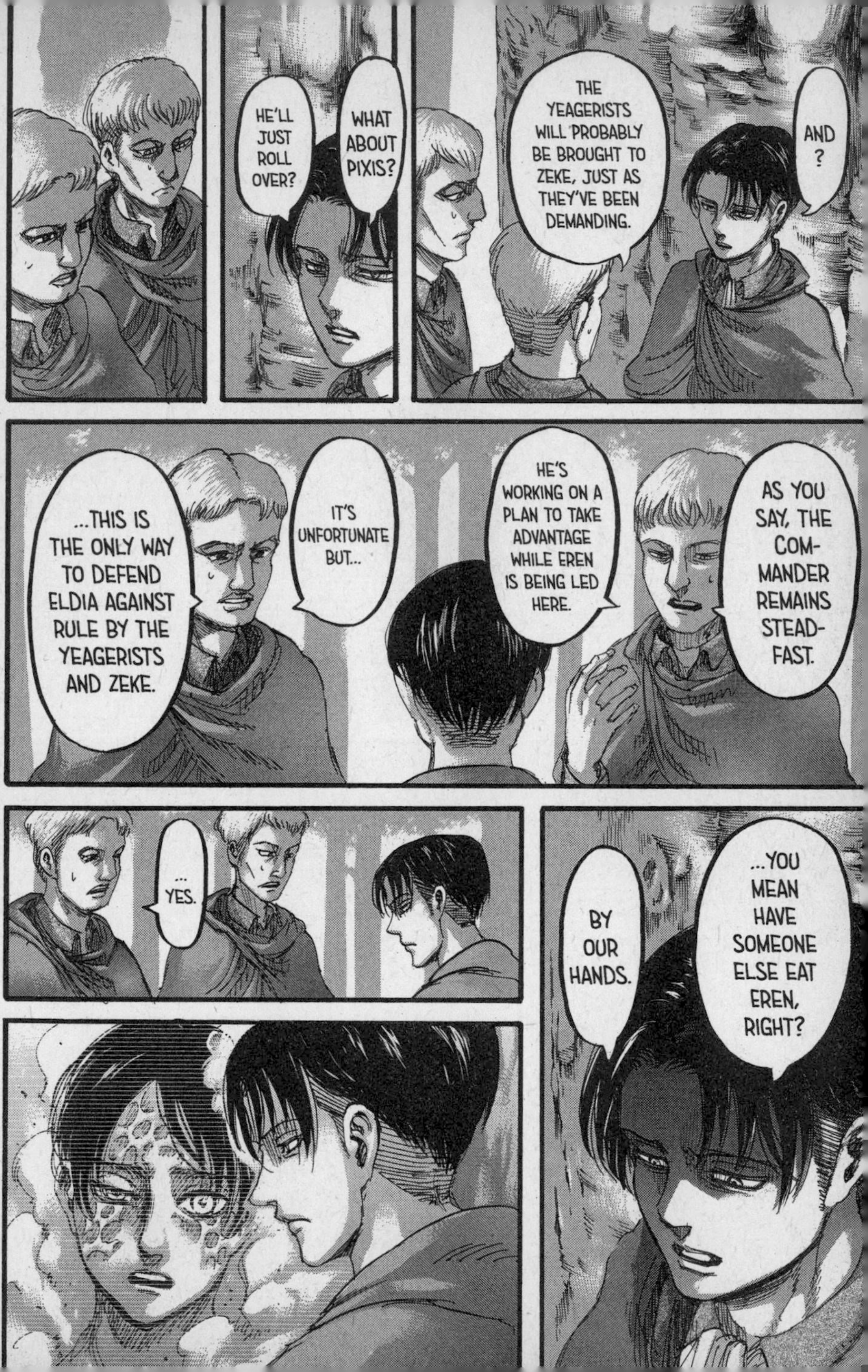
AND ?
THE YEAGERISTS WILL PROBABLY BE BROUGHT TO ZEKE, JUST AS THEY'VE BEEN DEMANDING.
WHAT ABOUT PIXIS?
HE'LL JUST ROLL OVER?
AS YOU SAY, THE COM-MANDER REMAINS STEAD-FAST.
HE'S WORKING ON A PLAN TO TAKE ADVANTAGE WHILE EREN IS BEING LED HERE.
IT'S UNFORTUNATE BUT...
...THIS IS THE ONLY WAY TO DEFEND ELDIA AGAINST RULE BY THE YEAGERISTS AND ZEKE.
...YOU MEAN HAVE SOMEONE ELSE EAT EREN, RIGHT?
BY OUR HANDS.
... YES.

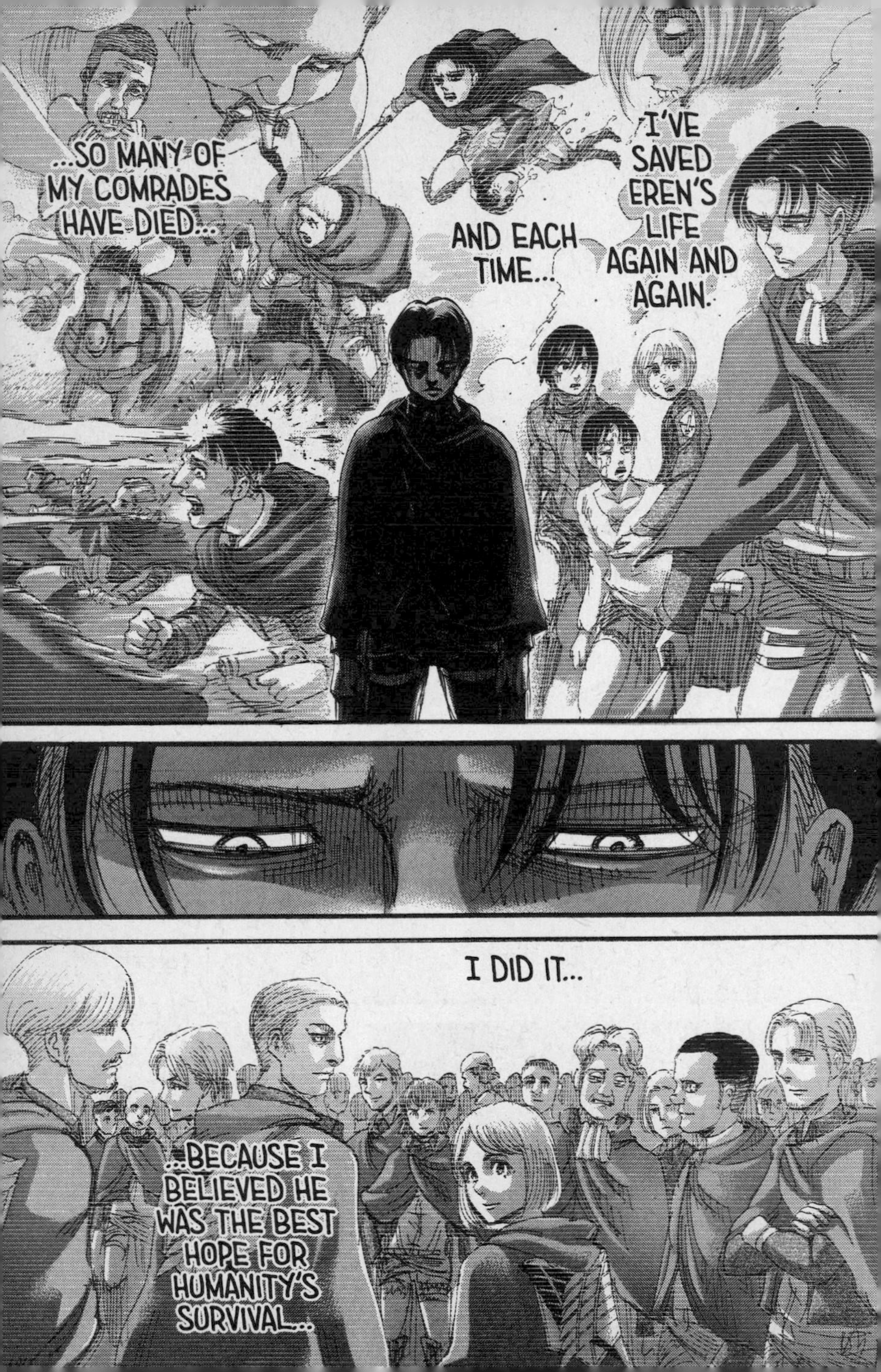
I'VE SAVED EREN'S LIFE AGAIN AND AGAIN.
AND EACH TIME...
...SO MANY OF MY COMRADES HAVE DIED...
I DID IT...
...BECAUSE I BELIEVED HE WAS THE BEST HOPE FOR HUMANITY'S SURVIVAL...

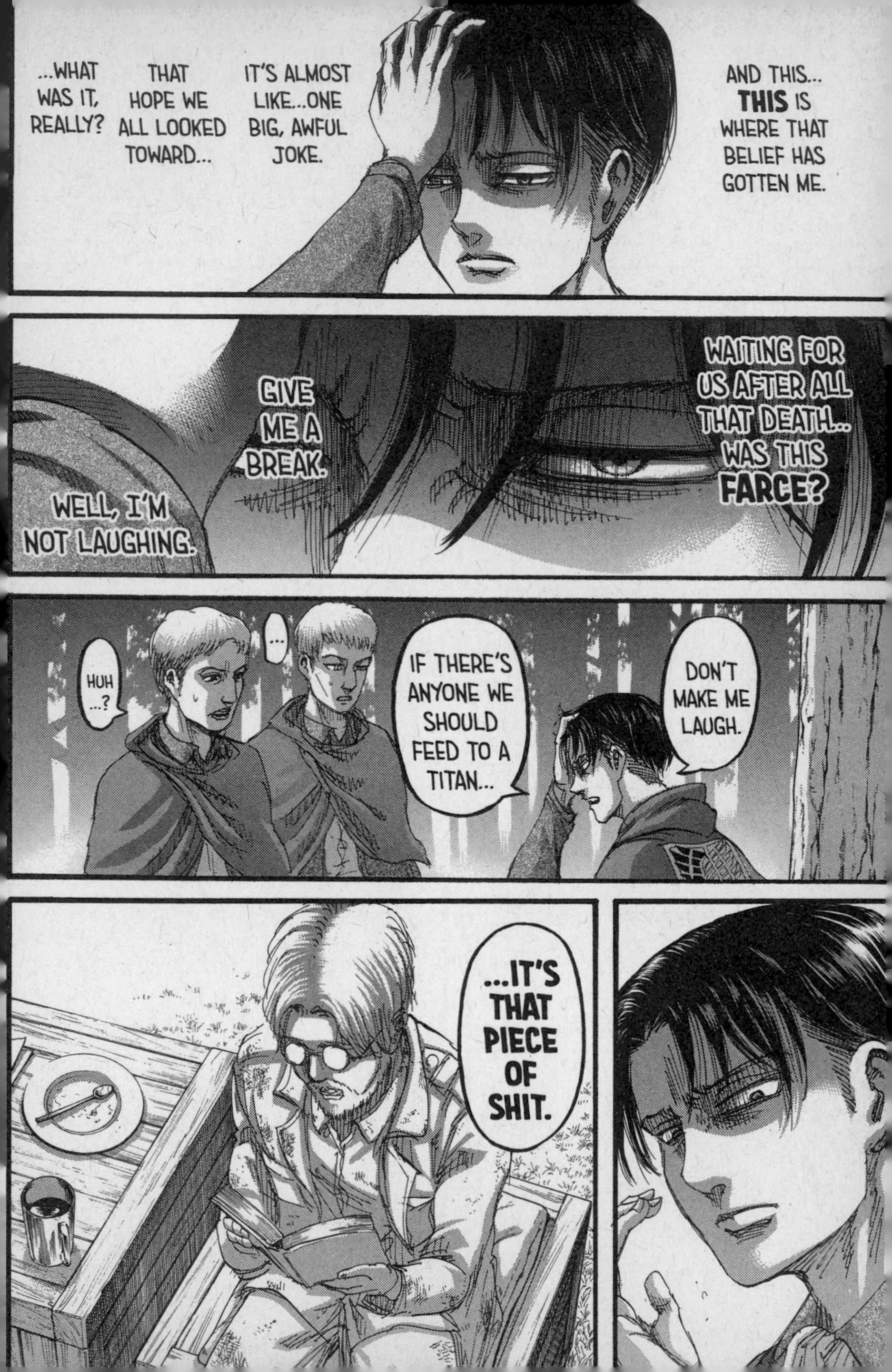
AND THIS... **THIS** IS WHERE THAT BELIEF HAS GOTTEN ME.
IT'S ALMOST LIKE...ONE BIG, AWFUL JOKE.
THAT HOPE WE ALL LOOKED TOWARD...
...WHAT WAS IT, REALLY?
WAITING FOR US AFTER ALL THAT DEATH... WAS THIS **FARCE?**
GIVE ME A BREAK.
WELL, I'M NOT LAUGHING.
DON'T MAKE ME LAUGH.
IF THERE'S ANYONE WE SHOULD FEED TO A TITAN...
...
HUH ...?
...IT'S THAT PIECE OF SHIT.

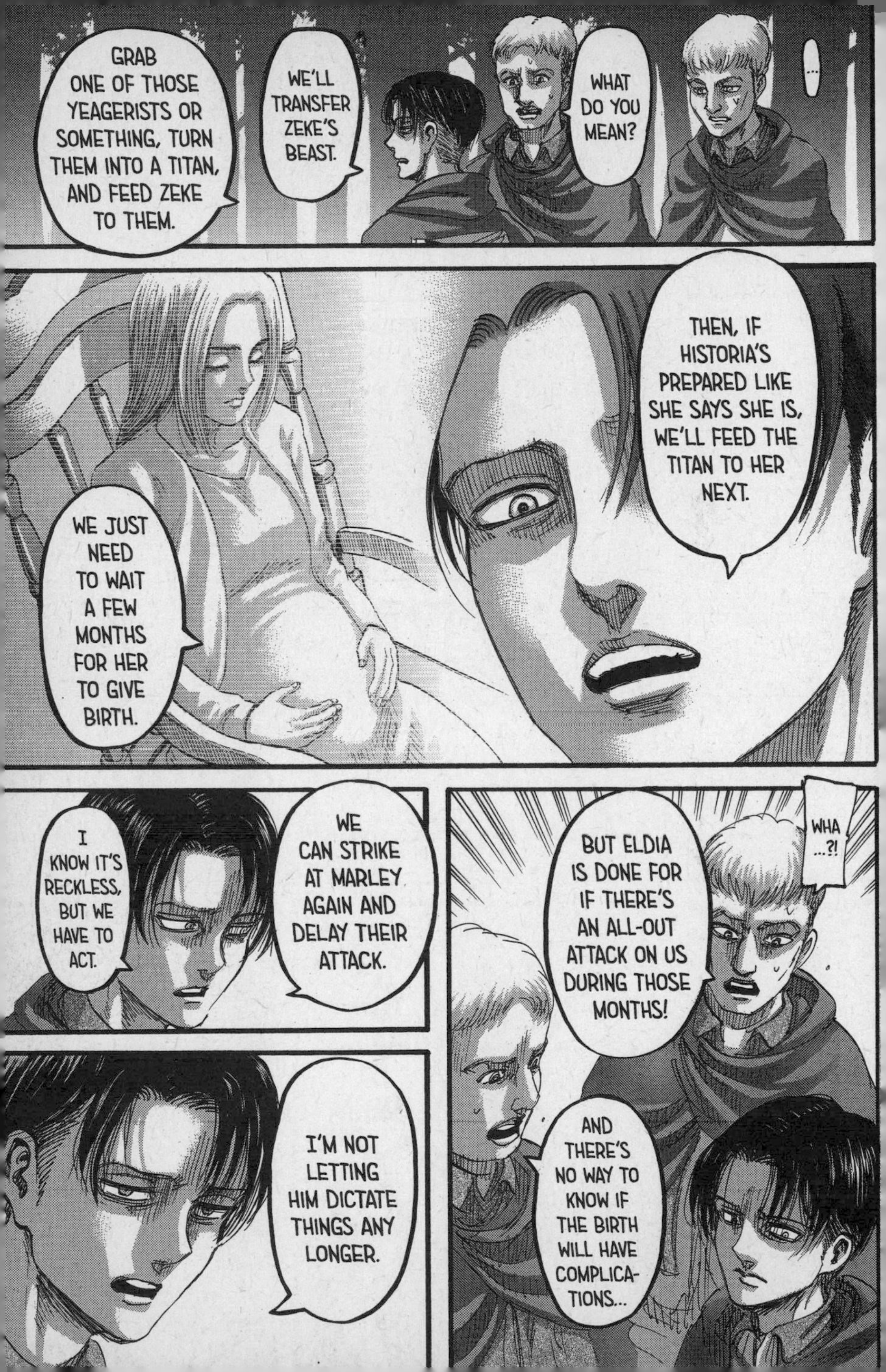
...
WHAT DO YOU MEAN?
WE'LL TRANSFER ZEKE'S BEAST.
GRAB ONE OF THOSE YEAGERISTS OR SOMETHING, TURN THEM INTO A TITAN, AND FEED ZEKE TO THEM.
THEN, IF HISTORIA'S PREPARED LIKE SHE SAYS SHE IS, WE'LL FEED THE TITAN TO HER NEXT.
WE JUST NEED TO WAIT A FEW MONTHS FOR HER TO GIVE BIRTH.
WHA ...?!
BUT ELDIA IS DONE FOR IF THERE'S AN ALL-OUT ATTACK ON US DURING THOSE MONTHS!
AND THERE'S NO WAY TO KNOW IF THE BIRTH WILL HAVE COMPLICATIONS...
WE CAN STRIKE AT MARLEY AGAIN AND DELAY THEIR ATTACK.
I KNOW IT'S RECKLESS, BUT WE HAVE TO ACT.
I'M NOT LETTING HIM DICTATE THINGS ANY LONGER.

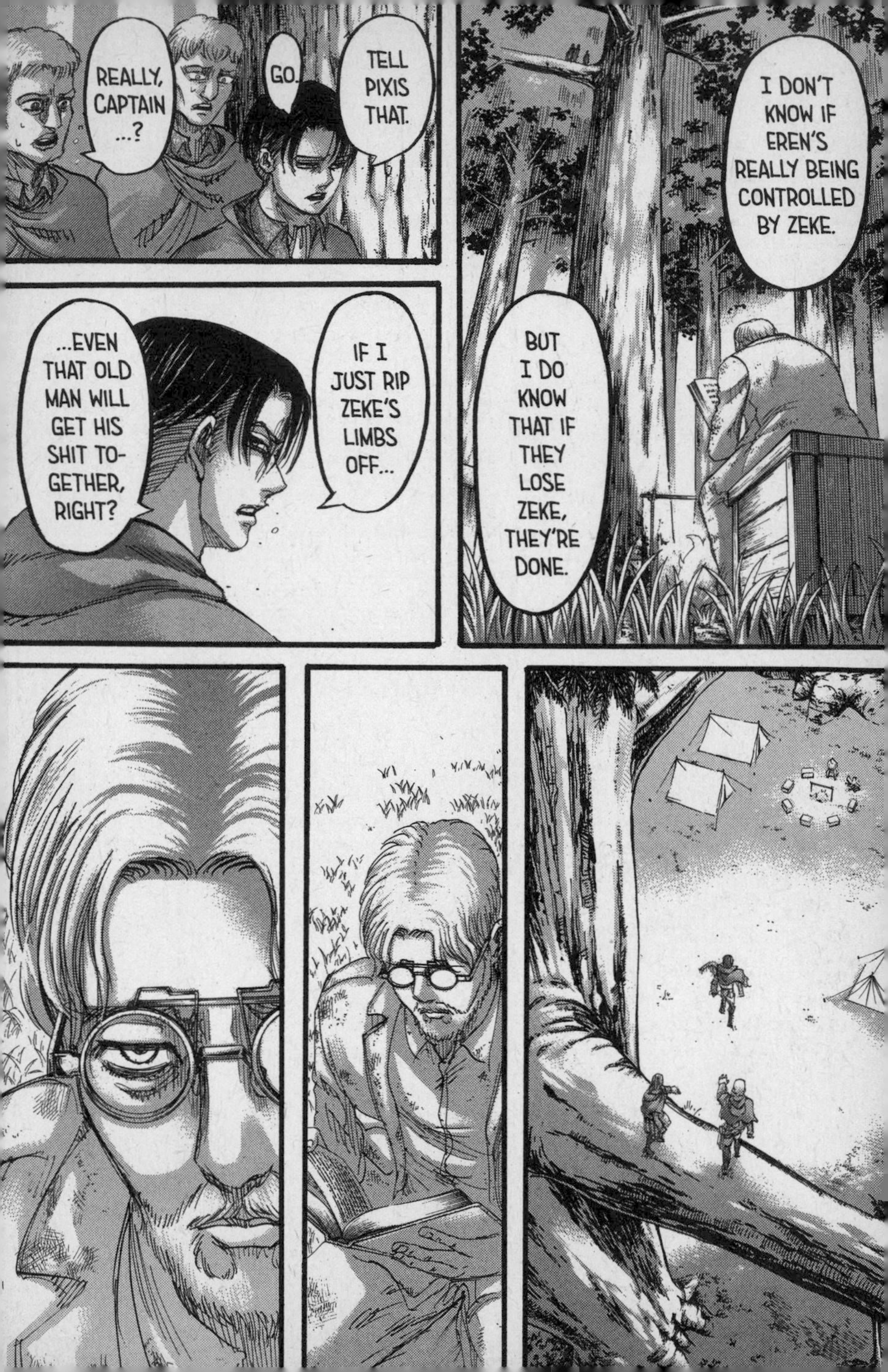
I DON'T KNOW IF EREN'S REALLY BEING CONTROLLED BY ZEKE.
BUT I DO KNOW THAT IF THEY LOSE ZEKE, THEY'RE DONE.
TELL PIXIS THAT.
GO.
REALLY, CAPTAIN ...?
IF I JUST RIP ZEKE'S LIMBS OFF...
...EVEN THAT OLD MAN WILL GET HIS SHIT TO-GETHER, RIGHT?

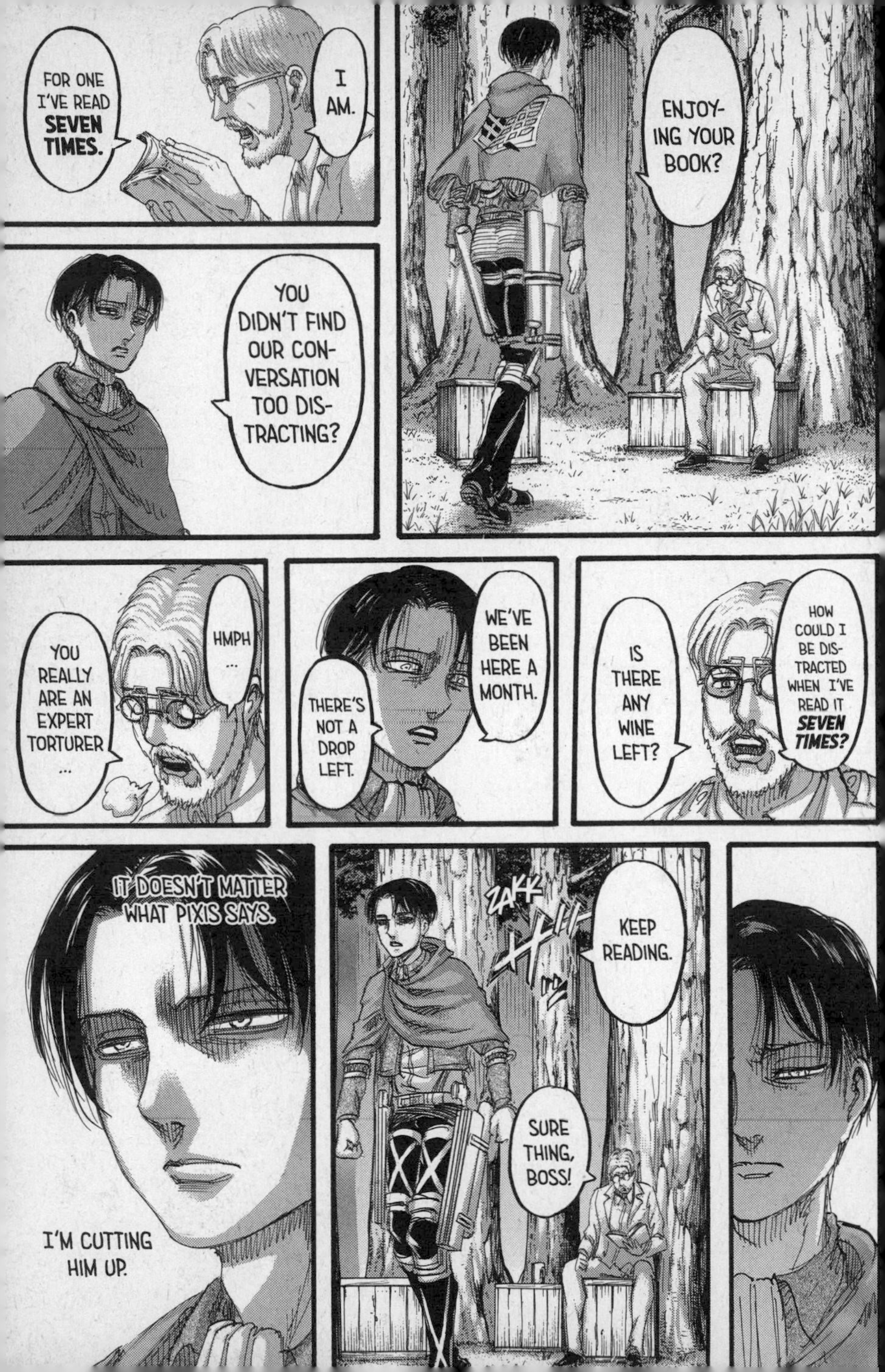
ENJOYING YOUR BOOK?
I AM.
FOR ONE I'VE READ **SEVEN TIMES.**
YOU DIDN'T FIND OUR CONVERSATION TOO DISTRACTING?
HOW COULD I BE DISTRACTED WHEN I'VE READ IT ***SEVEN TIMES?***
IS THERE ANY WINE LEFT?
WE'VE BEEN HERE A MONTH.
THERE'S NOT A DROP LEFT.
HMPH ...
YOU REALLY ARE AN EXPERT TORTURER ...
ZAKK
KEEP READING.
SURE THING, BOSS!
IT DOESN'T MATTER WHAT PIXIS SAYS.
I'M CUTTING HIM UP.

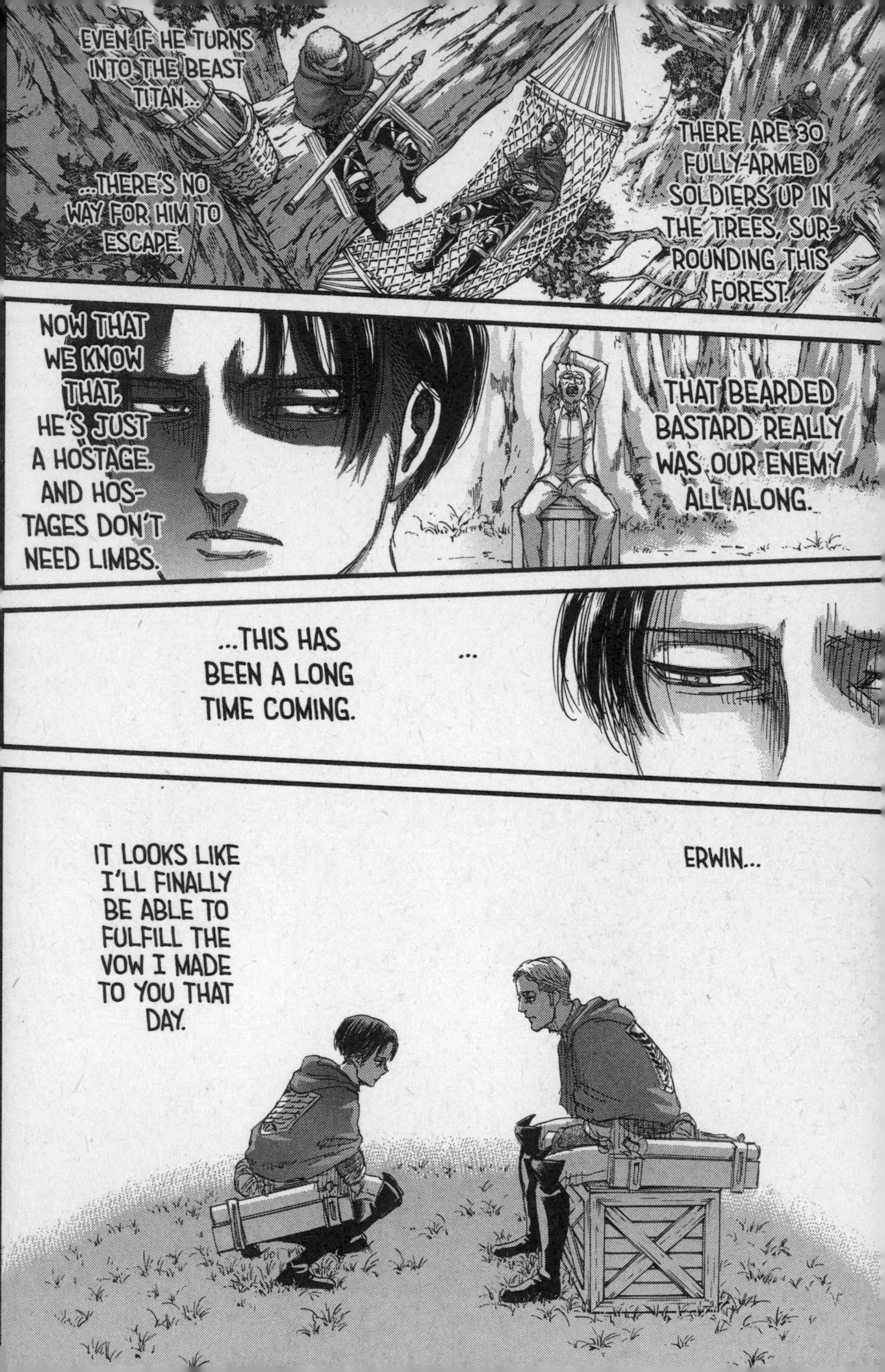

THERE ARE 30 FULLY-ARMED SOLDIERS UP IN THE TREES, SURROUNDING THIS FOREST.
EVEN IF HE TURNS INTO THE BEAST TITAN...
...THERE'S NO WAY FOR HIM TO ESCAPE.
THAT BEARDED BASTARD REALLY WAS OUR ENEMY ALL ALONG.
NOW THAT WE KNOW THAT, HE'S JUST A HOSTAGE.
AND HOSTAGES DON'T NEED LIMBS.
...
...THIS HAS BEEN A LONG TIME COMING.
ERWIN...
IT LOOKS LIKE I'LL FINALLY BE ABLE TO FULFILL THE VOW I MADE TO YOU THAT DAY.

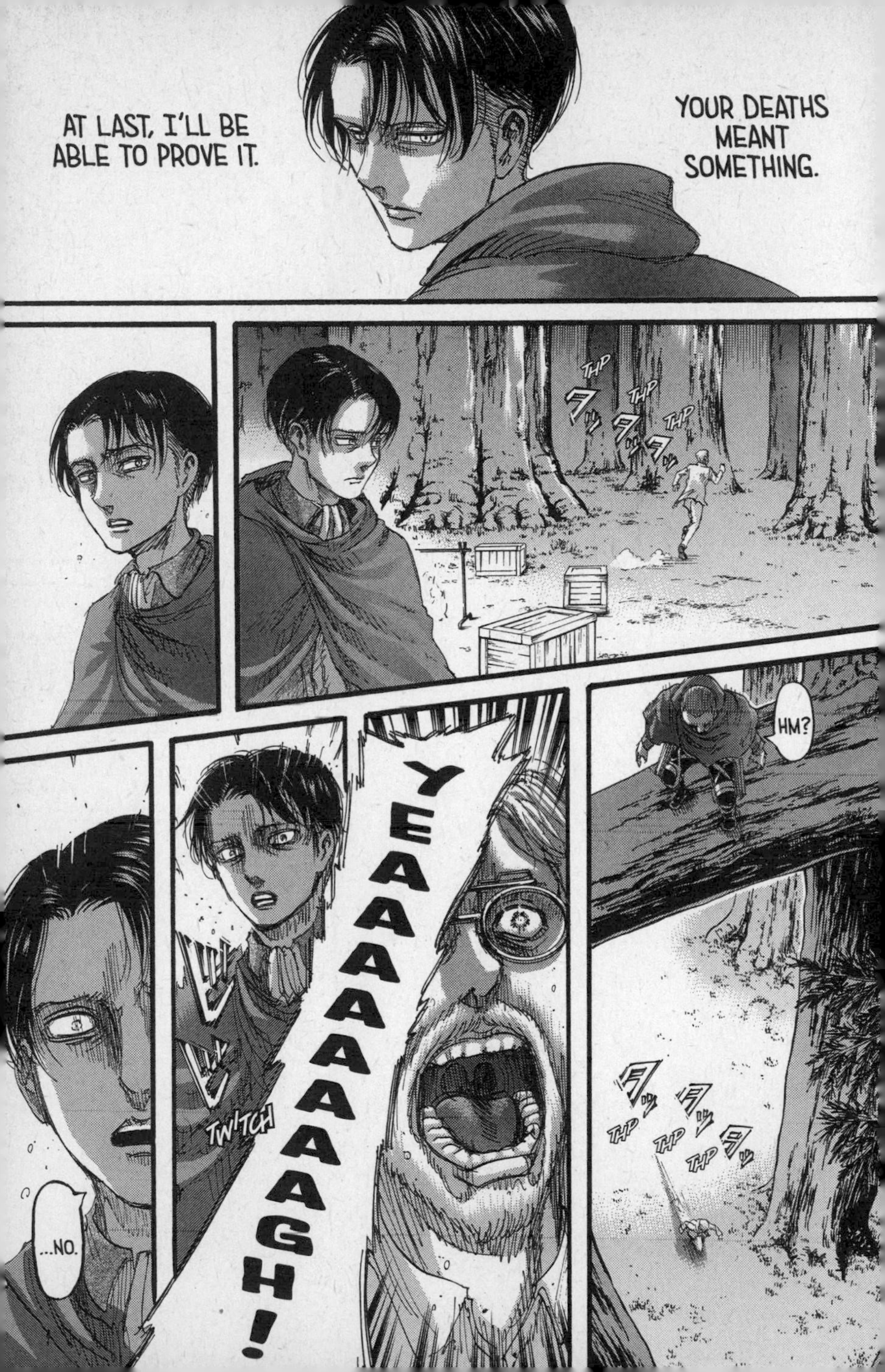
YOUR DEATHS MEANT SOMETHING.
AT LAST, I'LL BE ABLE TO PROVE IT.
THP
THP
THP
HM?
THP
THP
THP
YEAAAAAAAAGH!
TWITCH
...NO.

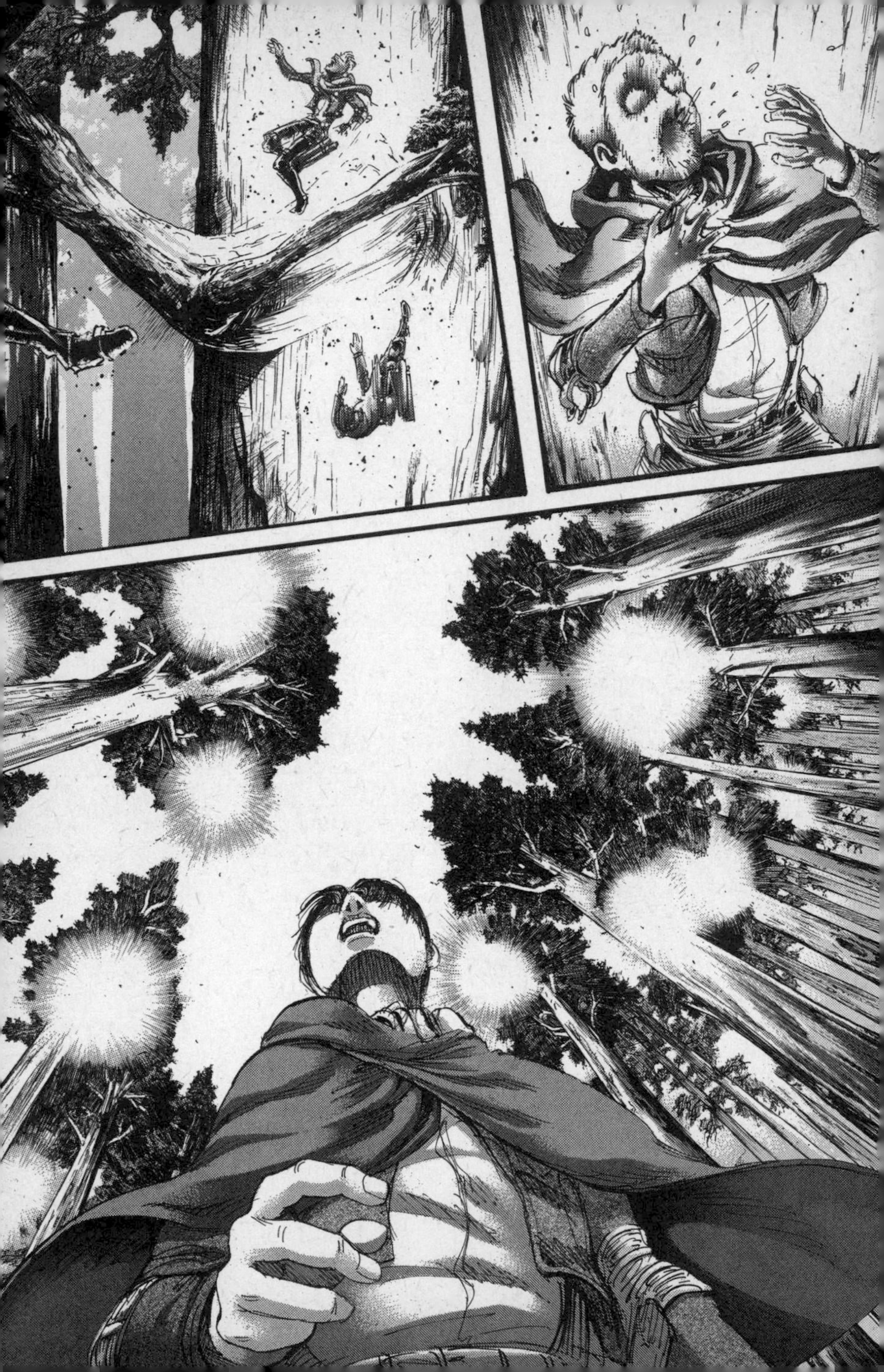

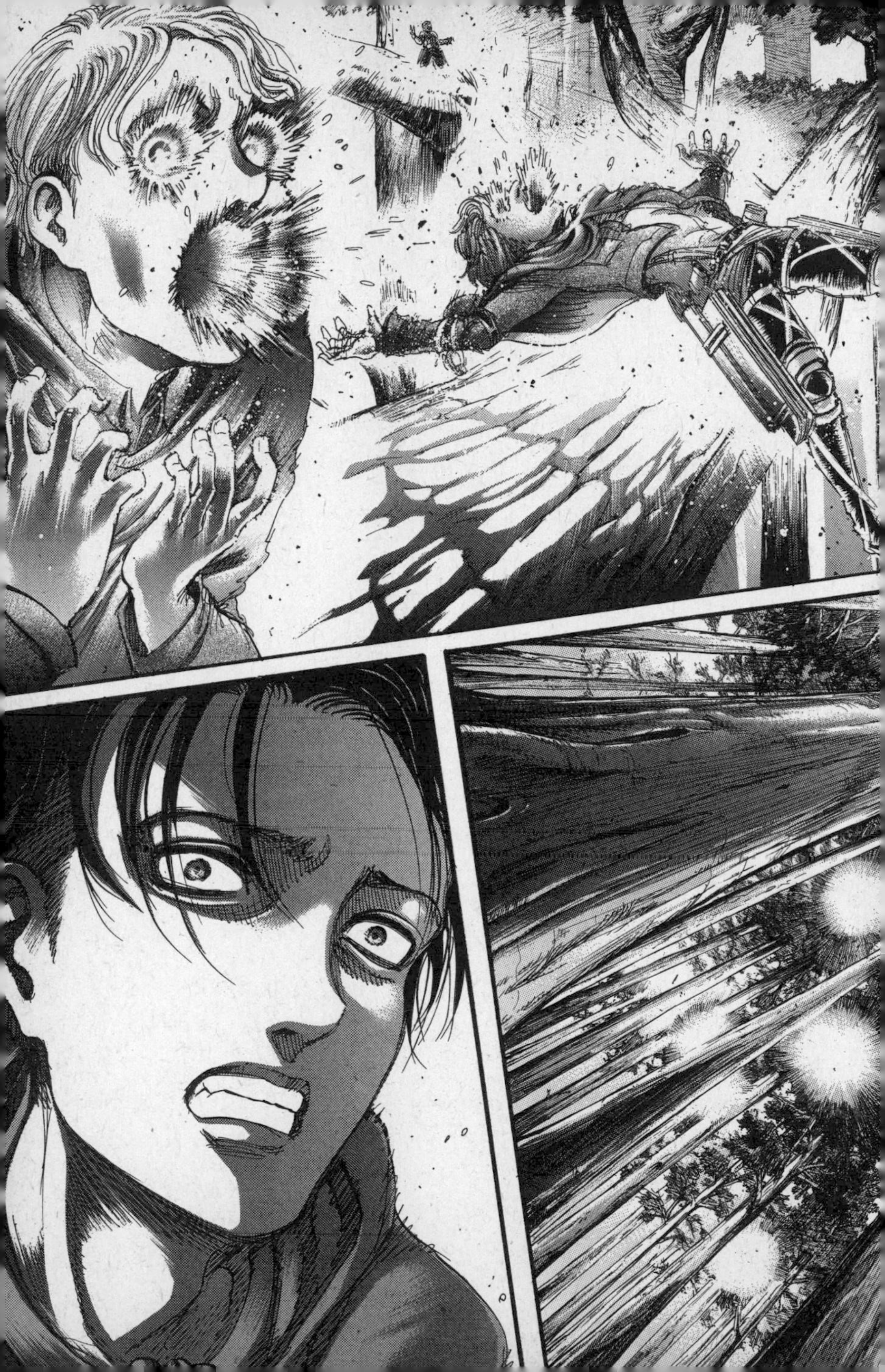

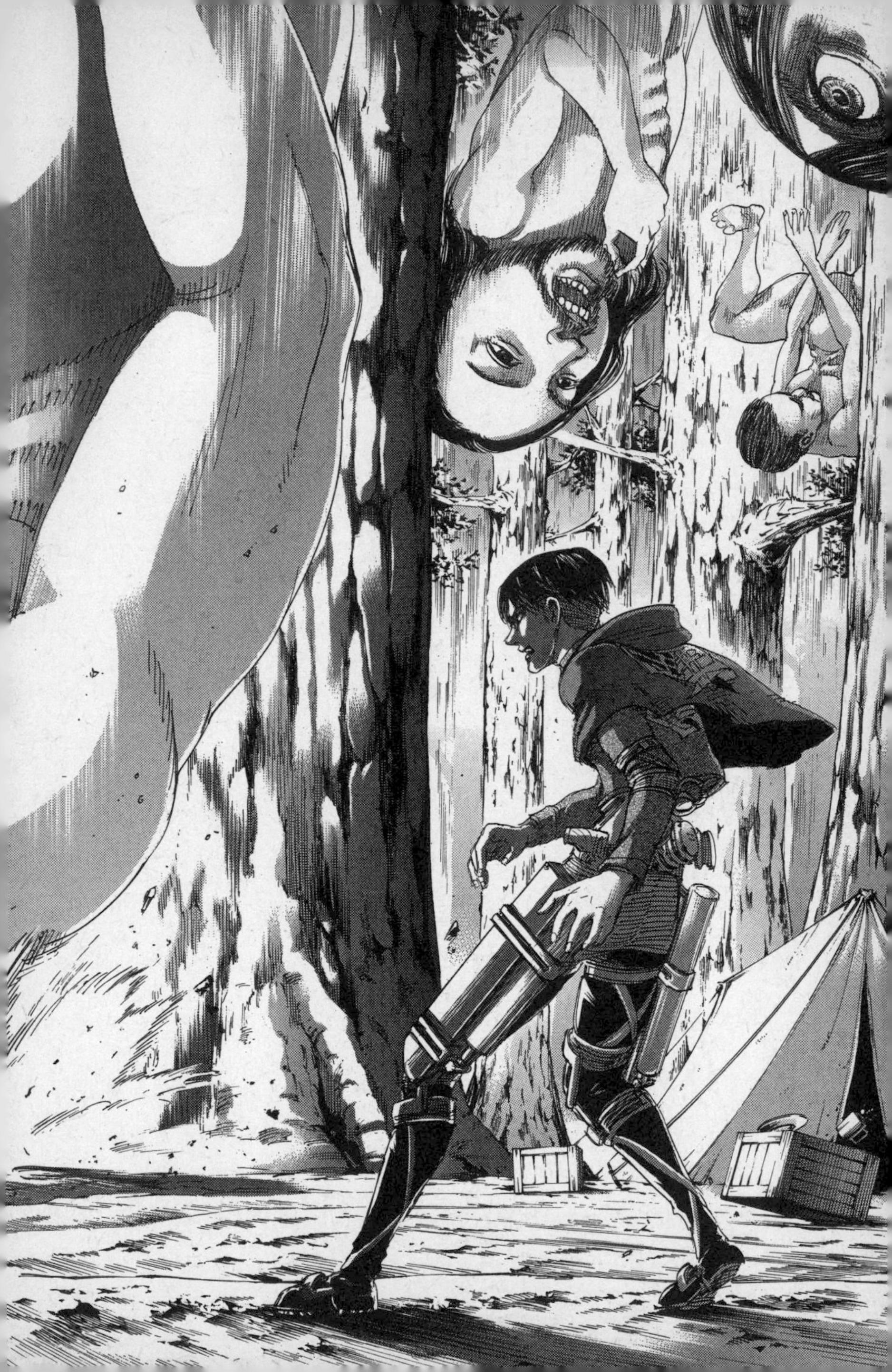

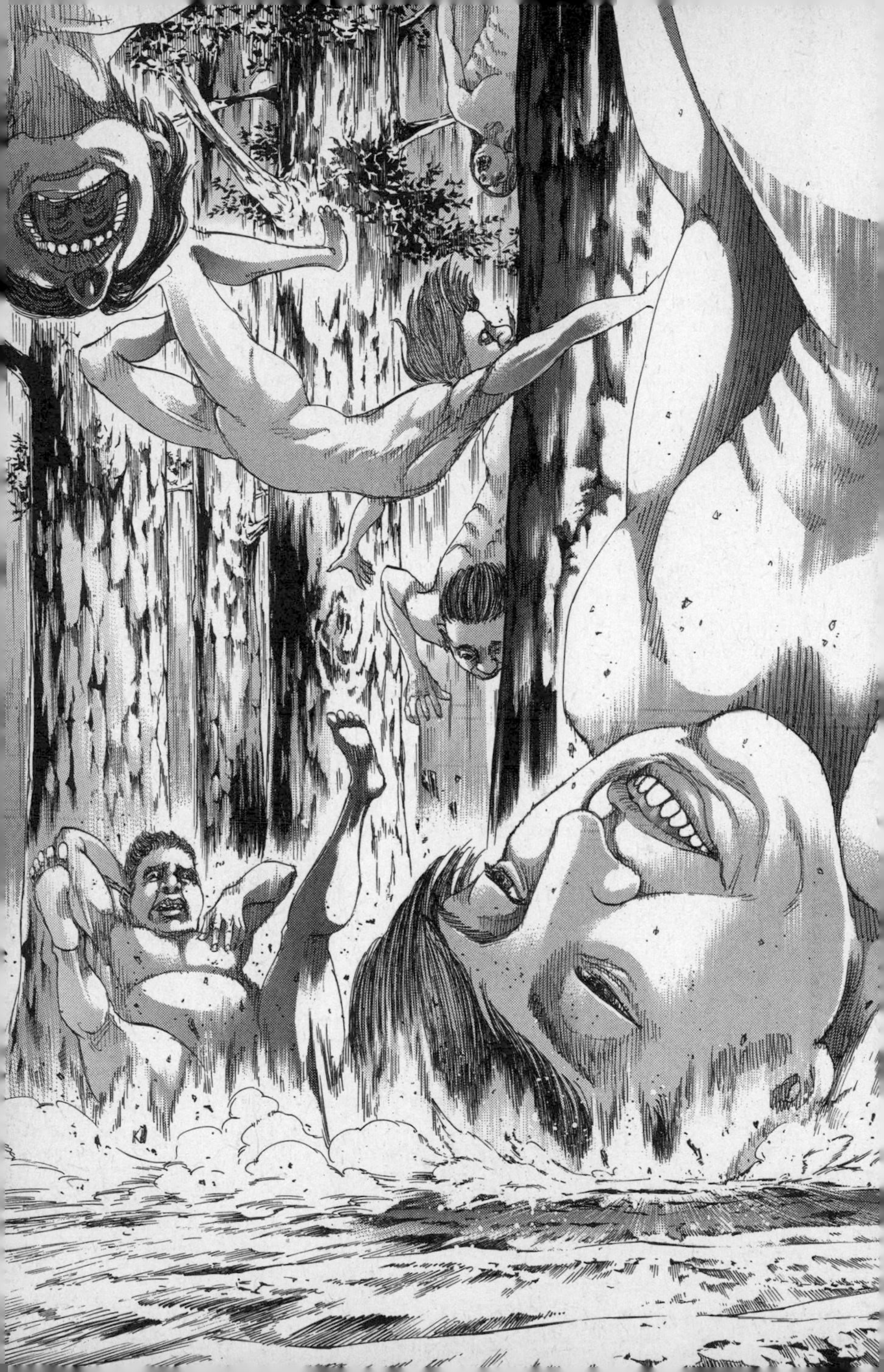

ATTACK on TITAN

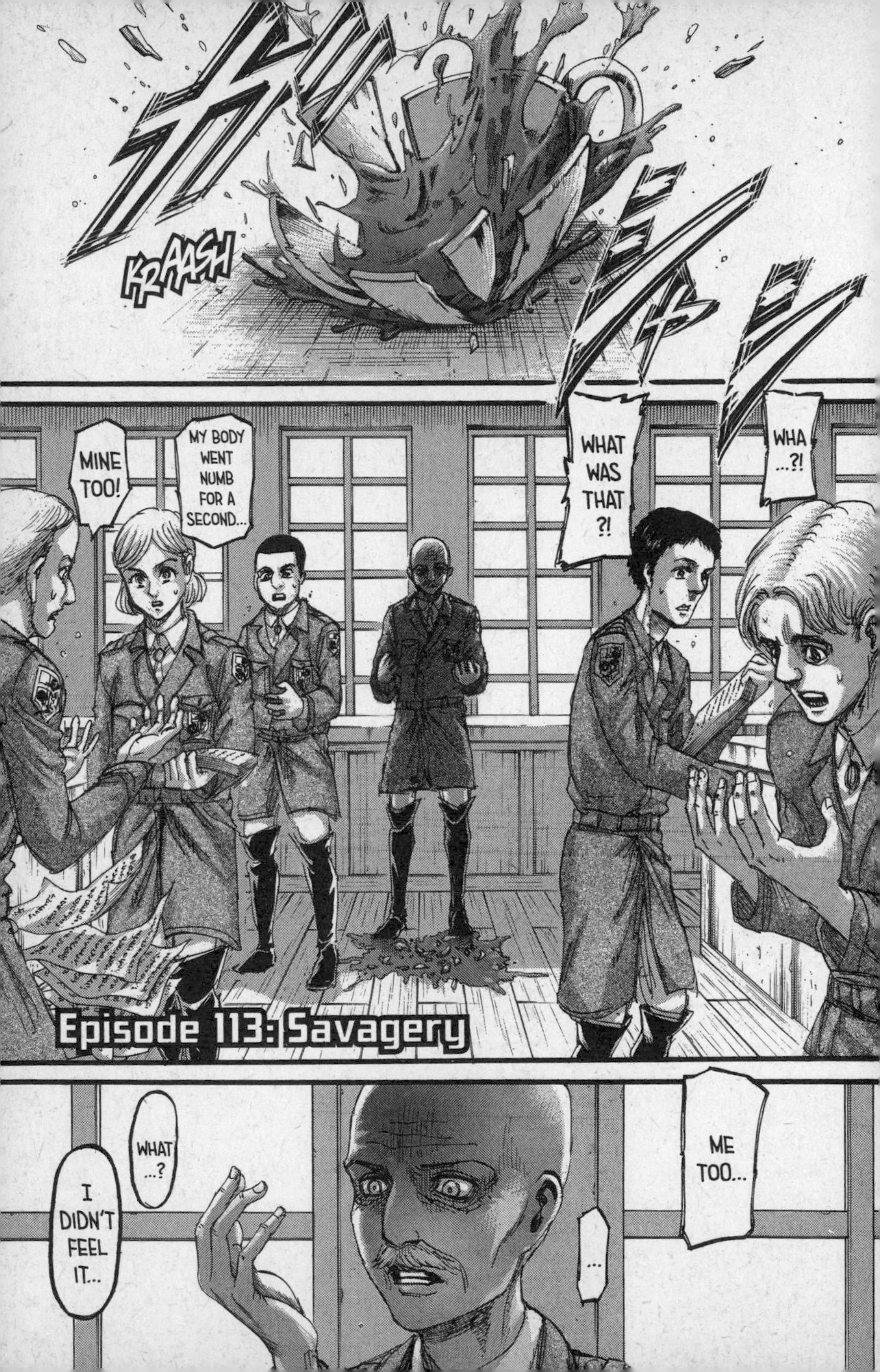
KRAASH
WHA ...?!
WHAT WAS THAT ?!
MY BODY WENT NUMB FOR A SECOND...
MINE TOO!
Episode 113: Savagery
ME TOO...
...
WHAT ...?
I DIDN'T FEEL IT...

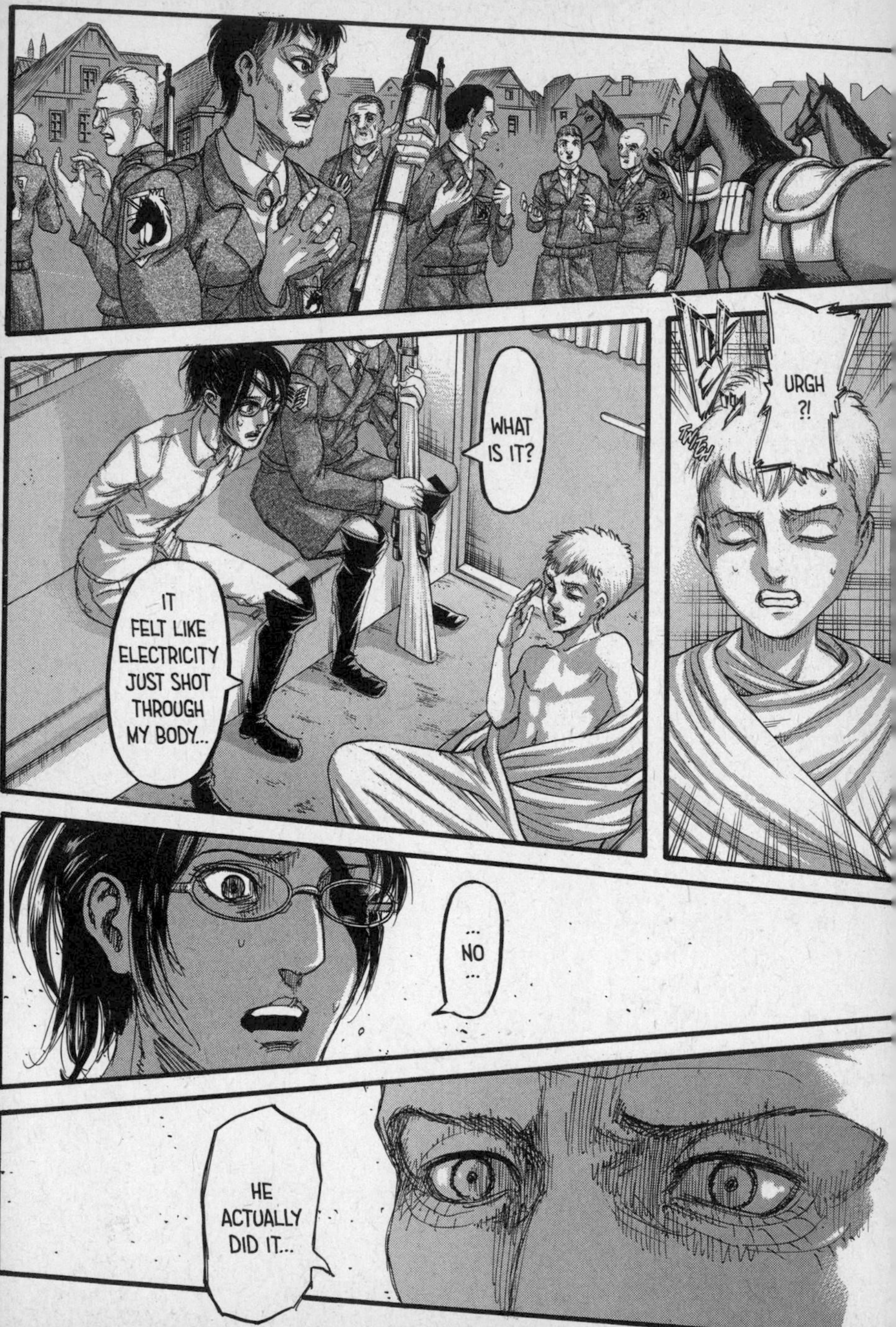
URGH ?!
WHAT IS IT?
IT FELT LIKE ELECTRICITY JUST SHOT THROUGH MY BODY...
... NO ...
HE ACTUALLY DID IT...

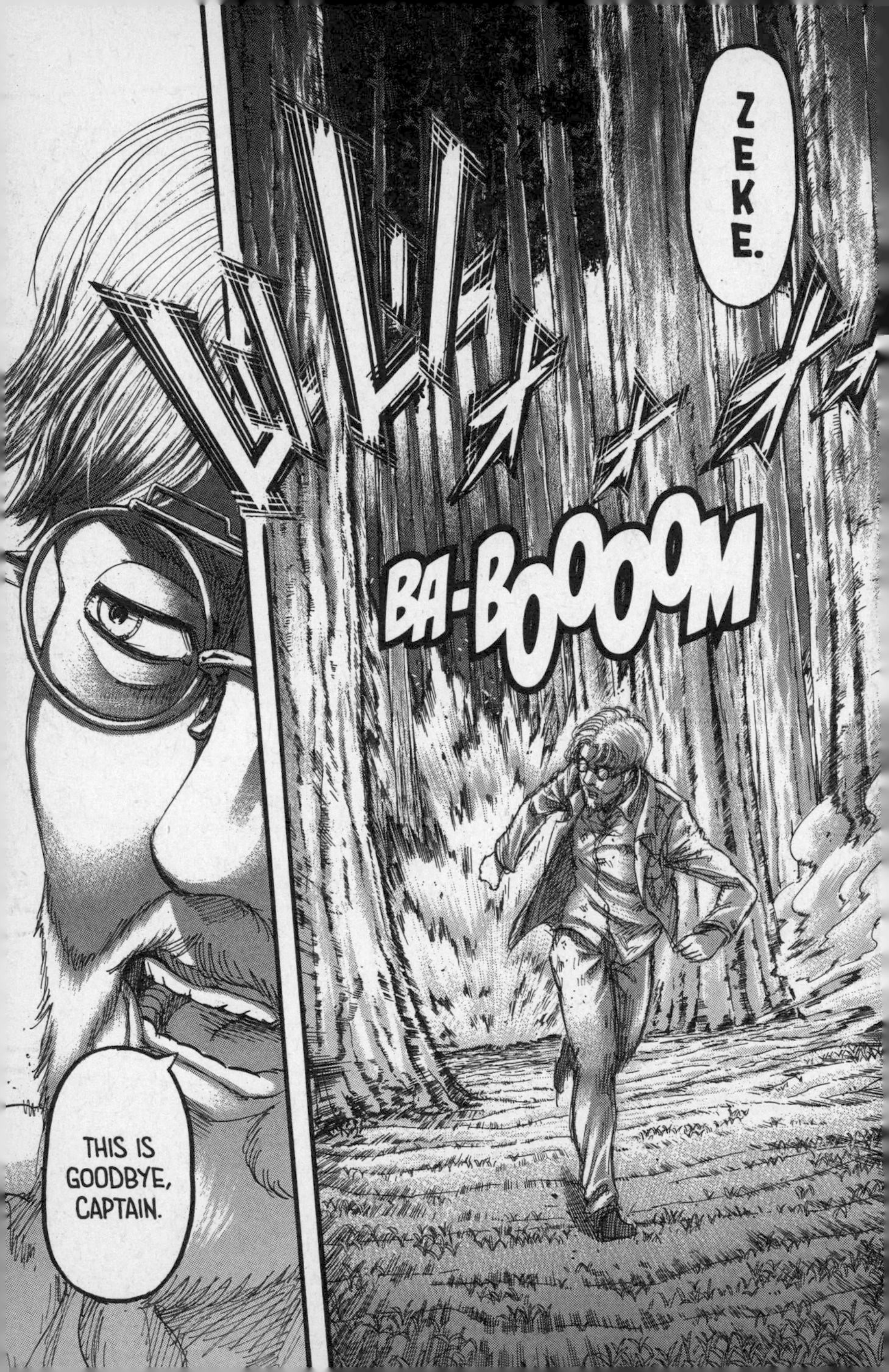
ZEKE.
BA-BOOOOM
THIS IS GOODBYE, CAPTAIN.

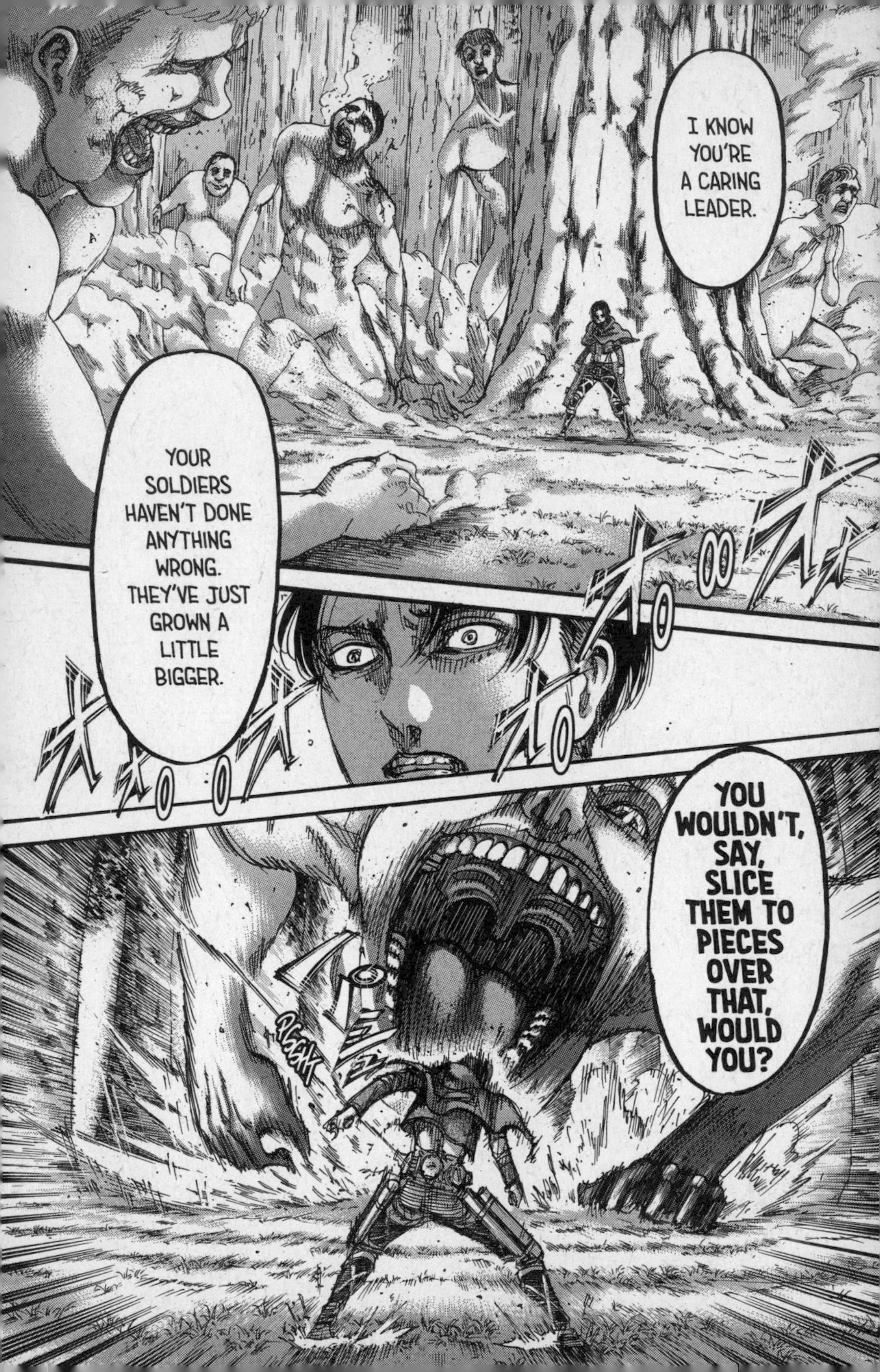
I KNOW YOU'RE A CARING LEADER.
YOUR SOLDIERS HAVEN'T DONE ANYTHING WRONG. THEY'VE JUST GROWN A LITTLE BIGGER.
YOU WOULDN'T, SAY, SLICE THEM TO PIECES OVER THAT, WOULD YOU?

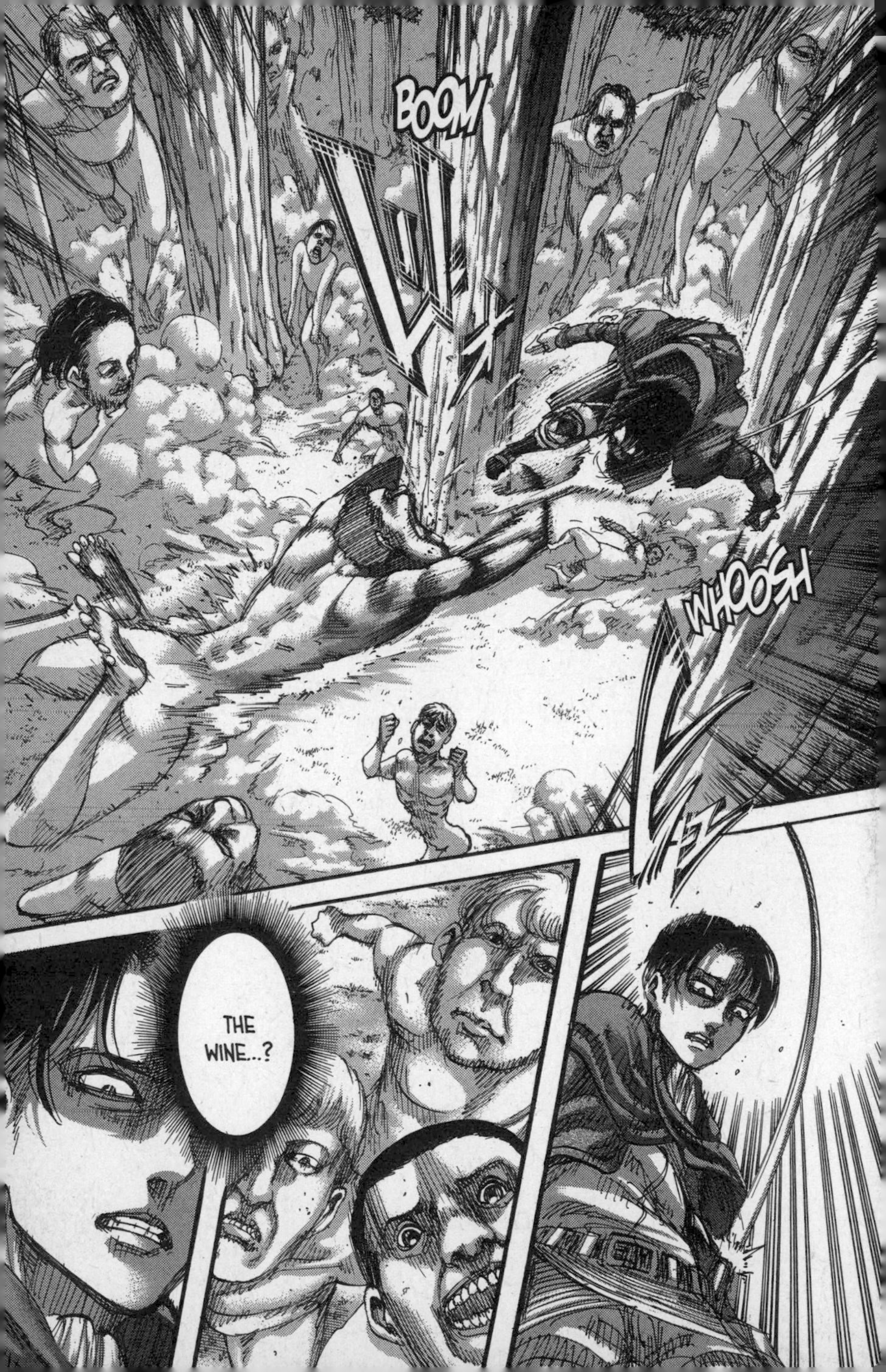
BOOM
WHOOSH
THE WINE...?

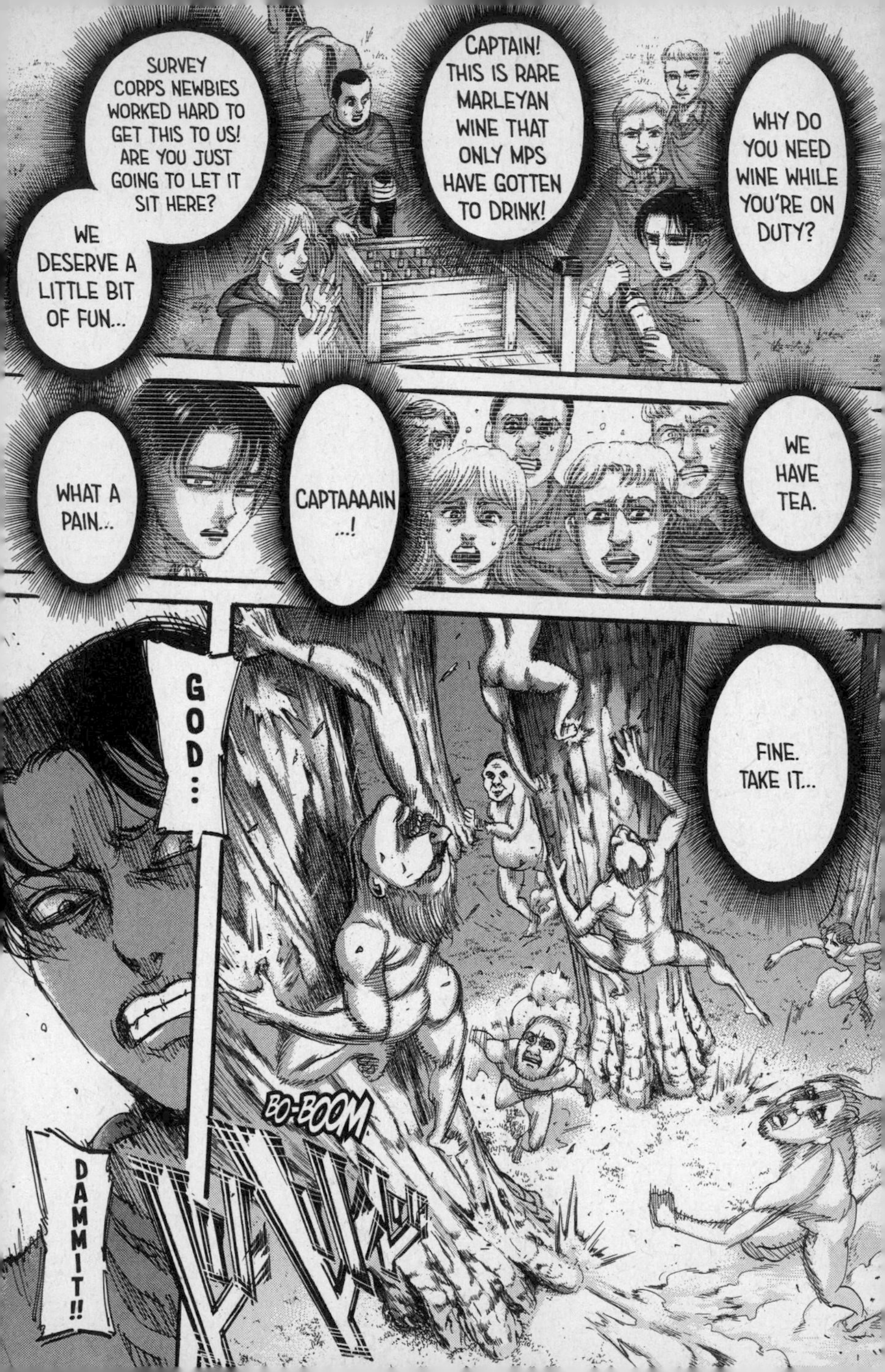

WHY DO YOU NEED WINE WHILE YOU'RE ON DUTY?
CAPTAIN! THIS IS RARE MARLEYAN WINE THAT ONLY MPS HAVE GOTTEN TO DRINK!
SURVEY CORPS NEWBIES WORKED HARD TO GET THIS TO US! ARE YOU JUST GOING TO LET IT SIT HERE?
WE DESERVE A LITTLE BIT OF FUN...
WE HAVE TEA.
CAPTAAAAIN ...!
WHAT A PAIN...
FINE. TAKE IT...
GOD...
BO-BOOM
DAMMIT!!

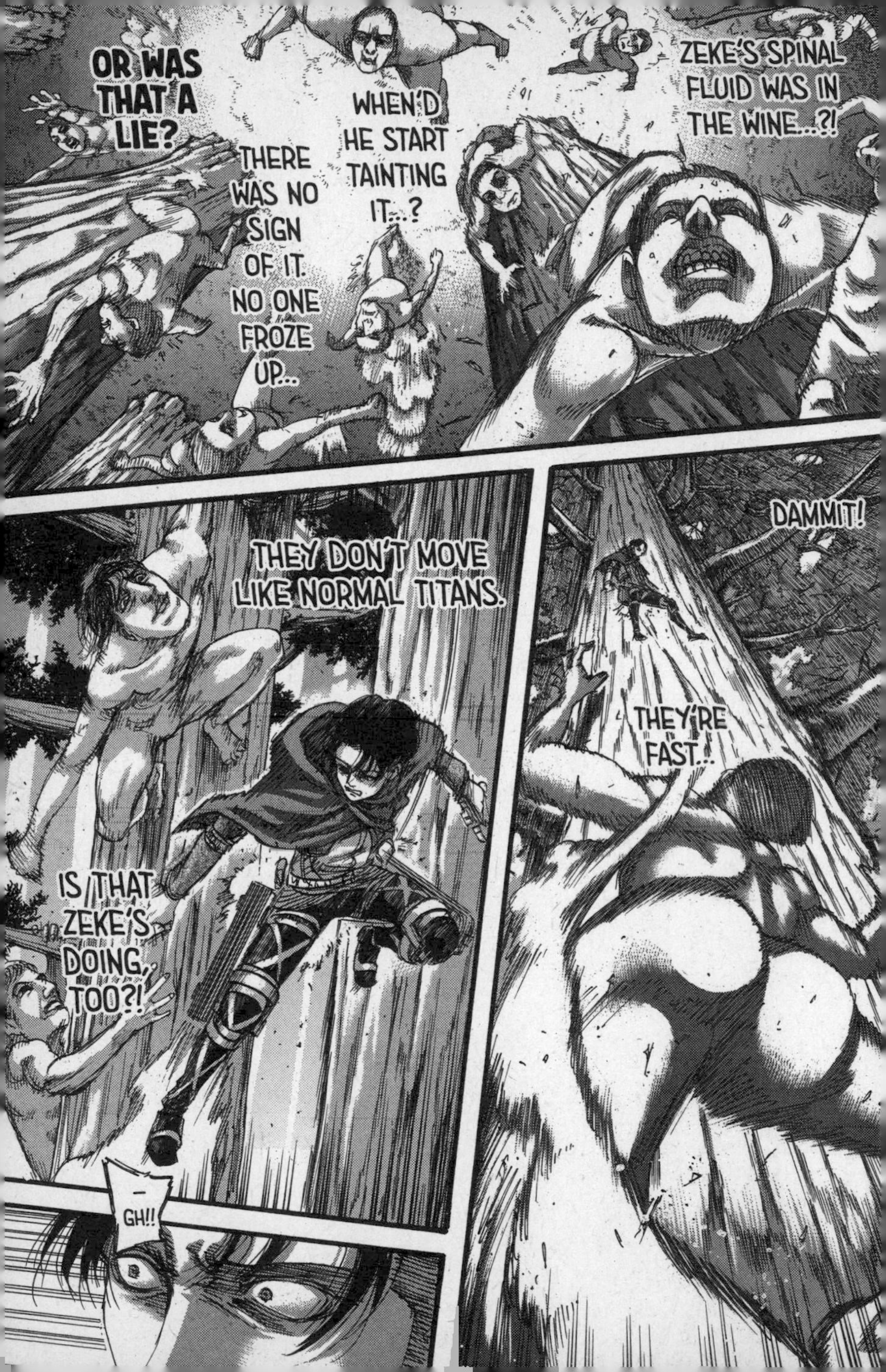
ZEKE'S SPINAL FLUID WAS IN THE WINE...?!
WHEN'D HE START TAINTING IT...?
THERE WAS NO SIGN OF IT. NO ONE FROZE UP...
OR WAS THAT A LIE?
DAMMIT!
THEY'RE FAST...
THEY DON'T MOVE LIKE NORMAL TITANS.
IS THAT ZEKE'S DOING, TOO?!
–GH!!

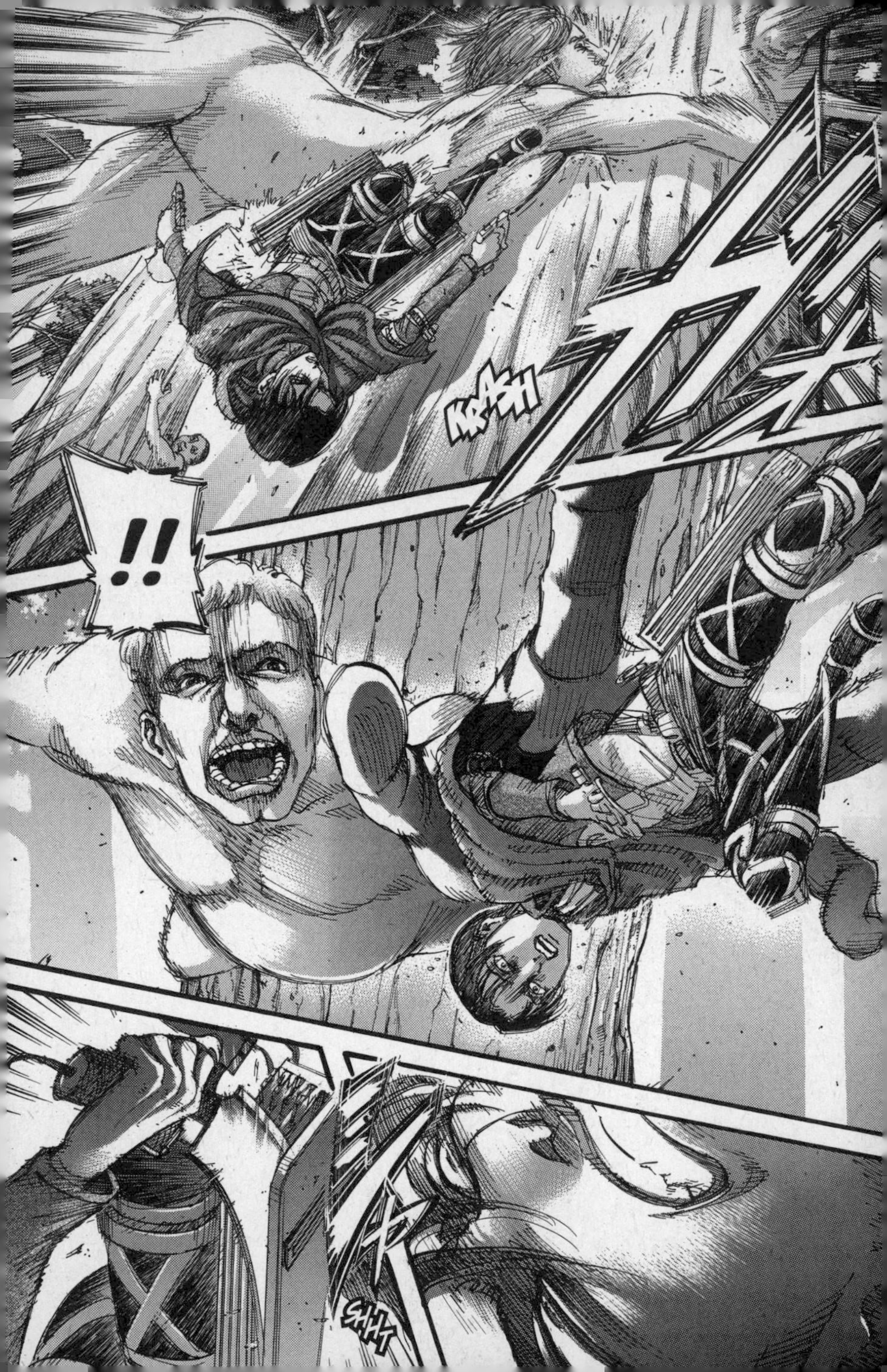
KRASH
!!
SHHK

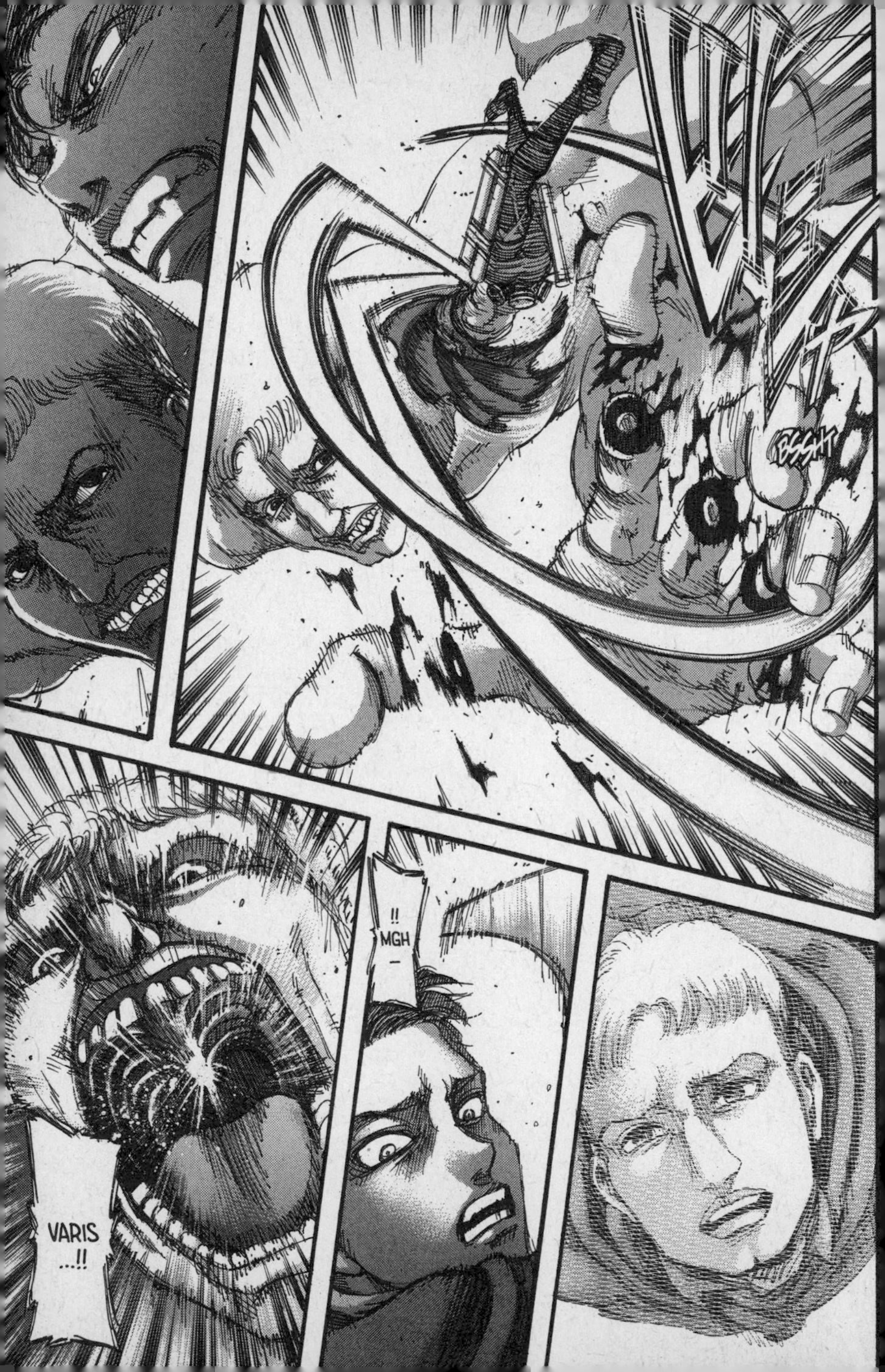
BSSHT
!! MGH —
VARIS ...!!

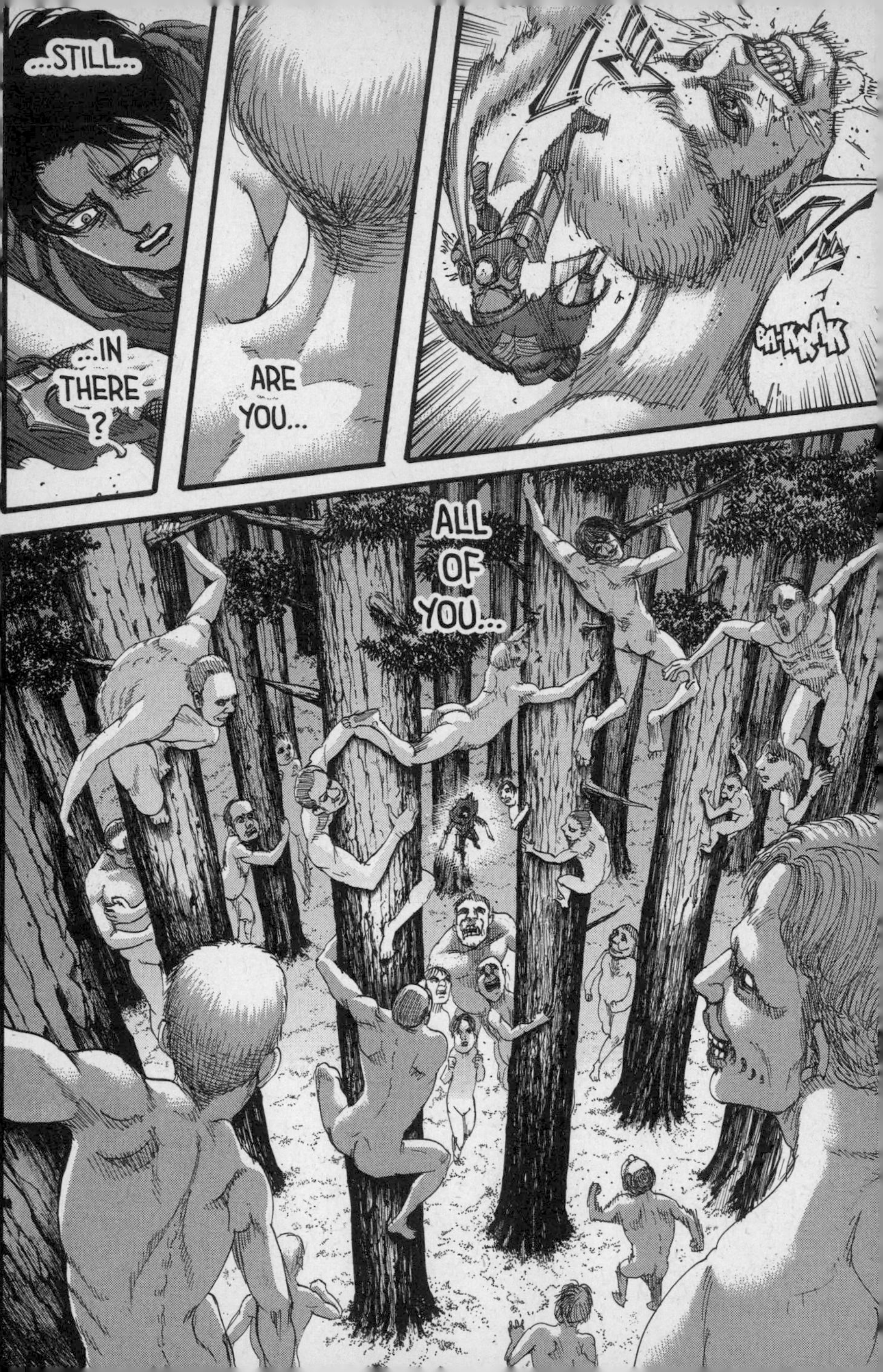
BA-KRAAK
ARE YOU...
...STILL...
...IN THERE ?
ALL OF YOU...

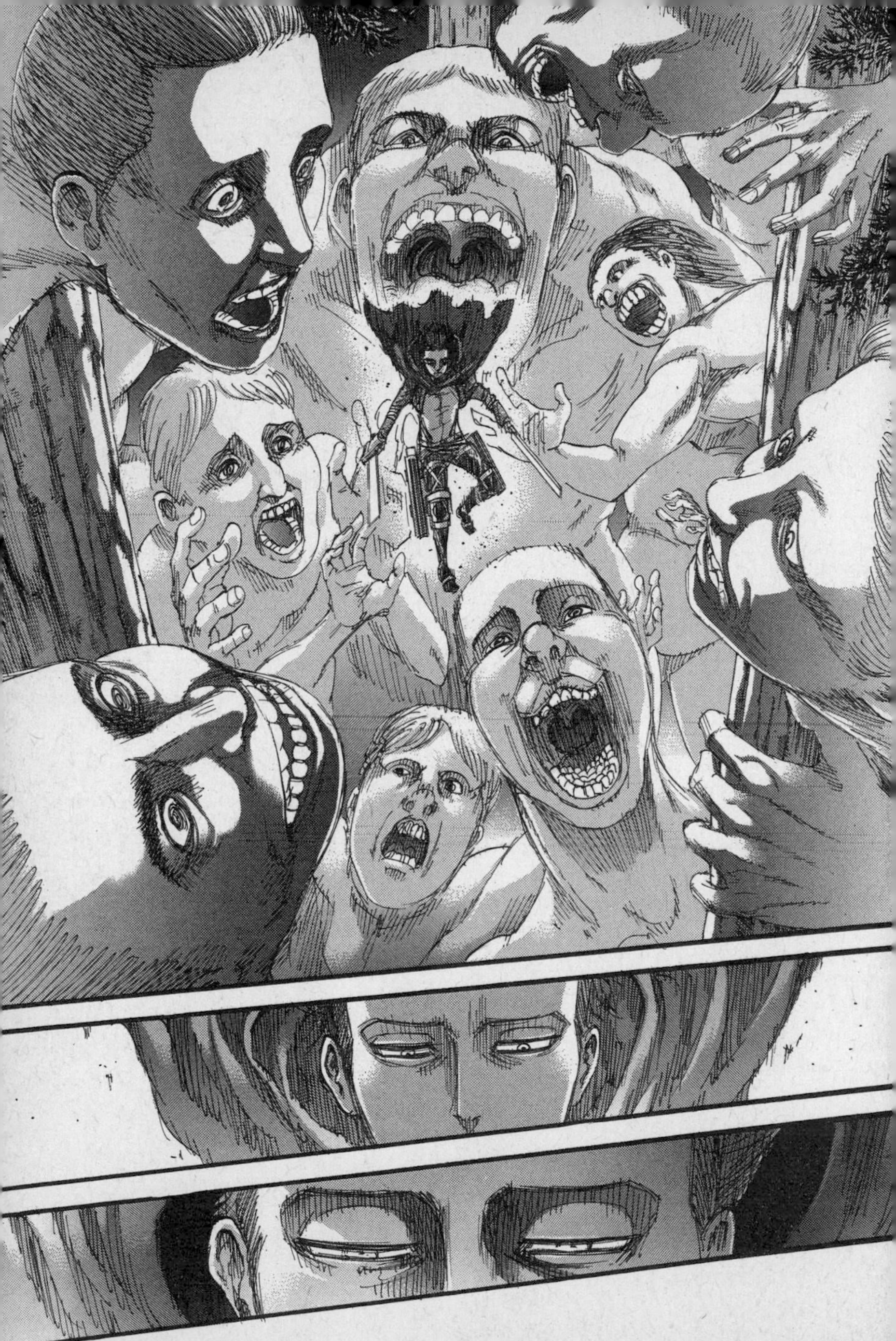

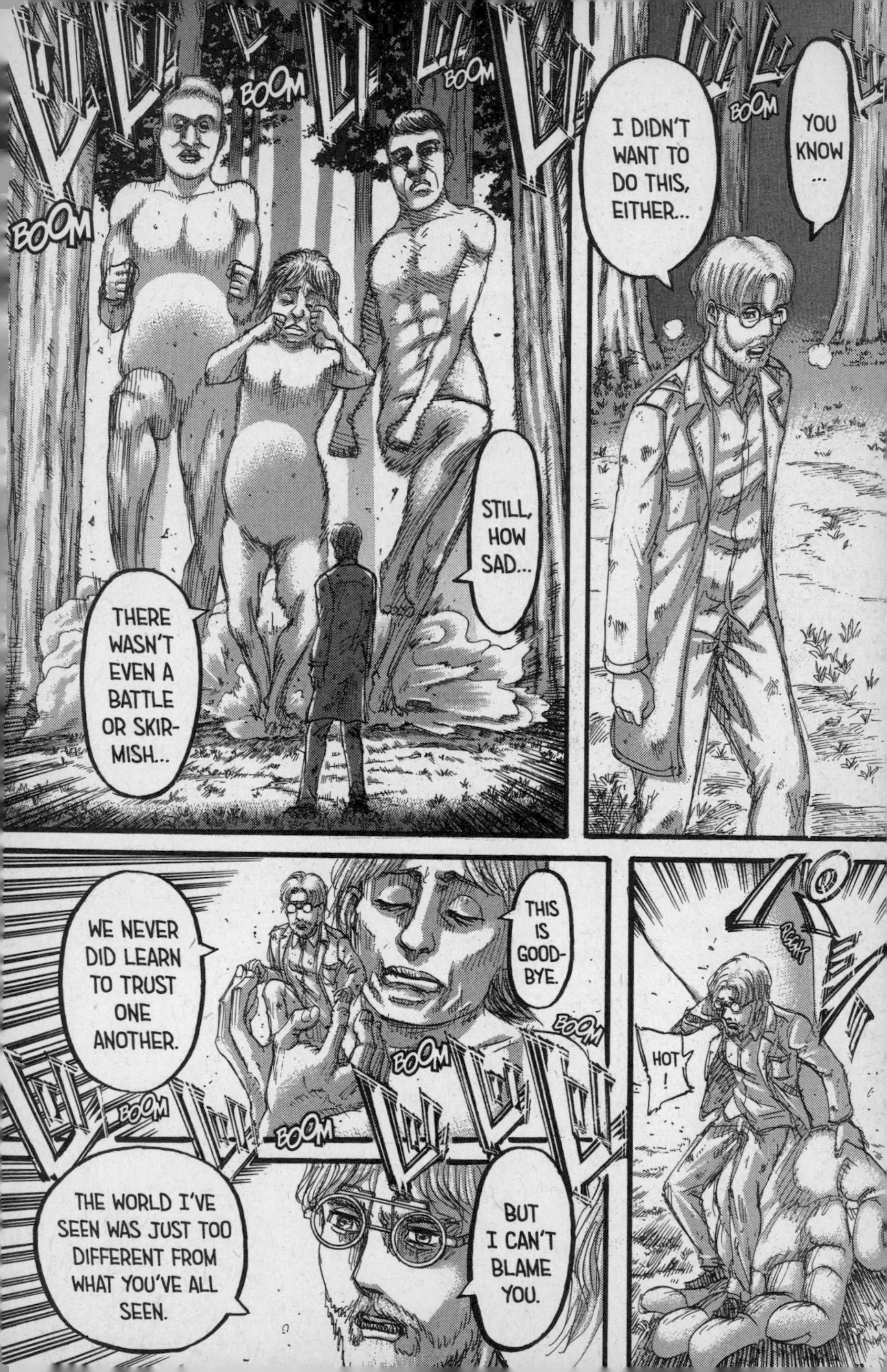

YOU KNOW...
BOOM
I DIDN'T WANT TO DO THIS, EITHER...
BOOM
BOOM
BOOM
STILL, HOW SAD...
THERE WASN'T EVEN A BATTLE OR SKIRMISH...
HOT!
THIS IS GOODBYE.
BOOM
BOOM
WE NEVER DID LEARN TO TRUST ONE ANOTHER.
BOOM
BOOM
BUT I CAN'T BLAME YOU.
THE WORLD I'VE SEEN WAS JUST TOO DIFFERENT FROM WHAT YOU'VE ALL SEEN.

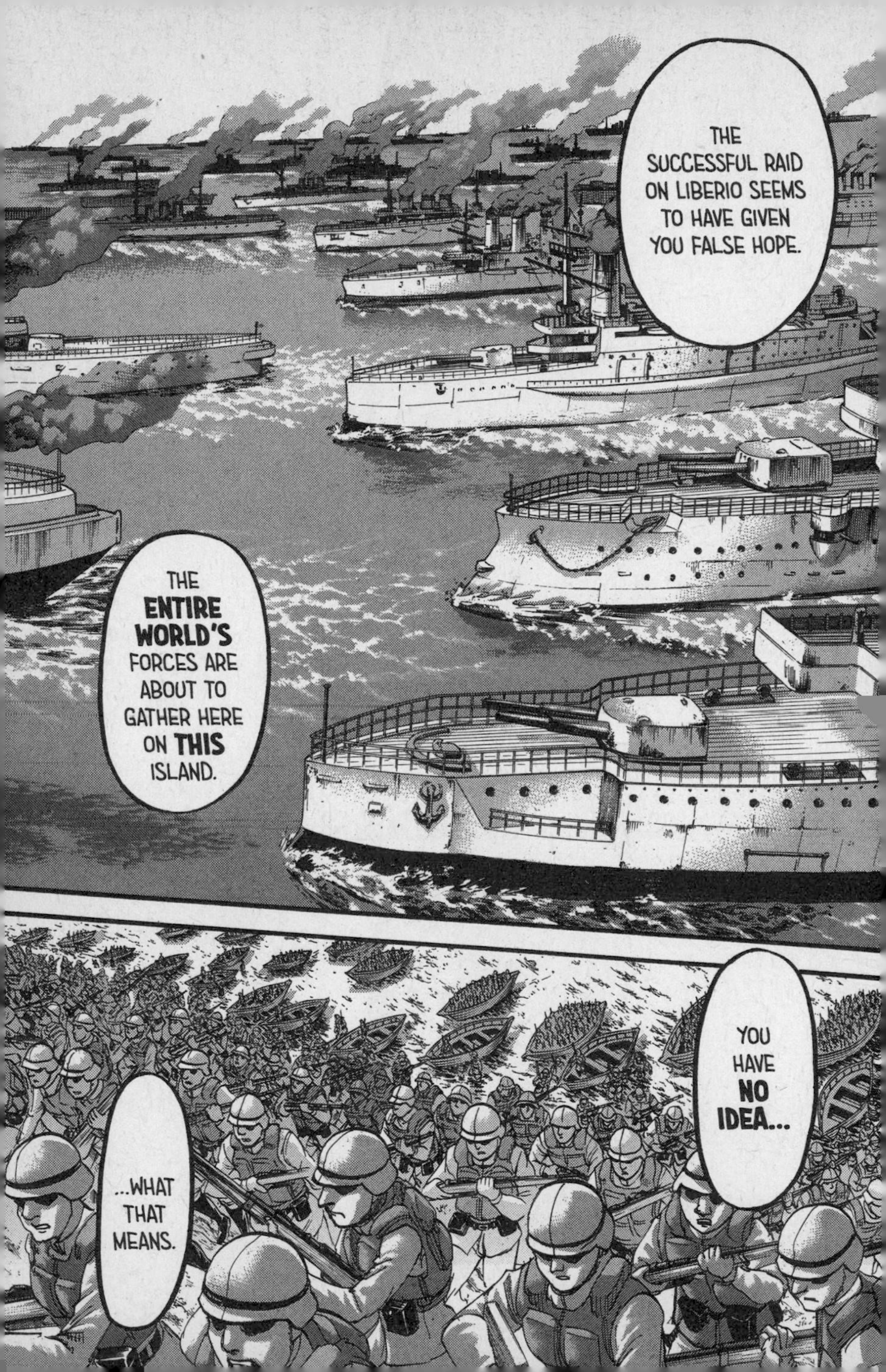
THE SUCCESSFUL RAID ON LIBERIO SEEMS TO HAVE GIVEN YOU FALSE HOPE.
THE **ENTIRE WORLD'S** FORCES ARE ABOUT TO GATHER HERE ON **THIS** ISLAND.
YOU HAVE **NO IDEA...**
...WHAT THAT MEANS.

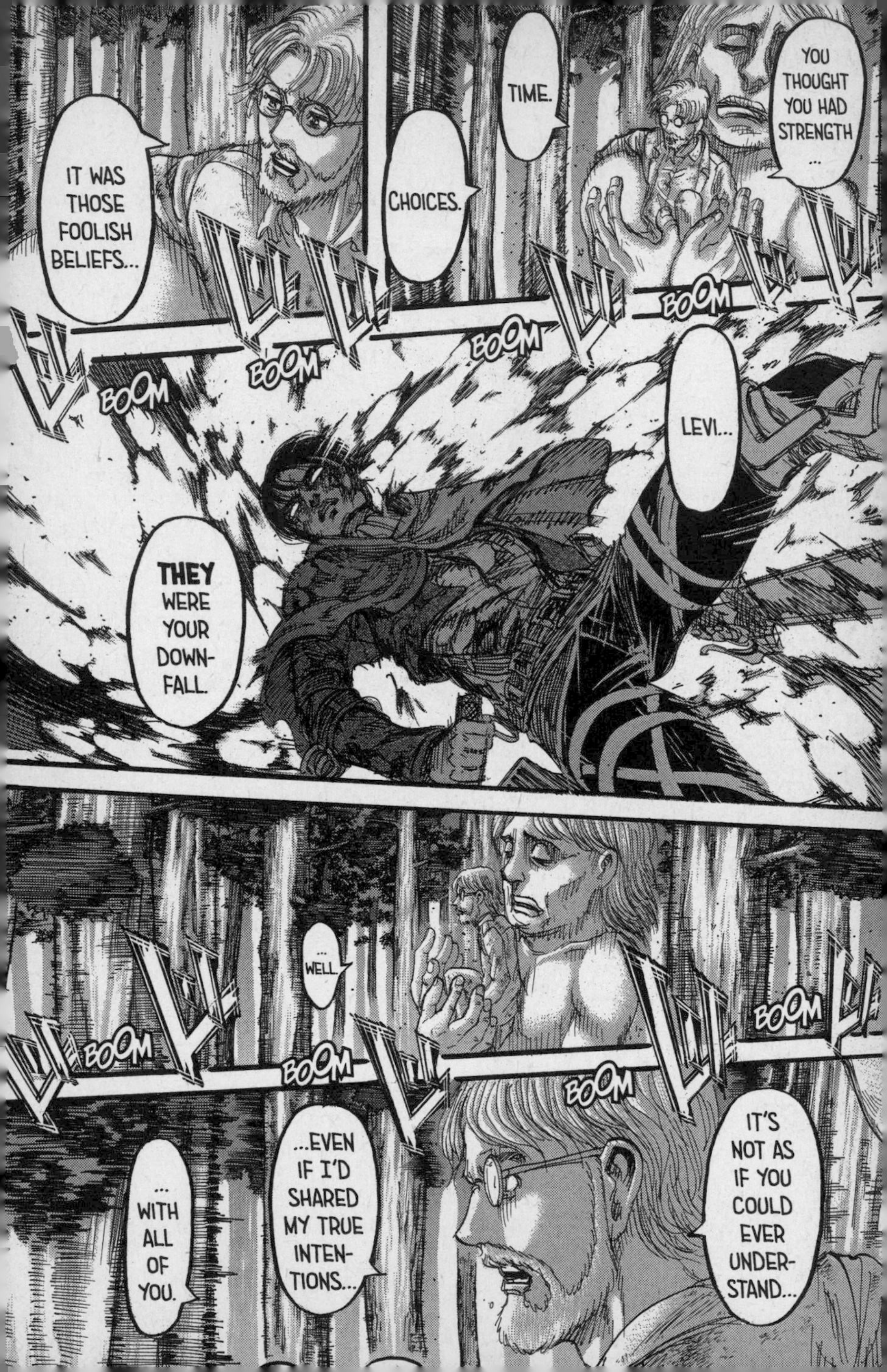
YOU THOUGHT YOU HAD STRENGTH ...
BOOM
TIME.
CHOICES.
BOOM
IT WAS THOSE FOOLISH BELIEFS...
BOOM
BOOM
LEVI...
THEY WERE YOUR DOWNFALL.
BOOM
... WELL.
BOOM
BOOM
BOOM
IT'S NOT AS IF YOU COULD EVER UNDERSTAND...
...EVEN IF I'D SHARED MY TRUE INTENTIONS...
... WITH ALL OF YOU.

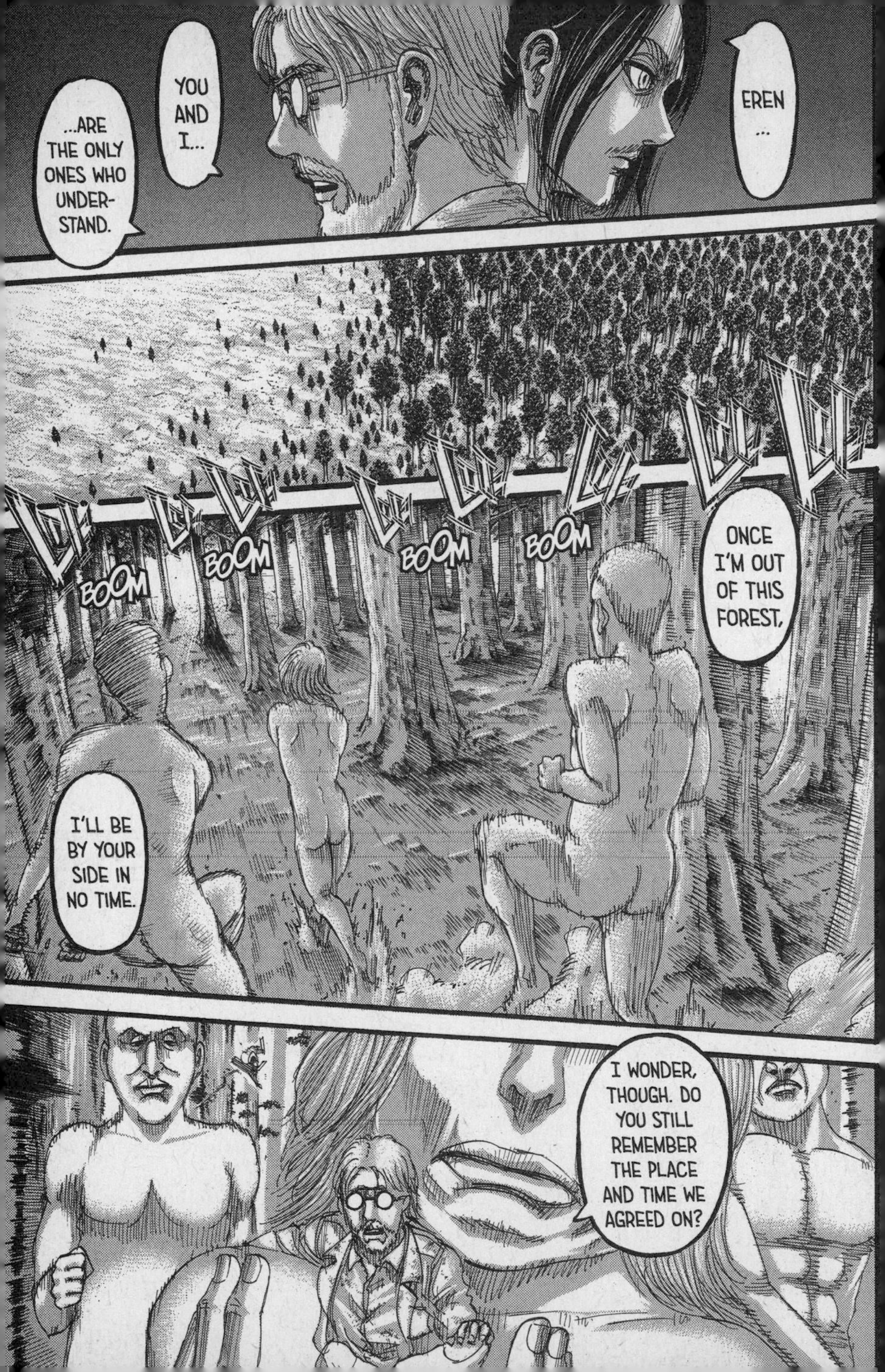
EREN ...
YOU AND I...
...ARE THE ONLY ONES WHO UNDER-STAND.
BOOM
BOOM
BOOM
BOOM
ONCE I'M OUT OF THIS FOREST,
I'LL BE BY YOUR SIDE IN NO TIME.
I WONDER, THOUGH. DO YOU STILL REMEMBER THE PLACE AND TIME WE AGREED ON?

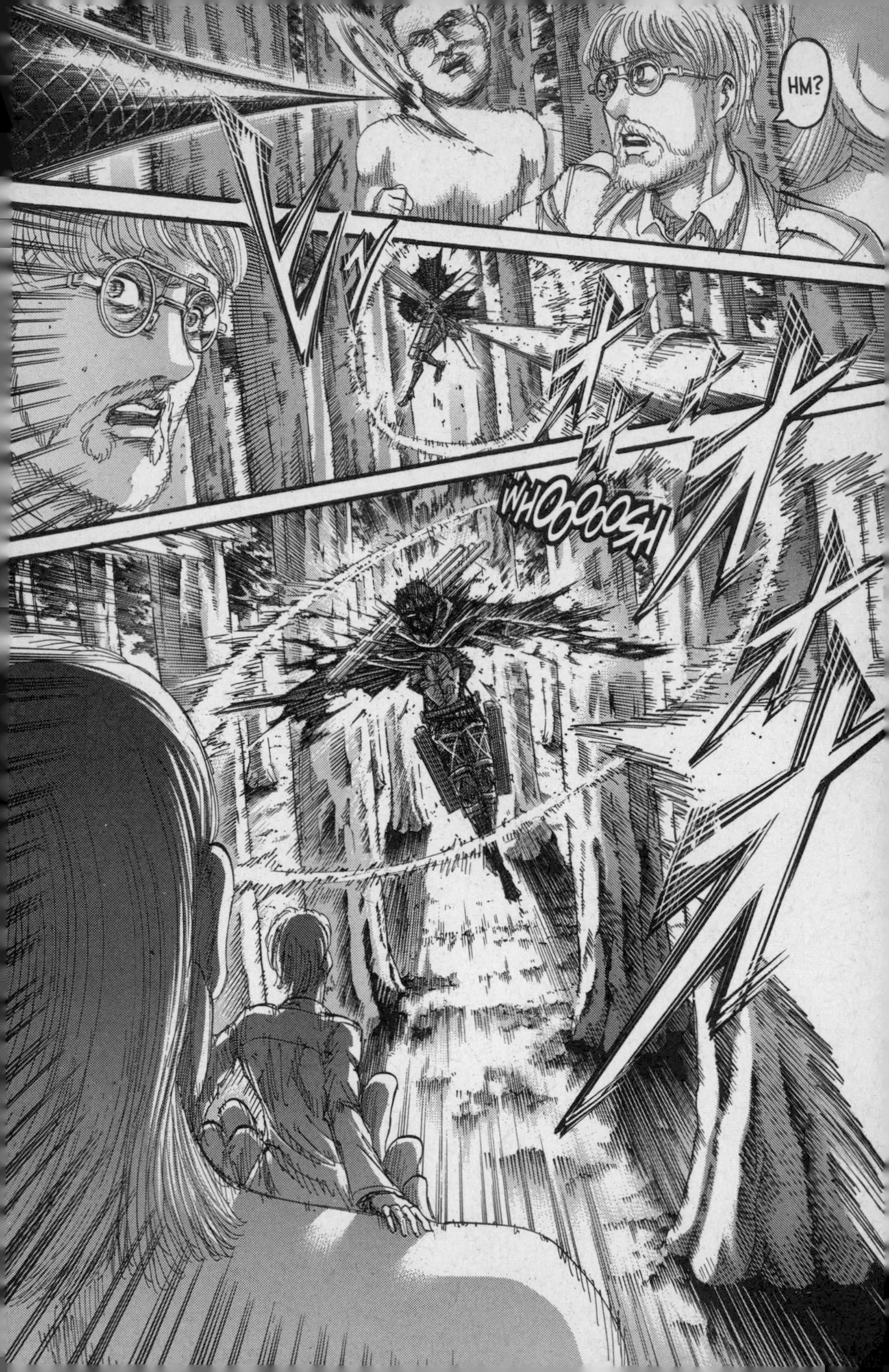
HM?
WHOOOOOSH

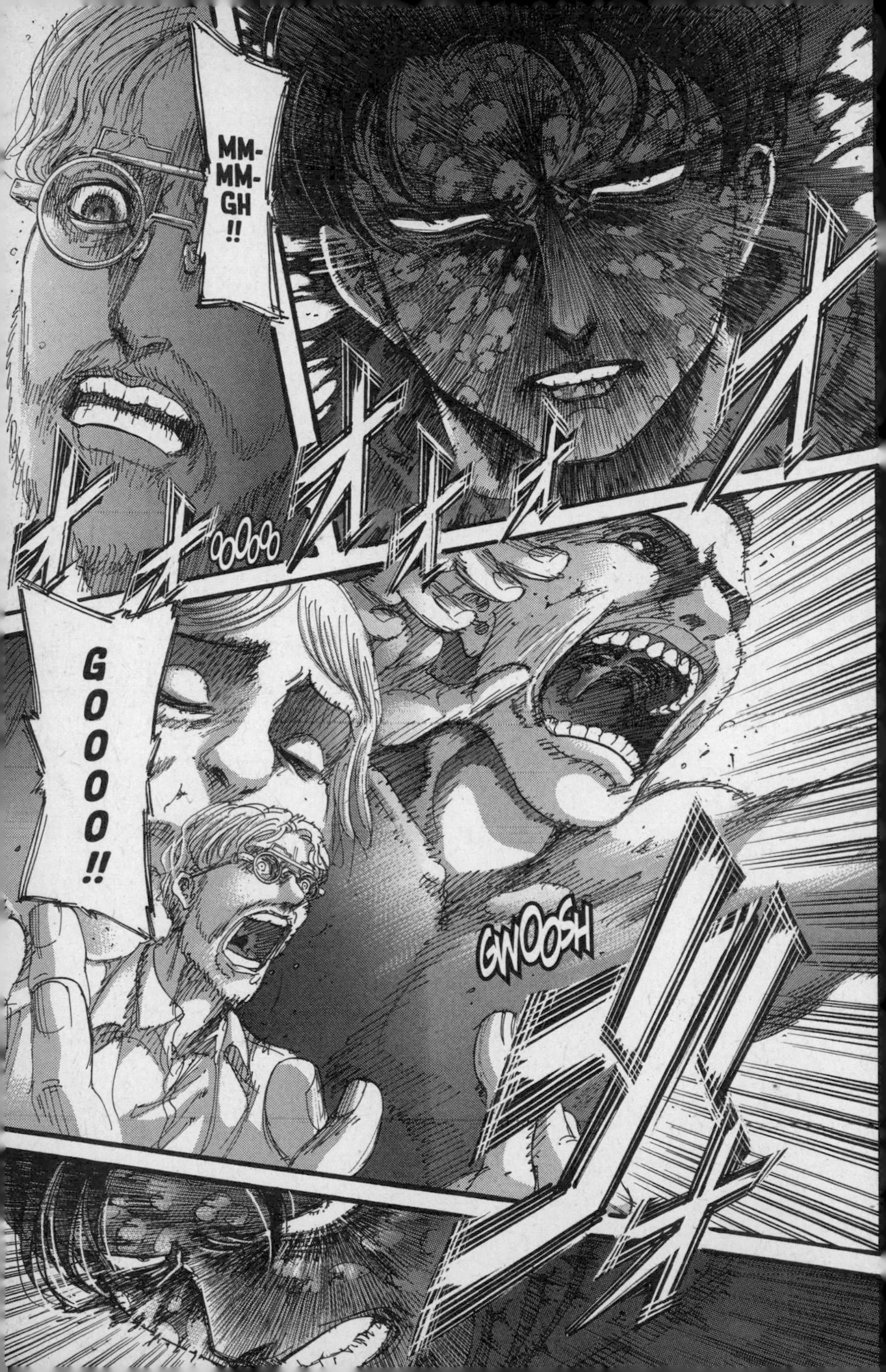
MM-MM-GH!!
OOOOO
GWOOSH
GOOOOO!!

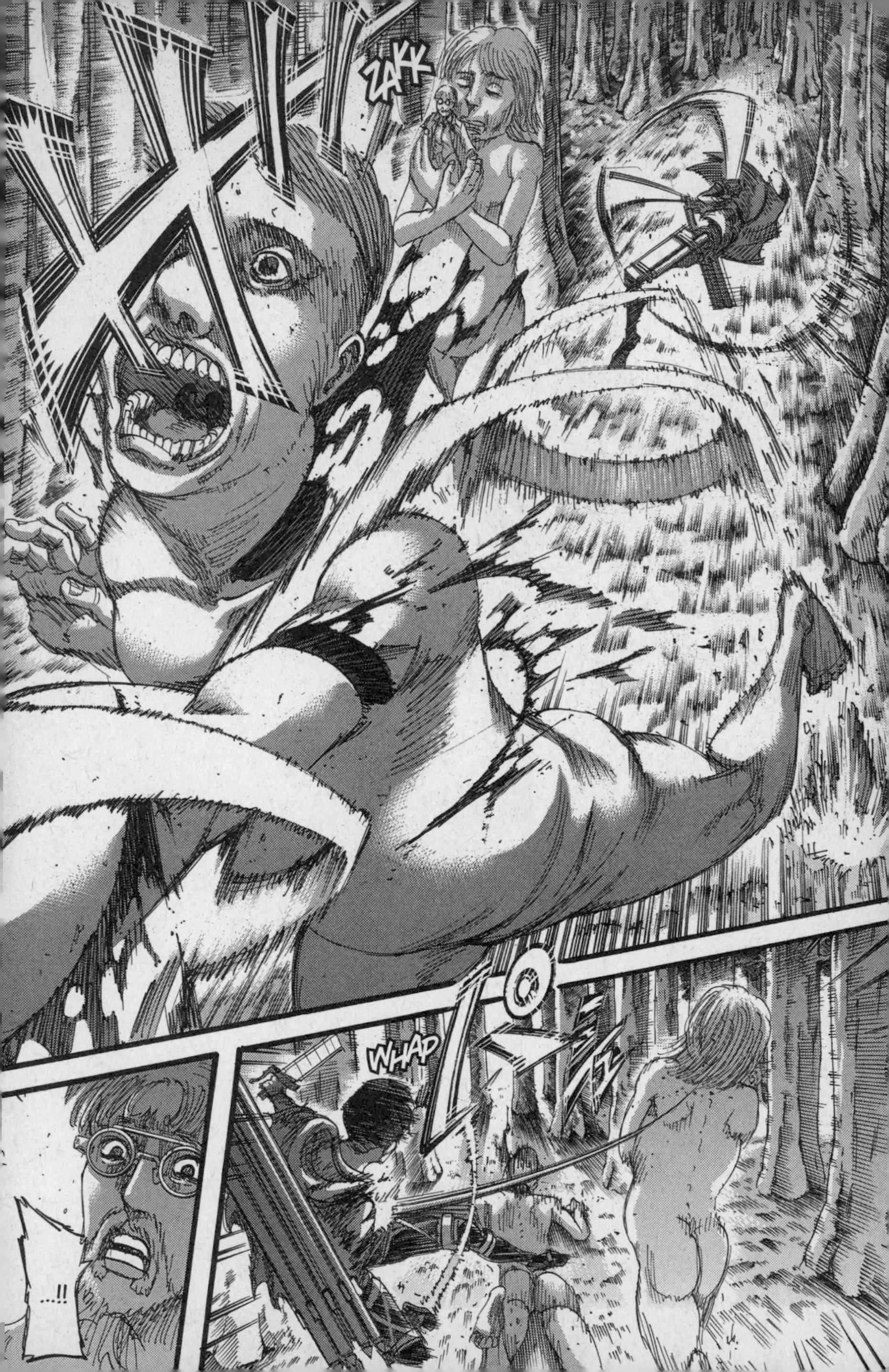
ZAKK
WHAP
...!!

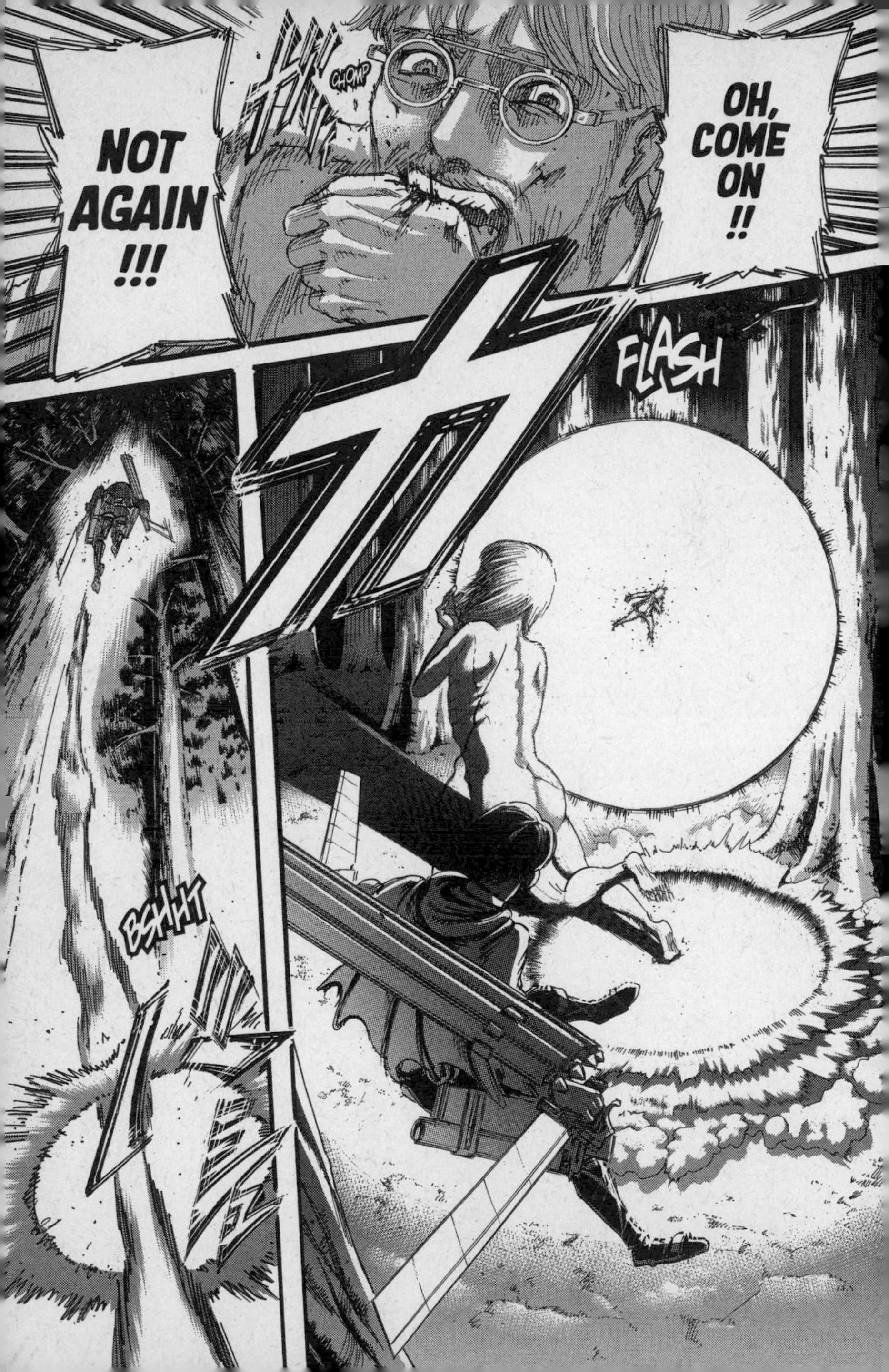
OH, COME ON !!
CHOMP
NOT AGAIN !!!
FLASH
BSHHT

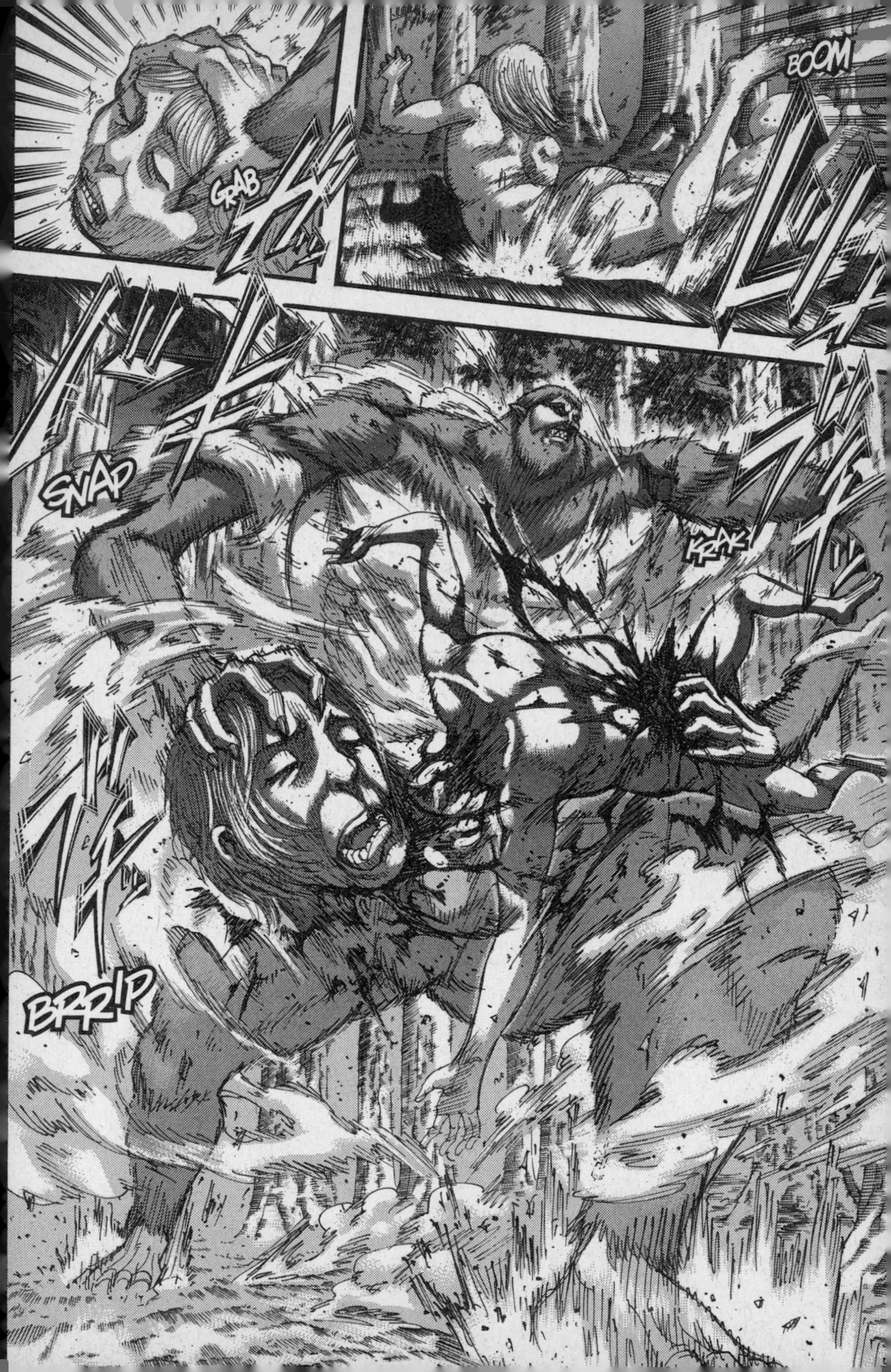
BOOM
GRAB
KRAK
SNAP
BRRIP

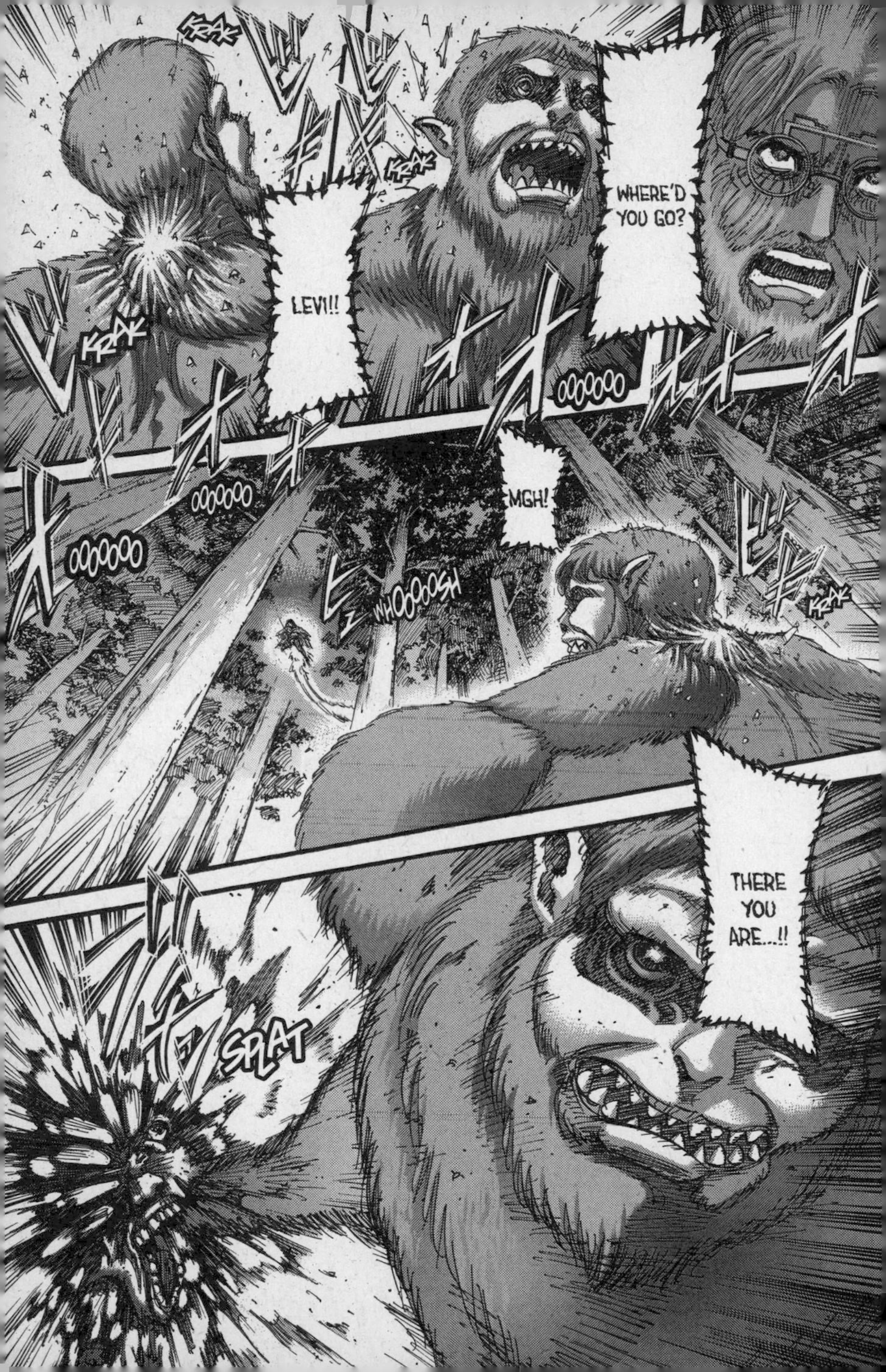
WHERE'D YOU GO?
LEVI!!
KRAK
KRAK
OOOOOOO
KRAK
OOOOOOO
OOOOOOO
MGH!
KRAK
WHOOOOOSH
THERE YOU ARE...!!
SPLAT

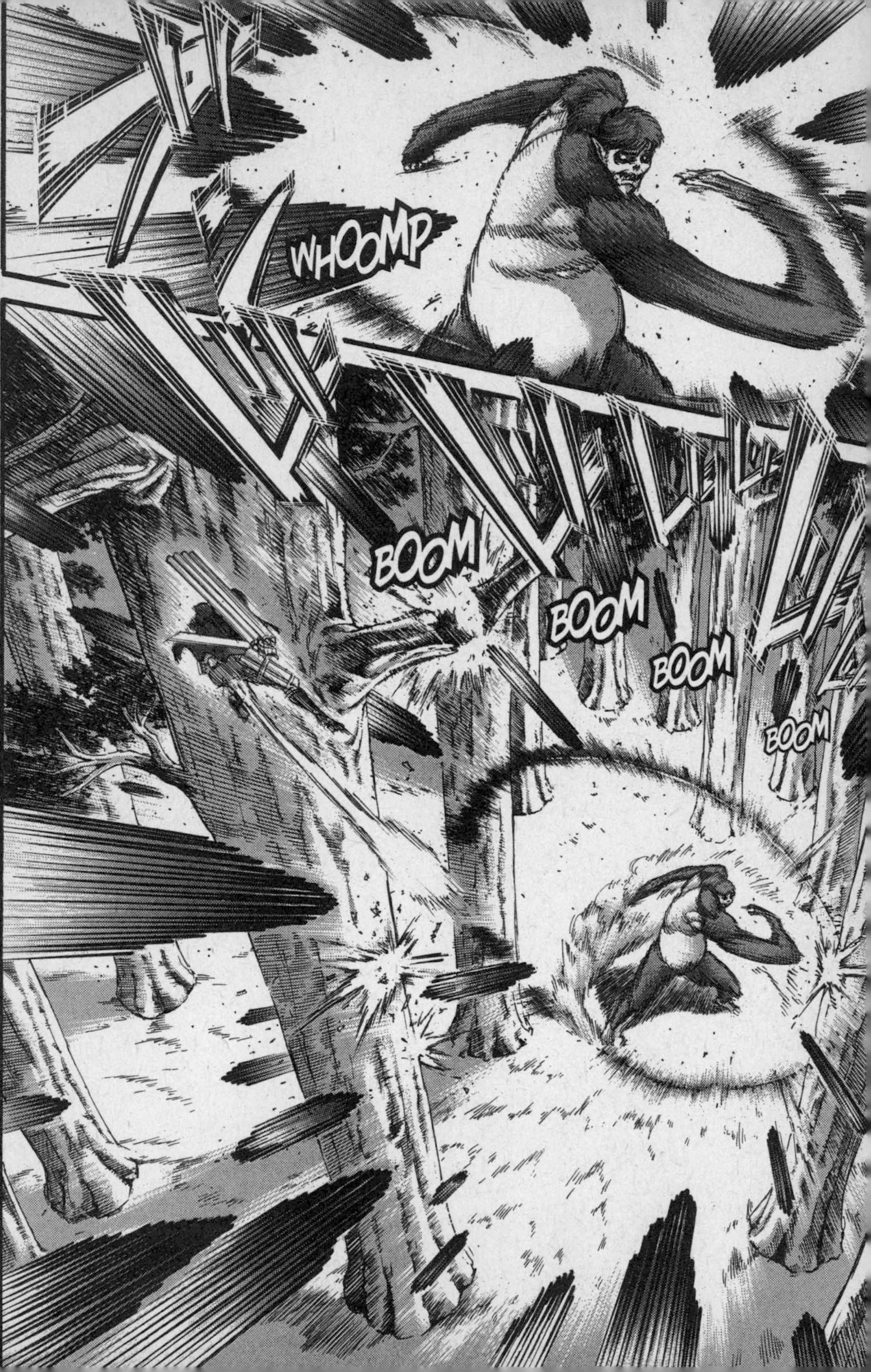
WHOOMP
BOOM
BOOM
BOOM
BOOM

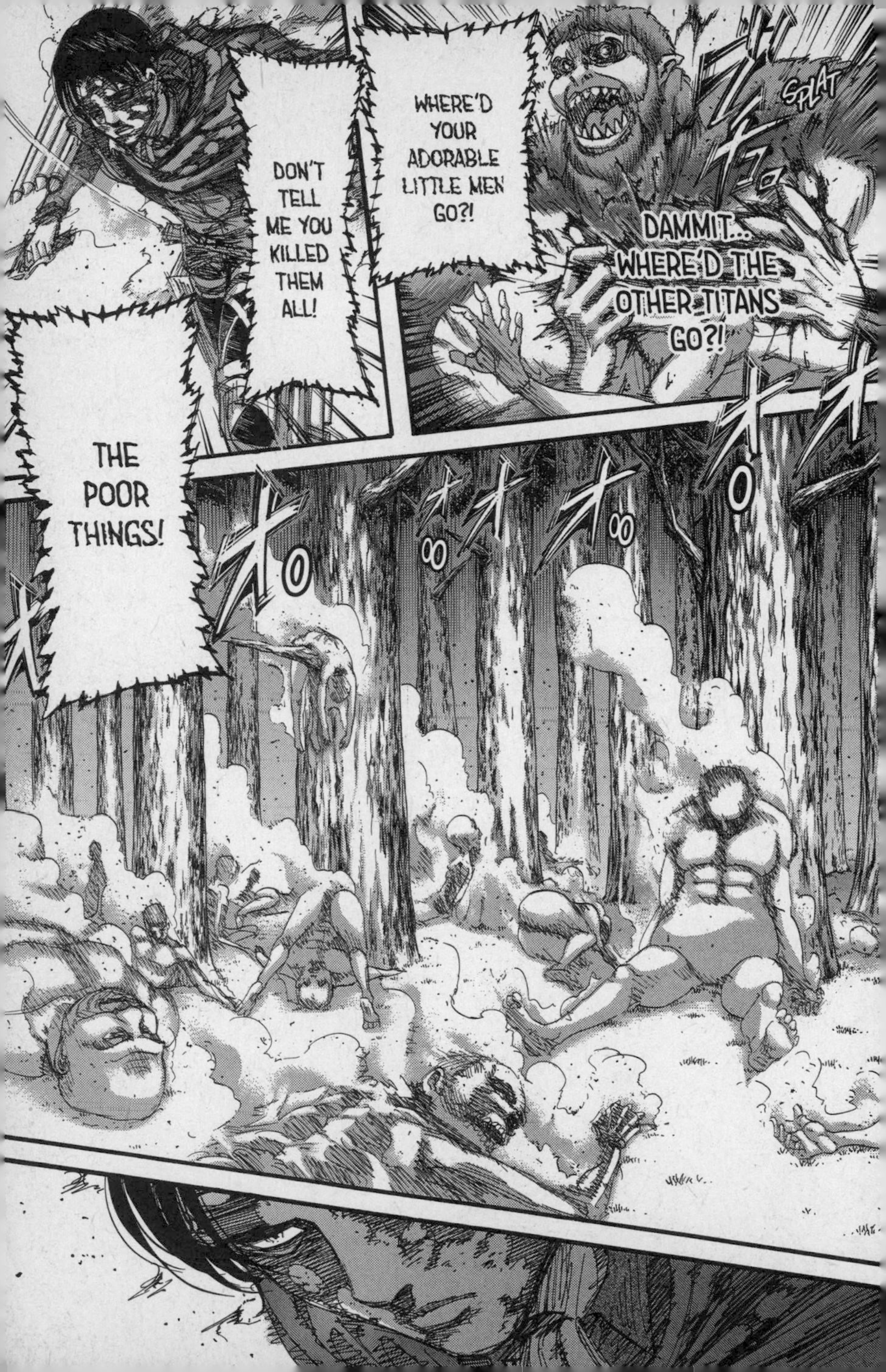
SPLAT
WHERE'D YOUR ADORABLE LITTLE MEN GO?!
DAMMIT... WHERE'D THE OTHER TITANS GO?!
DON'T TELL ME YOU KILLED THEM ALL!
THE POOR THINGS!

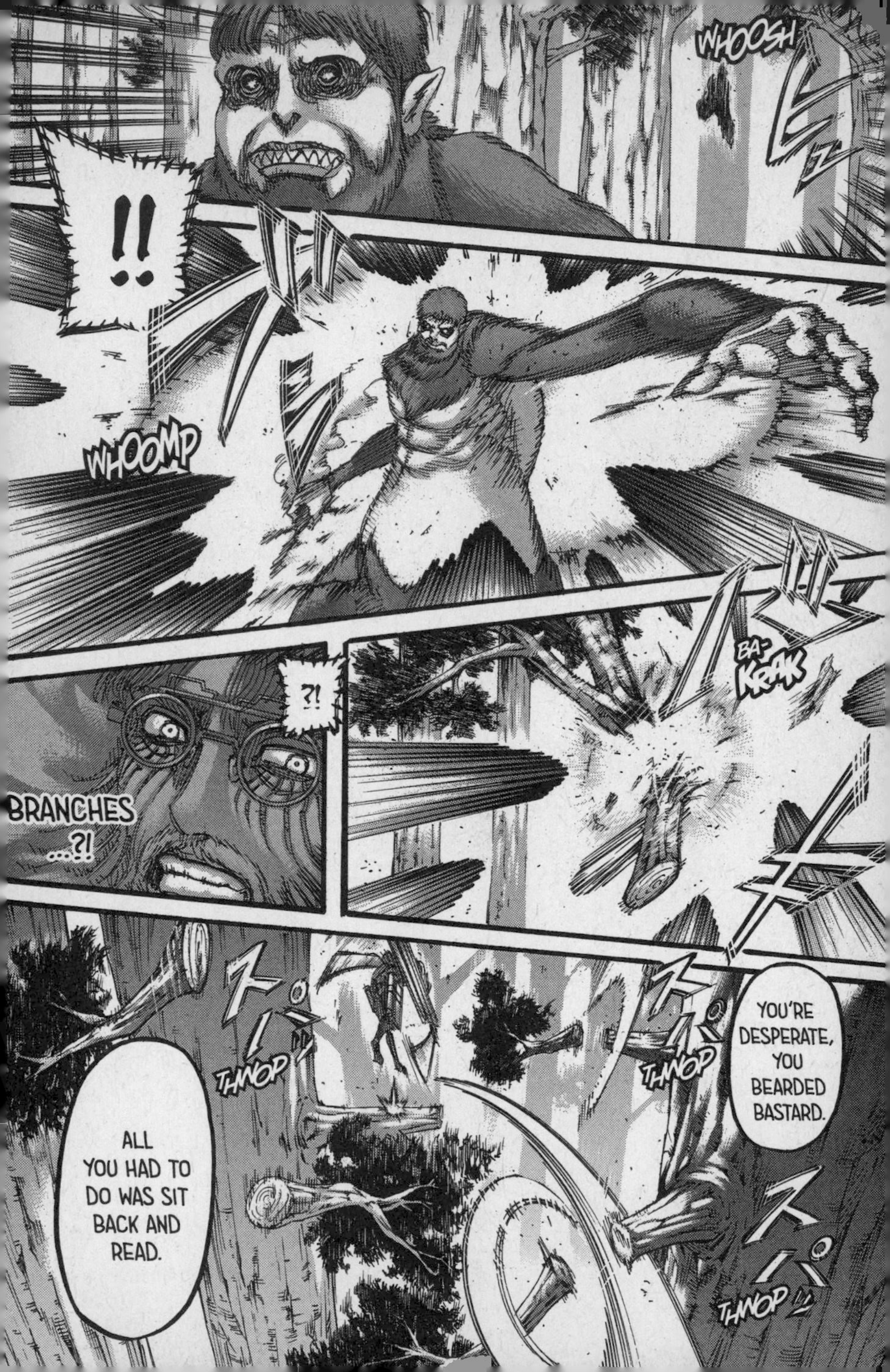

WHOOSH
!!
WHOOMP
BA-KRAK
?!
BRANCHES ...?!
YOU'RE DESPERATE, YOU BEARDED BASTARD.
THWOP
THWOP
ALL YOU HAD TO DO WAS SIT BACK AND READ.
THWOP!!

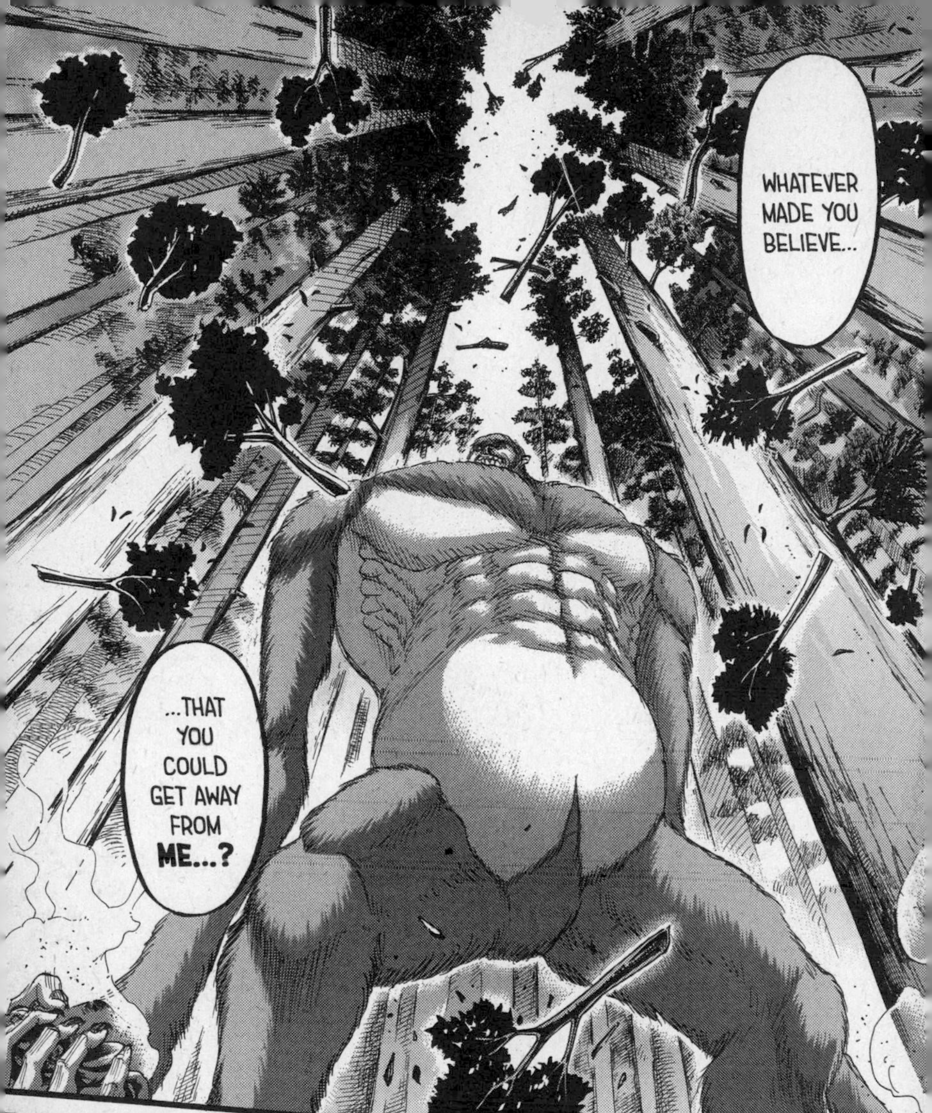
WHATEVER MADE YOU BELIEVE...
...THAT YOU COULD GET AWAY FROM **ME...?**

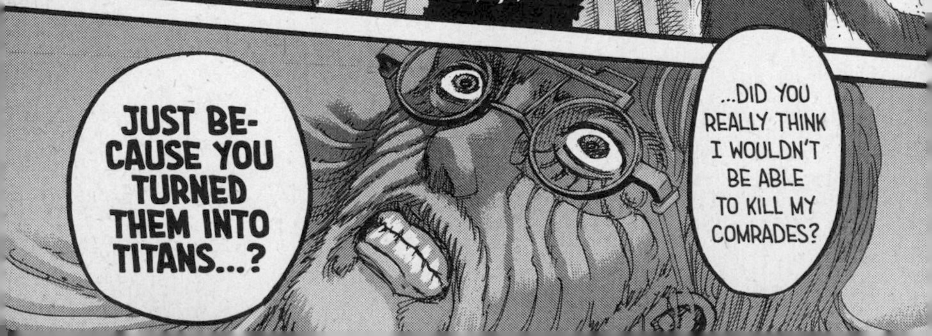
...DID YOU REALLY THINK I WOULDN'T BE ABLE TO KILL MY COMRADES?
JUST BE-CAUSE YOU TURNED THEM INTO TITANS...?

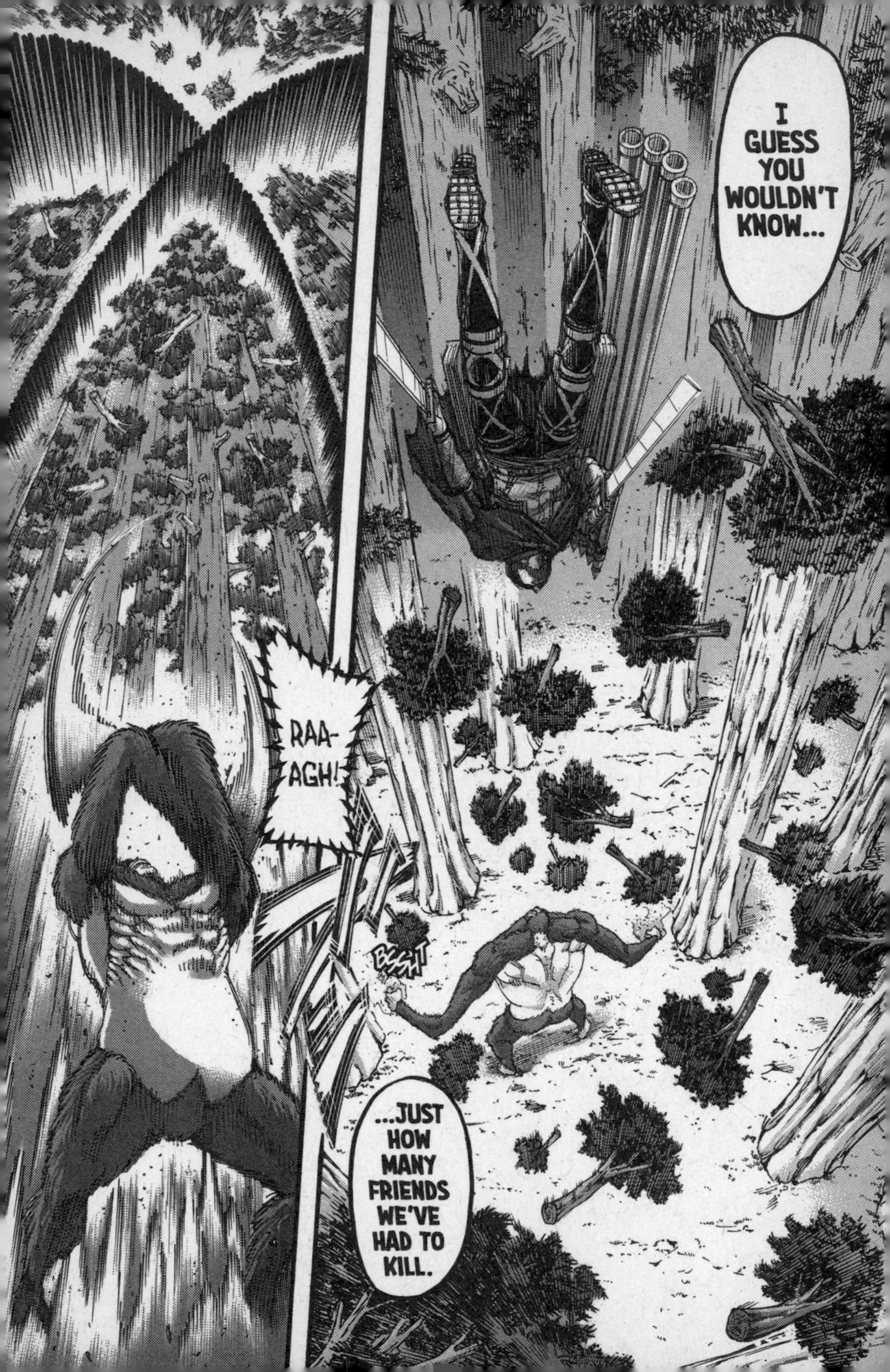
I GUESS YOU WOULDN'T KNOW...
BSSHT
...JUST HOW MANY FRIENDS WE'VE HAD TO KILL.
RAA-AGH!

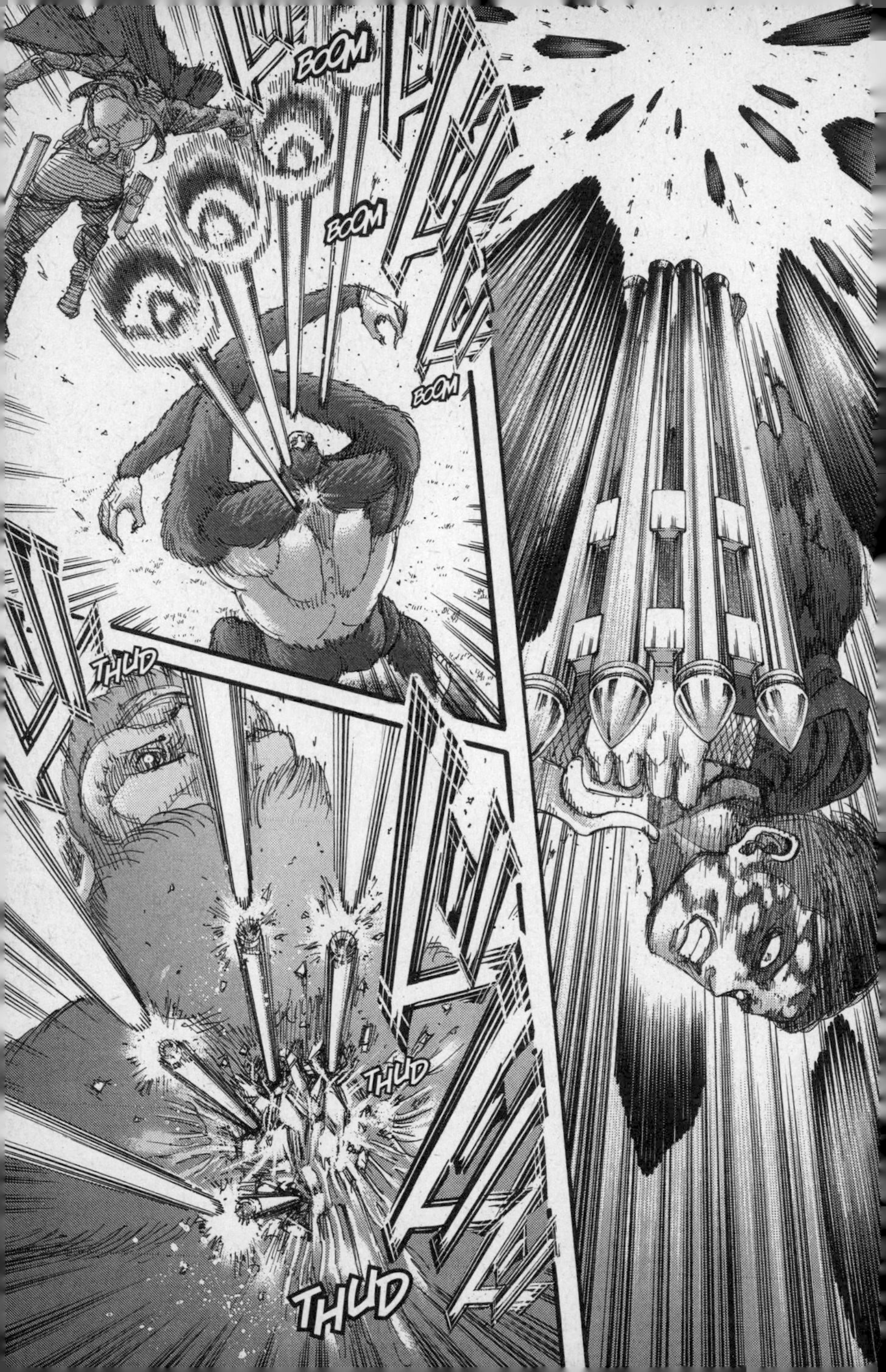
BOOM
BOOM
BOOM
THUD
THUD
THUD

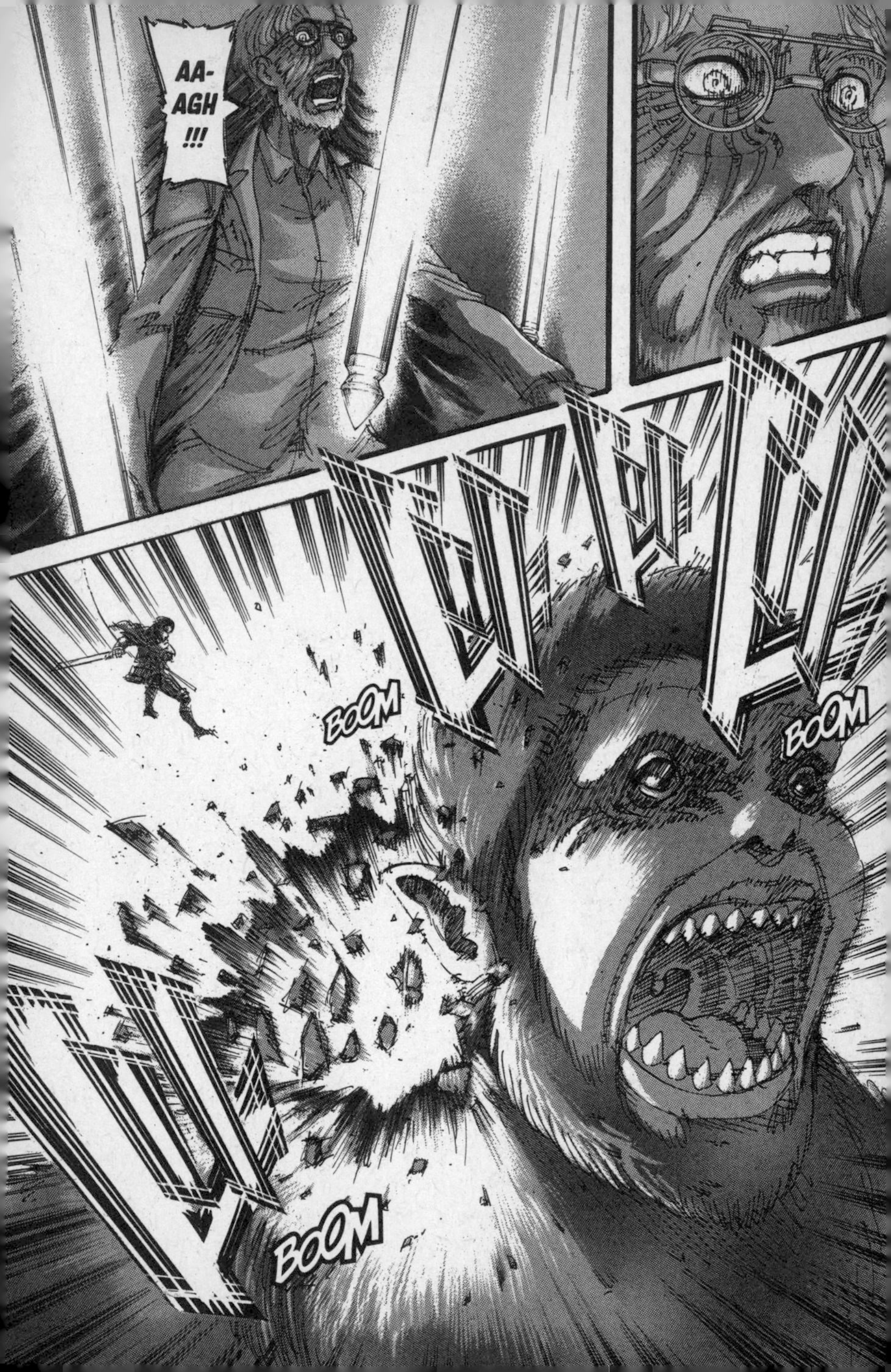
AA-AGH!!!
BOOM
BOOM
BOOM

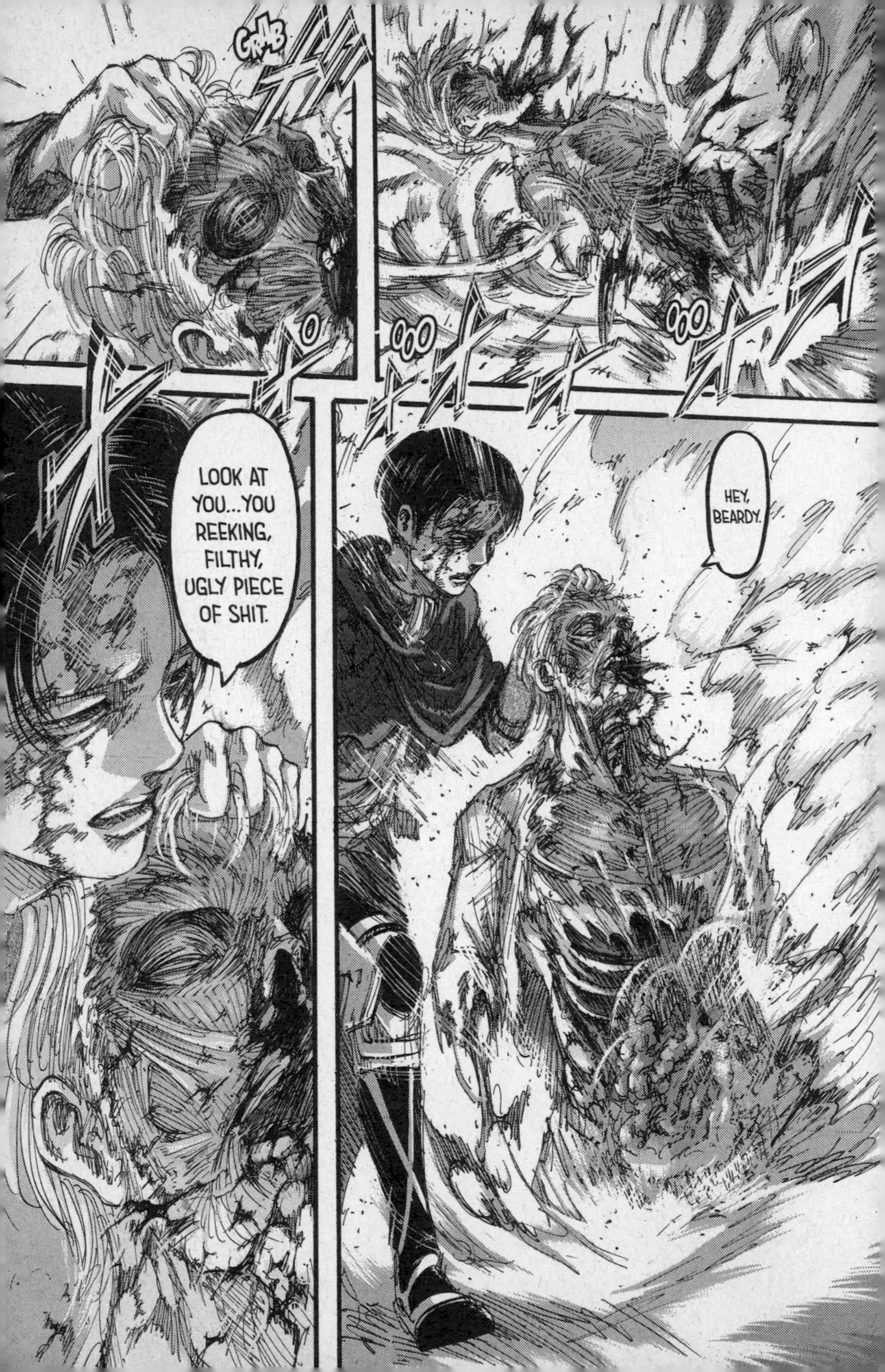
OOO
OOO
GRAB
O
HEY, BEARDY.
LOOK AT YOU...YOU REEKING, FILTHY, UGLY PIECE OF SHIT.

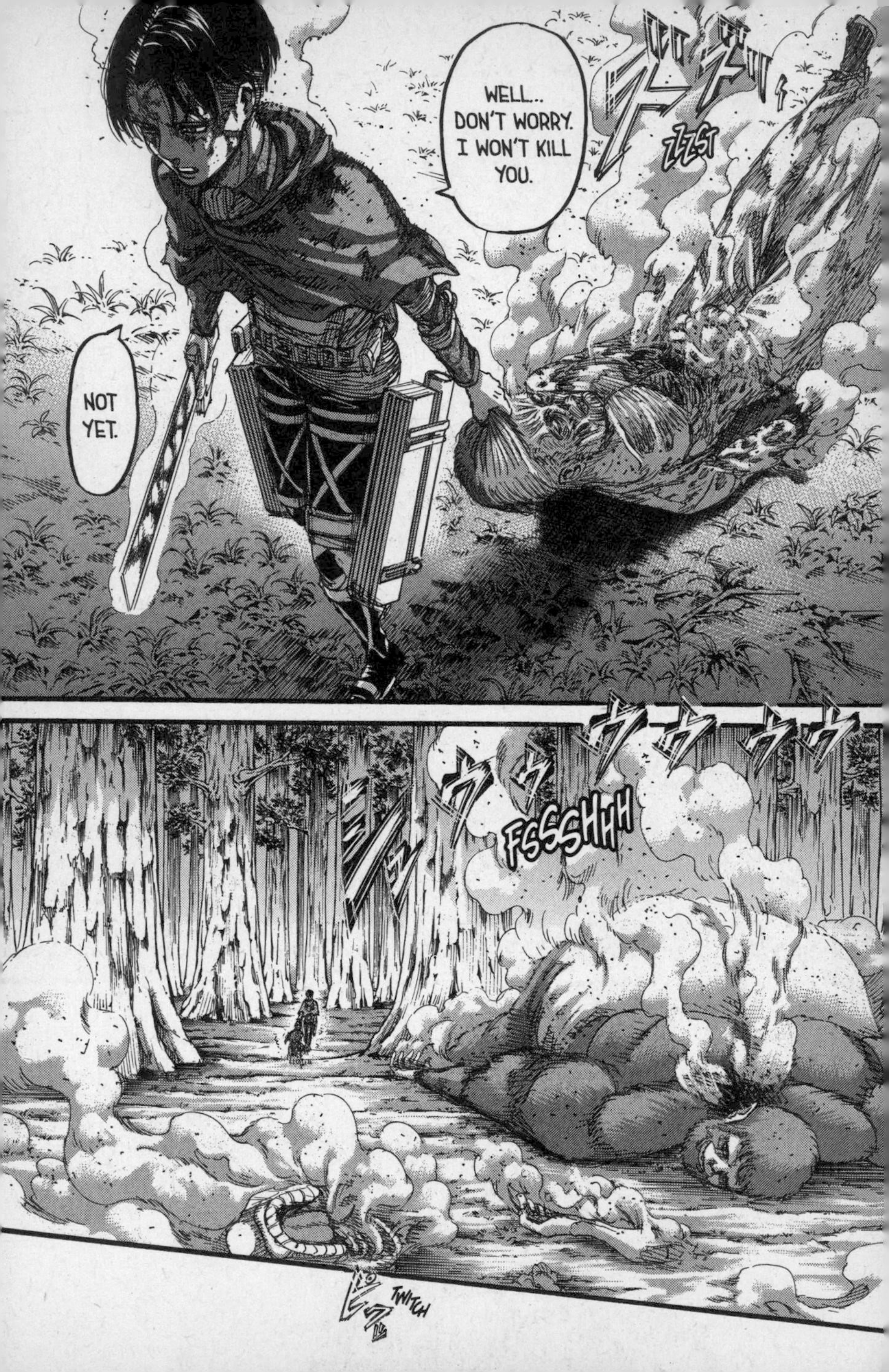
ZZZST
WELL... DON'T WORRY. I WON'T KILL YOU.
NOT YET.
FSSSHHH
TWITCH

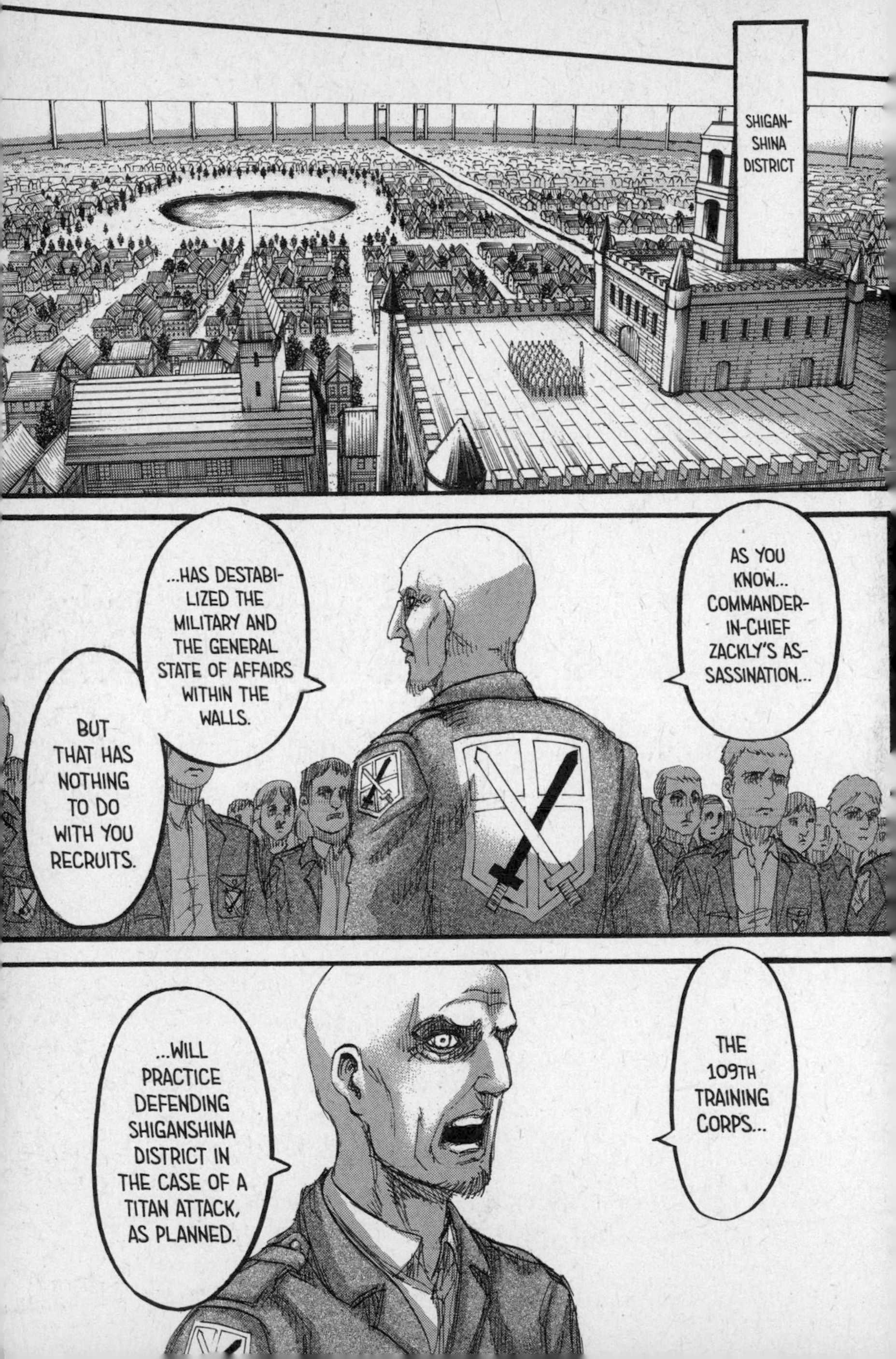
SHIGANSHINA DISTRICT
AS YOU KNOW... COMMANDER-IN-CHIEF ZACKLY'S ASSASSINATION...
...HAS DESTABILIZED THE MILITARY AND THE GENERAL STATE OF AFFAIRS WITHIN THE WALLS.
BUT THAT HAS NOTHING TO DO WITH YOU RECRUITS.
THE 109TH TRAINING CORPS...
...WILL PRACTICE DEFENDING SHIGANSHINA DISTRICT IN THE CASE OF A TITAN ATTACK, AS PLANNED.

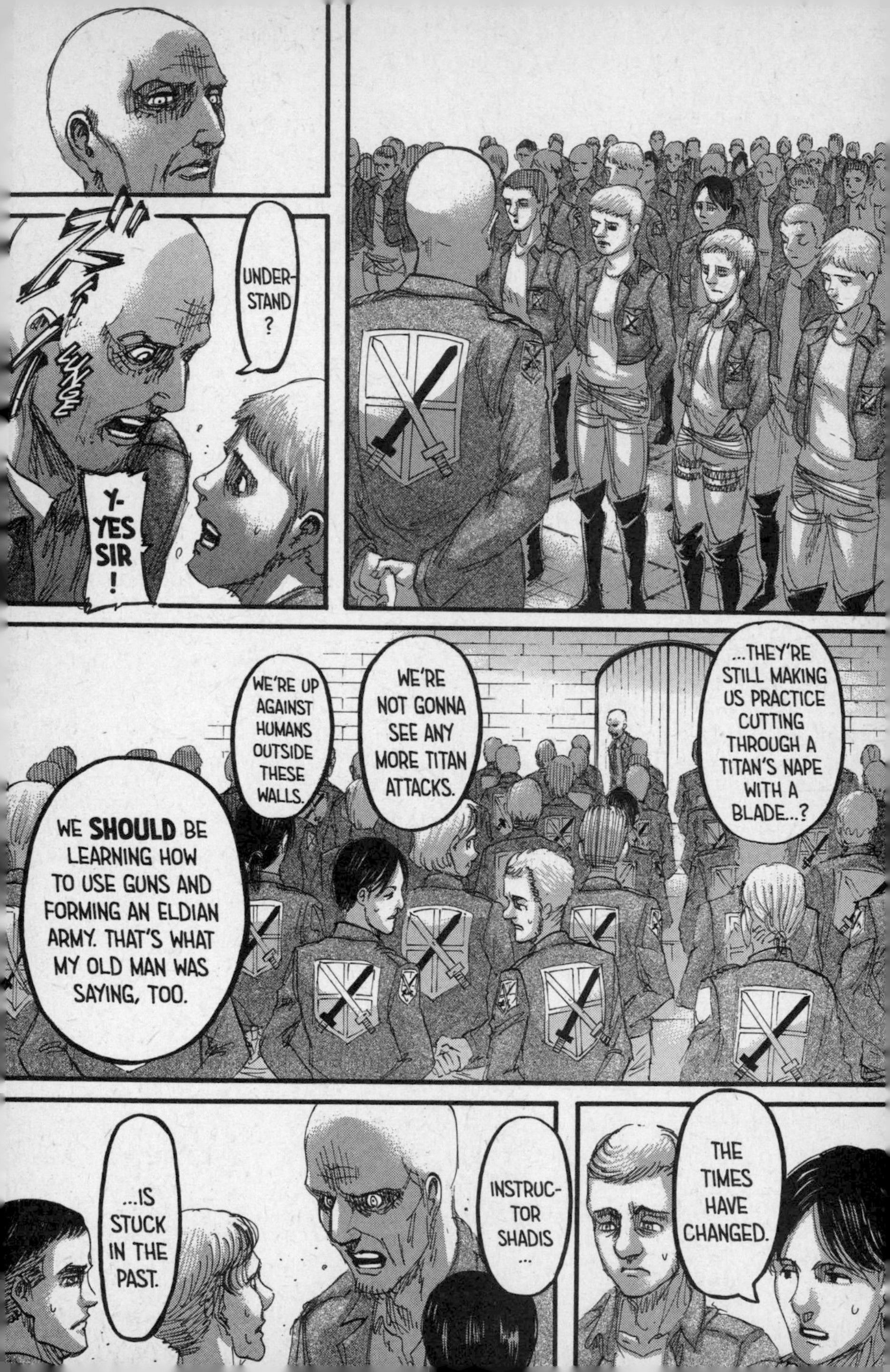
UNDERSTAND?
Y-YES SIR!
...THEY'RE STILL MAKING US PRACTICE CUTTING THROUGH A TITAN'S NAPE WITH A BLADE...?
WE'RE NOT GONNA SEE ANY MORE TITAN ATTACKS.
WE'RE UP AGAINST HUMANS OUTSIDE THESE WALLS.
WE **SHOULD** BE LEARNING HOW TO USE GUNS AND FORMING AN ELDIAN ARMY. THAT'S WHAT MY OLD MAN WAS SAYING, TOO.
THE TIMES HAVE CHANGED.
INSTRUCTOR SHADIS...
...IS STUCK IN THE PAST.

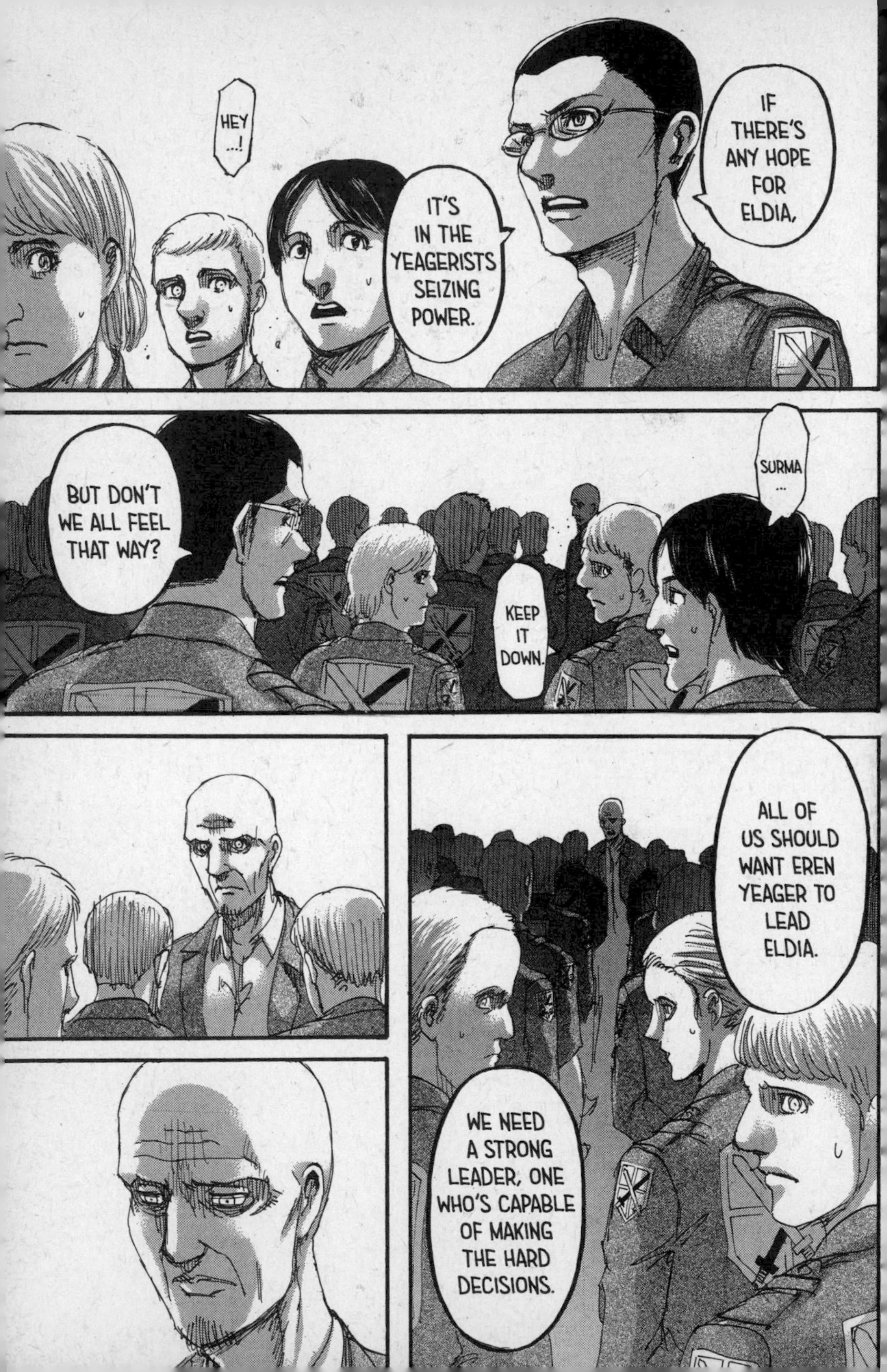
IF THERE'S ANY HOPE FOR ELDIA,
IT'S IN THE YEAGERISTS SEIZING POWER.
HEY ...!
SURMA ...
KEEP IT DOWN.
BUT DON'T WE ALL FEEL THAT WAY?
ALL OF US SHOULD WANT EREN YEAGER TO LEAD ELDIA.
WE NEED A STRONG LEADER, ONE WHO'S CAPABLE OF MAKING THE HARD DECISIONS.

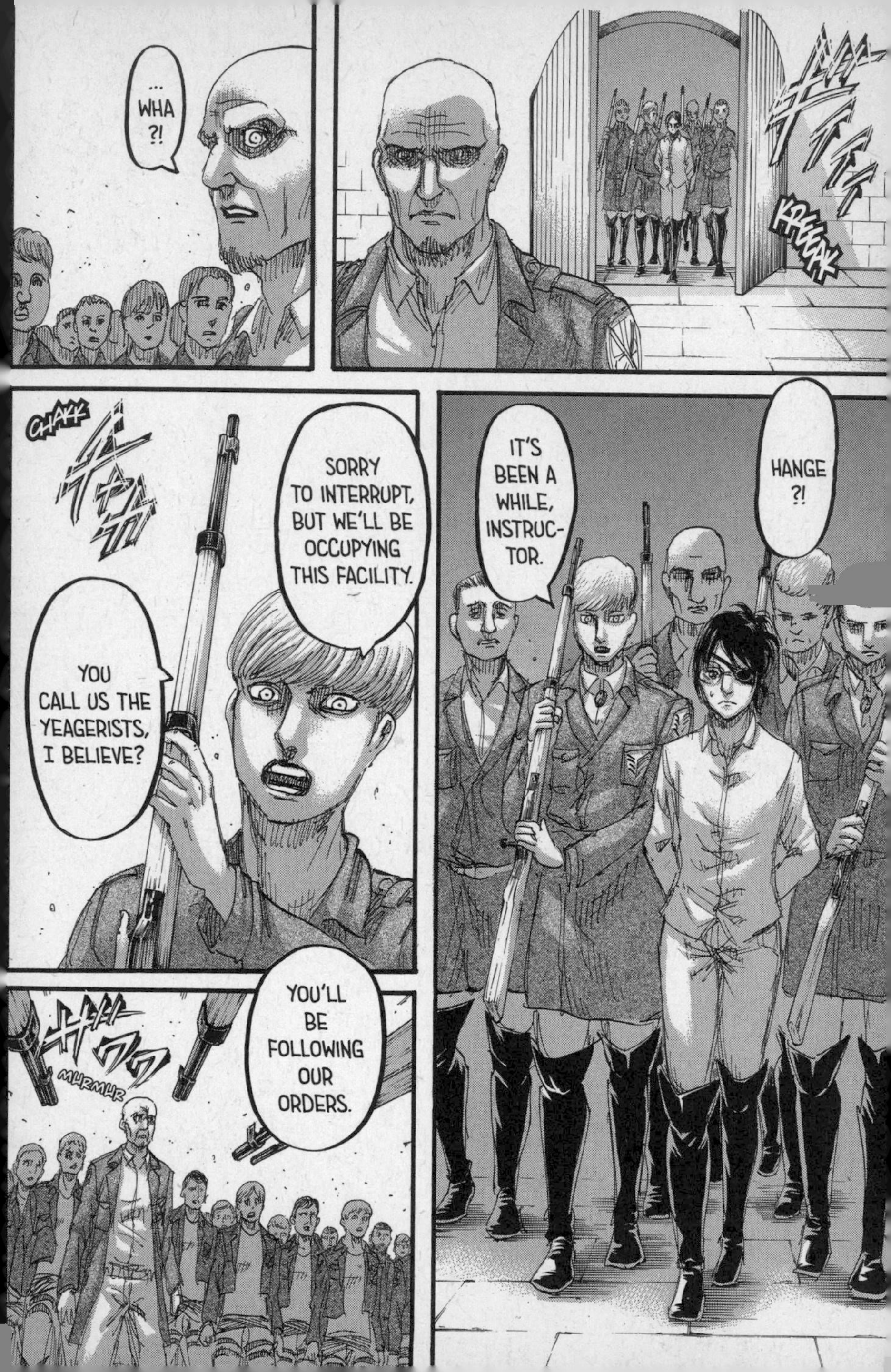
KREEAK
... WHA ?!
HANGE ?!
IT'S BEEN A WHILE, INSTRUCTOR.
CHAKK
SORRY TO INTERRUPT, BUT WE'LL BE OCCUPYING THIS FACILITY.
YOU CALL US THE YEAGERISTS, I BELIEVE?
YOU'LL BE FOLLOWING OUR ORDERS.
MURMUR

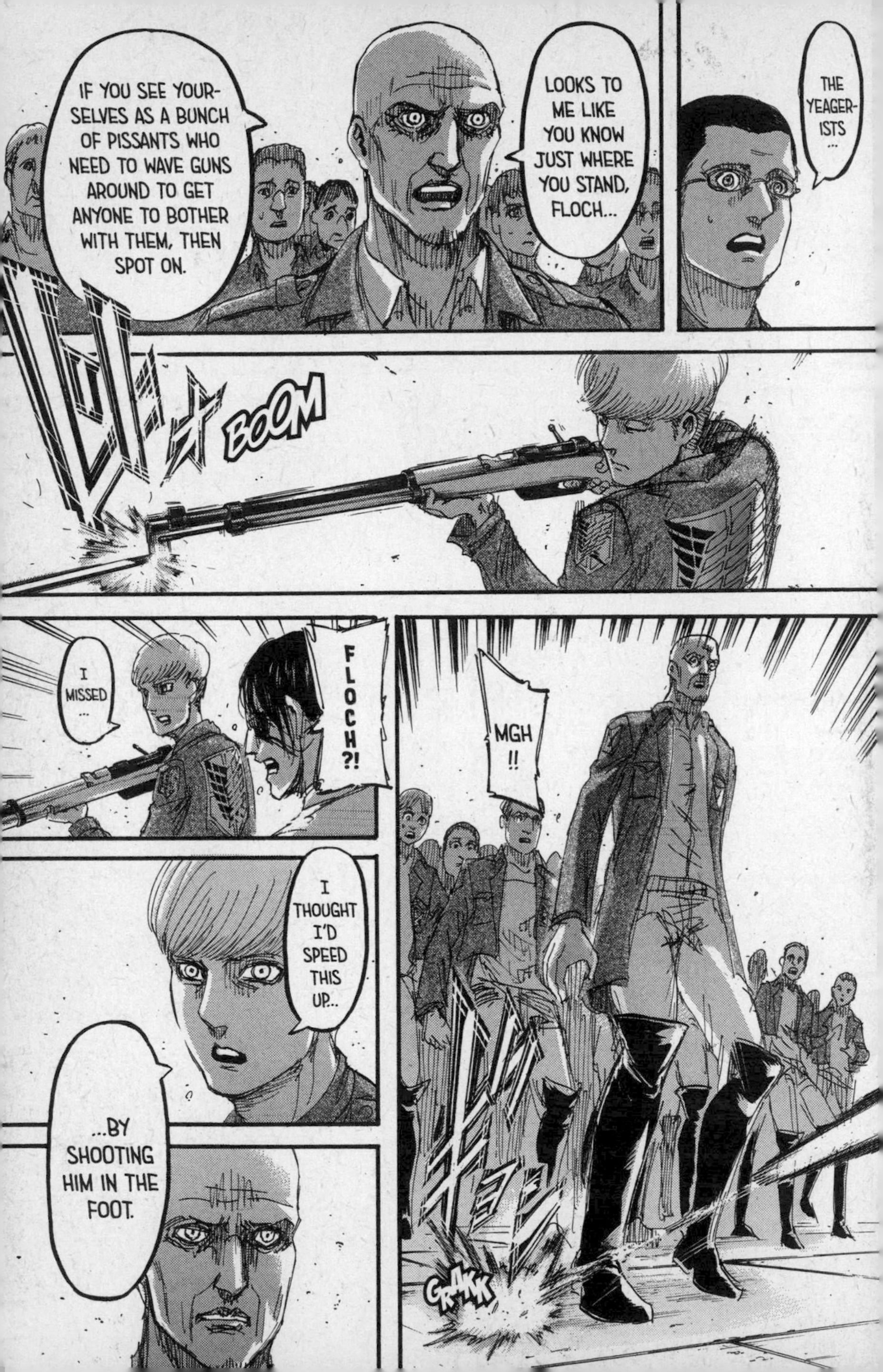
THE YEAGER-ISTS ...
LOOKS TO ME LIKE YOU KNOW JUST WHERE YOU STAND, FLOCH...
IF YOU SEE YOUR-SELVES AS A BUNCH OF PISSANTS WHO NEED TO WAVE GUNS AROUND TO GET ANYONE TO BOTHER WITH THEM, THEN SPOT ON.
BOOM
MGH !!
GRAKK
FLOCH?!
I MISSED ...
I THOUGHT I'D SPEED THIS UP...
...BY SHOOTING HIM IN THE FOOT.

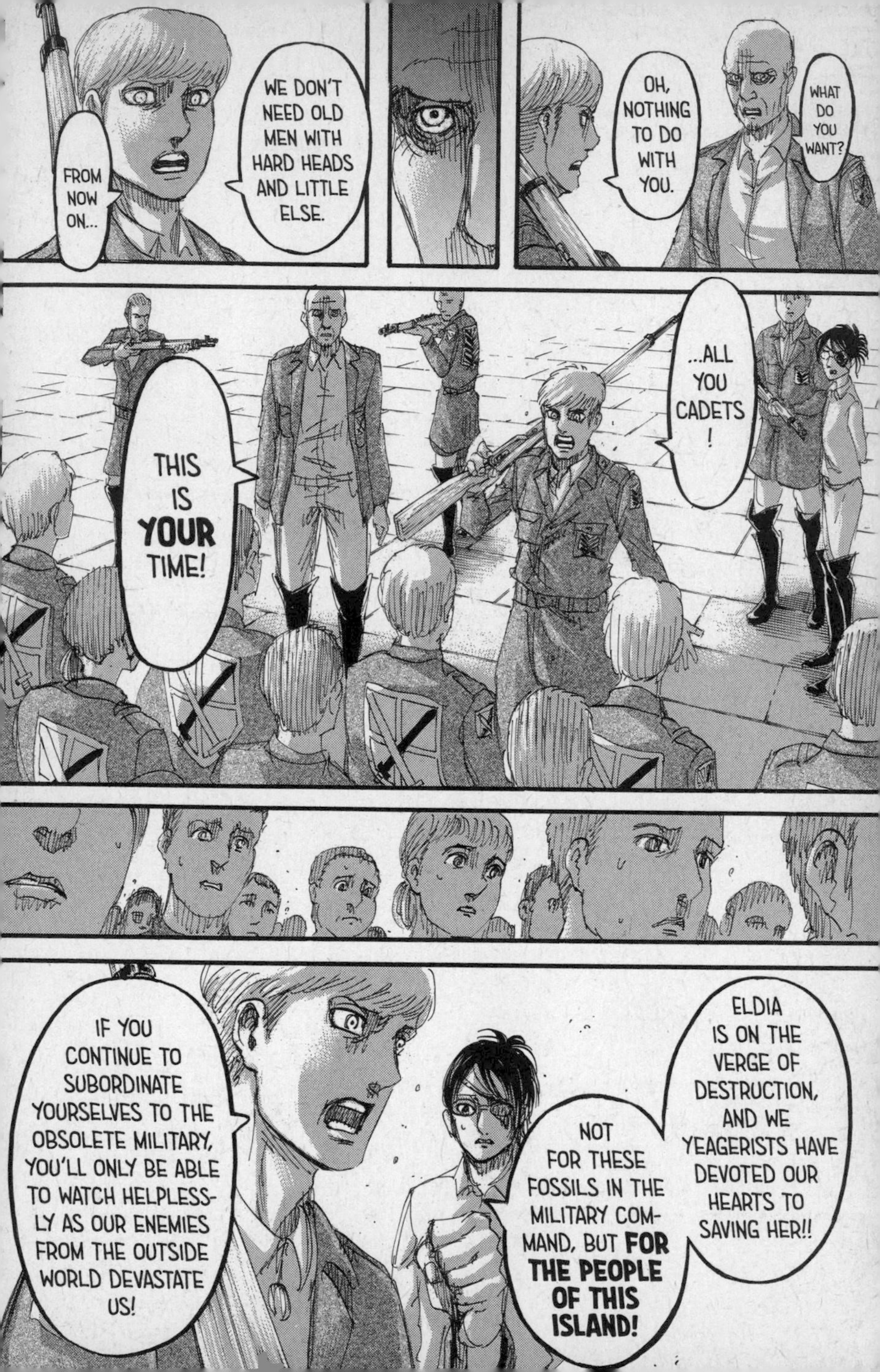
WHAT DO YOU WANT?
OH, NOTHING TO DO WITH YOU.
WE DON'T NEED OLD MEN WITH HARD HEADS AND LITTLE ELSE.
FROM NOW ON...
...ALL YOU CADETS!
THIS IS **YOUR** TIME!
ELDIA IS ON THE VERGE OF DESTRUCTION, AND WE YEAGERISTS HAVE DEVOTED OUR HEARTS TO SAVING HER!!
NOT FOR THESE FOSSILS IN THE MILITARY COMMAND, BUT **FOR THE PEOPLE OF THIS ISLAND!**
IF YOU CONTINUE TO SUBORDINATE YOURSELVES TO THE OBSOLETE MILITARY, YOU'LL ONLY BE ABLE TO WATCH HELPLESSLY AS OUR ENEMIES FROM THE OUTSIDE WORLD DEVASTATE US!

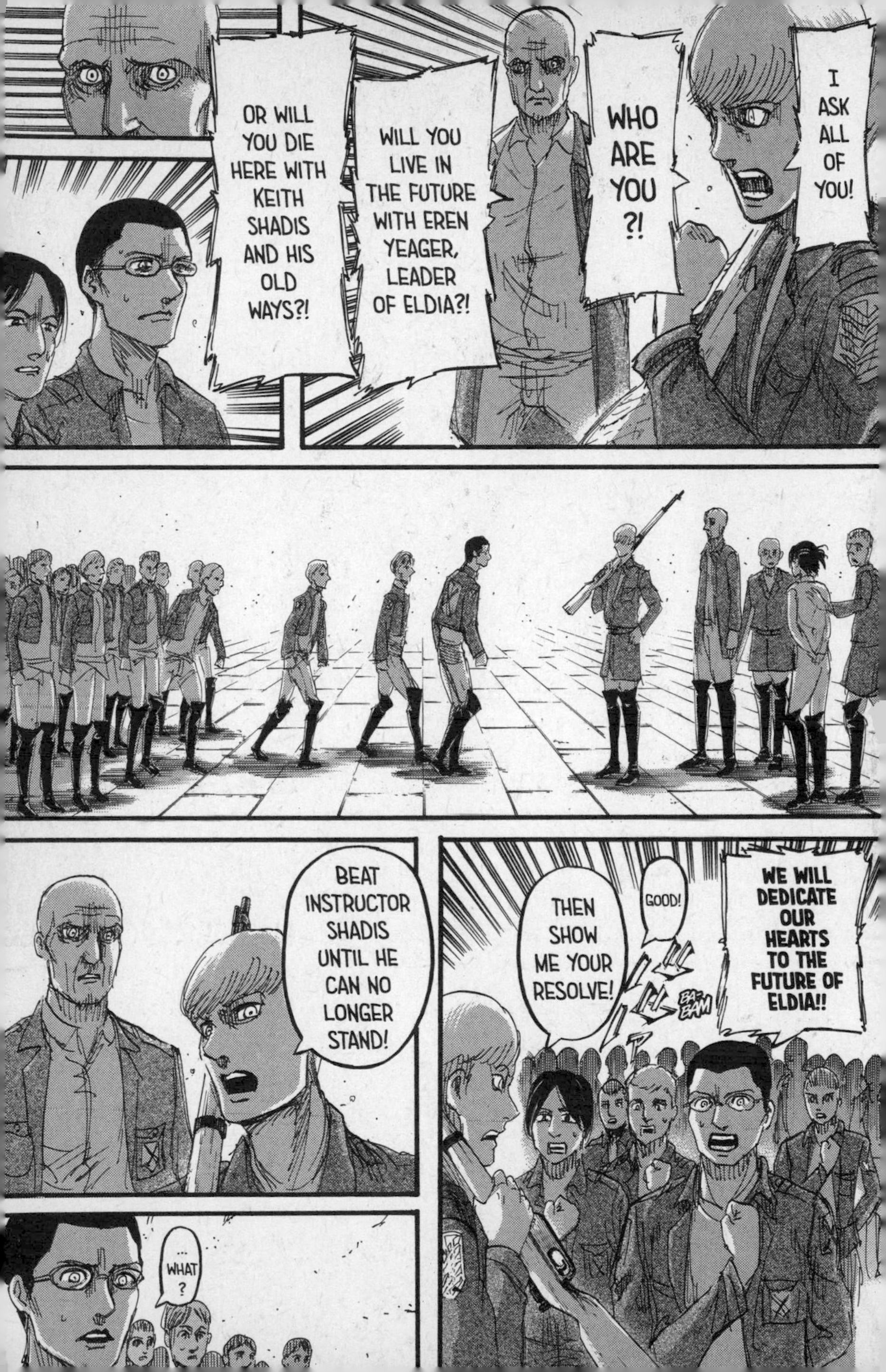
I ASK ALL OF YOU!
WHO ARE YOU?!
WILL YOU LIVE IN THE FUTURE WITH EREN YEAGER, LEADER OF ELDIA?!
OR WILL YOU DIE HERE WITH KEITH SHADIS AND HIS OLD WAYS?!
WE WILL DEDICATE OUR HEARTS TO THE FUTURE OF ELDIA!!
GOOD!
THEN SHOW ME YOUR RESOLVE!
BA-BAM
BEAT INSTRUCTOR SHADIS UNTIL HE CAN NO LONGER STAND!
...WHAT?

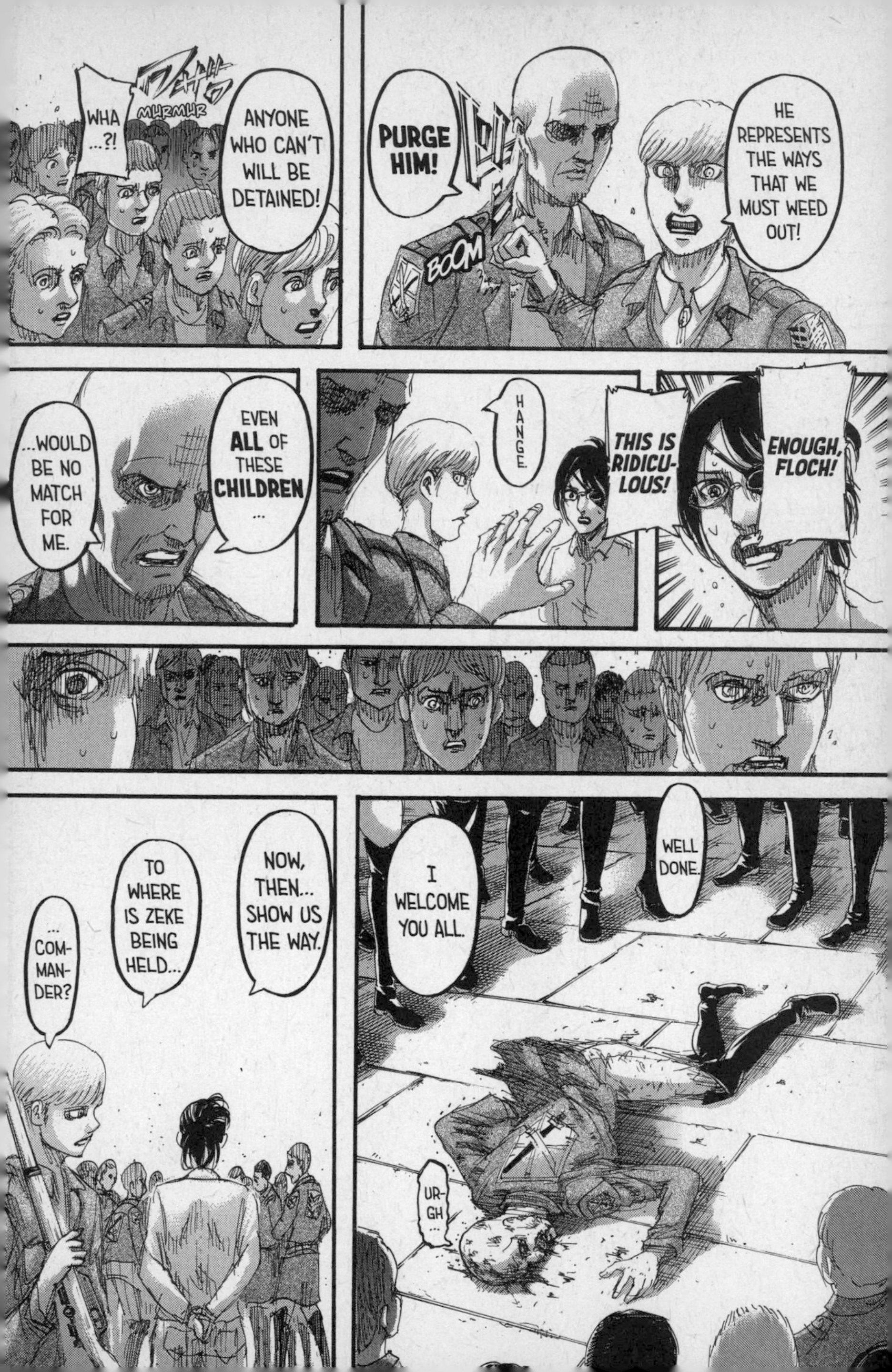
HE REPRESENTS THE WAYS THAT WE MUST WEED OUT!
PURGE HIM!
BOOM
ANYONE WHO CAN'T WILL BE DETAINED!
MURMUR
WHA ...?!
ENOUGH, FLOCH!
THIS IS RIDICULOUS!
HANGE.
EVEN ALL OF THESE CHILDREN ...
...WOULD BE NO MATCH FOR ME.
WELL DONE.
I WELCOME YOU ALL.
URGH ...
NOW, THEN... SHOW US THE WAY.
TO WHERE IS ZEKE BEING HELD...
... COMMANDER?

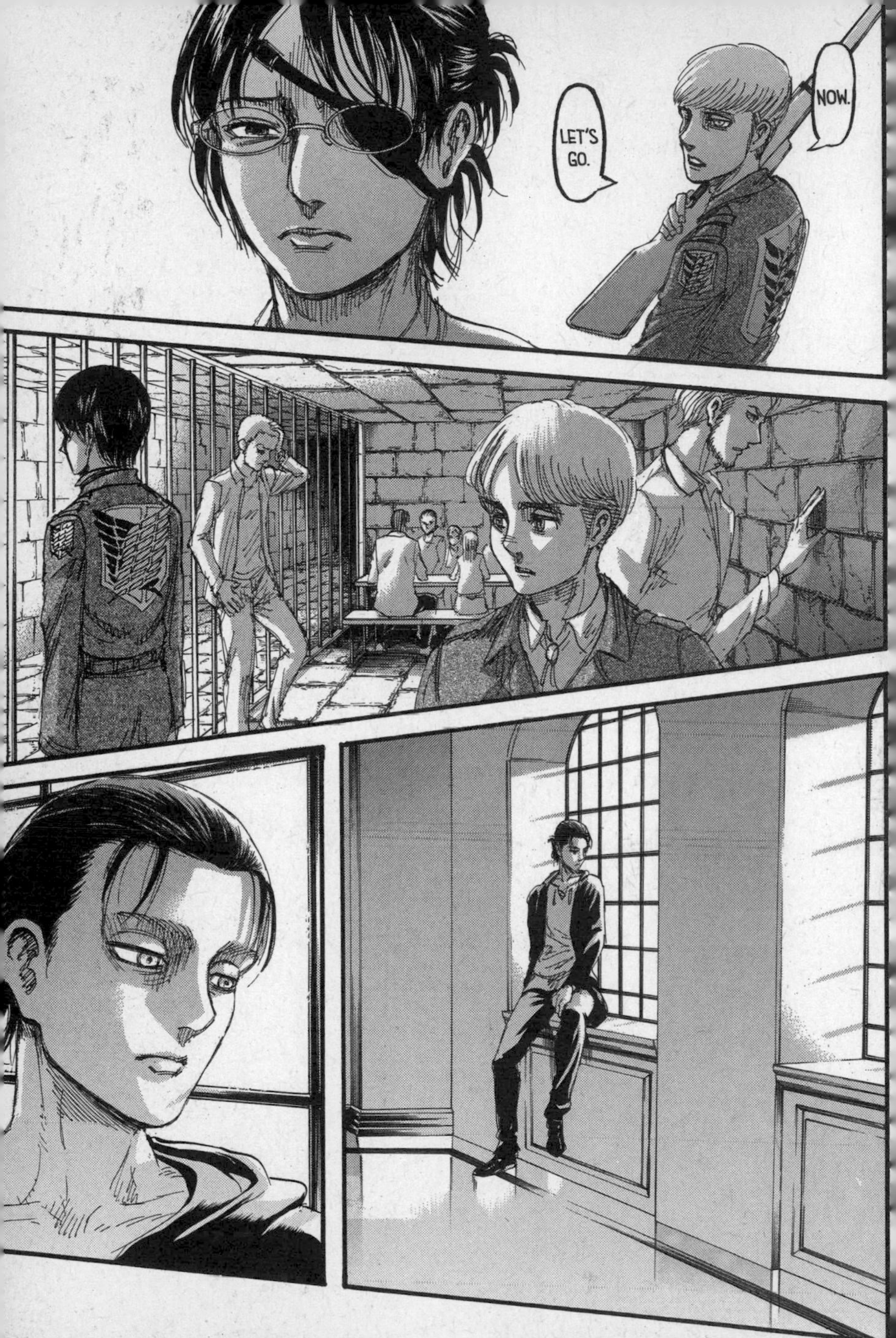
NOW.
LET'S GO.

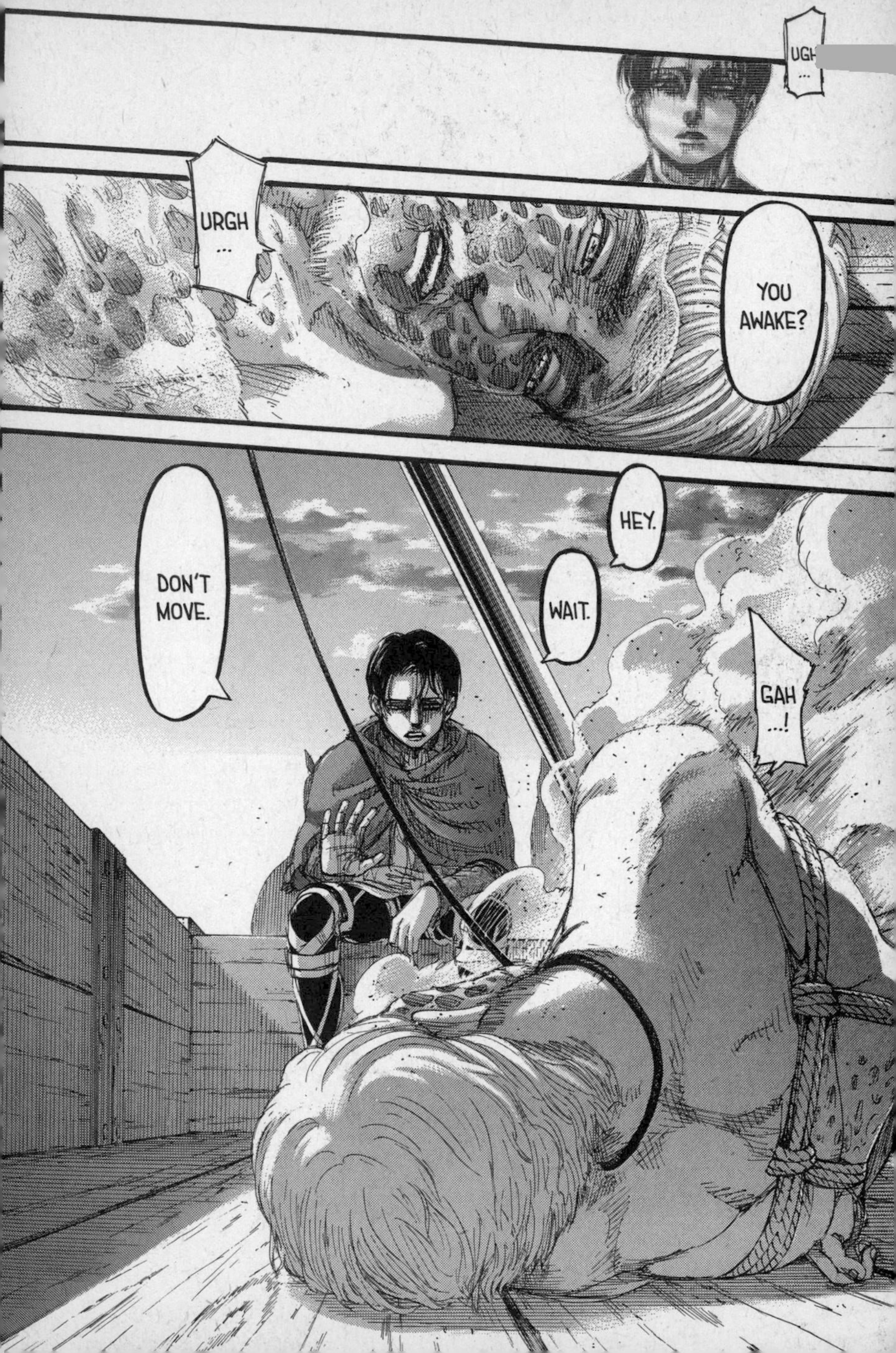
UGH ...
URGH ...
YOU AWAKE?
HEY.
WAIT.
GAH ...!
DON'T MOVE.

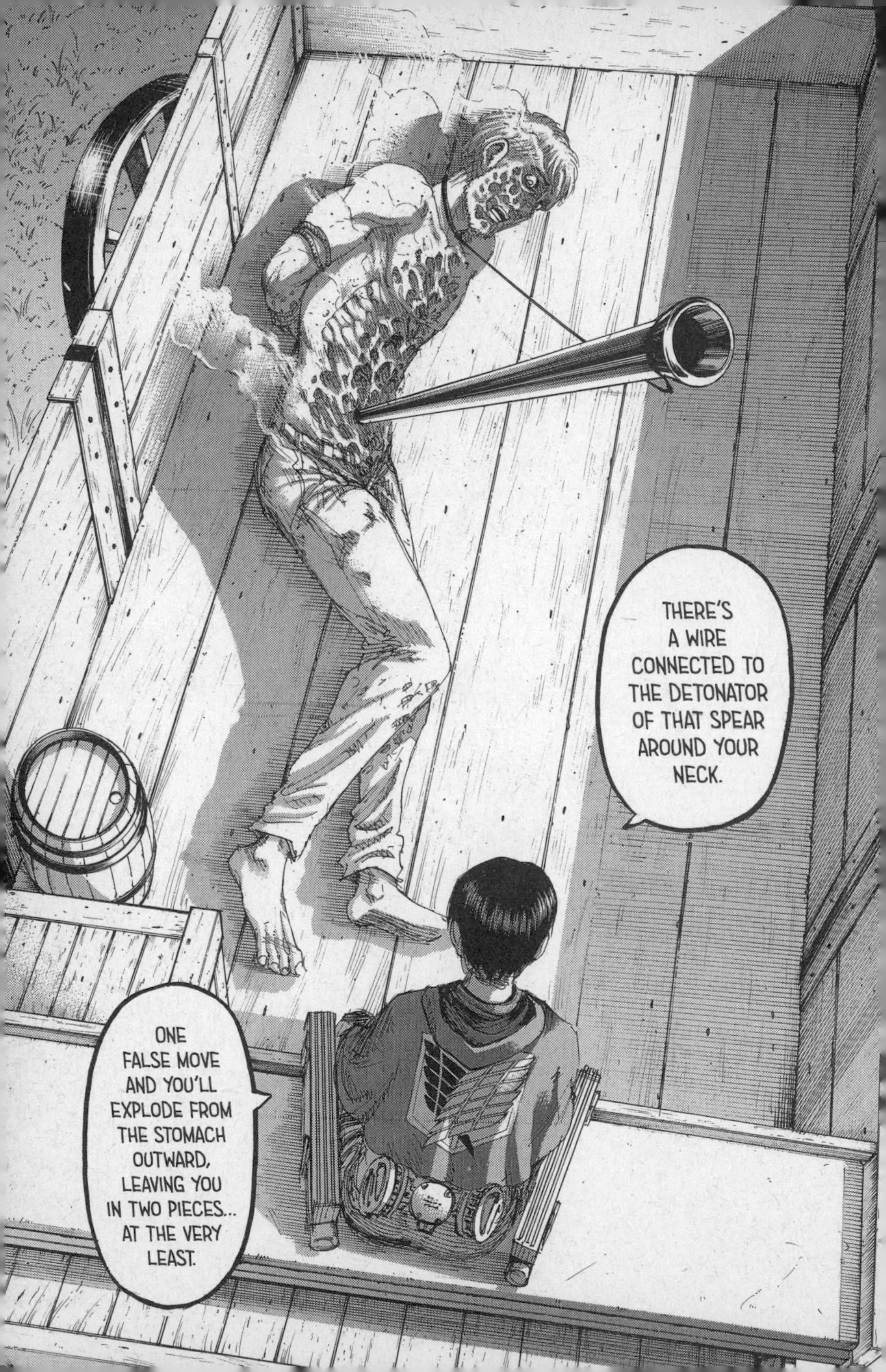
THERE'S A WIRE CONNECTED TO THE DETONATOR OF THAT SPEAR AROUND YOUR NECK.
ONE FALSE MOVE AND YOU'LL EXPLODE FROM THE STOMACH OUTWARD, LEAVING YOU IN TWO PIECES... AT THE VERY LEAST.

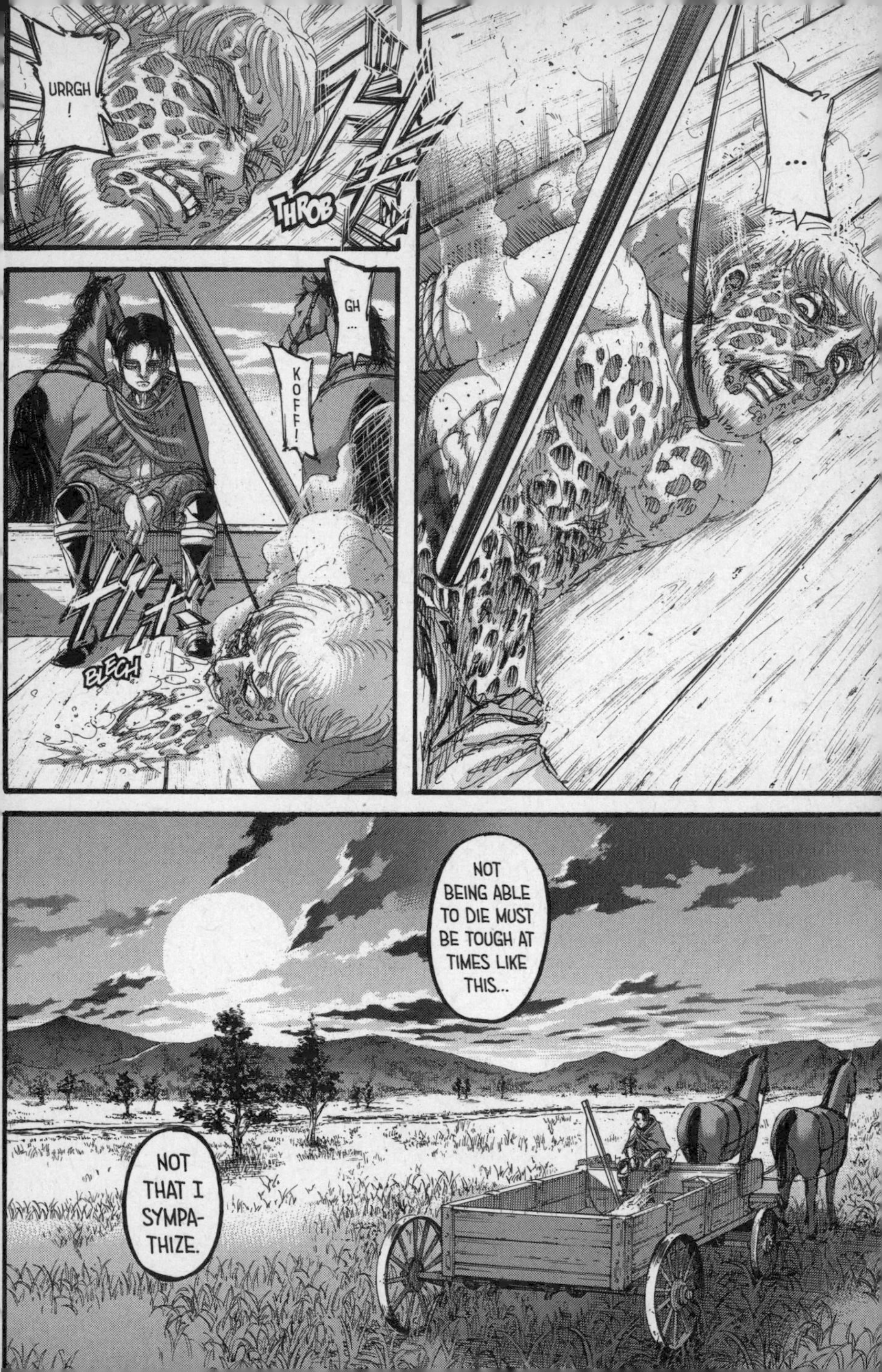
...
URRGH !
THROB
GH ...
KOFF!
BLECH
NOT BEING ABLE TO DIE MUST BE TOUGH AT TIMES LIKE THIS...
NOT THAT I SYMPA-THIZE.

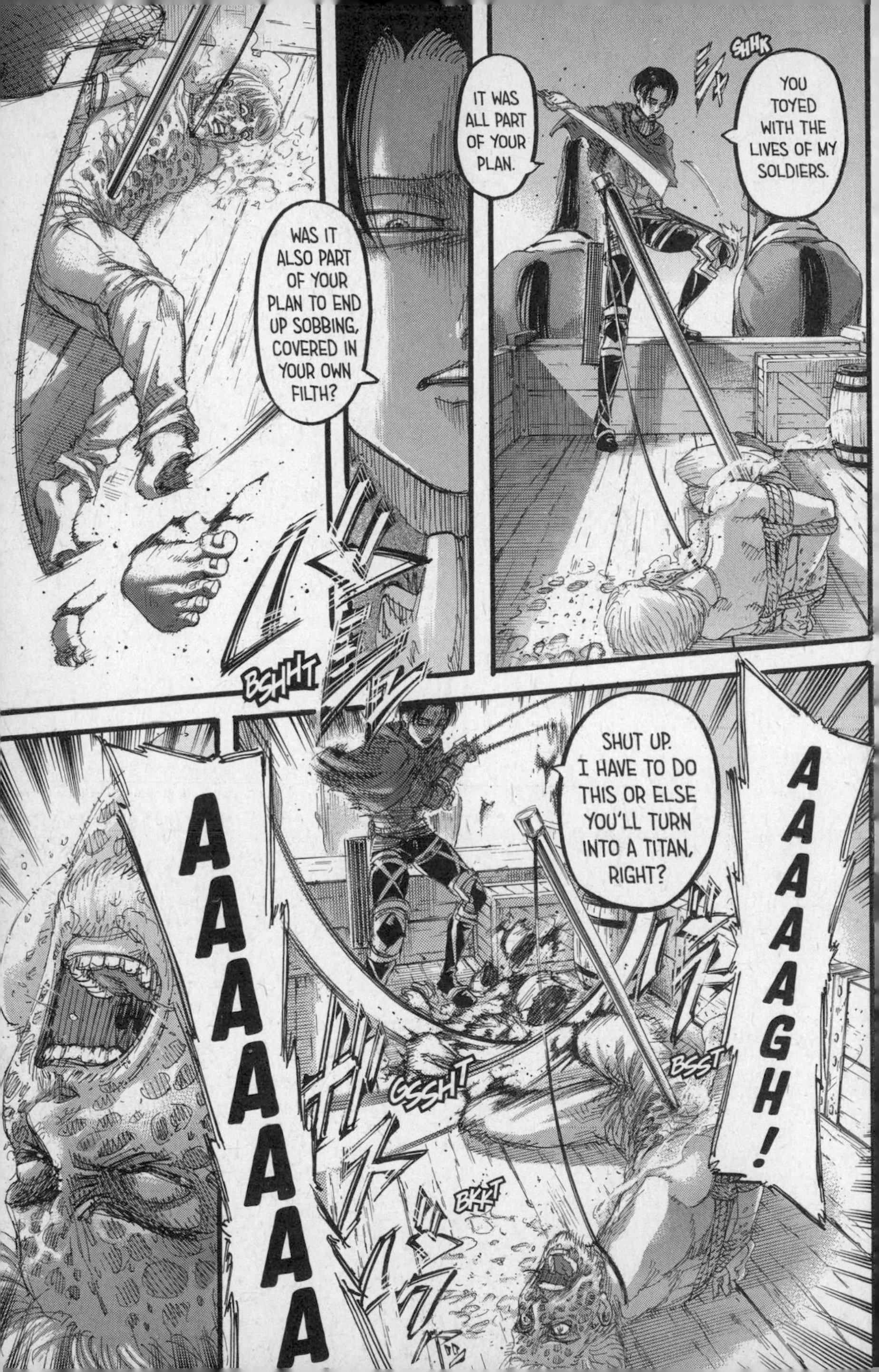
SHHK
YOU TOYED WITH THE LIVES OF MY SOLDIERS.
IT WAS ALL PART OF YOUR PLAN.
WAS IT ALSO PART OF YOUR PLAN TO END UP SOBBING, COVERED IN YOUR OWN FILTH?
BSHHT
AAAAAAGH!
SHUT UP. I HAVE TO DO THIS OR ELSE YOU'LL TURN INTO A TITAN, RIGHT?
BSST
GSSHT
BKKT
AAAAAAAAA

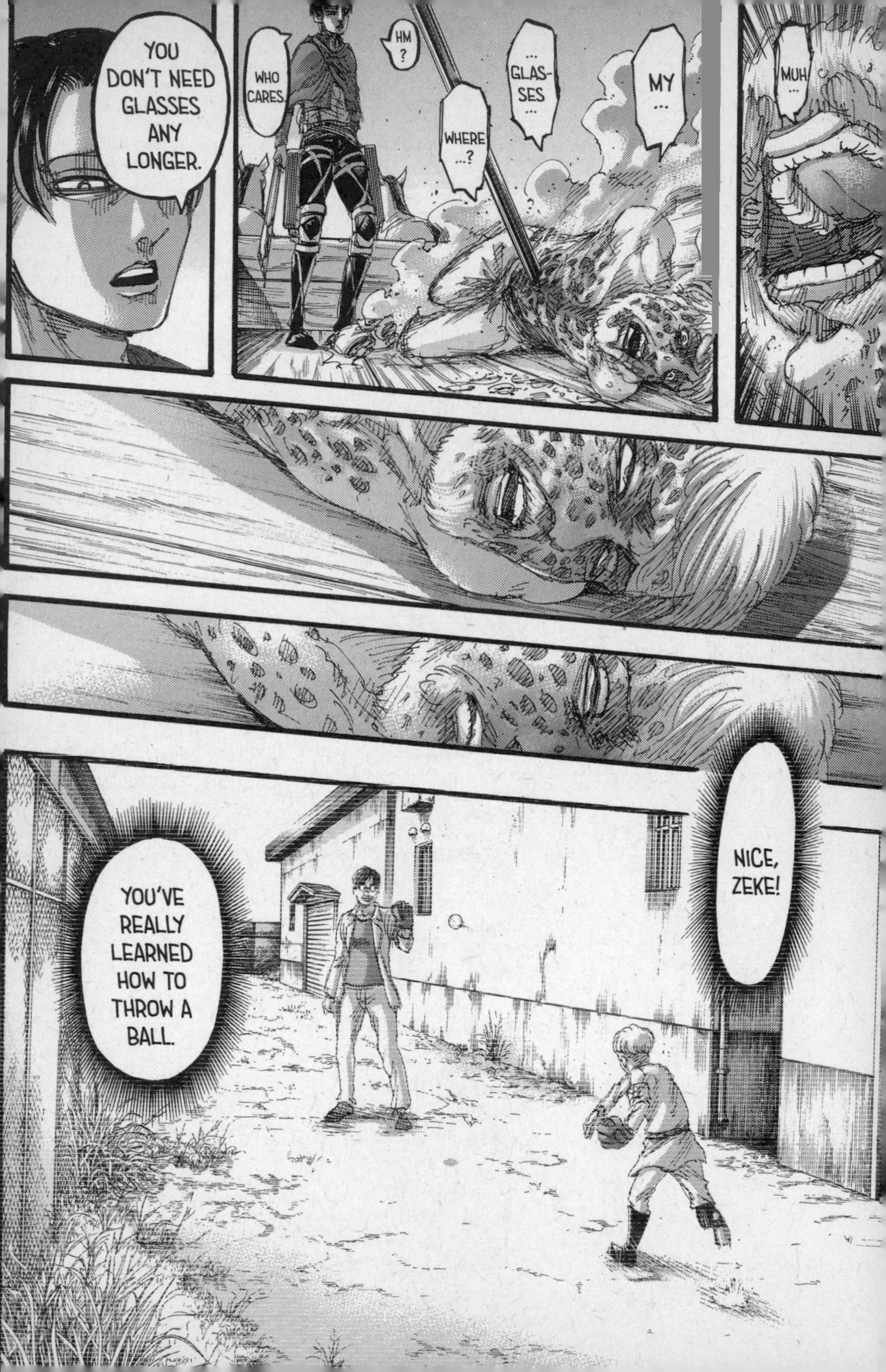
MUH ...
MY ...
... GLASSES ...
WHERE ...?
HM ?
WHO CARES.
YOU DON'T NEED GLASSES ANY LONGER.
NICE, ZEKE!
YOU'VE REALLY LEARNED HOW TO THROW A BALL.

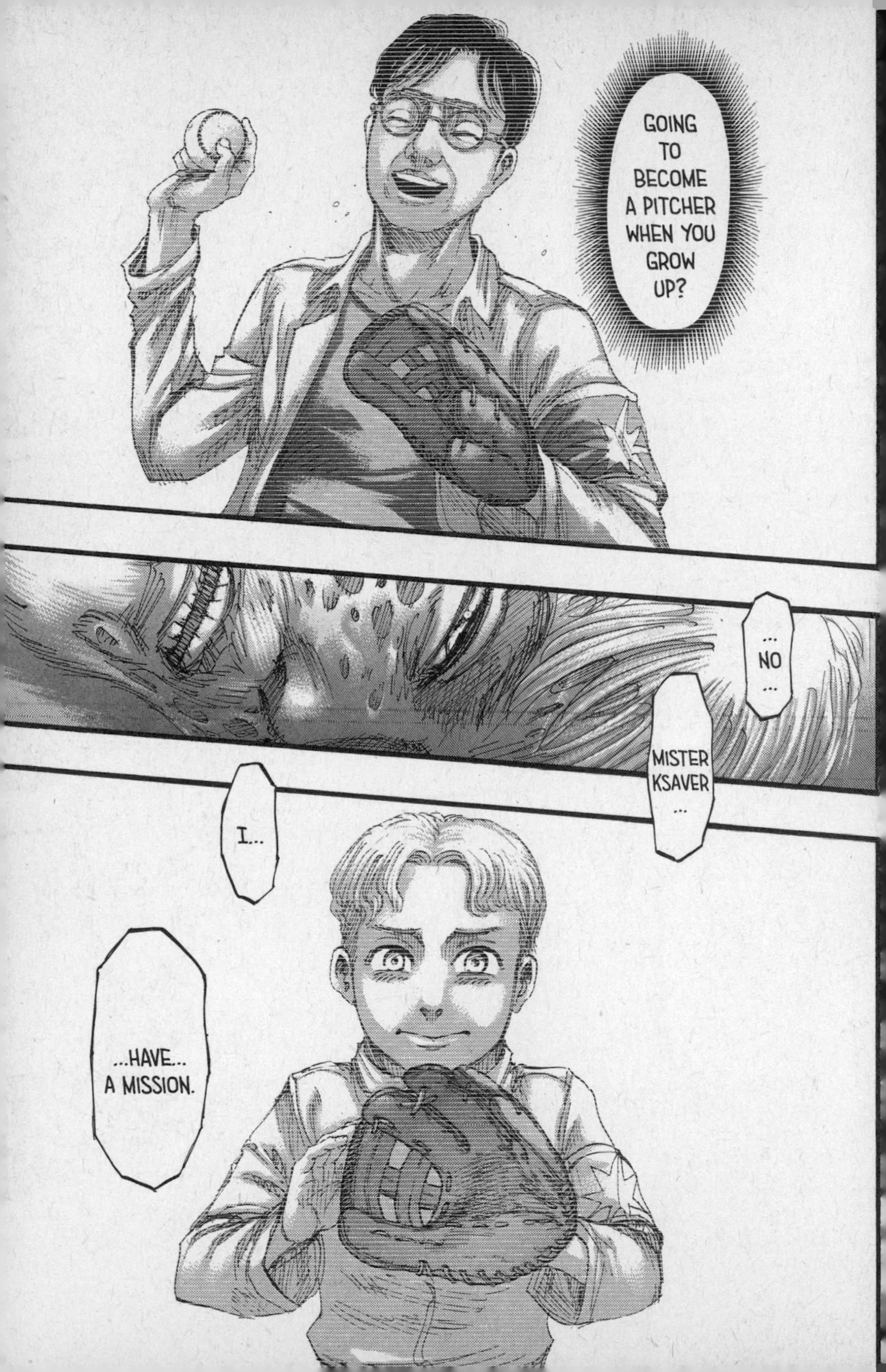
GOING TO BECOME A PITCHER WHEN YOU GROW UP?
... NO ...
MISTER KSAVER ...
I...
...HAVE... A MISSION.

ATTACK on TITAN

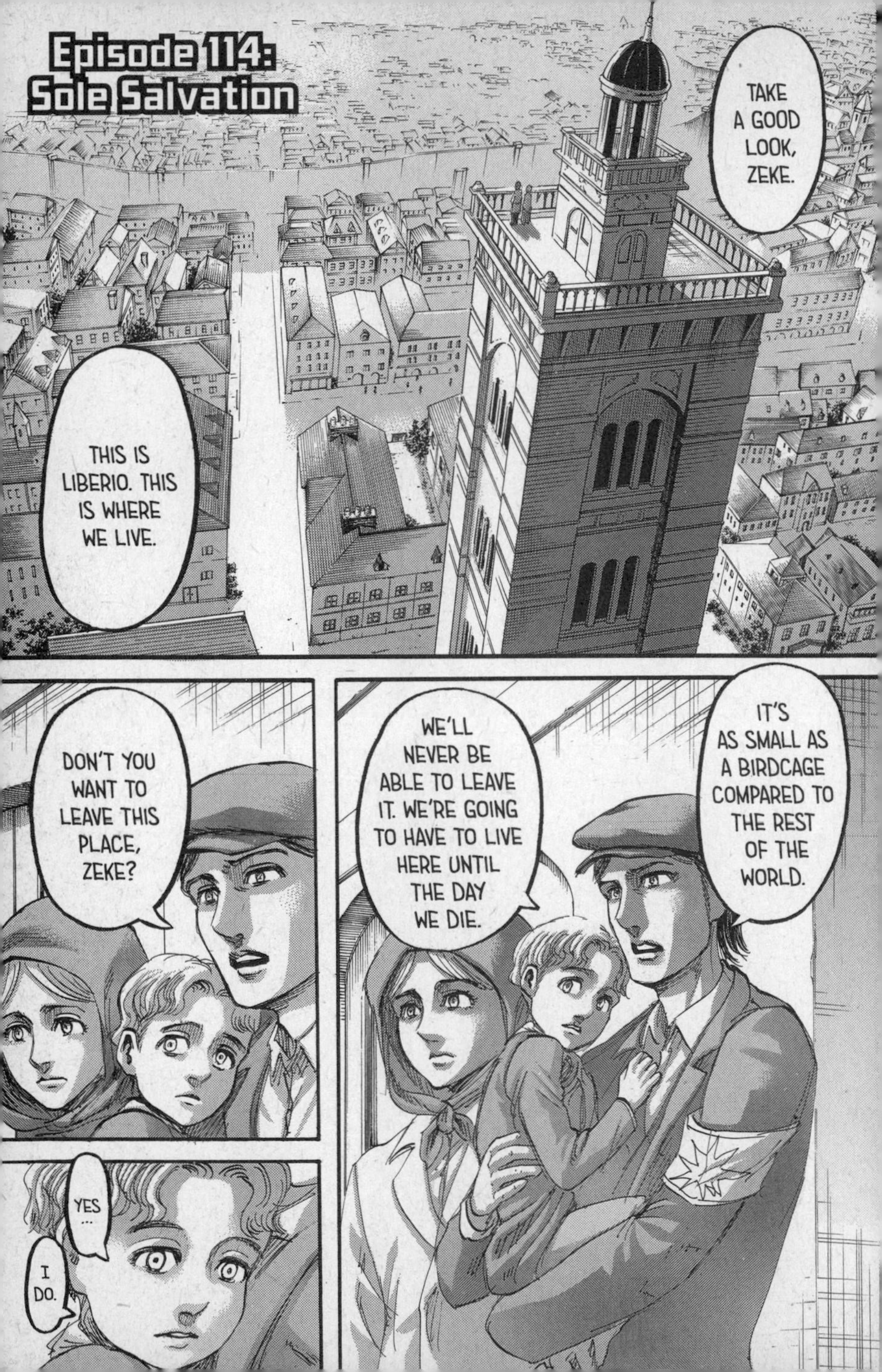
Episode 114: Sole Salvation
TAKE A GOOD LOOK, ZEKE.
THIS IS LIBERIO. THIS IS WHERE WE LIVE.
IT'S AS SMALL AS A BIRDCAGE COMPARED TO THE REST OF THE WORLD.
WE'LL NEVER BE ABLE TO LEAVE IT. WE'RE GOING TO HAVE TO LIVE HERE UNTIL THE DAY WE DIE.
DON'T YOU WANT TO LEAVE THIS PLACE, ZEKE?
YES...
I DO.

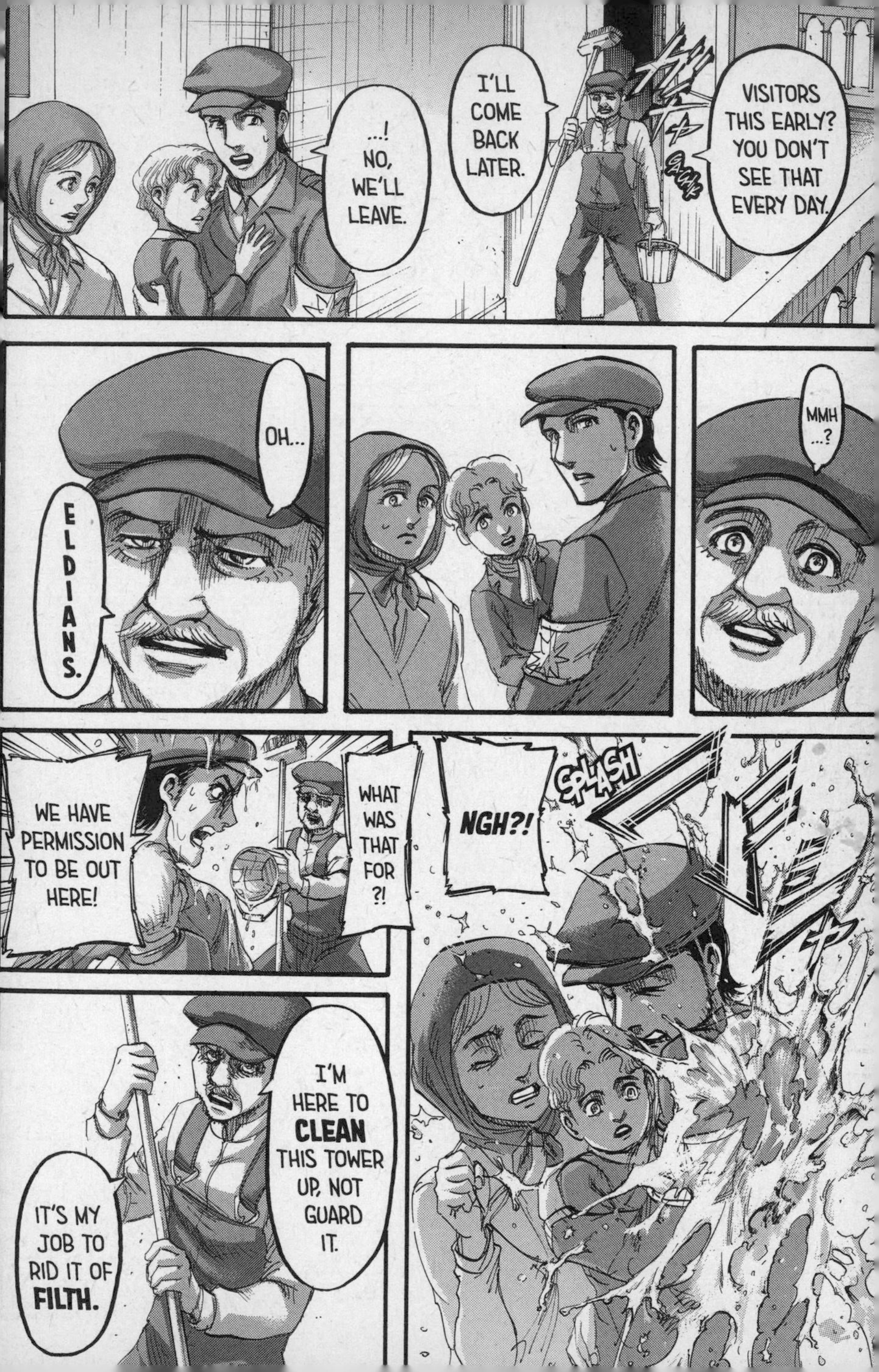
GACK
VISITORS THIS EARLY? YOU DON'T SEE THAT EVERY DAY.
I'LL COME BACK LATER.
...! NO, WE'LL LEAVE.
MMH ...?
OH...
ELDIANS.
SPLASH
NGH?!
WHAT WAS THAT FOR?!
WE HAVE PERMISSION TO BE OUT HERE!
I'M HERE TO **CLEAN** THIS TOWER UP, NOT GUARD IT.
IT'S MY JOB TO RID IT OF **FILTH.**

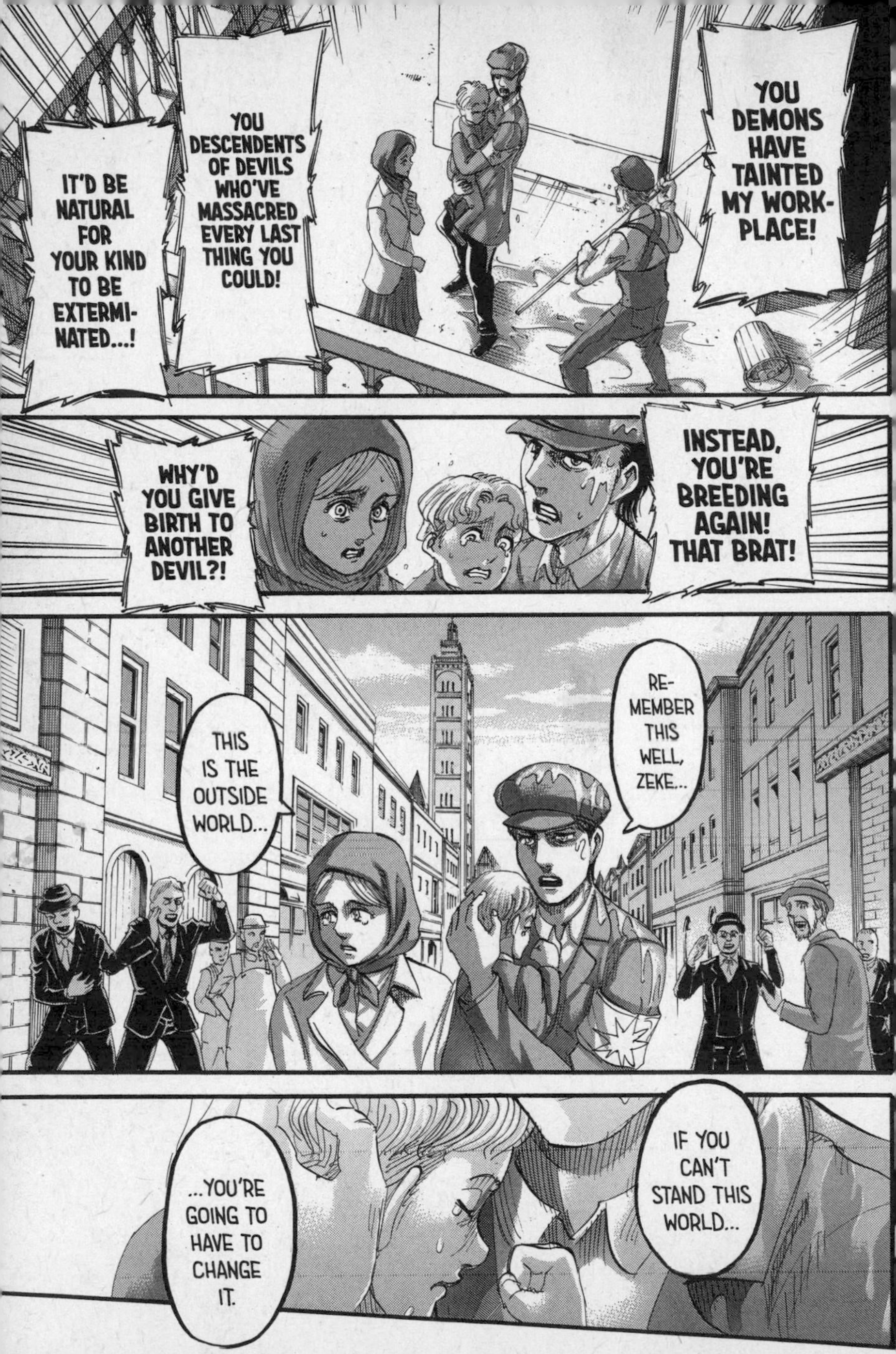
YOU DEMONS HAVE TAINTED MY WORK-PLACE!
YOU DESCENDENTS OF DEVILS WHO'VE MASSACRED EVERY LAST THING YOU COULD!
IT'D BE NATURAL FOR YOUR KIND TO BE EXTERMINATED...!
INSTEAD, YOU'RE BREEDING AGAIN! THAT BRAT!
WHY'D YOU GIVE BIRTH TO ANOTHER DEVIL?!
RE-MEMBER THIS WELL, ZEKE...
THIS IS THE OUTSIDE WORLD...
IF YOU CAN'T STAND THIS WORLD...
...YOU'RE GOING TO HAVE TO CHANGE IT.

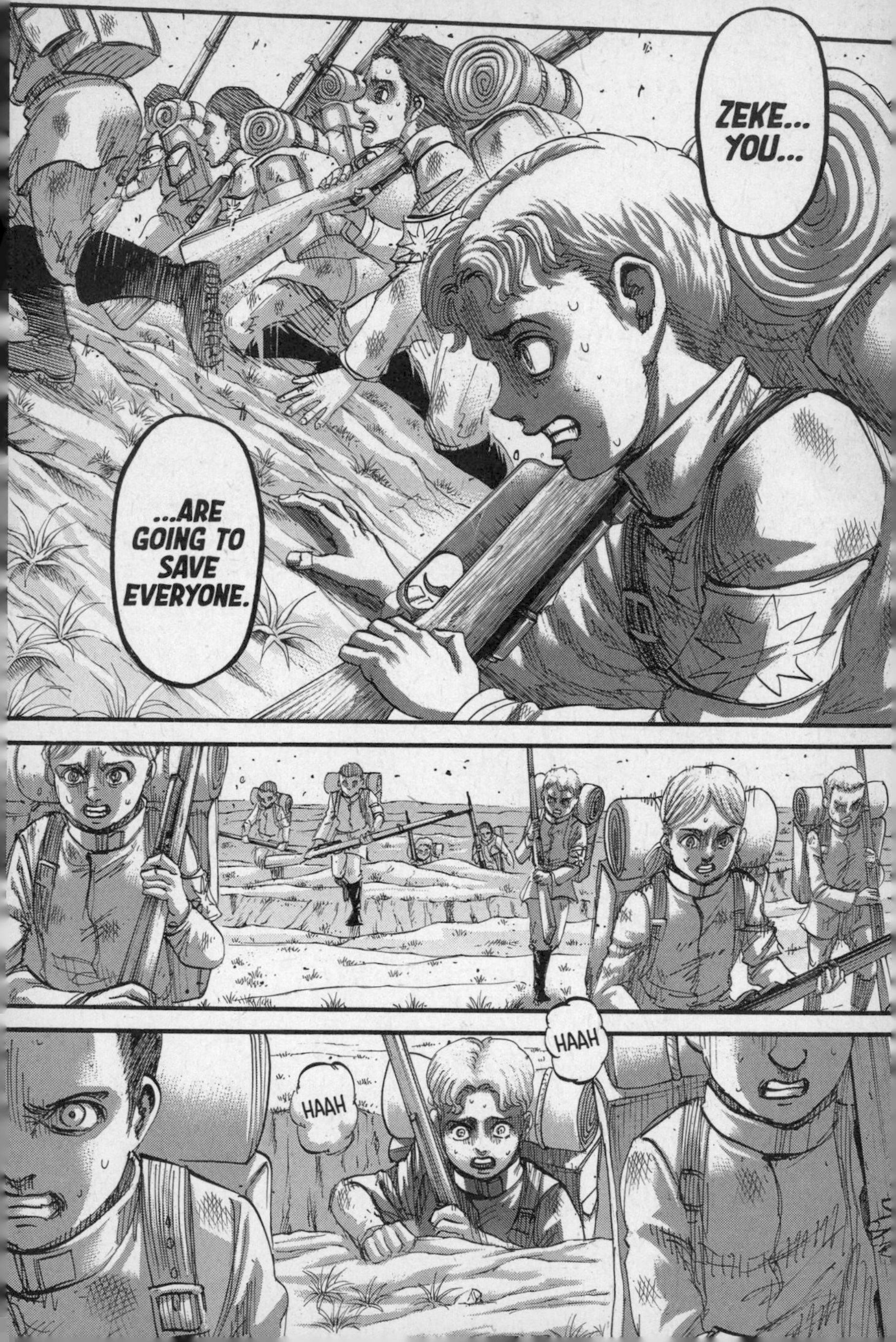
ZEKE... YOU...
...ARE GOING TO SAVE EVERYONE.
HAAH
HAAH

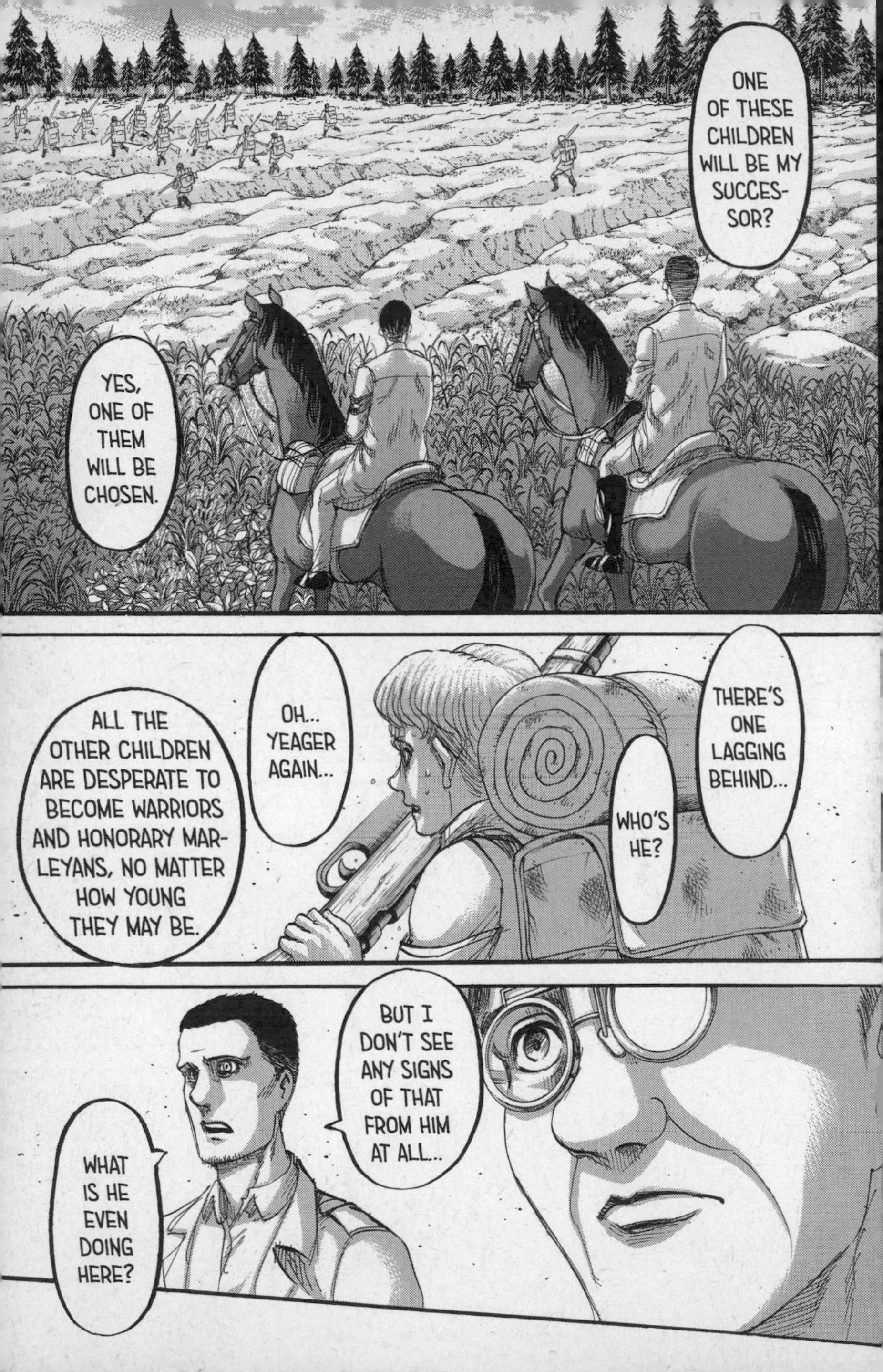
ONE OF THESE CHILDREN WILL BE MY SUCCESSOR?
YES, ONE OF THEM WILL BE CHOSEN.
THERE'S ONE LAGGING BEHIND...
WHO'S HE?
OH... YEAGER AGAIN...
ALL THE OTHER CHILDREN ARE DESPERATE TO BECOME WARRIORS AND HONORARY MARLEYANS, NO MATTER HOW YOUNG THEY MAY BE.
BUT I DON'T SEE ANY SIGNS OF THAT FROM HIM AT ALL...
WHAT IS HE EVEN DOING HERE?

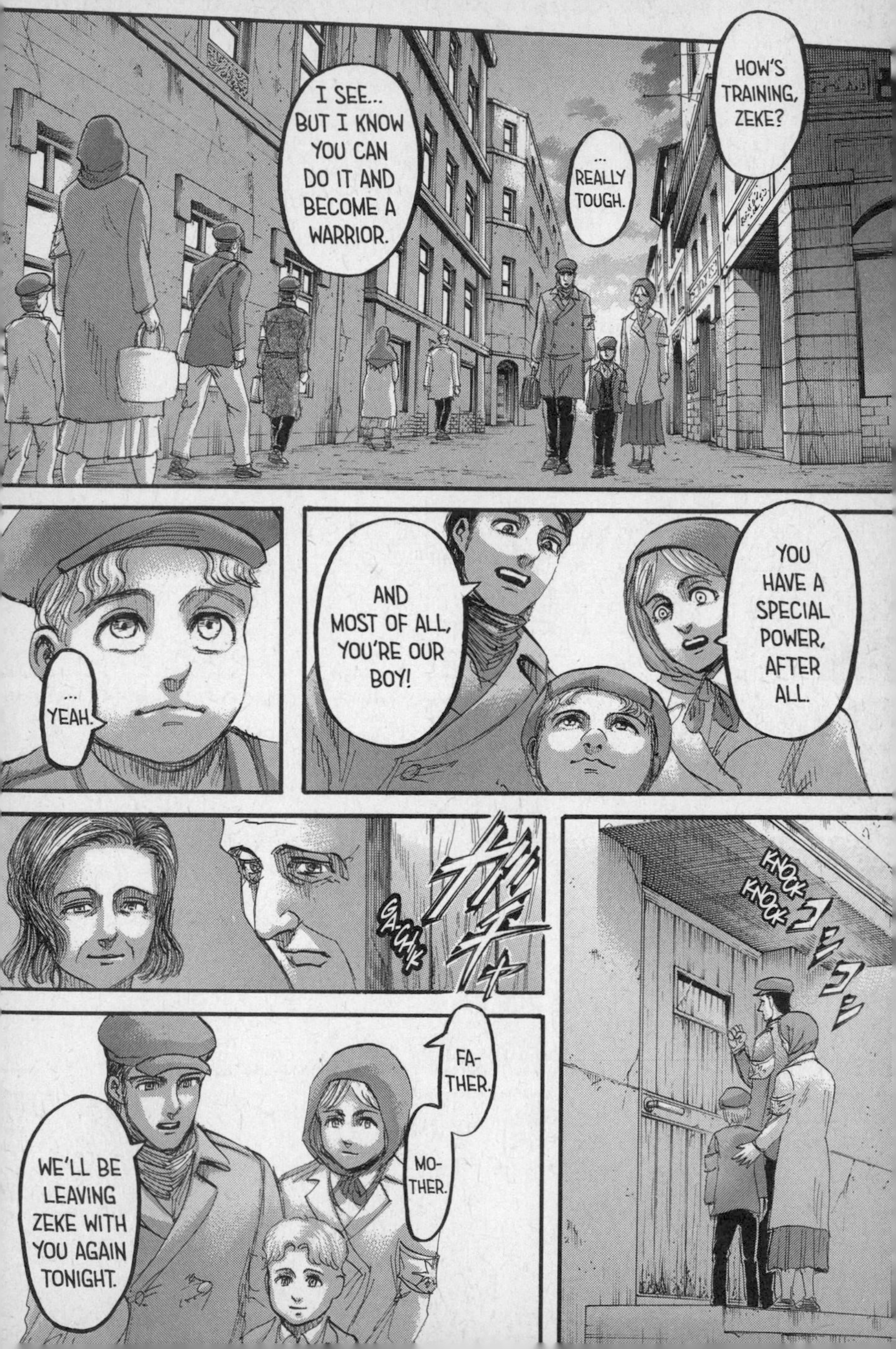
HOW'S TRAINING, ZEKE?
... REALLY TOUGH.
I SEE... BUT I KNOW YOU CAN DO IT AND BECOME A WARRIOR.
YOU HAVE A SPECIAL POWER, AFTER ALL.
AND MOST OF ALL, YOU'RE OUR BOY!
... YEAH.
KNOCK KNOCK
GA-CHIK
FA-THER.
MO-THER.
WE'LL BE LEAVING ZEKE WITH YOU AGAIN TONIGHT.

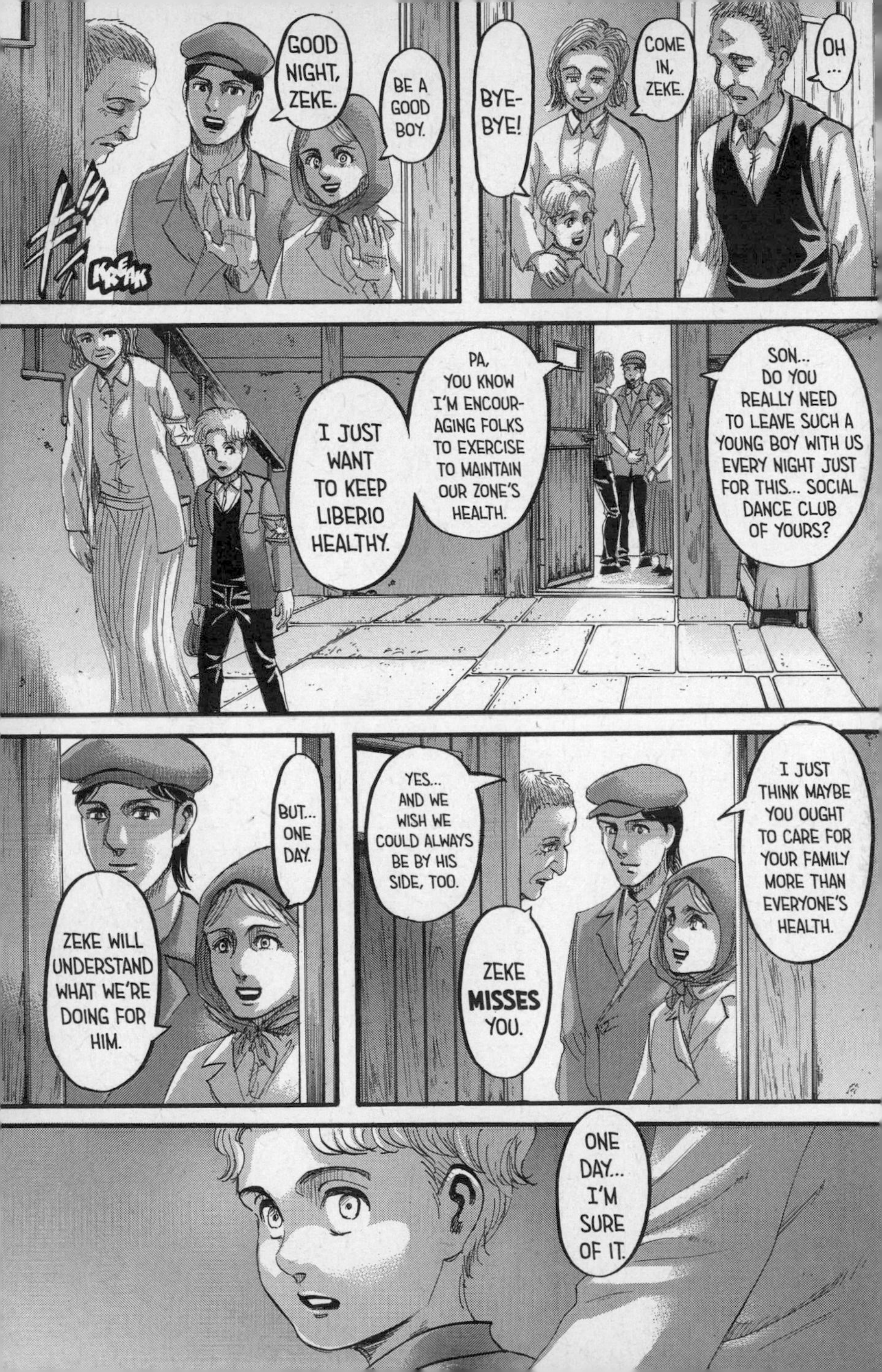
OH ...
COME IN, ZEKE.
BYE-BYE!
BE A GOOD BOY.
GOOD NIGHT, ZEKE.
KREAK
SON... DO YOU REALLY NEED TO LEAVE SUCH A YOUNG BOY WITH US EVERY NIGHT JUST FOR THIS... SOCIAL DANCE CLUB OF YOURS?
PA, YOU KNOW I'M ENCOURAGING FOLKS TO EXERCISE TO MAINTAIN OUR ZONE'S HEALTH.
I JUST WANT TO KEEP LIBERIO HEALTHY.
I JUST THINK MAYBE YOU OUGHT TO CARE FOR YOUR FAMILY MORE THAN EVERYONE'S HEALTH.
YES... AND WE WISH WE COULD ALWAYS BE BY HIS SIDE, TOO.
ZEKE **MISSES** YOU.
BUT... ONE DAY.
ZEKE WILL UNDERSTAND WHAT WE'RE DOING FOR HIM.
ONE DAY... I'M SURE OF IT.

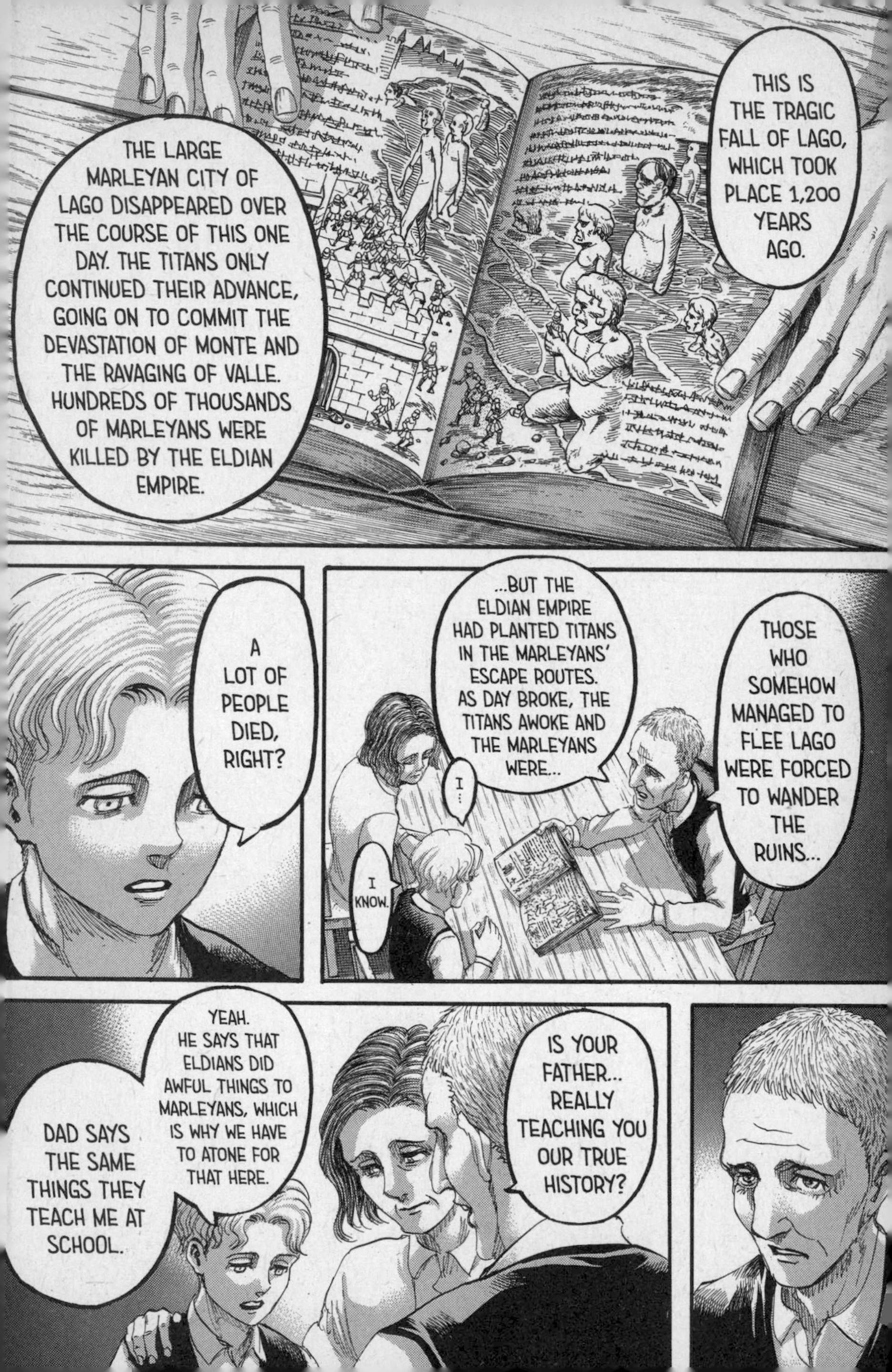
THIS IS THE TRAGIC FALL OF LAGO, WHICH TOOK PLACE 1,200 YEARS AGO.
THE LARGE MARLEYAN CITY OF LAGO DISAPPEARED OVER THE COURSE OF THIS ONE DAY. THE TITANS ONLY CONTINUED THEIR ADVANCE, GOING ON TO COMMIT THE DEVASTATION OF MONTE AND THE RAVAGING OF VALLE. HUNDREDS OF THOUSANDS OF MARLEYANS WERE KILLED BY THE ELDIAN EMPIRE.
THOSE WHO SOMEHOW MANAGED TO FLEE LAGO WERE FORCED TO WANDER THE RUINS...
...BUT THE ELDIAN EMPIRE HAD PLANTED TITANS IN THE MARLEYANS' ESCAPE ROUTES. AS DAY BROKE, THE TITANS AWOKE AND THE MARLEYANS WERE...
I...
I KNOW.
A LOT OF PEOPLE DIED, RIGHT?
IS YOUR FATHER... REALLY TEACHING YOU OUR TRUE HISTORY?
YEAH. HE SAYS THAT ELDIANS DID AWFUL THINGS TO MARLEYANS, WHICH IS WHY WE HAVE TO ATONE FOR THAT HERE.
DAD SAYS THE SAME THINGS THEY TEACH ME AT SCHOOL.

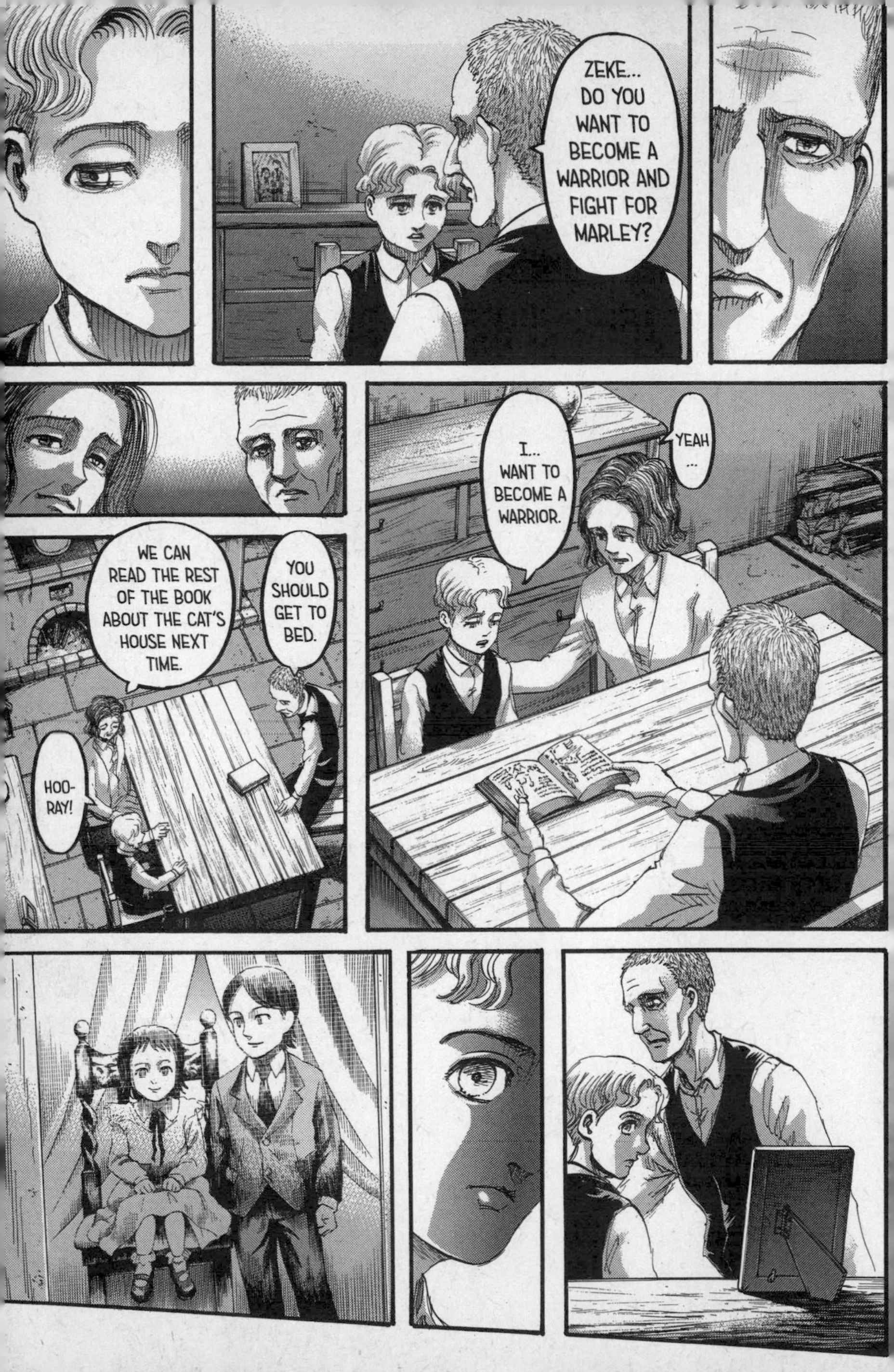
ZEKE... DO YOU WANT TO BECOME A WARRIOR AND FIGHT FOR MARLEY?
I... WANT TO BECOME A WARRIOR.
YEAH ...
YOU SHOULD GET TO BED.
WE CAN READ THE REST OF THE BOOK ABOUT THE CAT'S HOUSE NEXT TIME.
HOO-RAY!

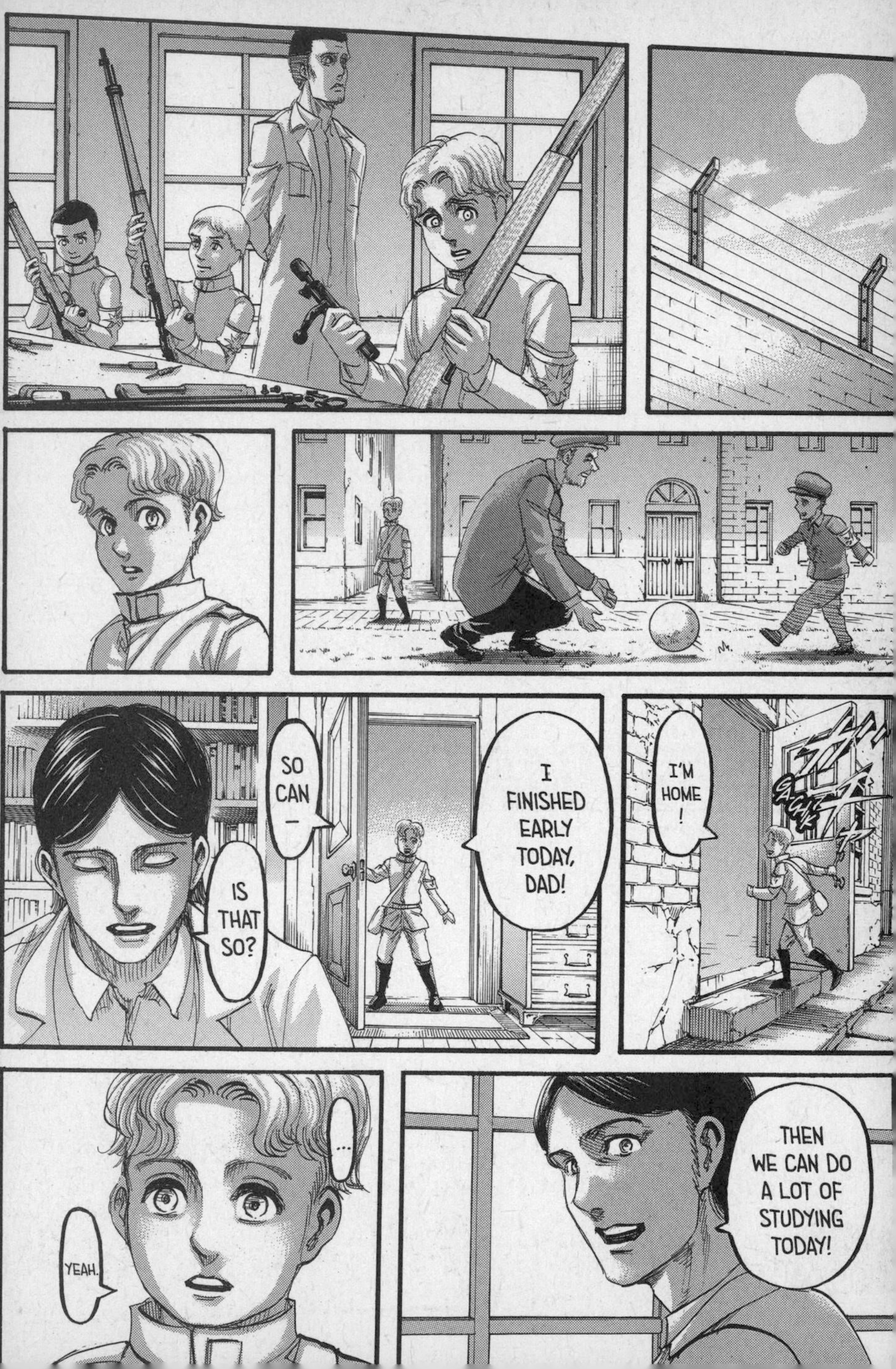
I'M HOME!
GA-CHIK
I FINISHED EARLY TODAY, DAD!
SO CAN—
IS THAT SO?
THEN WE CAN DO A LOT OF STUDYING TODAY!
...
YEAH.

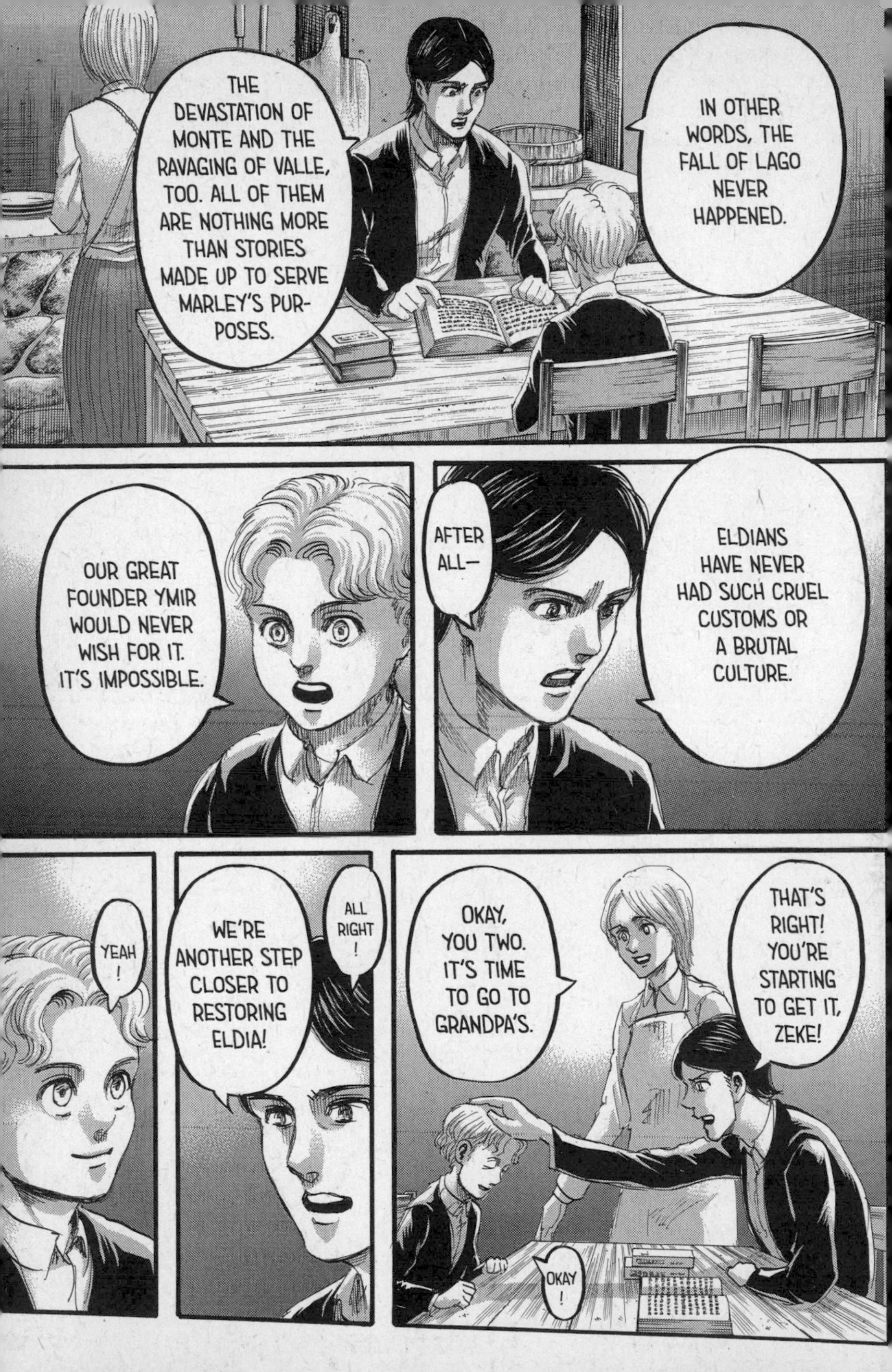
IN OTHER WORDS, THE FALL OF LAGO NEVER HAPPENED.
THE DEVASTATION OF MONTE AND THE RAVAGING OF VALLE, TOO. ALL OF THEM ARE NOTHING MORE THAN STORIES MADE UP TO SERVE MARLEY'S PURPOSES.
ELDIANS HAVE NEVER HAD SUCH CRUEL CUSTOMS OR A BRUTAL CULTURE.
AFTER ALL—
OUR GREAT FOUNDER YMIR WOULD NEVER WISH FOR IT. IT'S IMPOSSIBLE.
THAT'S RIGHT! YOU'RE STARTING TO GET IT, ZEKE!
OKAY, YOU TWO. IT'S TIME TO GO TO GRANDPA'S.
OKAY!
ALL RIGHT!
WE'RE ANOTHER STEP CLOSER TO RESTORING ELDIA!
YEAH!

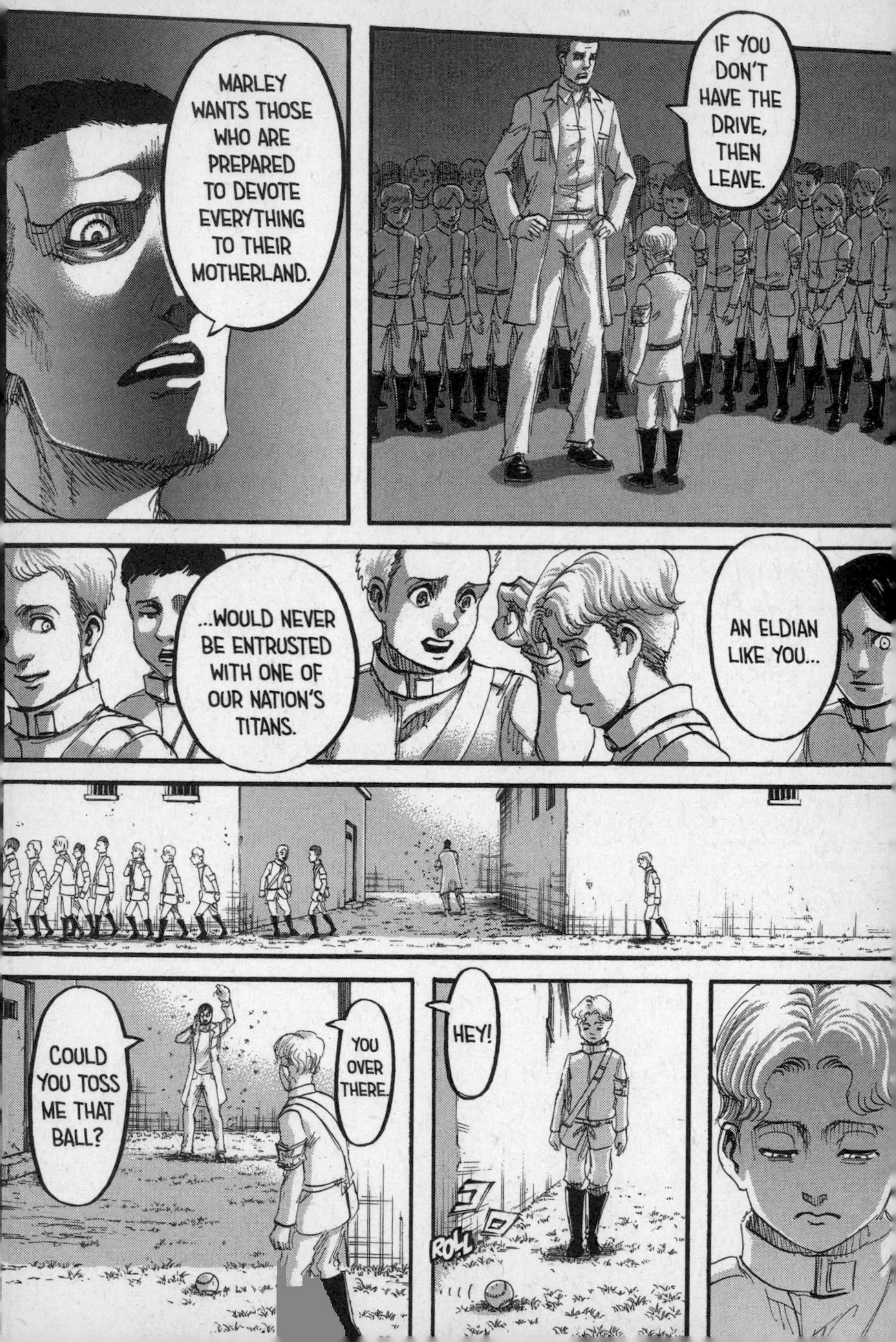
IF YOU DON'T HAVE THE DRIVE, THEN LEAVE.
MARLEY WANTS THOSE WHO ARE PREPARED TO DEVOTE EVERYTHING TO THEIR MOTHERLAND.
AN ELDIAN LIKE YOU...
...WOULD NEVER BE ENTRUSTED WITH ONE OF OUR NATION'S TITANS.
HEY!
ROLL
YOU OVER THERE.
COULD YOU TOSS ME THAT BALL?

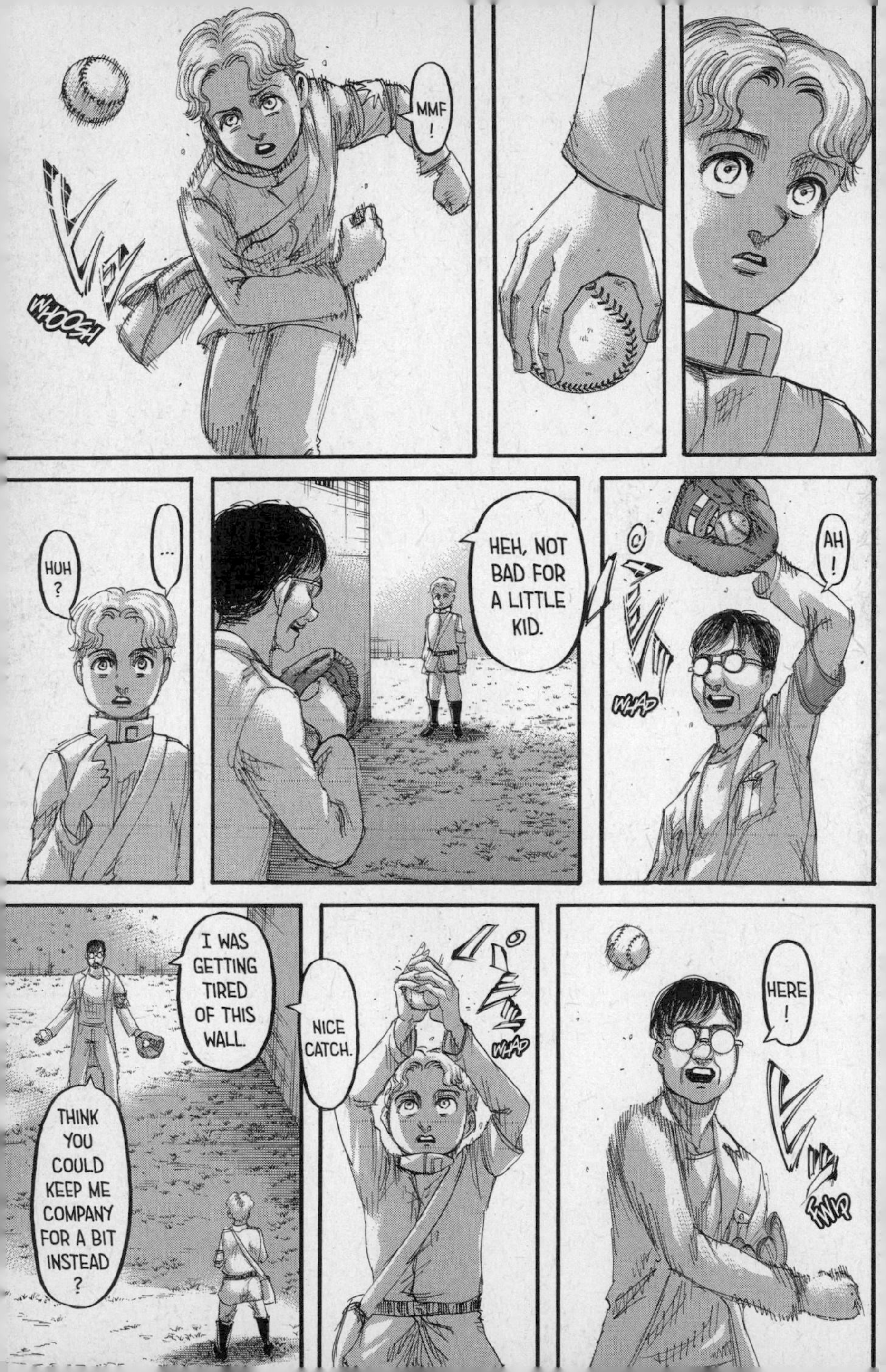
MMF!
WHOOSH
AH!
WHAP
HEH, NOT BAD FOR A LITTLE KID.
...
HUH?
HERE!
FWIP
NICE CATCH.
WHAP
I WAS GETTING TIRED OF THIS WALL.
THINK YOU COULD KEEP ME COMPANY FOR A BIT INSTEAD?

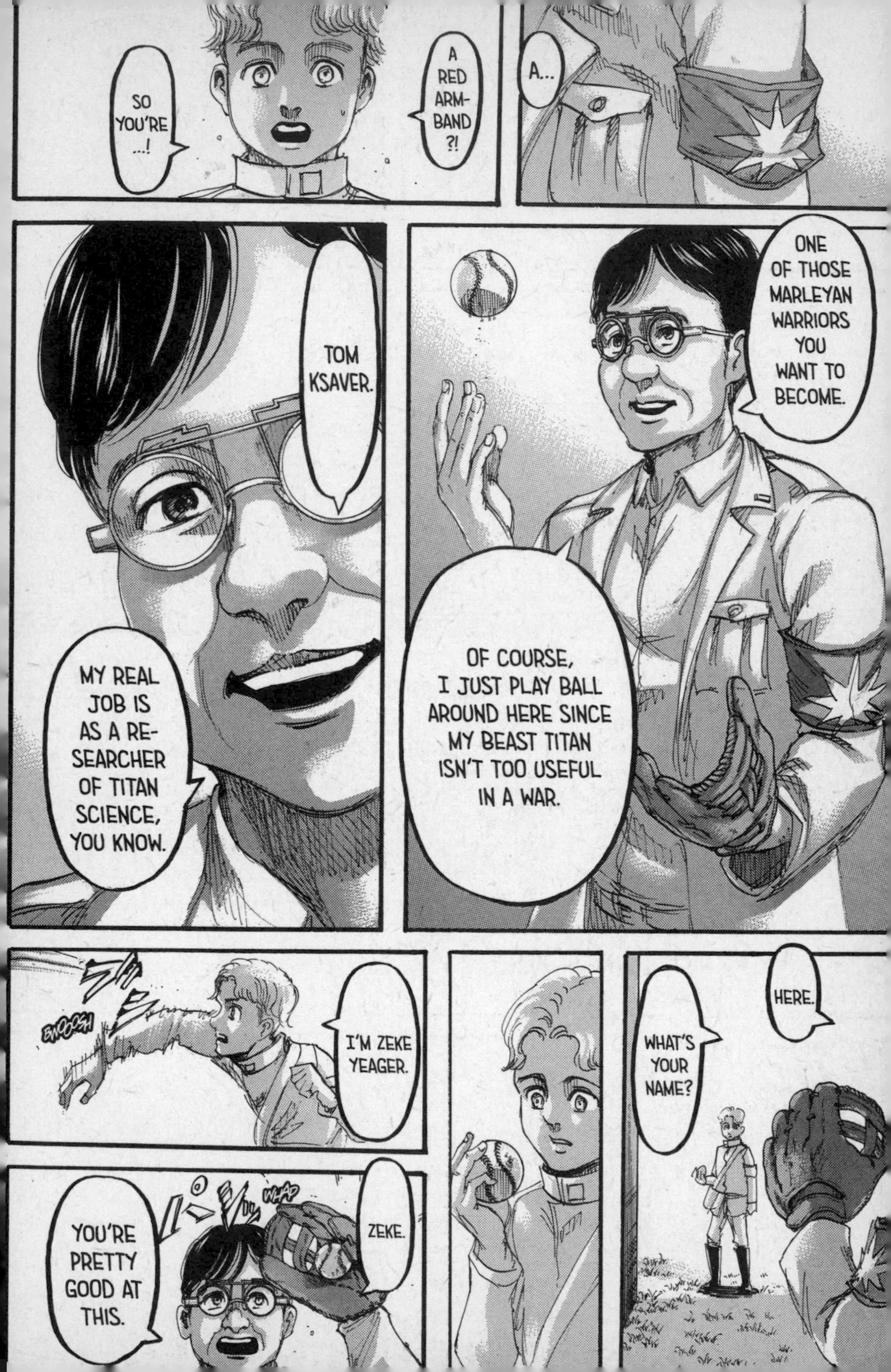
A...
A RED ARM-BAND ?!
SO YOU'RE ...!
ONE OF THOSE MARLEYAN WARRIORS YOU WANT TO BECOME.
OF COURSE, I JUST PLAY BALL AROUND HERE SINCE MY BEAST TITAN ISN'T TOO USEFUL IN A WAR.
TOM KSAVER.
MY REAL JOB IS AS A RE-SEARCHER OF TITAN SCIENCE, YOU KNOW.
HERE.
WHAT'S YOUR NAME?
SWOOSH
I'M ZEKE YEAGER.
ZEKE.
WHAP
YOU'RE PRETTY GOOD AT THIS.

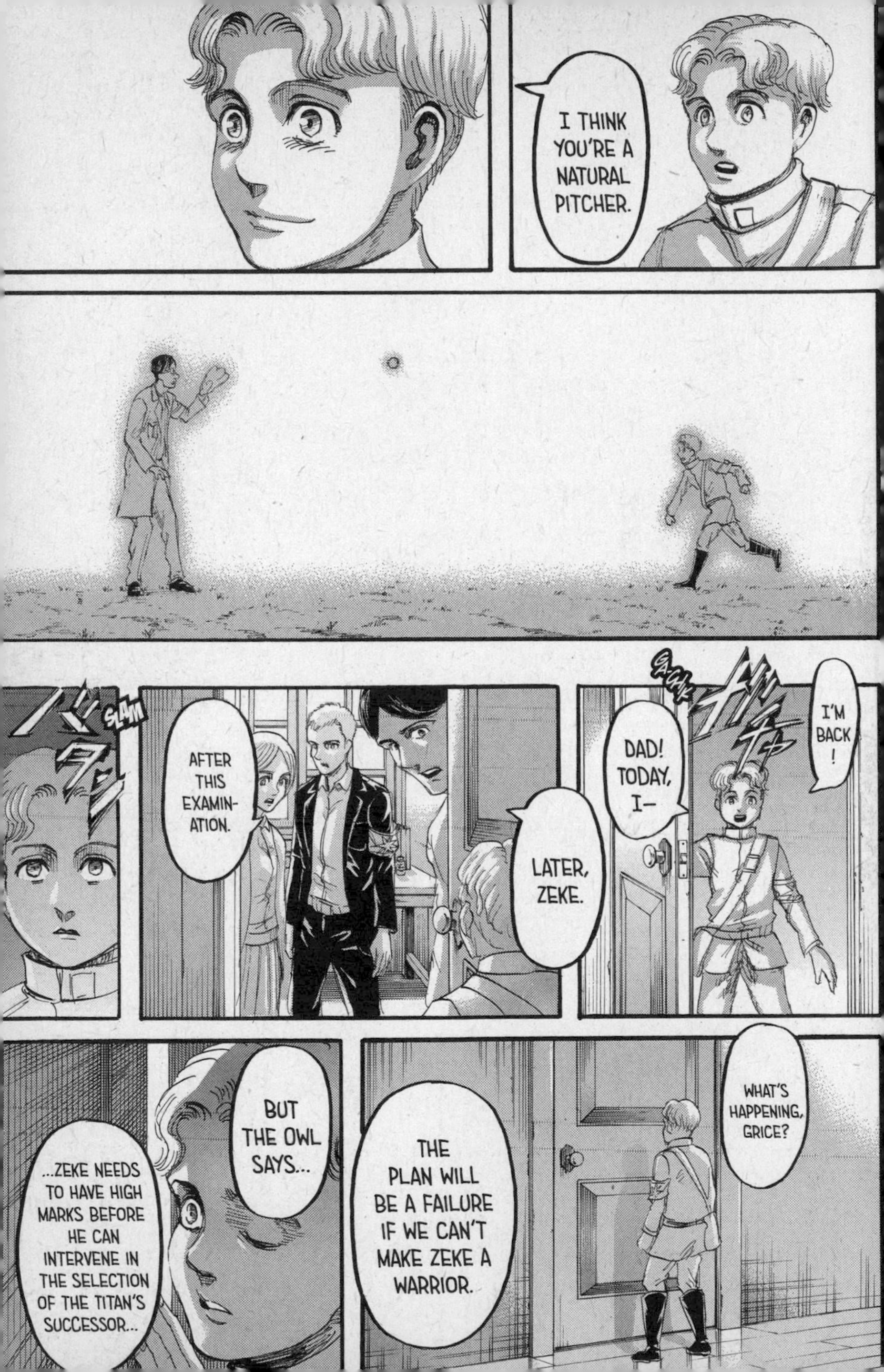

I THINK YOU'RE A NATURAL PITCHER.
I'M BACK!
GACHAK
DAD! TODAY, I—
LATER, ZEKE.
AFTER THIS EXAMINATION.
SLAM
WHAT'S HAPPENING, GRICE?
THE PLAN WILL BE A FAILURE IF WE CAN'T MAKE ZEKE A WARRIOR.
BUT THE OWL SAYS...
...ZEKE NEEDS TO HAVE HIGH MARKS BEFORE HE CAN INTERVENE IN THE SELECTION OF THE TITAN'S SUCCESSOR...

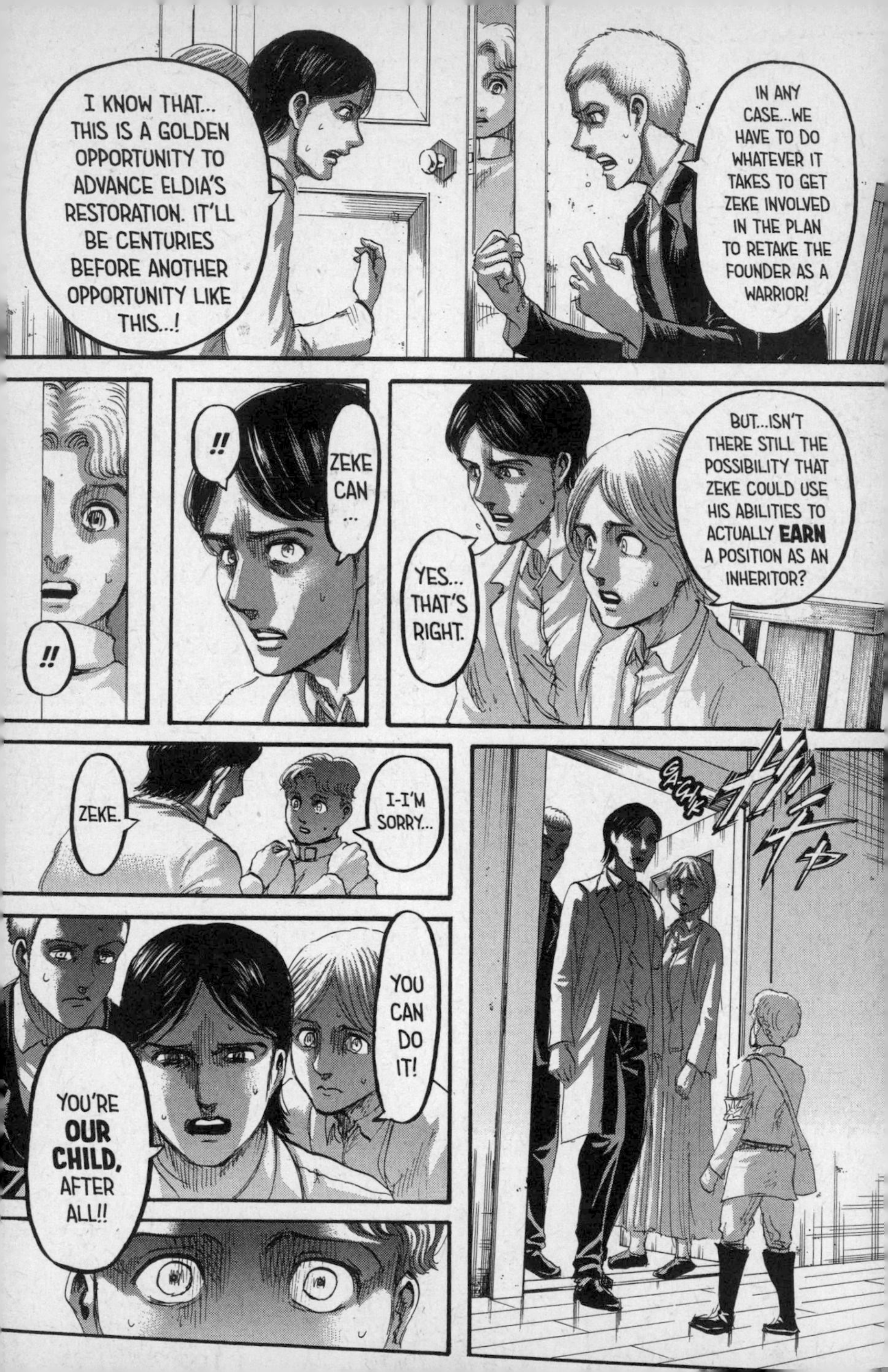
IN ANY CASE...WE HAVE TO DO WHATEVER IT TAKES TO GET ZEKE INVOLVED IN THE PLAN TO RETAKE THE FOUNDER AS A WARRIOR!
I KNOW THAT... THIS IS A GOLDEN OPPORTUNITY TO ADVANCE ELDIA'S RESTORATION. IT'LL BE CENTURIES BEFORE ANOTHER OPPORTUNITY LIKE THIS...!
BUT...ISN'T THERE STILL THE POSSIBILITY THAT ZEKE COULD USE HIS ABILITIES TO ACTUALLY **EARN** A POSITION AS AN INHERITOR?
YES... THAT'S RIGHT.
!!
ZEKE CAN ...
!!
GA-CHAK
ZEKE.
I-I'M SORRY...
YOU CAN DO IT!
YOU'RE **OUR CHILD,** AFTER ALL!!

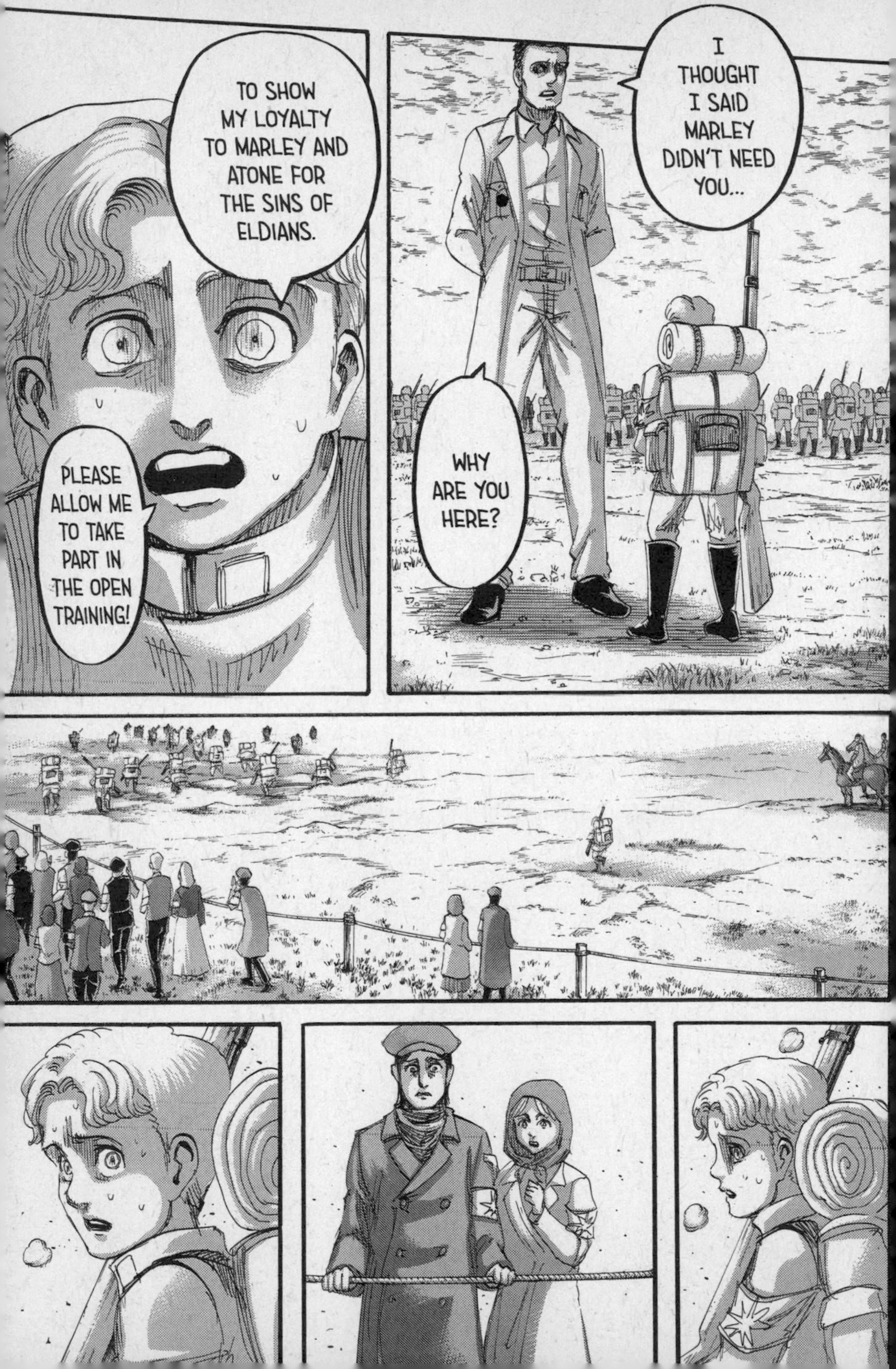
I THOUGHT I SAID MARLEY DIDN'T NEED YOU...
WHY ARE YOU HERE?
TO SHOW MY LOYALTY TO MARLEY AND ATONE FOR THE SINS OF ELDIANS.
PLEASE ALLOW ME TO TAKE PART IN THE OPEN TRAINING!

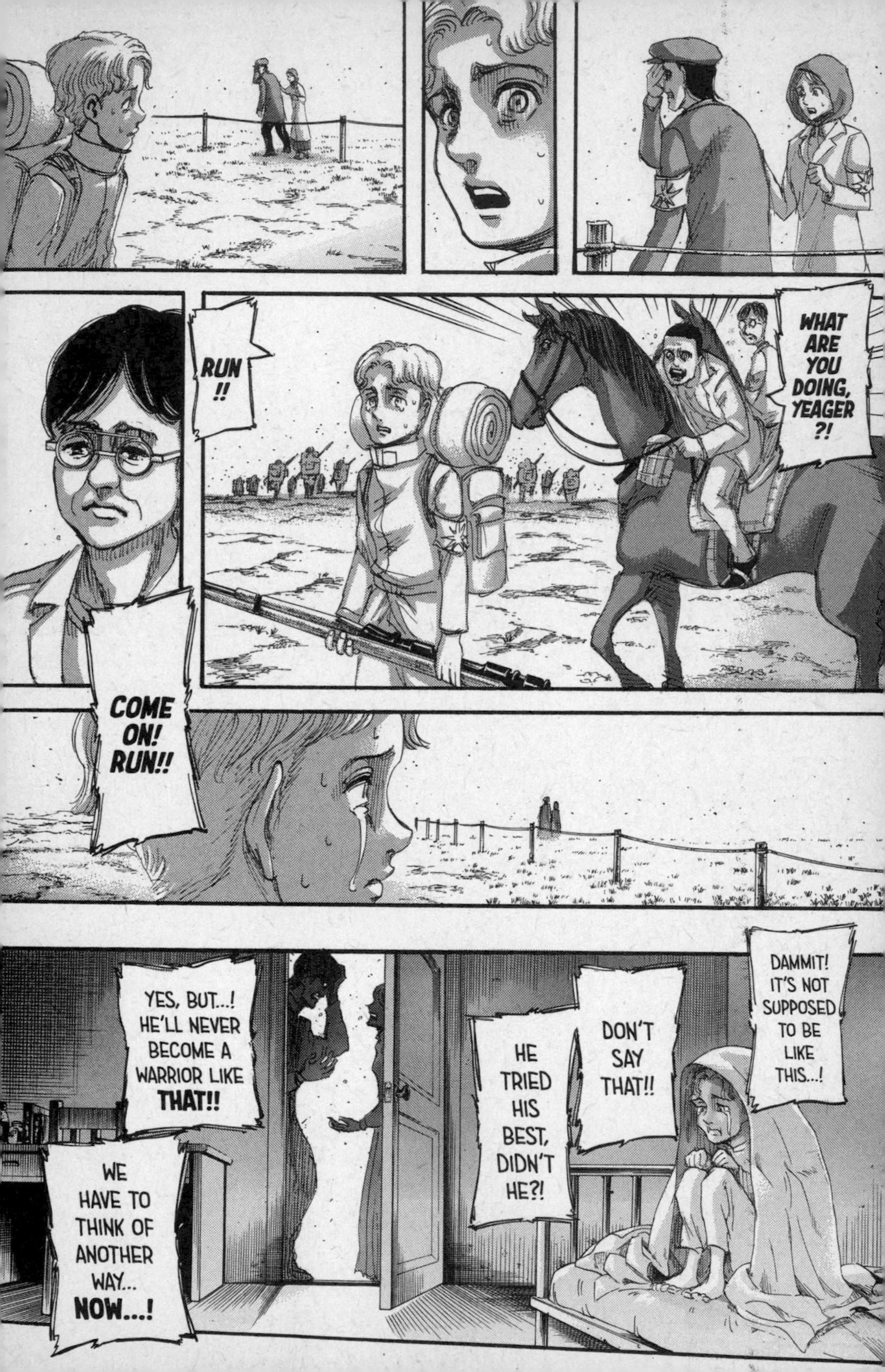

WHAT ARE YOU DOING, YEAGER?!
RUN!!
COME ON! RUN!!
DAMMIT! IT'S NOT SUPPOSED TO BE LIKE THIS...!
DON'T SAY THAT!!
HE TRIED HIS BEST, DIDN'T HE?!
YES, BUT...! HE'LL NEVER BECOME A WARRIOR LIKE **THAT!!**
WE HAVE TO THINK OF ANOTHER WAY... **NOW...!**

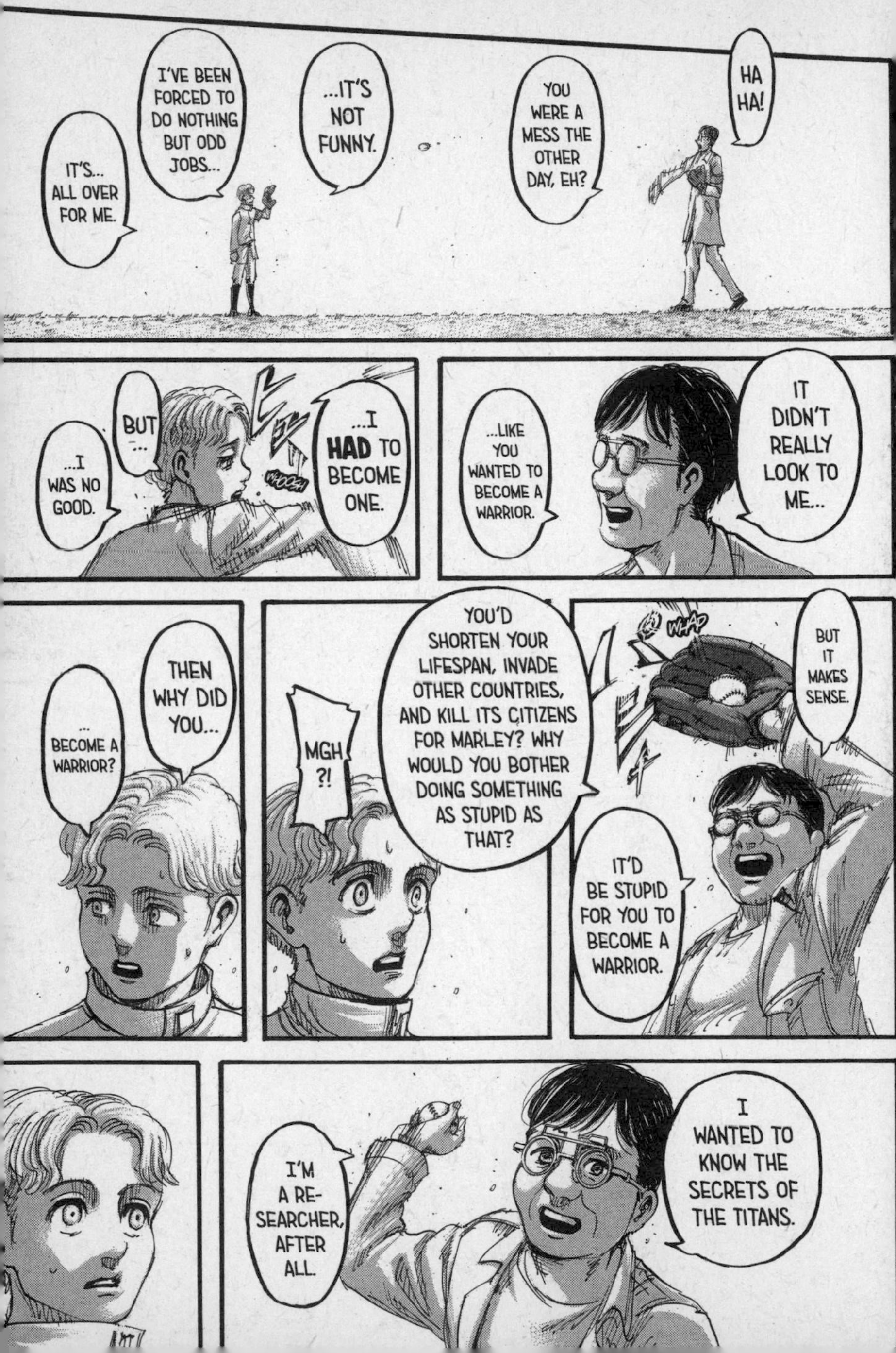
HA HA!
YOU WERE A MESS THE OTHER DAY, EH?
...IT'S NOT FUNNY.
I'VE BEEN FORCED TO DO NOTHING BUT ODD JOBS...
IT'S... ALL OVER FOR ME.
IT DIDN'T REALLY LOOK TO ME...
...LIKE YOU WANTED TO BECOME A WARRIOR.
...I **HAD** TO BECOME ONE.
WHOOSH
BUT...
...I WAS NO GOOD.
BUT IT MAKES SENSE.
WHAP
IT'D BE STUPID FOR YOU TO BECOME A WARRIOR.
YOU'D SHORTEN YOUR LIFESPAN, INVADE OTHER COUNTRIES, AND KILL ITS CITIZENS FOR MARLEY? WHY WOULD YOU BOTHER DOING SOMETHING AS STUPID AS THAT?
MGH?!
THEN WHY DID YOU...
...BECOME A WARRIOR?
I WANTED TO KNOW THE SECRETS OF THE TITANS.
I'M A RESEARCHER, AFTER ALL.

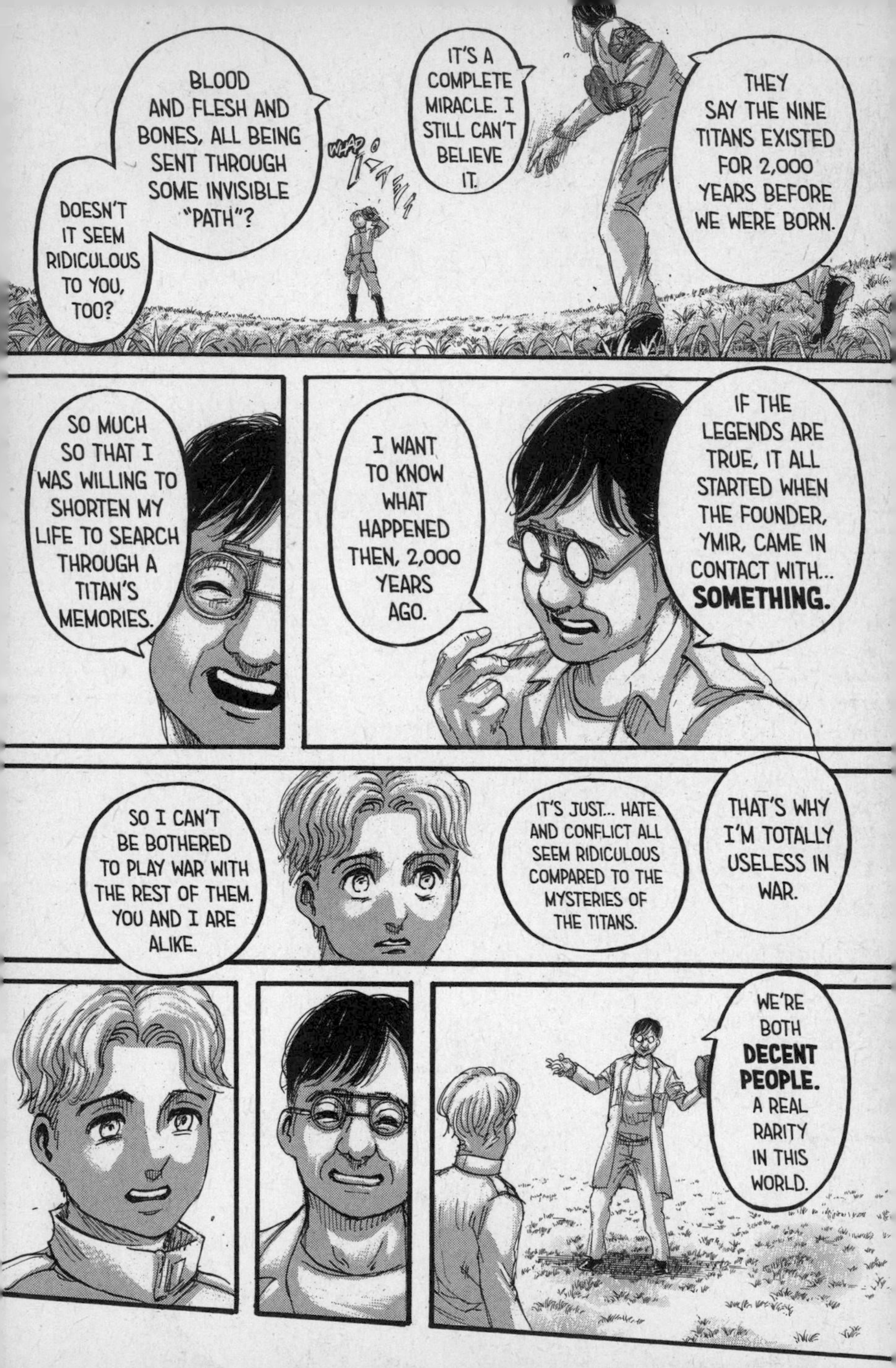
THEY SAY THE NINE TITANS EXISTED FOR 2,000 YEARS BEFORE WE WERE BORN.
IT'S A COMPLETE MIRACLE. I STILL CAN'T BELIEVE IT.
WHAP
BLOOD AND FLESH AND BONES, ALL BEING SENT THROUGH SOME INVISIBLE "PATH"?
DOESN'T IT SEEM RIDICULOUS TO YOU, TOO?
IF THE LEGENDS ARE TRUE, IT ALL STARTED WHEN THE FOUNDER, YMIR, CAME IN CONTACT WITH... **SOMETHING.**
I WANT TO KNOW WHAT HAPPENED THEN, 2,000 YEARS AGO.
SO MUCH SO THAT I WAS WILLING TO SHORTEN MY LIFE TO SEARCH THROUGH A TITAN'S MEMORIES.
THAT'S WHY I'M TOTALLY USELESS IN WAR.
IT'S JUST... HATE AND CONFLICT ALL SEEM RIDICULOUS COMPARED TO THE MYSTERIES OF THE TITANS.
SO I CAN'T BE BOTHERED TO PLAY WAR WITH THE REST OF THEM. YOU AND I ARE ALIKE.
WE'RE BOTH **DECENT PEOPLE.** A REAL RARITY IN THIS WORLD.

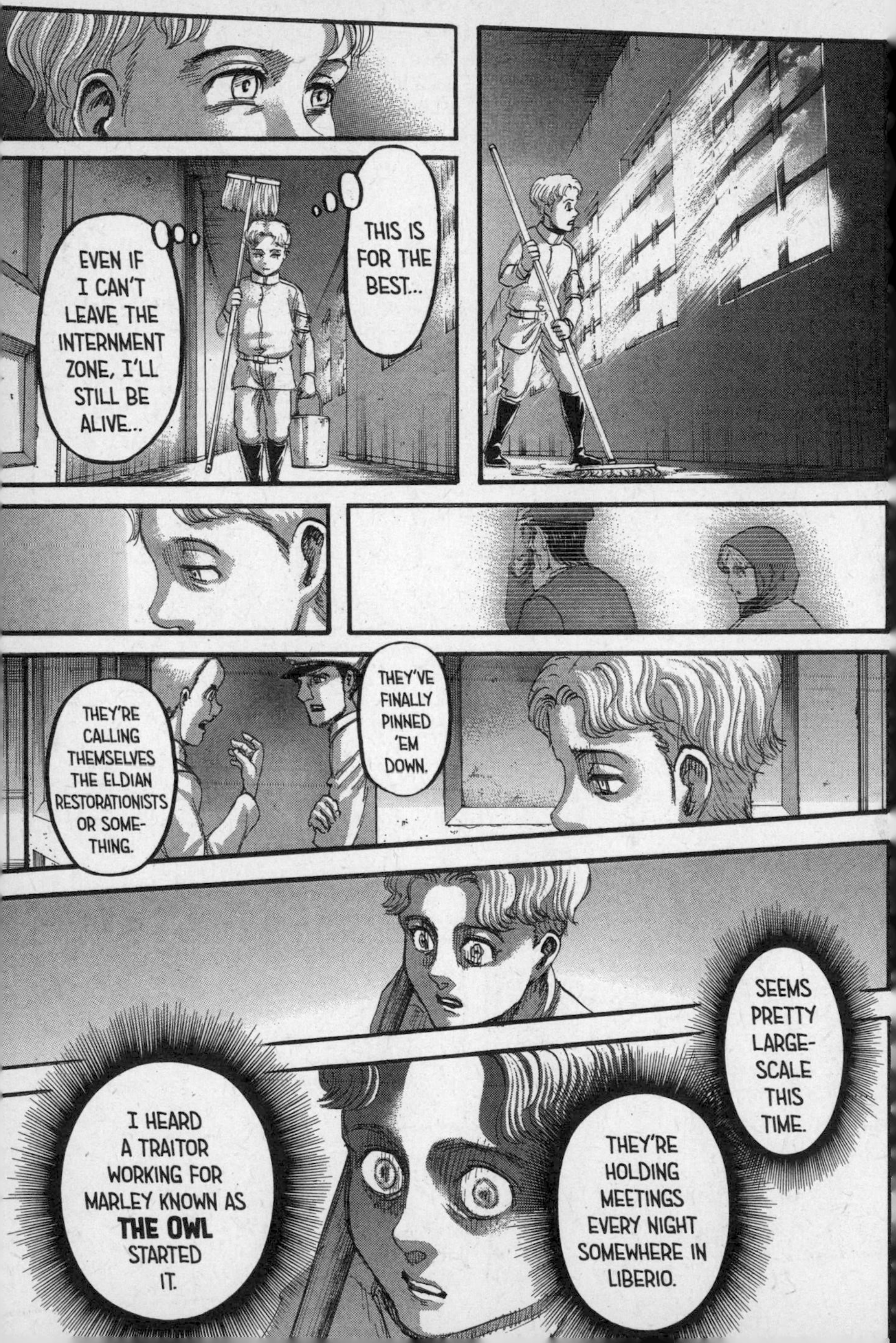
THIS IS FOR THE BEST...
EVEN IF I CAN'T LEAVE THE INTERNMENT ZONE, I'LL STILL BE ALIVE...
THEY'VE FINALLY PINNED 'EM DOWN.
THEY'RE CALLING THEMSELVES THE ELDIAN RESTORATIONISTS OR SOME-THING.
SEEMS PRETTY LARGE-SCALE THIS TIME.
THEY'RE HOLDING MEETINGS EVERY NIGHT SOMEWHERE IN LIBERIO.
I HEARD A TRAITOR WORKING FOR MARLEY KNOWN AS **THE OWL** STARTED IT.

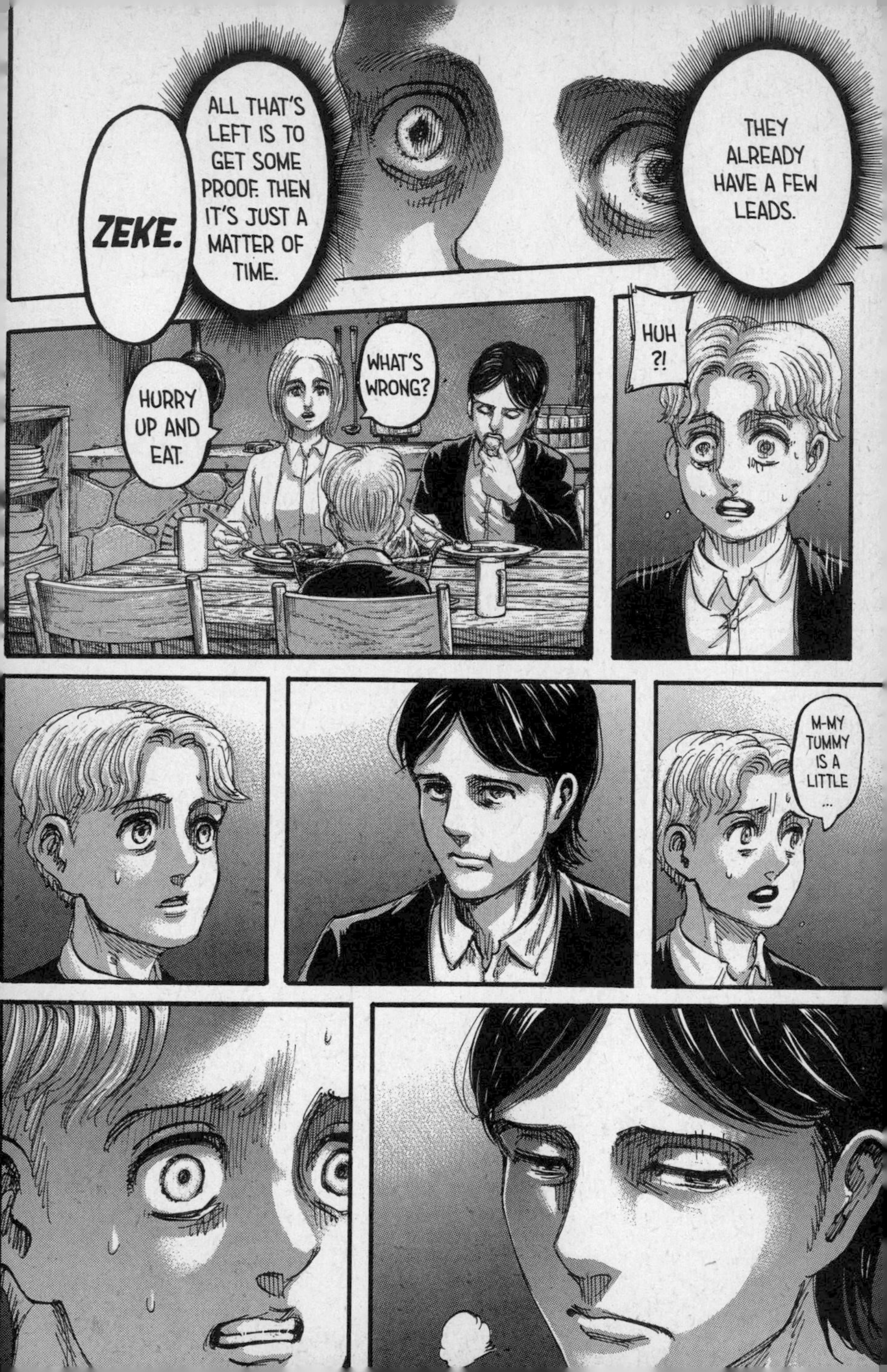
THEY ALREADY HAVE A FEW LEADS.
ALL THAT'S LEFT IS TO GET SOME PROOF. THEN IT'S JUST A MATTER OF TIME.
ZEKE.
HUH ?!
WHAT'S WRONG?
HURRY UP AND EAT.
M-MY TUMMY IS A LITTLE ...

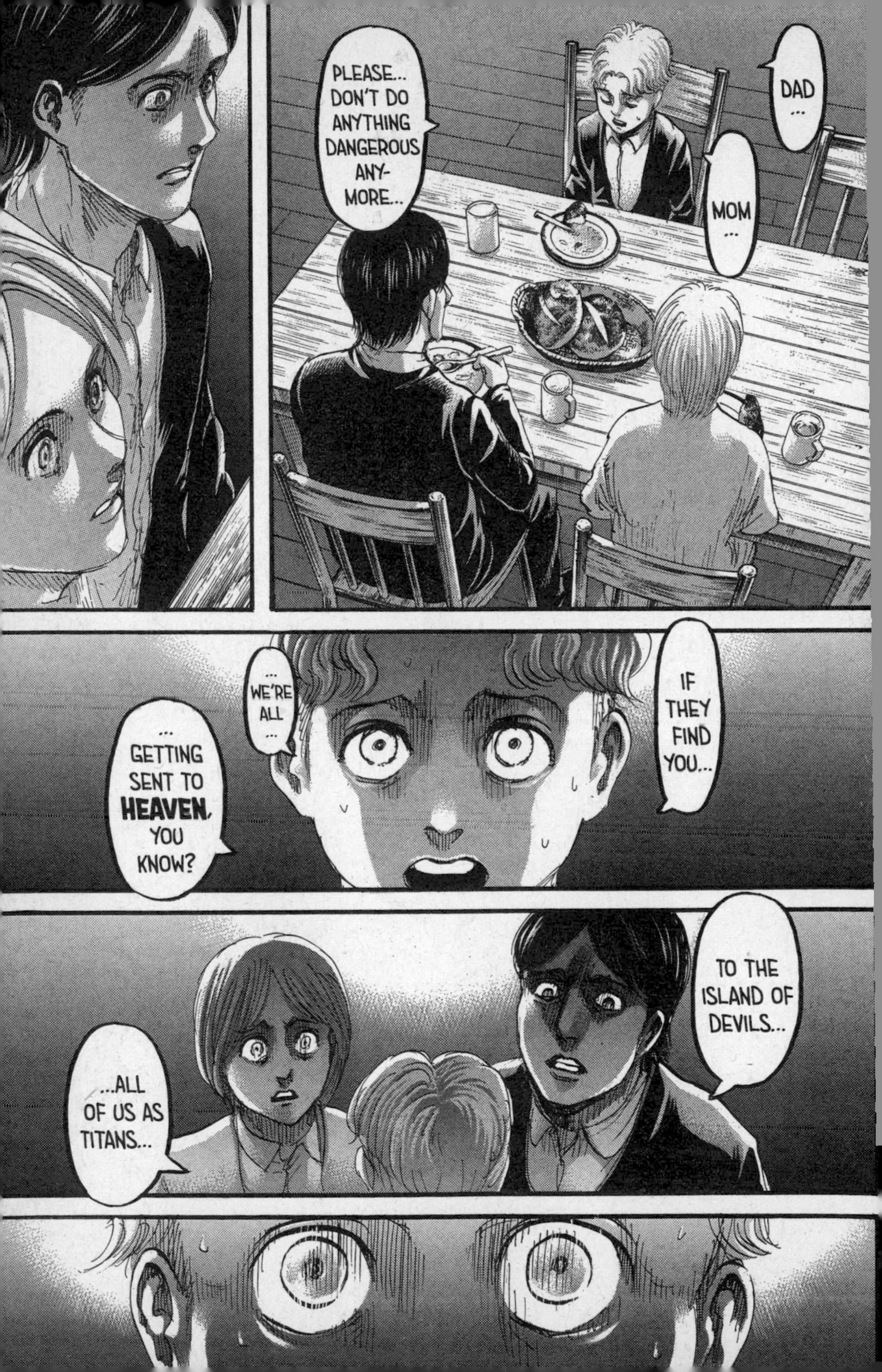
DAD ...
MOM ...
PLEASE... DON'T DO ANYTHING DANGEROUS ANY-MORE...
IF THEY FIND YOU...
... WE'RE ALL ...
... GETTING SENT TO **HEAVEN**, YOU KNOW?
TO THE ISLAND OF DEVILS...
...ALL OF US AS TITANS...

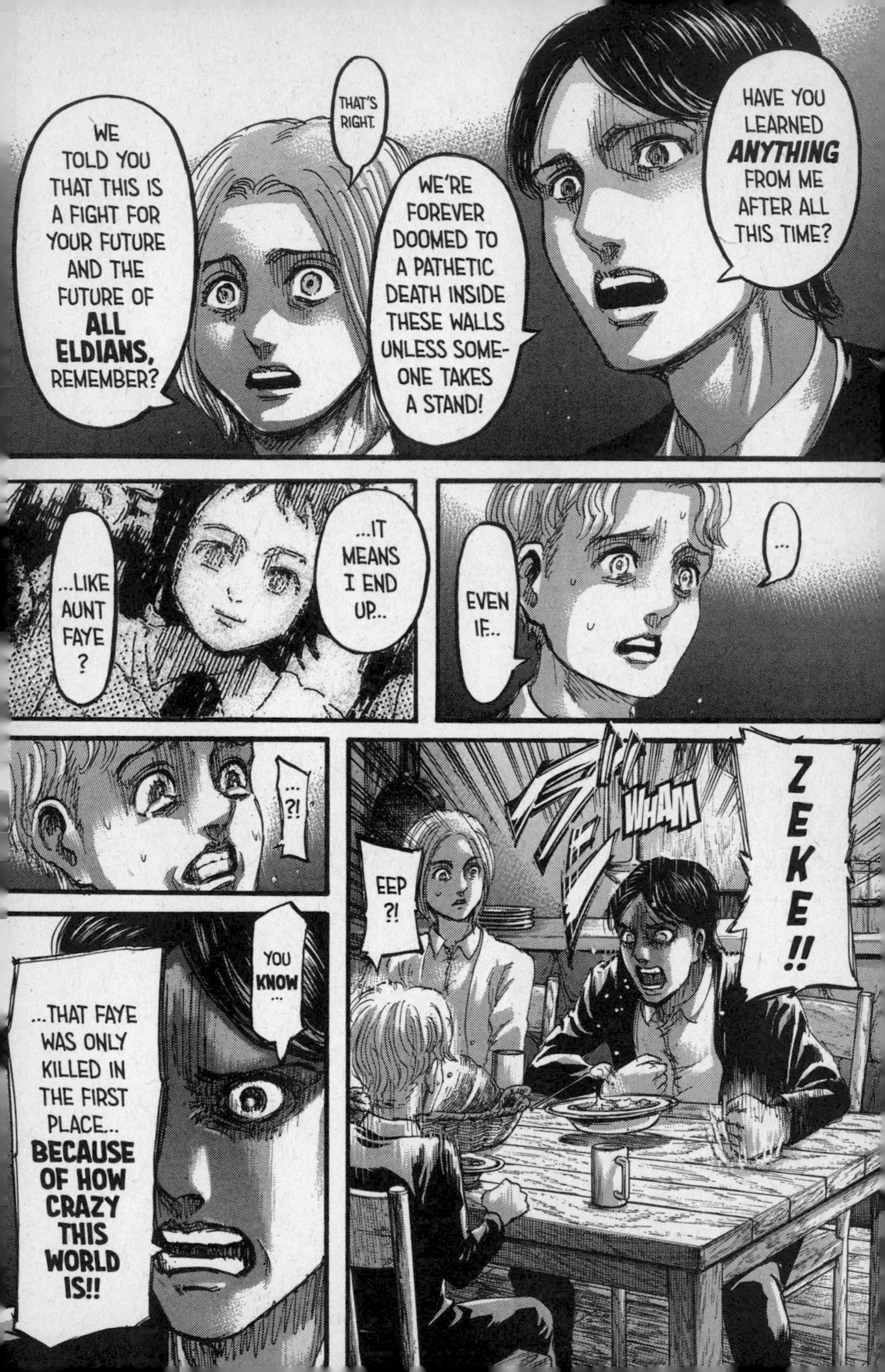
HAVE YOU LEARNED **ANYTHING** FROM ME AFTER ALL THIS TIME?
WE'RE FOREVER DOOMED TO A PATHETIC DEATH INSIDE THESE WALLS UNLESS SOME-ONE TAKES A STAND!
THAT'S RIGHT.
WE TOLD YOU THAT THIS IS A FIGHT FOR YOUR FUTURE AND THE FUTURE OF **ALL ELDIANS,** REMEMBER?
...
EVEN IF...
...IT MEANS I END UP...
...LIKE AUNT FAYE ?
ZEKE!!
WHAM
EEP ?!
...?!
YOU **KNOW** ...
...THAT FAYE WAS ONLY KILLED IN THE FIRST PLACE... **BECAUSE OF HOW CRAZY THIS WORLD IS!!**

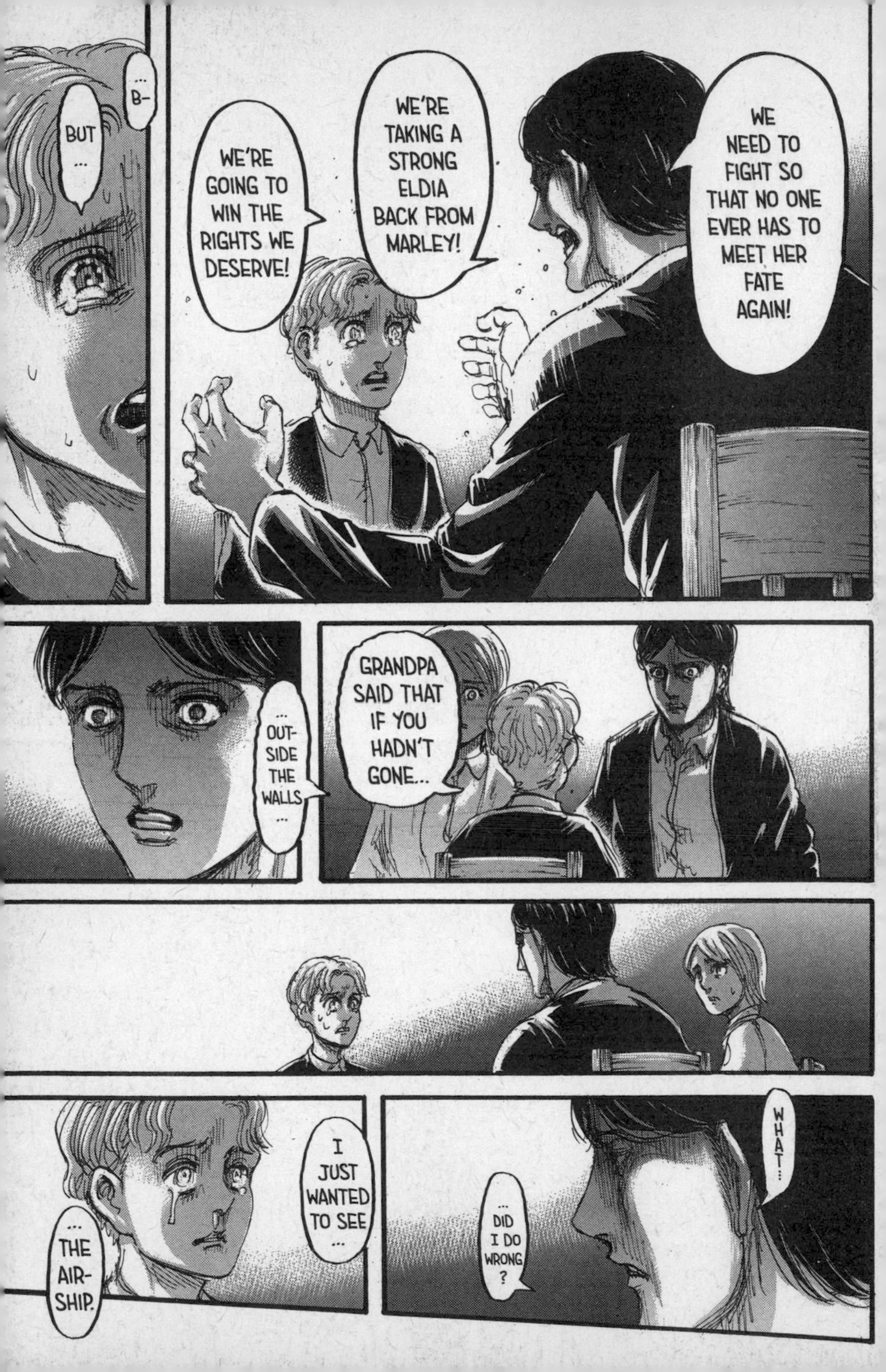
WE NEED TO FIGHT SO THAT NO ONE EVER HAS TO MEET HER FATE AGAIN!
WE'RE TAKING A STRONG ELDIA BACK FROM MARLEY!
WE'RE GOING TO WIN THE RIGHTS WE DESERVE!
... B-
BUT ...
GRANDPA SAID THAT IF YOU HADN'T GONE...
... OUT-SIDE THE WALLS ...
WHAT...
... DID I DO WRONG?
I JUST WANTED TO SEE ...
... THE AIR-SHIP.

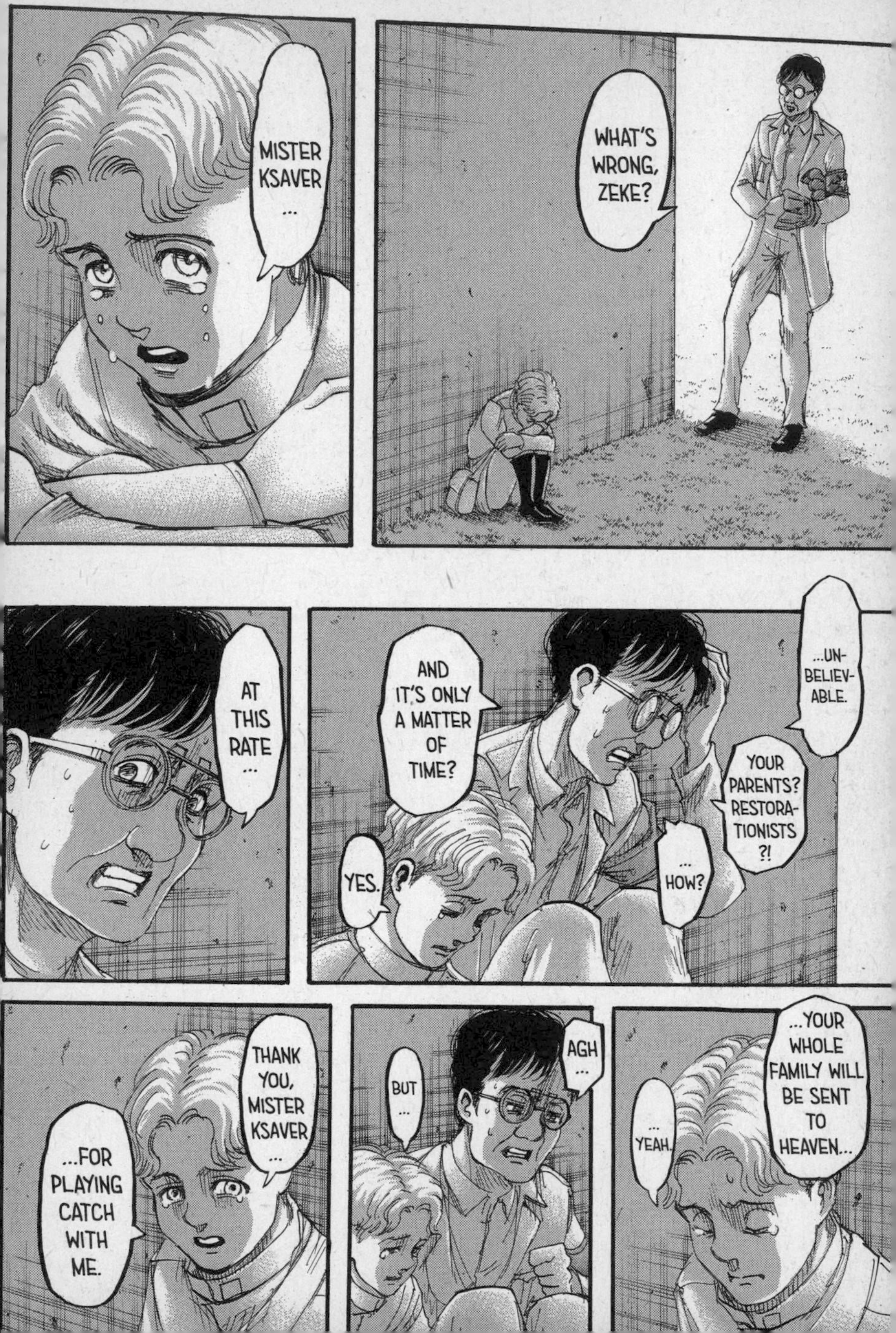
WHAT'S WRONG, ZEKE?
MISTER KSAVER ...
...UN-BELIEV-ABLE.
YOUR PARENTS? RESTORA-TIONISTS ?!
... HOW?
AND IT'S ONLY A MATTER OF TIME?
YES.
AT THIS RATE ...
...YOUR WHOLE FAMILY WILL BE SENT TO HEAVEN...
... YEAH.
AGH ...
BUT ...
THANK YOU, MISTER KSAVER ...
...FOR PLAYING CATCH WITH ME.

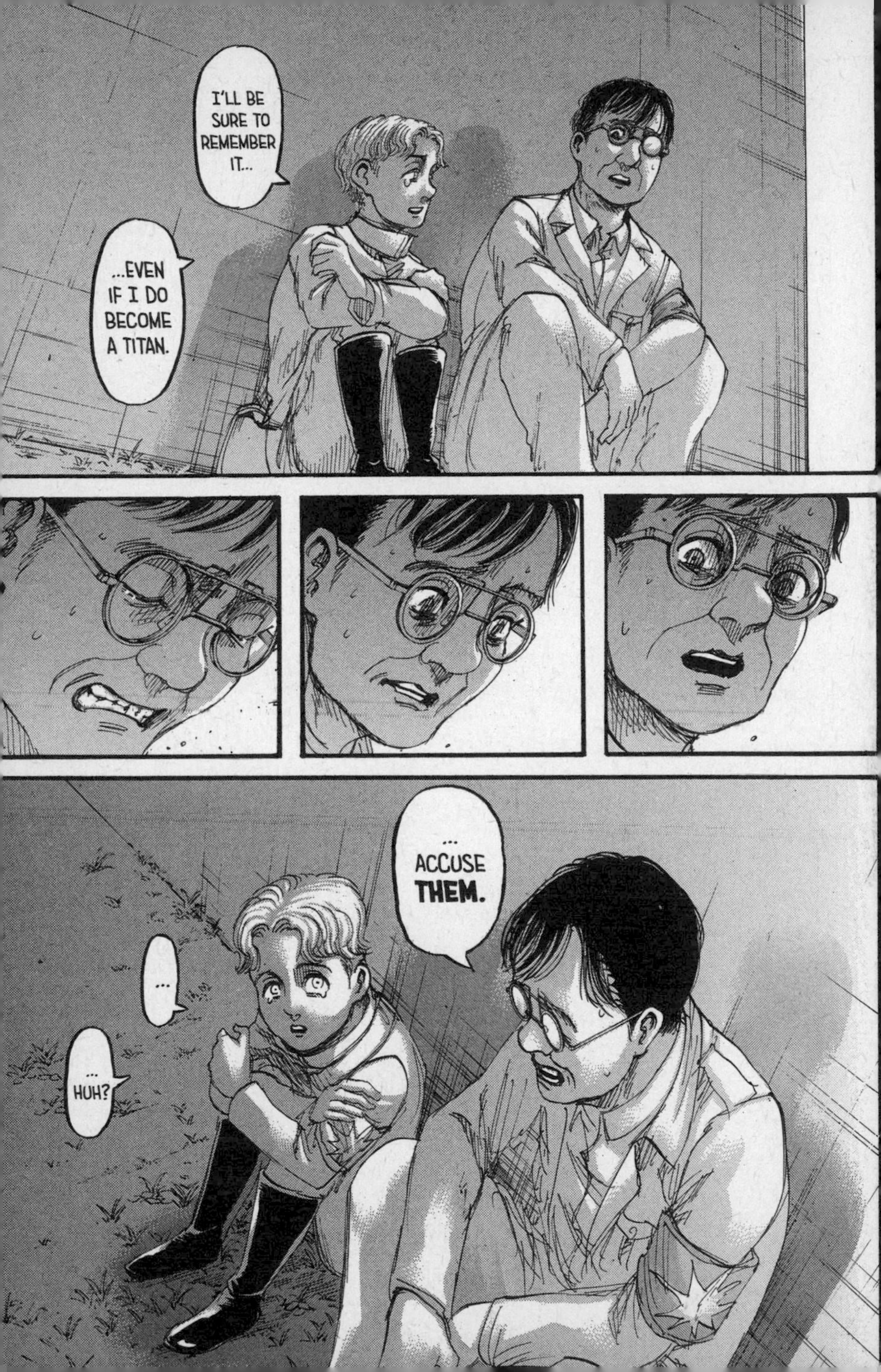
I'LL BE SURE TO REMEMBER IT...
...EVEN IF I DO BECOME A TITAN.
... ACCUSE **THEM.**
...
... HUH?

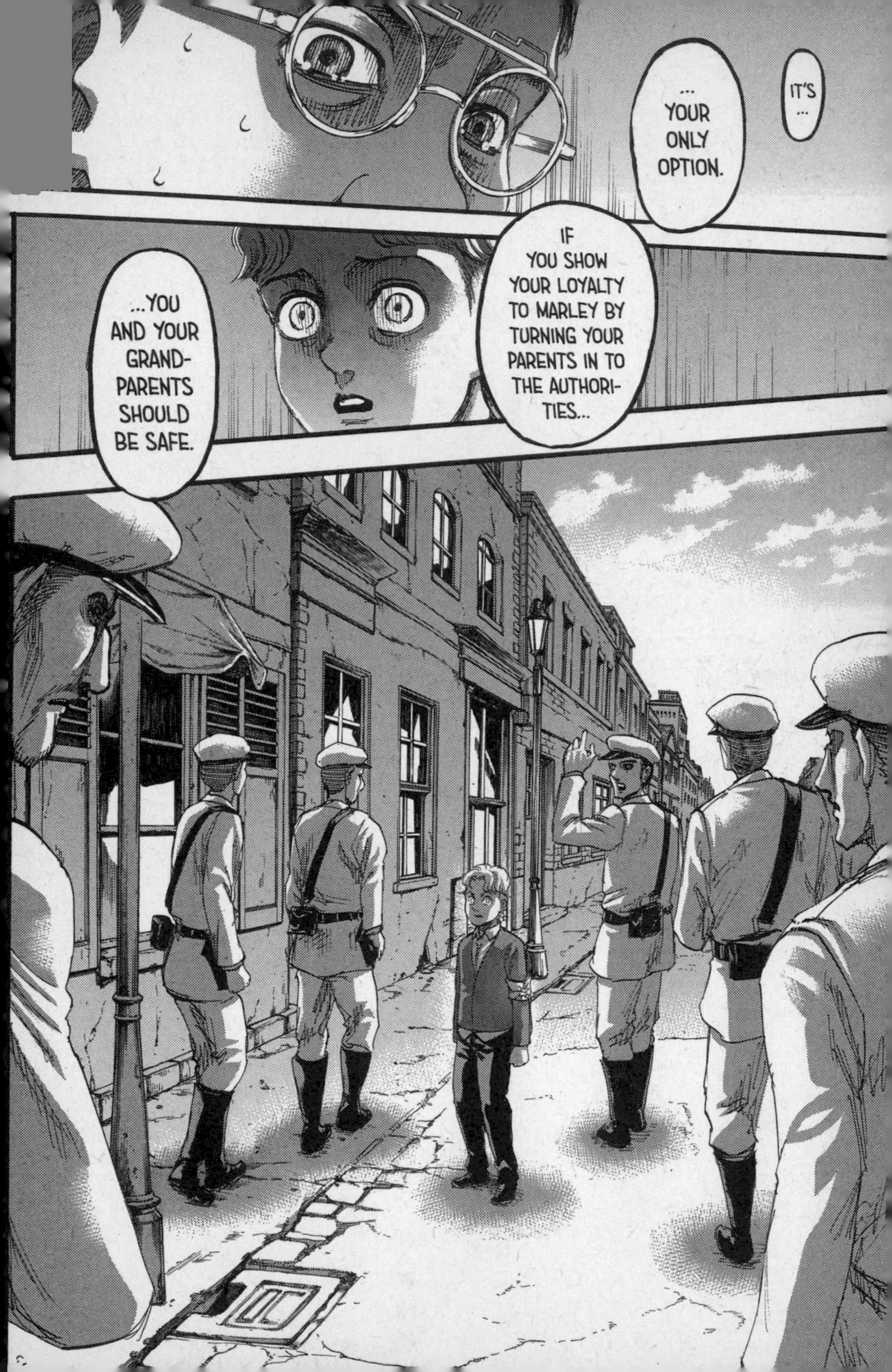
IT'S ...
... YOUR ONLY OPTION.
IF YOU SHOW YOUR LOYALTY TO MARLEY BY TURNING YOUR PARENTS IN TO THE AUTHORITIES...
...YOU AND YOUR GRANDPARENTS SHOULD BE SAFE.

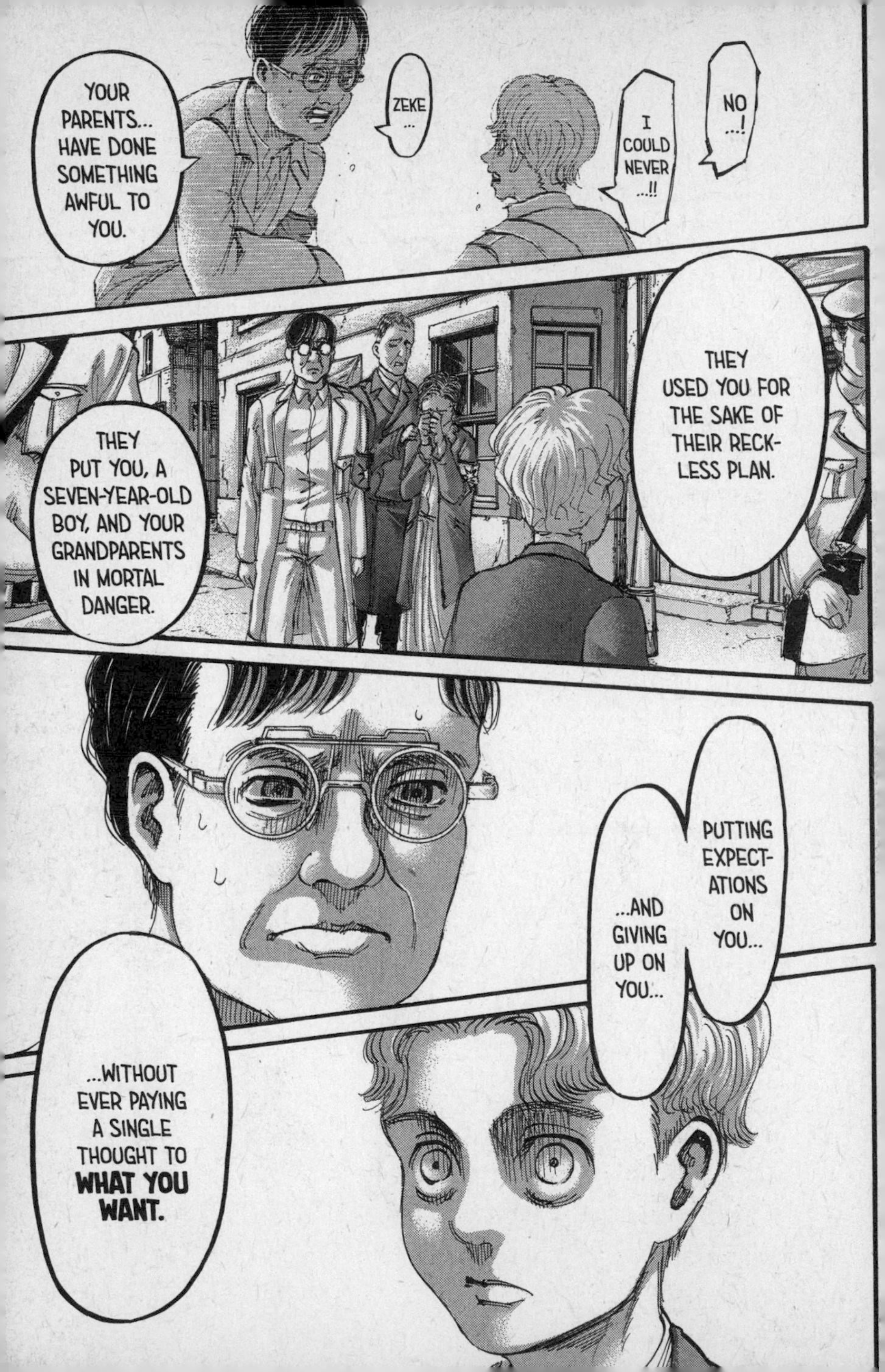
NO ...!
I COULD NEVER ...!!
ZEKE ...
YOUR PARENTS... HAVE DONE SOMETHING AWFUL TO YOU.
THEY USED YOU FOR THE SAKE OF THEIR RECKLESS PLAN.
THEY PUT YOU, A SEVEN-YEAR-OLD BOY, AND YOUR GRANDPARENTS IN MORTAL DANGER.
PUTTING EXPECTATIONS ON YOU...
...AND GIVING UP ON YOU...
...WITHOUT EVER PAYING A SINGLE THOUGHT TO **WHAT YOU WANT.**

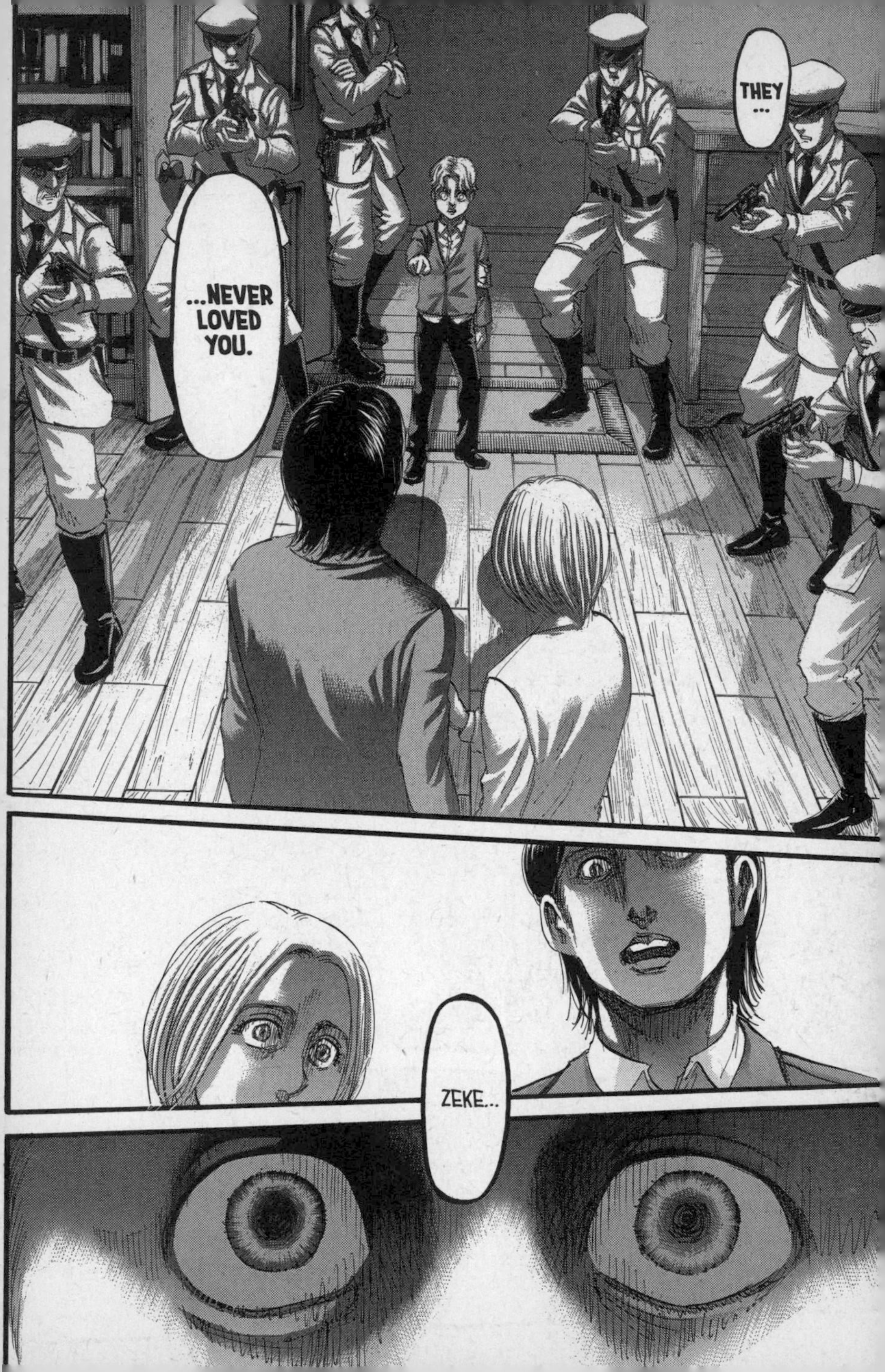
THEY ...
...NEVER LOVED YOU.
ZEKE...

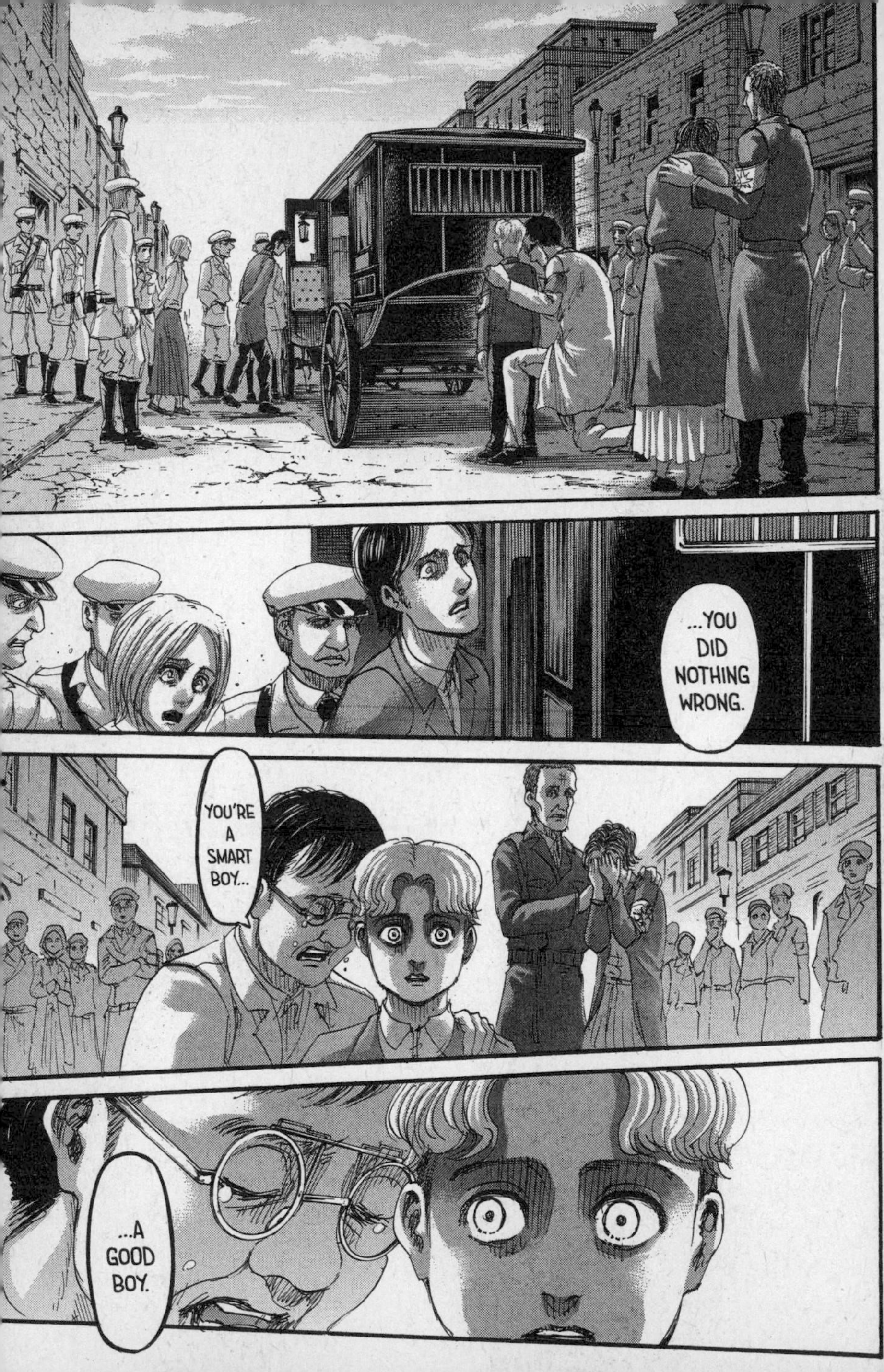
...YOU DID NOTHING WRONG.
YOU'RE A SMART BOY...
...A GOOD BOY.

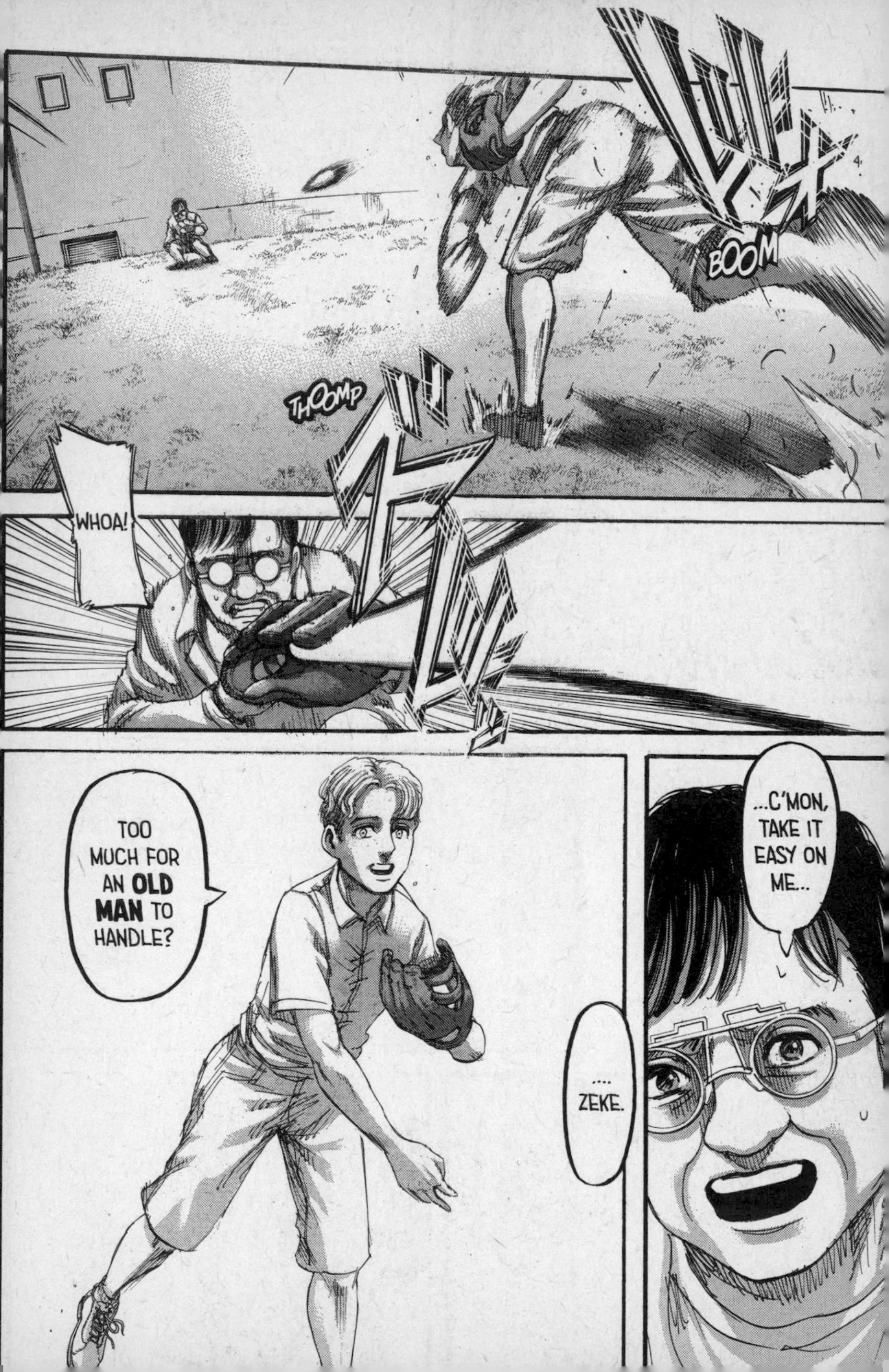
BOOM
THOOMP
WHOA!
...C'MON, TAKE IT EASY ON ME...
.... ZEKE.
TOO MUCH FOR AN OLD MAN TO HANDLE?

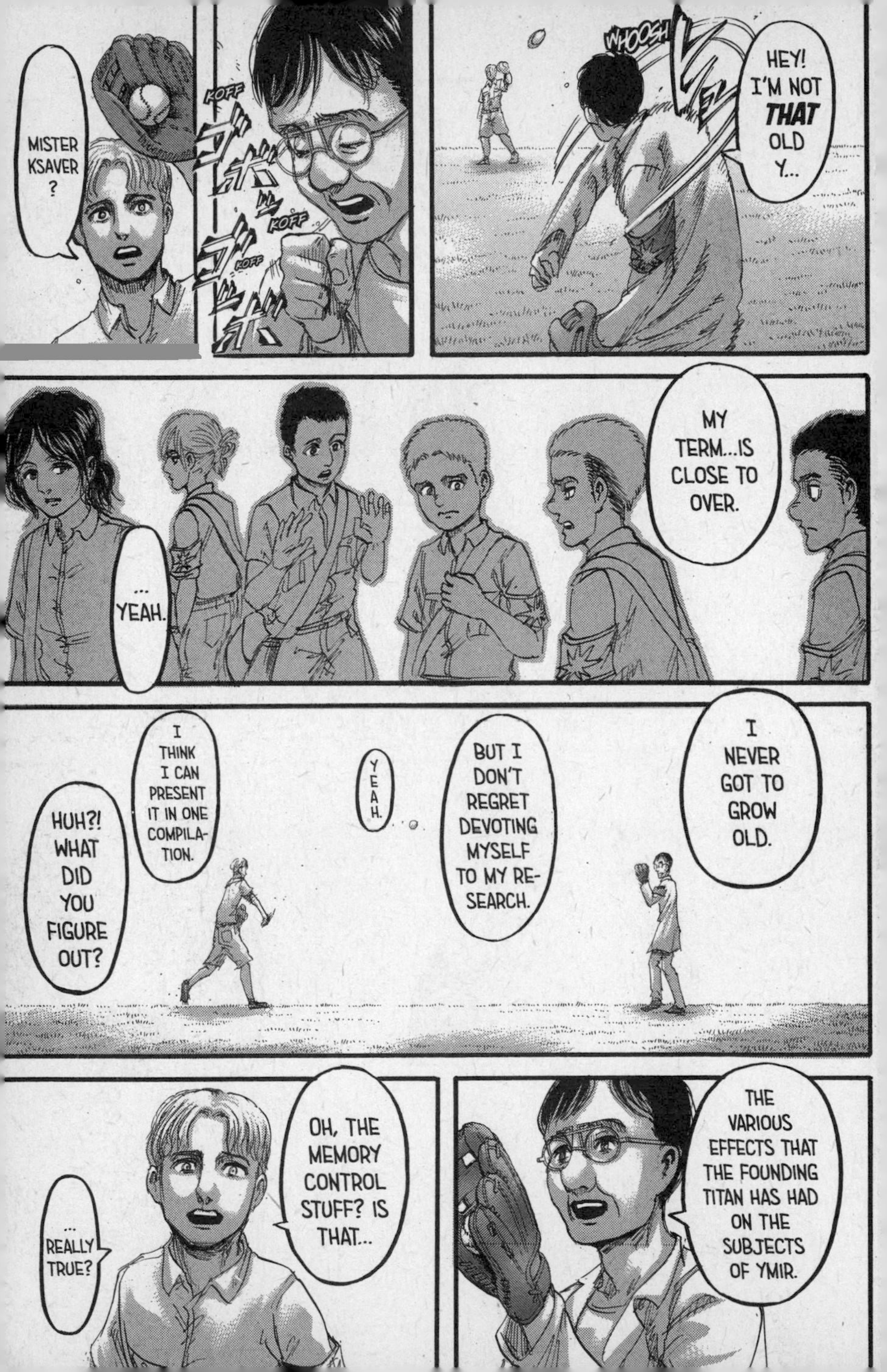
WHOOSH
HEY! I'M NOT THAT OLD Y...
KOFF
KOFF
KOFF
MISTER KSAVER?
MY TERM...IS CLOSE TO OVER.
... YEAH.
I NEVER GOT TO GROW OLD.
BUT I DON'T REGRET DEVOTING MYSELF TO MY RE-SEARCH.
YEAH.
I THINK I CAN PRESENT IT IN ONE COMPILA-TION.
HUH?! WHAT DID YOU FIGURE OUT?
THE VARIOUS EFFECTS THAT THE FOUNDING TITAN HAS HAD ON THE SUBJECTS OF YMIR.
OH, THE MEMORY CONTROL STUFF? IS THAT...
... REALLY TRUE?

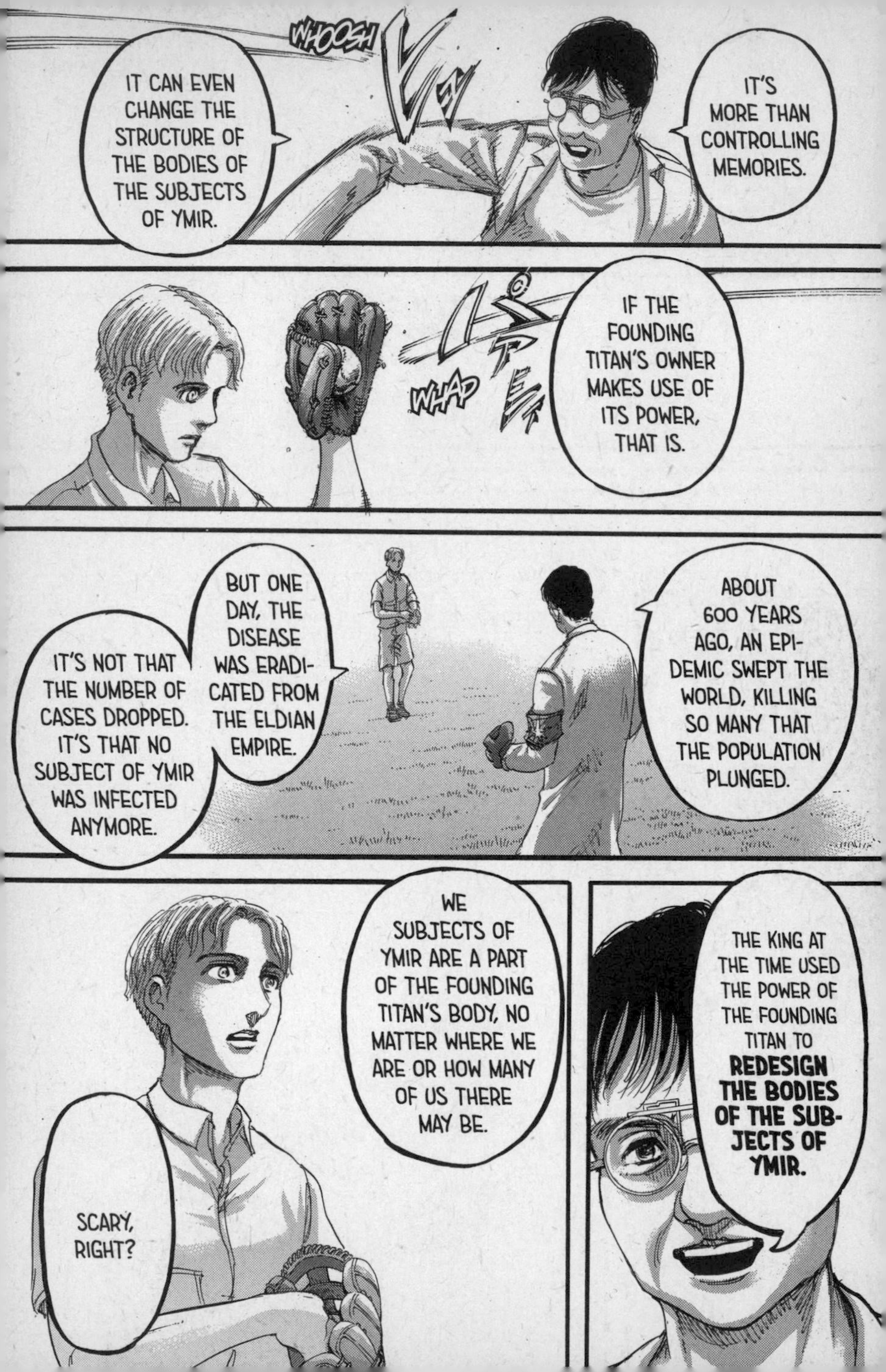
IT'S MORE THAN CONTROLLING MEMORIES.
WHOOSH
IT CAN EVEN CHANGE THE STRUCTURE OF THE BODIES OF THE SUBJECTS OF YMIR.
IF THE FOUNDING TITAN'S OWNER MAKES USE OF ITS POWER, THAT IS.
WHAP
ABOUT 600 YEARS AGO, AN EPIDEMIC SWEPT THE WORLD, KILLING SO MANY THAT THE POPULATION PLUNGED.
BUT ONE DAY, THE DISEASE WAS ERADICATED FROM THE ELDIAN EMPIRE.
IT'S NOT THAT THE NUMBER OF CASES DROPPED. IT'S THAT NO SUBJECT OF YMIR WAS INFECTED ANYMORE.
THE KING AT THE TIME USED THE POWER OF THE FOUNDING TITAN TO **REDESIGN THE BODIES OF THE SUBJECTS OF YMIR.**
WE SUBJECTS OF YMIR ARE A PART OF THE FOUNDING TITAN'S BODY, NO MATTER WHERE WE ARE OR HOW MANY OF US THERE MAY BE.
SCARY, RIGHT?

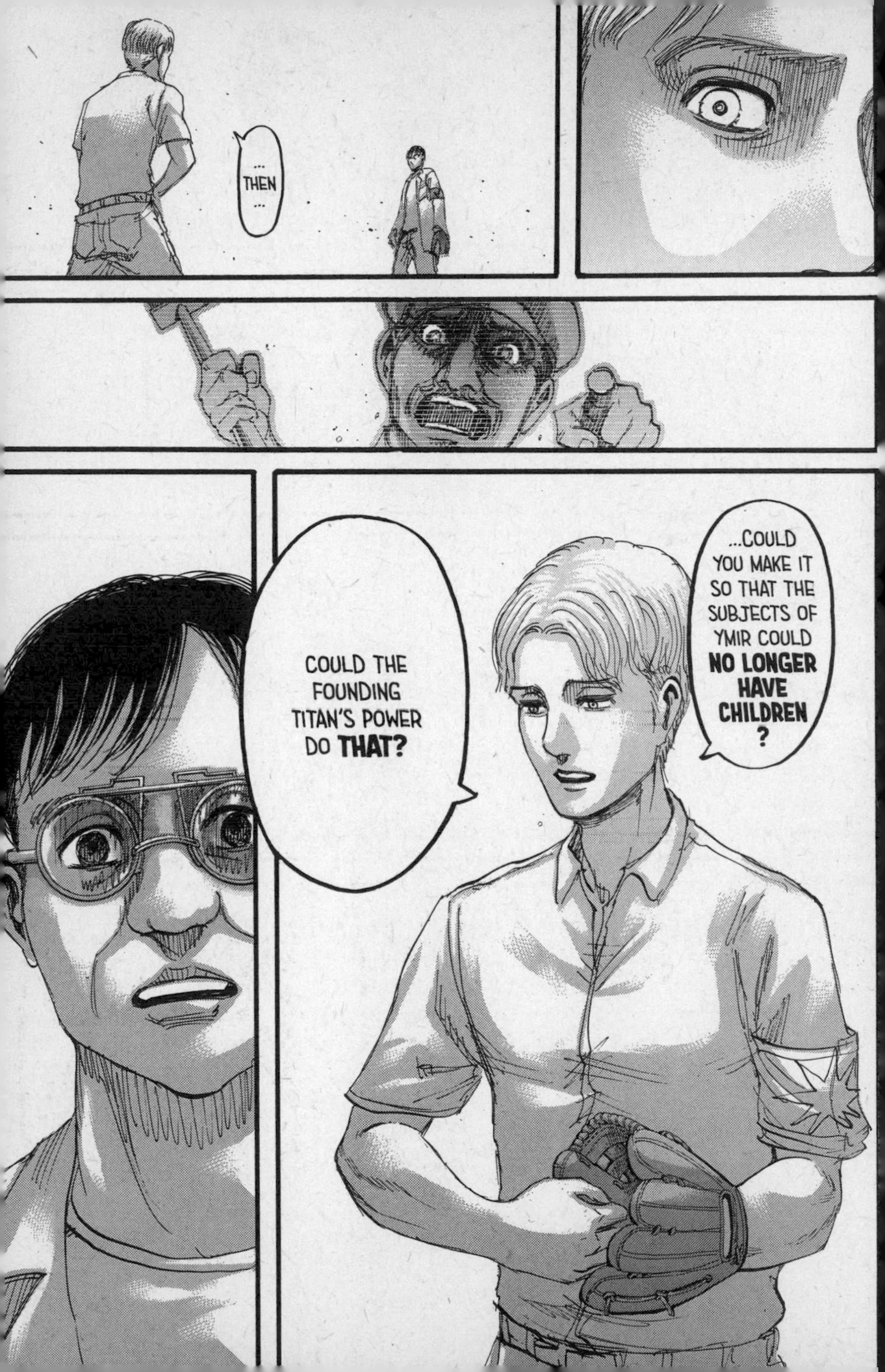

... THEN ...
...COULD YOU MAKE IT SO THAT THE SUBJECTS OF YMIR COULD **NO LONGER HAVE CHILDREN** ?
COULD THE FOUNDING TITAN'S POWER DO **THAT?**

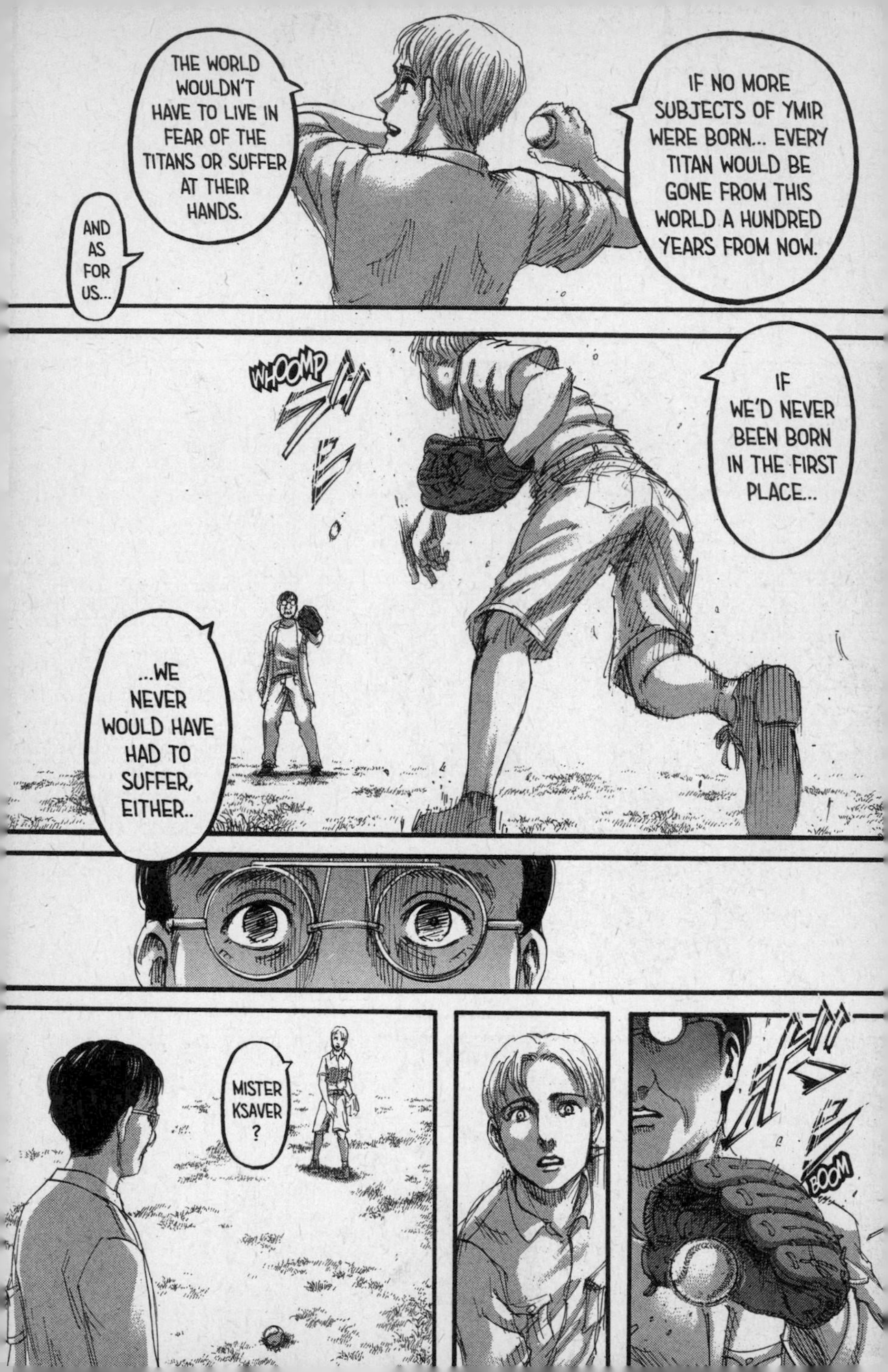
IF NO MORE SUBJECTS OF YMIR WERE BORN... EVERY TITAN WOULD BE GONE FROM THIS WORLD A HUNDRED YEARS FROM NOW.
THE WORLD WOULDN'T HAVE TO LIVE IN FEAR OF THE TITANS OR SUFFER AT THEIR HANDS.
AND AS FOR US...
IF WE'D NEVER BEEN BORN IN THE FIRST PLACE...
WHOOMP
...WE NEVER WOULD HAVE HAD TO SUFFER, EITHER..
BOOM
MISTER KSAVER ?

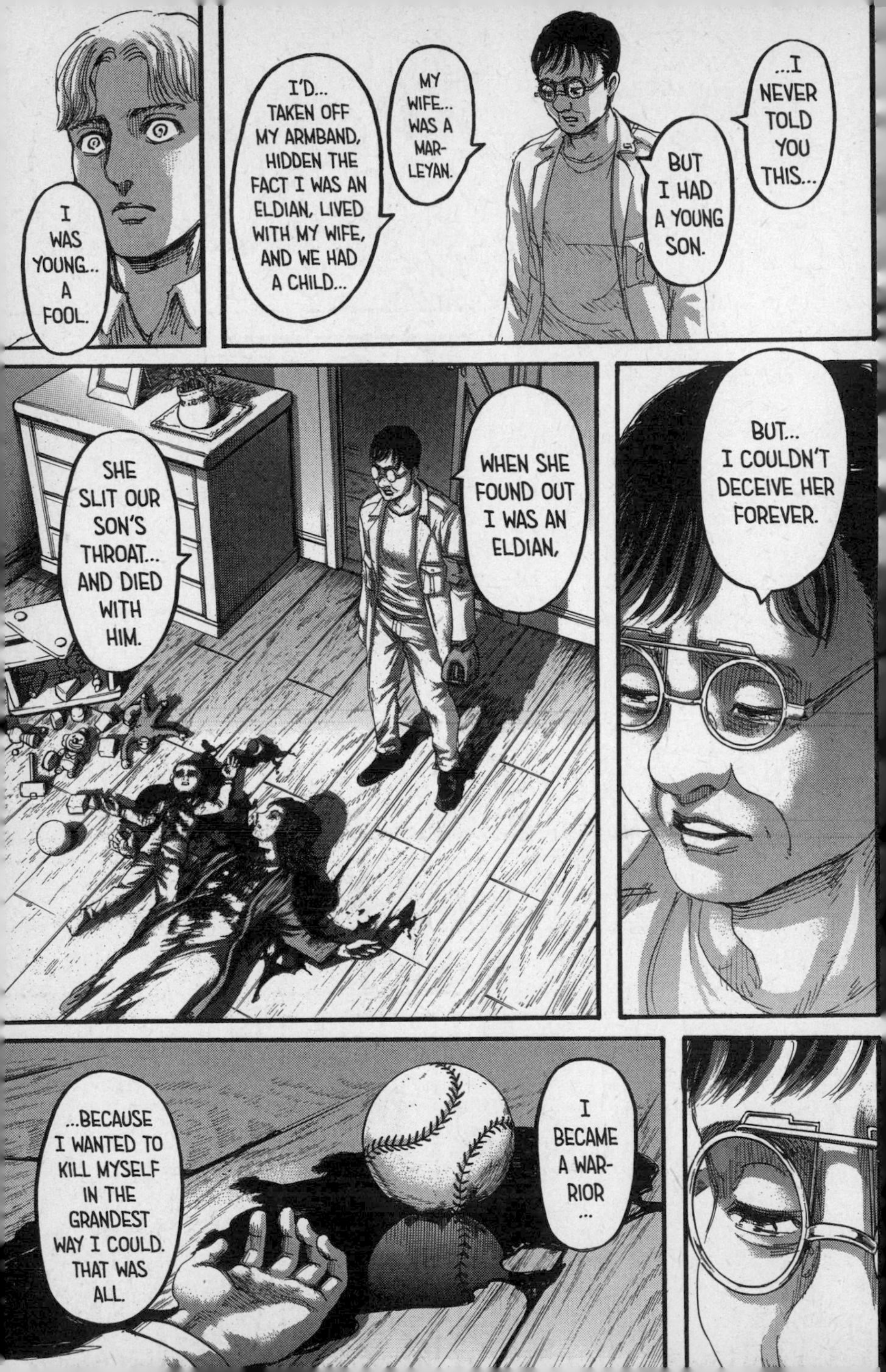
...I NEVER TOLD YOU THIS...
BUT I HAD A YOUNG SON.
MY WIFE... WAS A MAR-LEYAN.
I'D... TAKEN OFF MY ARMBAND, HIDDEN THE FACT I WAS AN ELDIAN, LIVED WITH MY WIFE, AND WE HAD A CHILD...
I WAS YOUNG... A FOOL.
BUT... I COULDN'T DECEIVE HER FOREVER.
WHEN SHE FOUND OUT I WAS AN ELDIAN,
SHE SLIT OUR SON'S THROAT... AND DIED WITH HIM.
I BECAME A WAR-RIOR...
...BECAUSE I WANTED TO KILL MYSELF IN THE GRANDEST WAY I COULD. THAT WAS ALL.

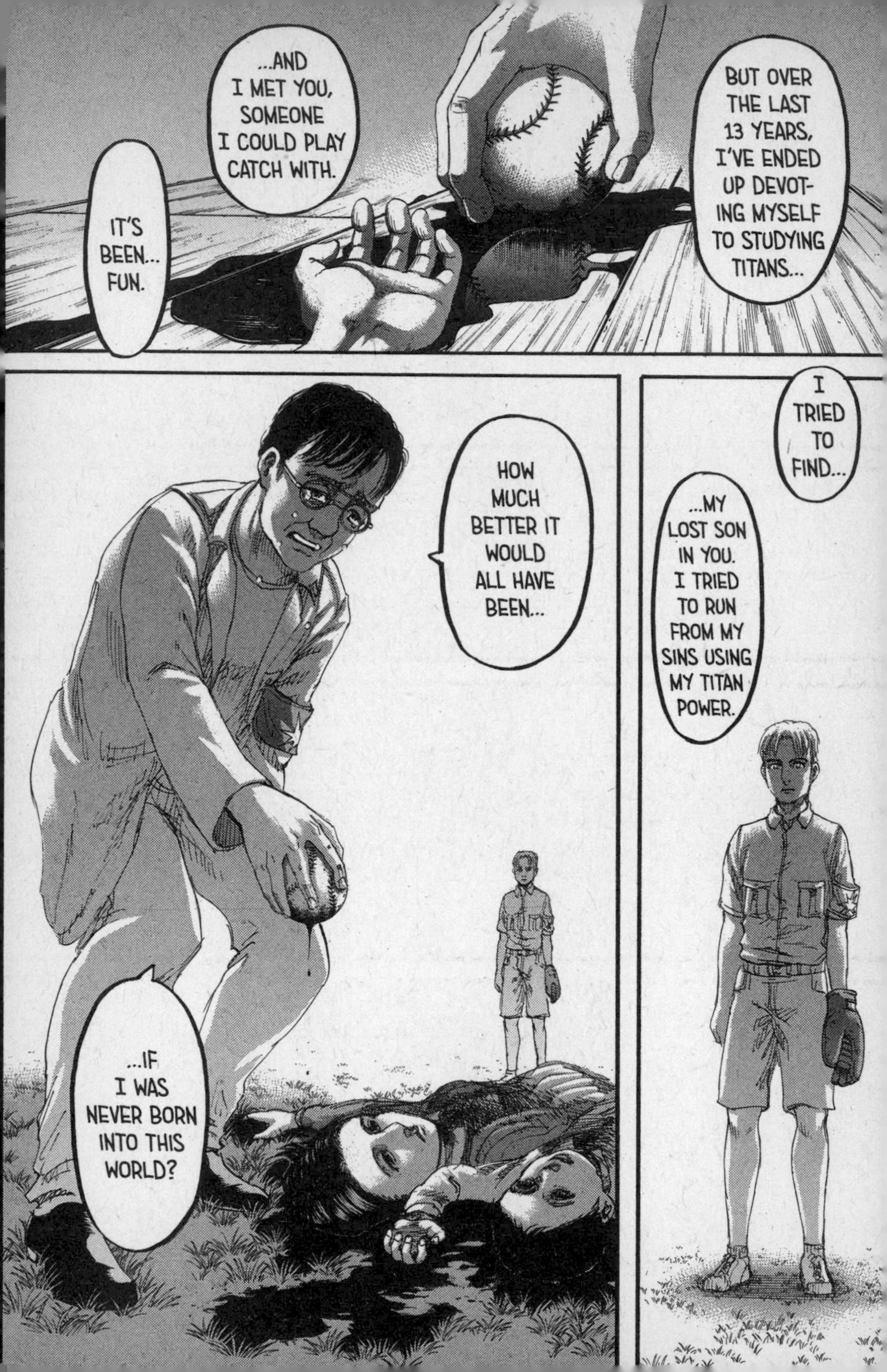
BUT OVER THE LAST 13 YEARS, I'VE ENDED UP DEVOTING MYSELF TO STUDYING TITANS...
...AND I MET YOU, SOMEONE I COULD PLAY CATCH WITH.
IT'S BEEN... FUN.
I TRIED TO FIND...
...MY LOST SON IN YOU. I TRIED TO RUN FROM MY SINS USING MY TITAN POWER.
HOW MUCH BETTER IT WOULD ALL HAVE BEEN...
...IF I WAS NEVER BORN INTO THIS WORLD?

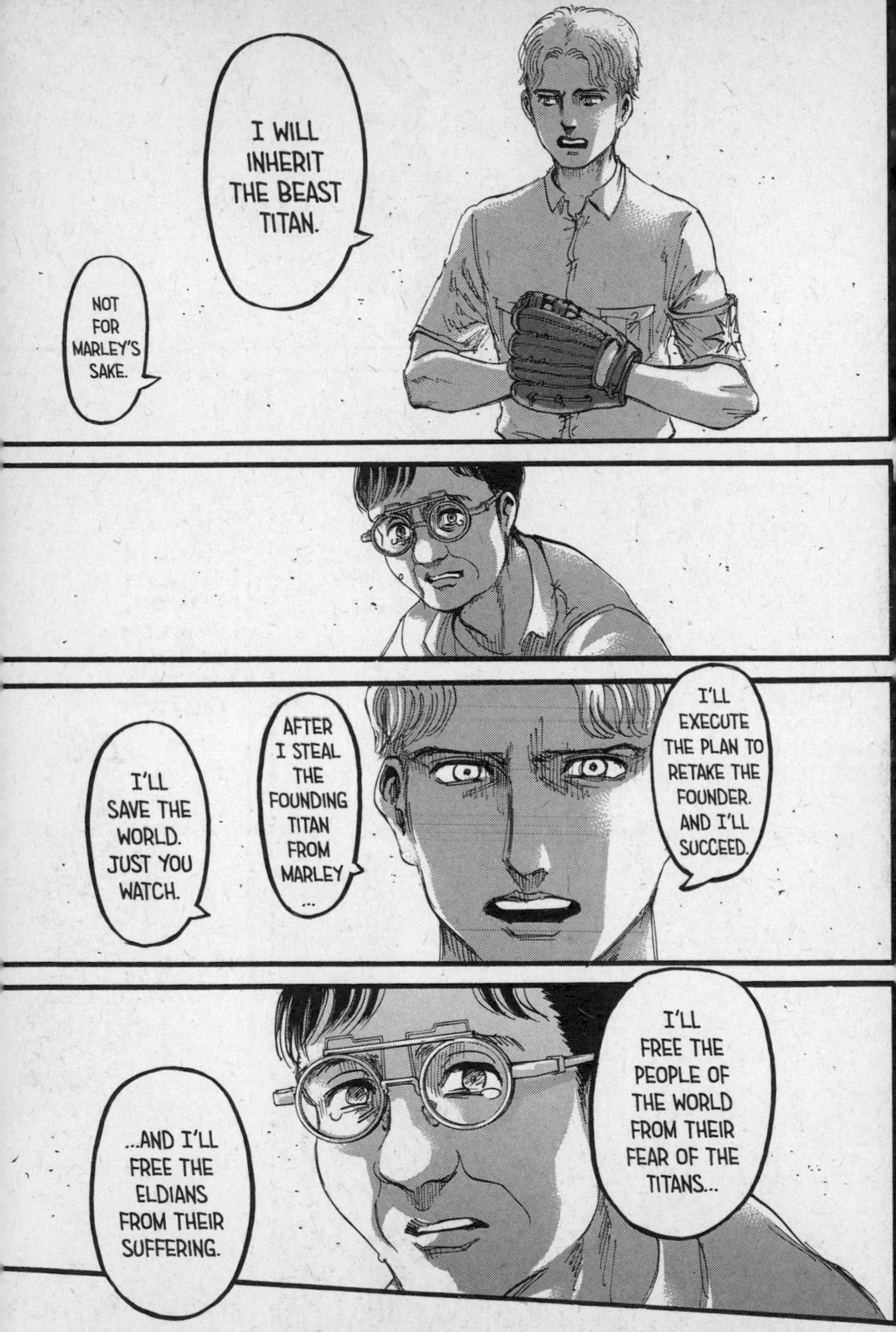
I WILL INHERIT THE BEAST TITAN.
NOT FOR MARLEY'S SAKE.
I'LL EXECUTE THE PLAN TO RETAKE THE FOUNDER. AND I'LL SUCCEED.
AFTER I STEAL THE FOUNDING TITAN FROM MARLEY ...
I'LL SAVE THE WORLD. JUST YOU WATCH.
I'LL FREE THE PEOPLE OF THE WORLD FROM THEIR FEAR OF THE TITANS...
...AND I'LL FREE THE ELDIANS FROM THEIR SUFFERING.

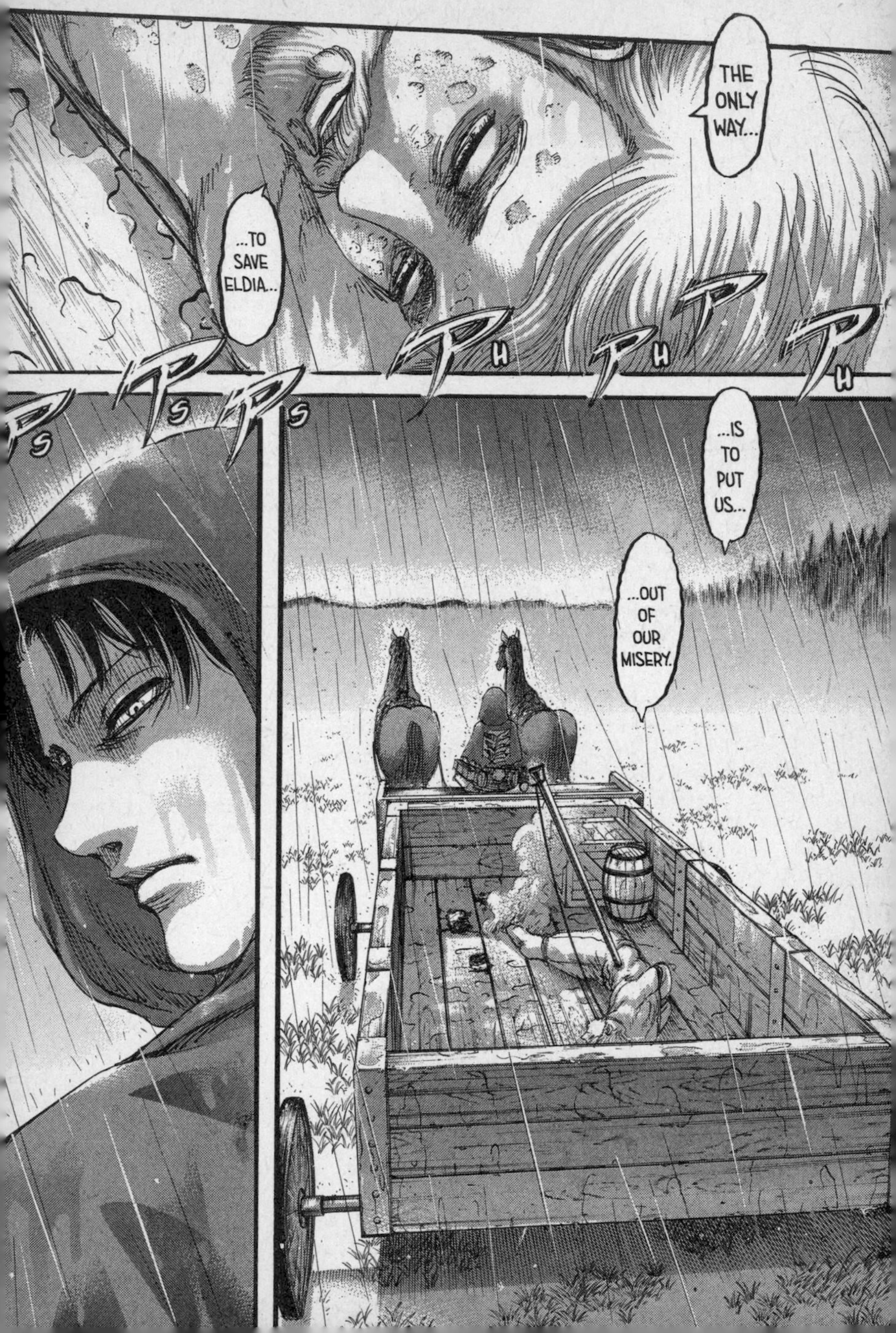
THE ONLY WAY...
...TO SAVE ELDIA...
...IS TO PUT US...
...OUT OF OUR MISERY.

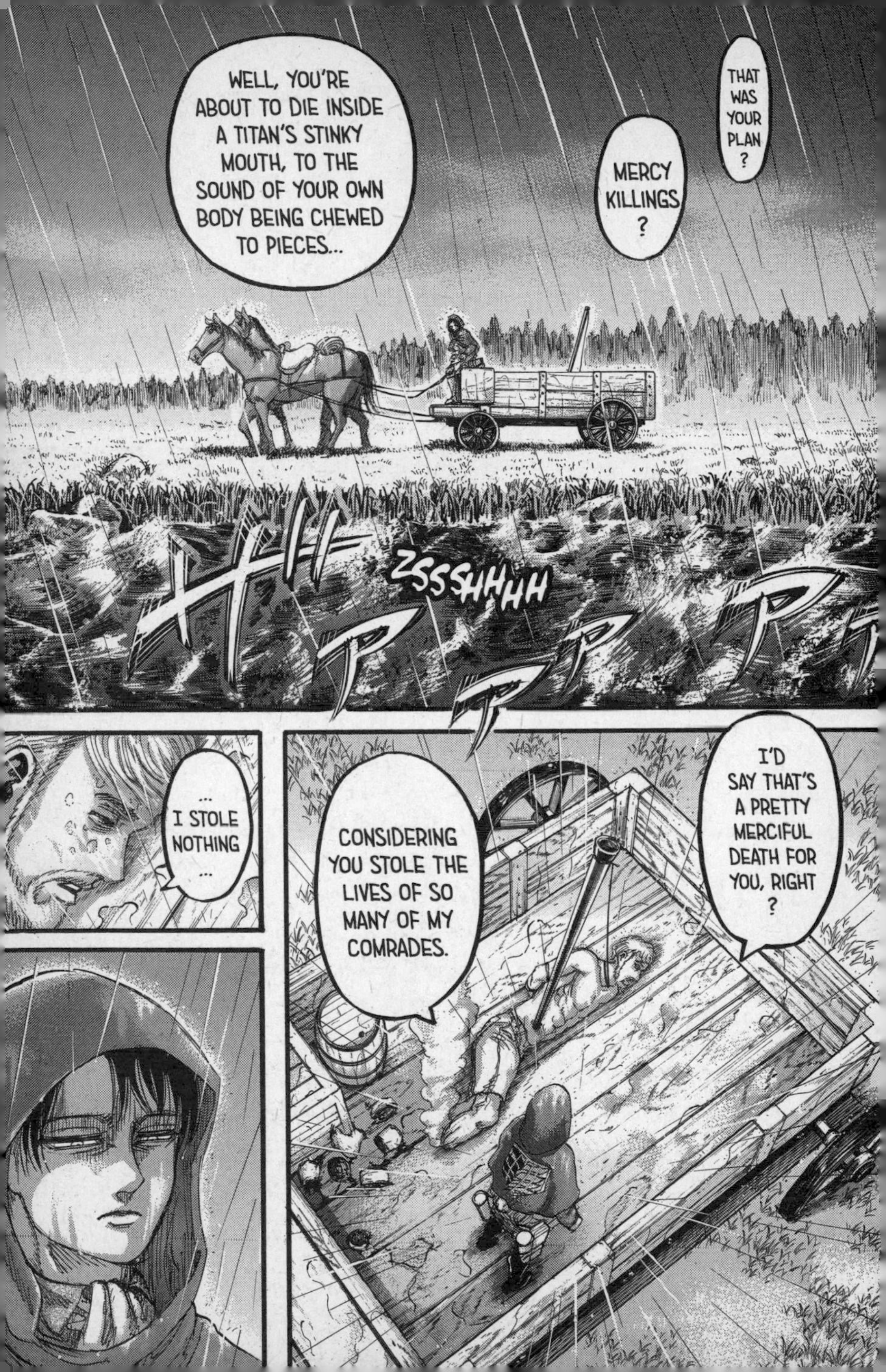
THAT WAS YOUR PLAN?
MERCY KILLINGS?
WELL, YOU'RE ABOUT TO DIE INSIDE A TITAN'S STINKY MOUTH, TO THE SOUND OF YOUR OWN BODY BEING CHEWED TO PIECES...
ZSSSHHHH
I'D SAY THAT'S A PRETTY MERCIFUL DEATH FOR YOU, RIGHT?
CONSIDERING YOU STOLE THE LIVES OF SO MANY OF MY COMRADES.
... I STOLE NOTHING ...

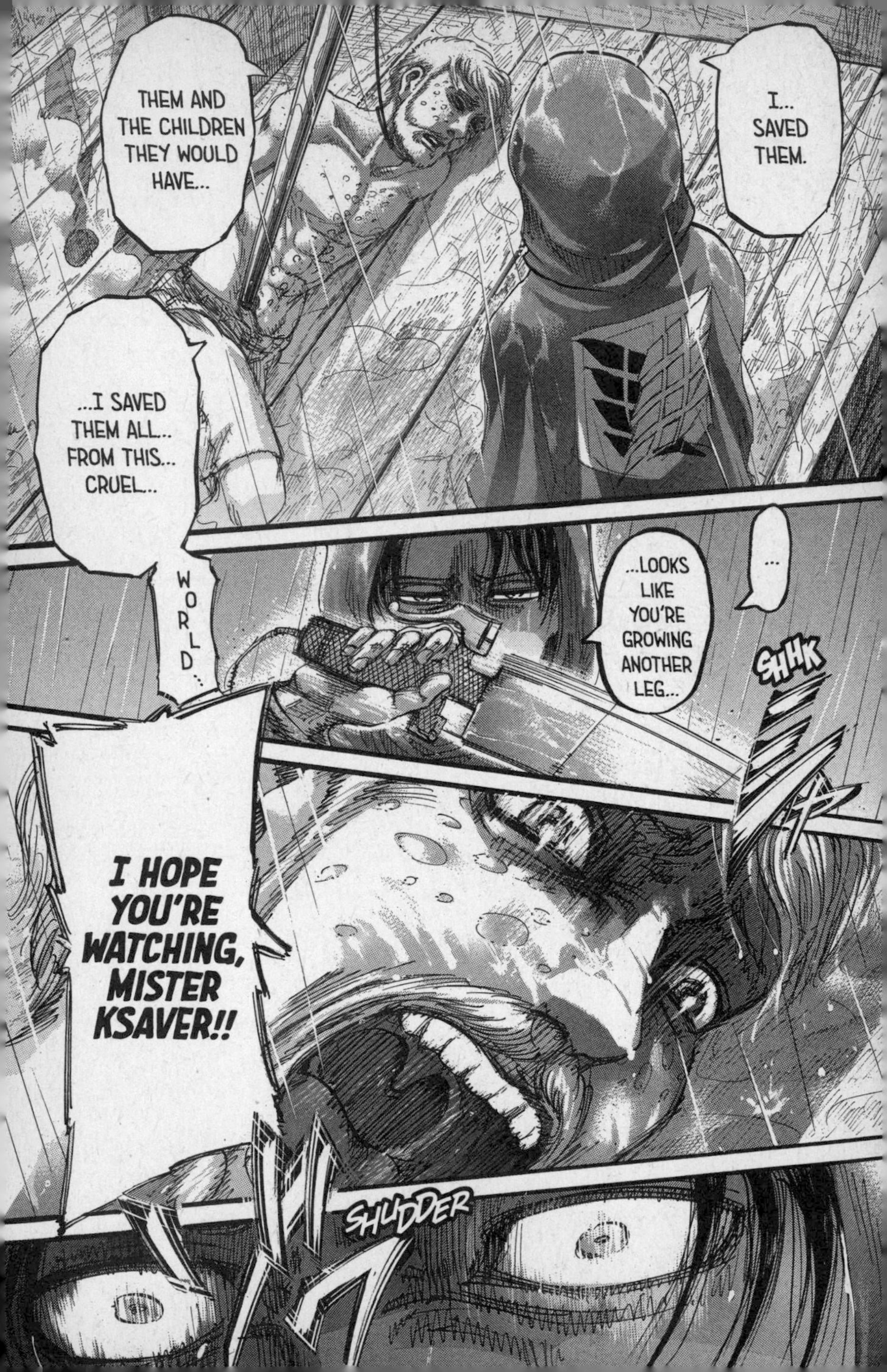
I... SAVED THEM.
THEM AND THE CHILDREN THEY WOULD HAVE...
...I SAVED THEM ALL... FROM THIS... CRUEL...
WORLD...
...
...LOOKS LIKE YOU'RE GROWING ANOTHER LEG...
SHHK
I HOPE YOU'RE WATCHING, MISTER KSAVER!!
SHUDDER

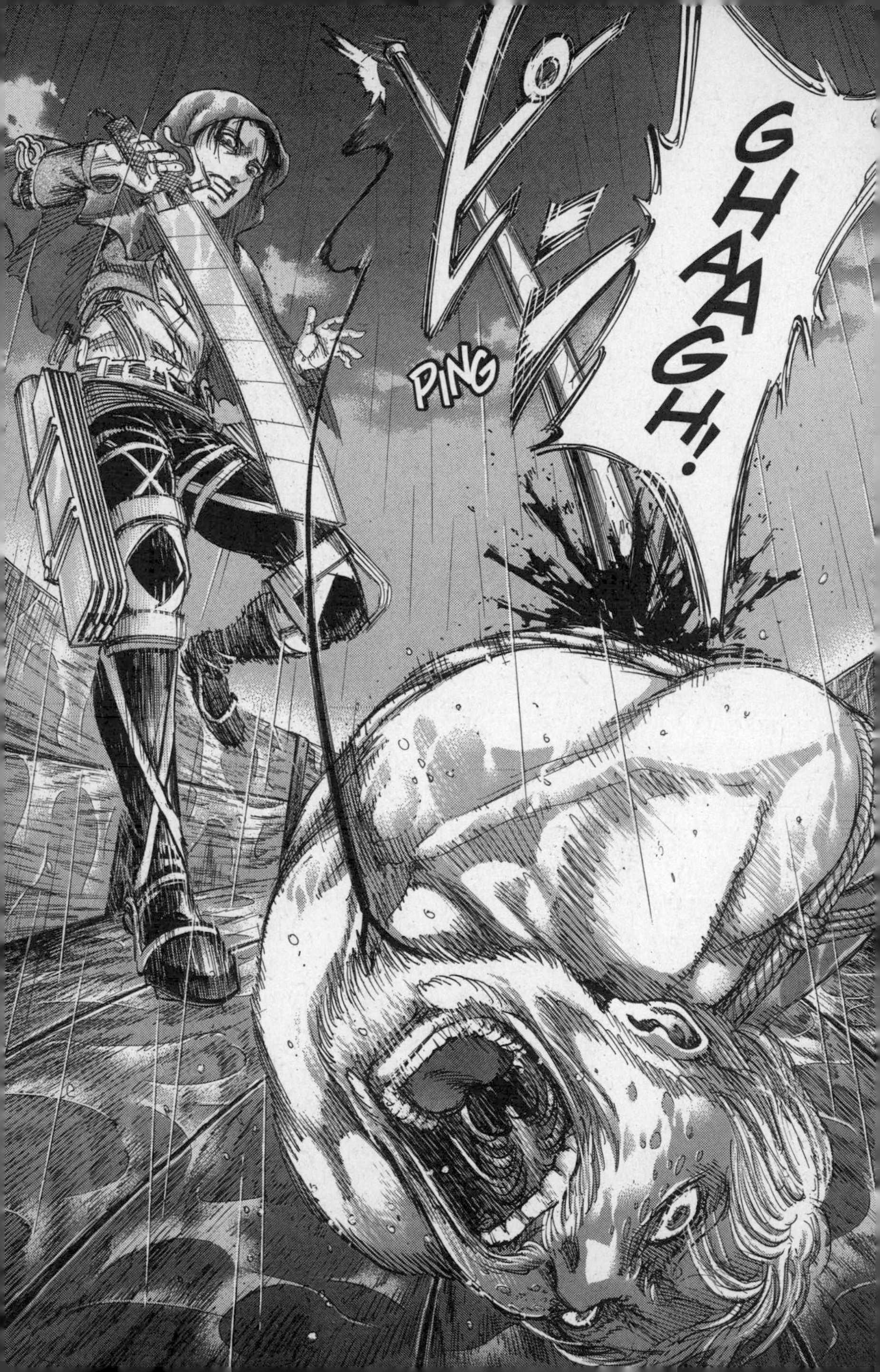
GHAAAGH!
PING

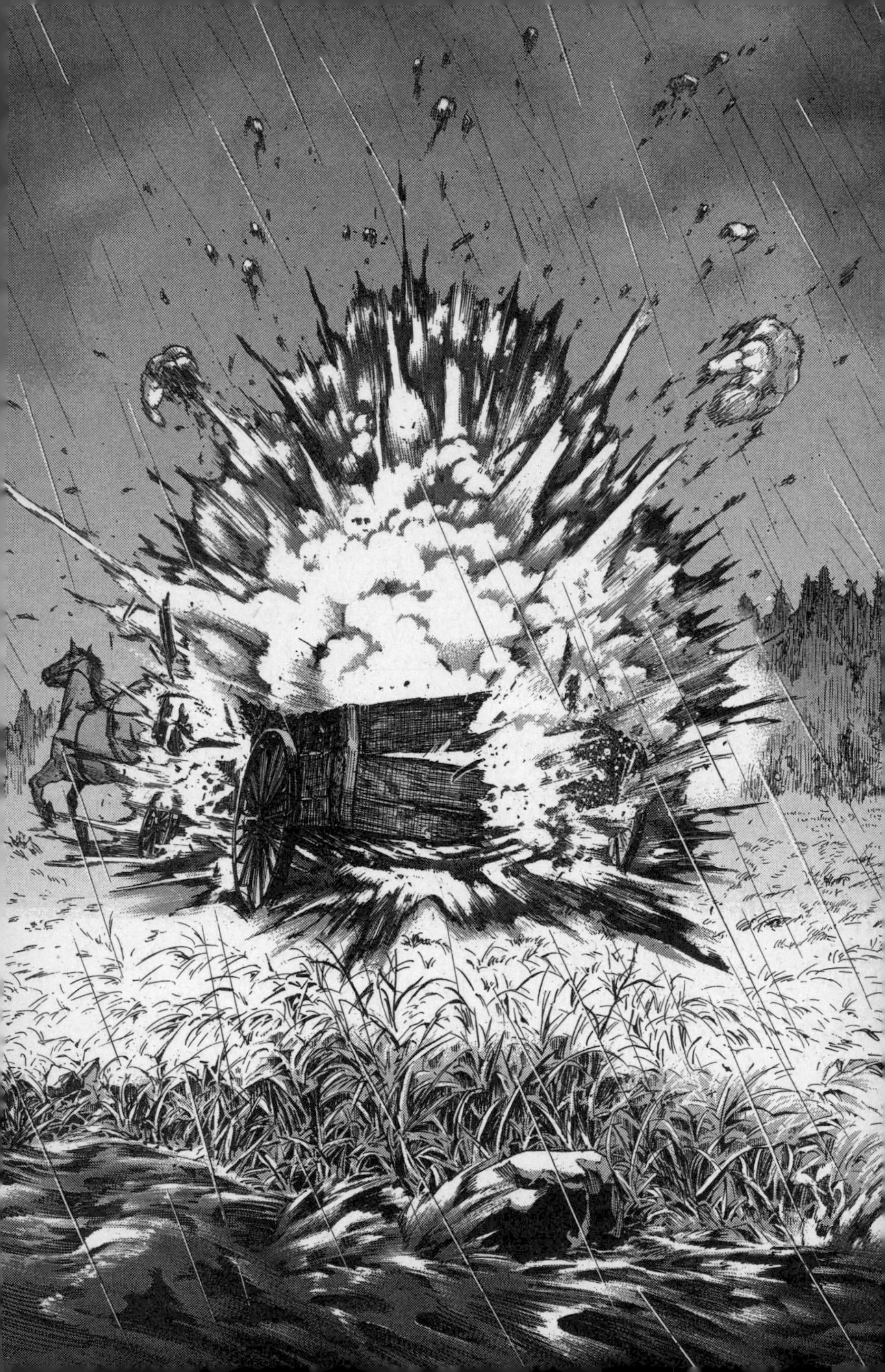

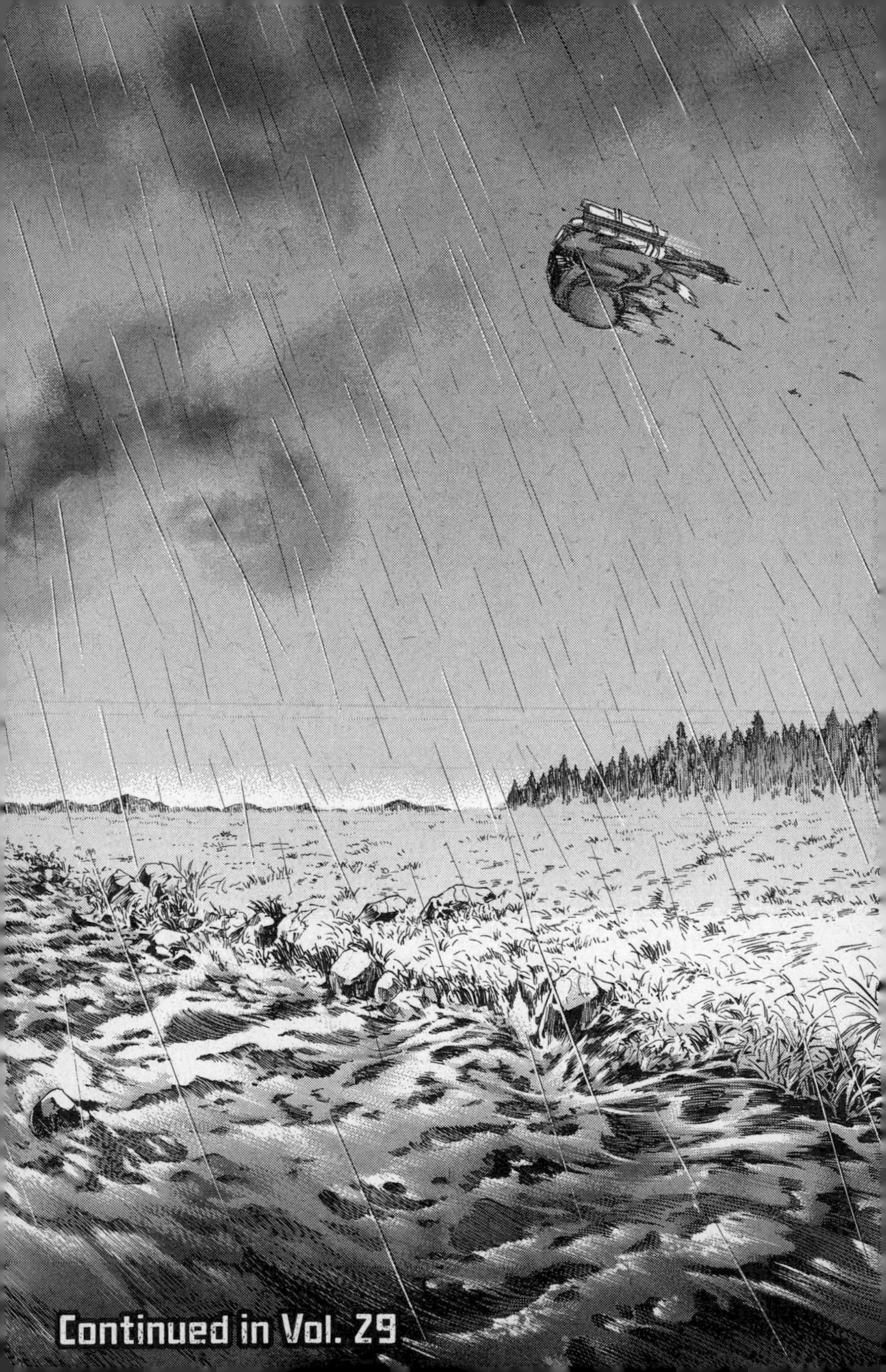
Continued in Vol. 29

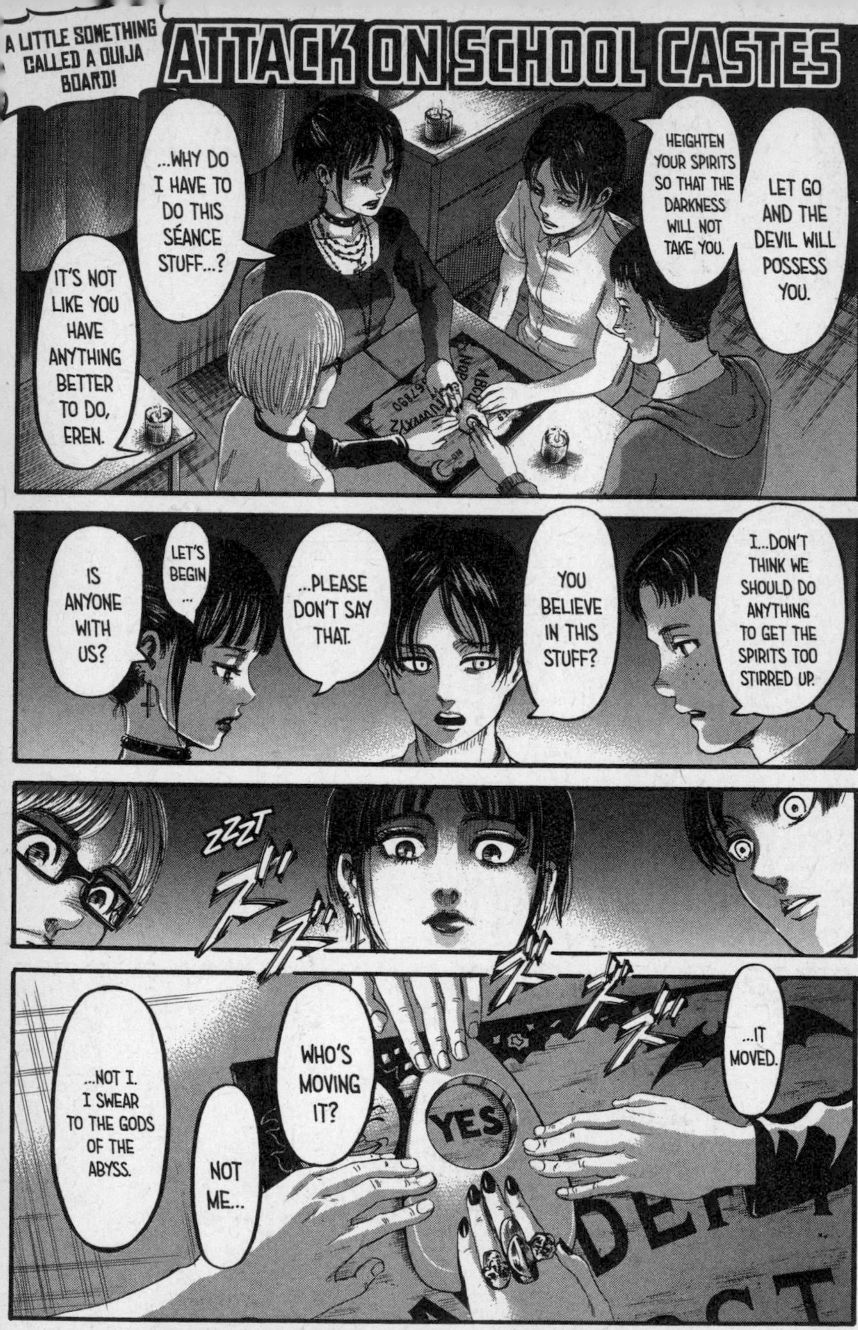
ATTACK ON SCHOOL CASTES
A LITTLE SOMETHING CALLED A OUIJA BOARD!
LET GO AND THE DEVIL WILL POSSESS YOU.
HEIGHTEN YOUR SPIRITS SO THAT THE DARKNESS WILL NOT TAKE YOU.
...WHY DO I HAVE TO DO THIS SÉANCE STUFF...?
IT'S NOT LIKE YOU HAVE ANYTHING BETTER TO DO, EREN.
I...DON'T THINK WE SHOULD DO ANYTHING TO GET THE SPIRITS TOO STIRRED UP.
YOU BELIEVE IN THIS STUFF?
...PLEASE DON'T SAY THAT.
LET'S BEGIN...
IS ANYONE WITH US?
ZZZT
...IT MOVED.
YES
WHO'S MOVING IT?
NOT ME...
...NOT I. I SWEAR TO THE GODS OF THE ABYSS.

COMING SOON

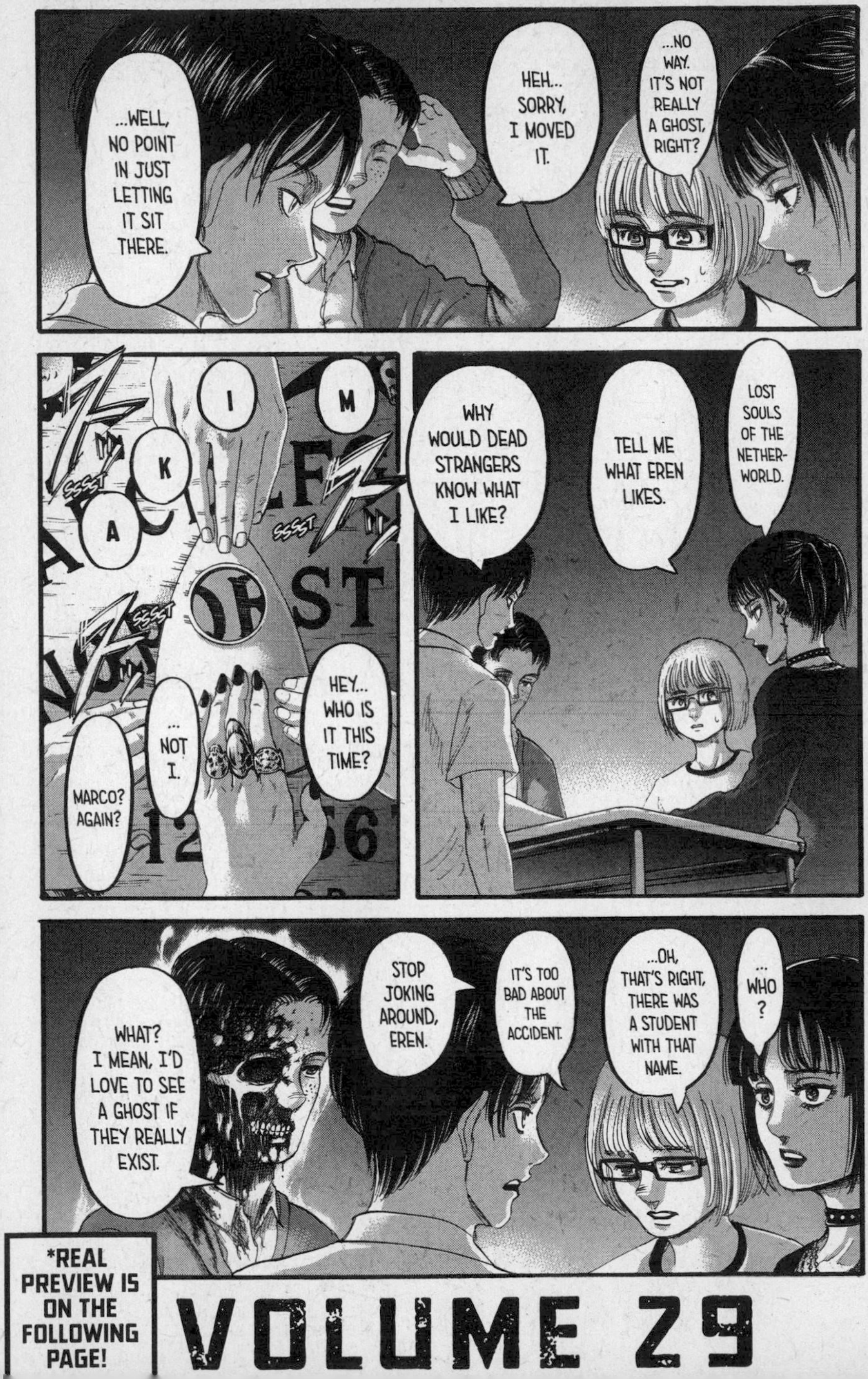
...NO WAY. IT'S NOT REALLY A GHOST, RIGHT?
HEH... SORRY, I MOVED IT.
...WELL, NO POINT IN JUST LETTING IT SIT THERE.
LOST SOULS OF THE NETHER-WORLD.
TELL ME WHAT EREN LIKES.
WHY WOULD DEAD STRANGERS KNOW WHAT I LIKE?
M
I
K
A
SSSST
SSSST
SSSST
HEY... WHO IS IT THIS TIME?
... NOT I.
MARCO? AGAIN?
... WHO ?
...OH, THAT'S RIGHT, THERE WAS A STUDENT WITH THAT NAME.
IT'S TOO BAD ABOUT THE ACCIDENT.
STOP JOKING AROUND, EREN.
WHAT? I MEAN, I'D LOVE TO SEE A GHOST IF THEY REALLY EXIST.
*REAL PREVIEW IS ON THE FOLLOWING PAGE!
VOLUME 29

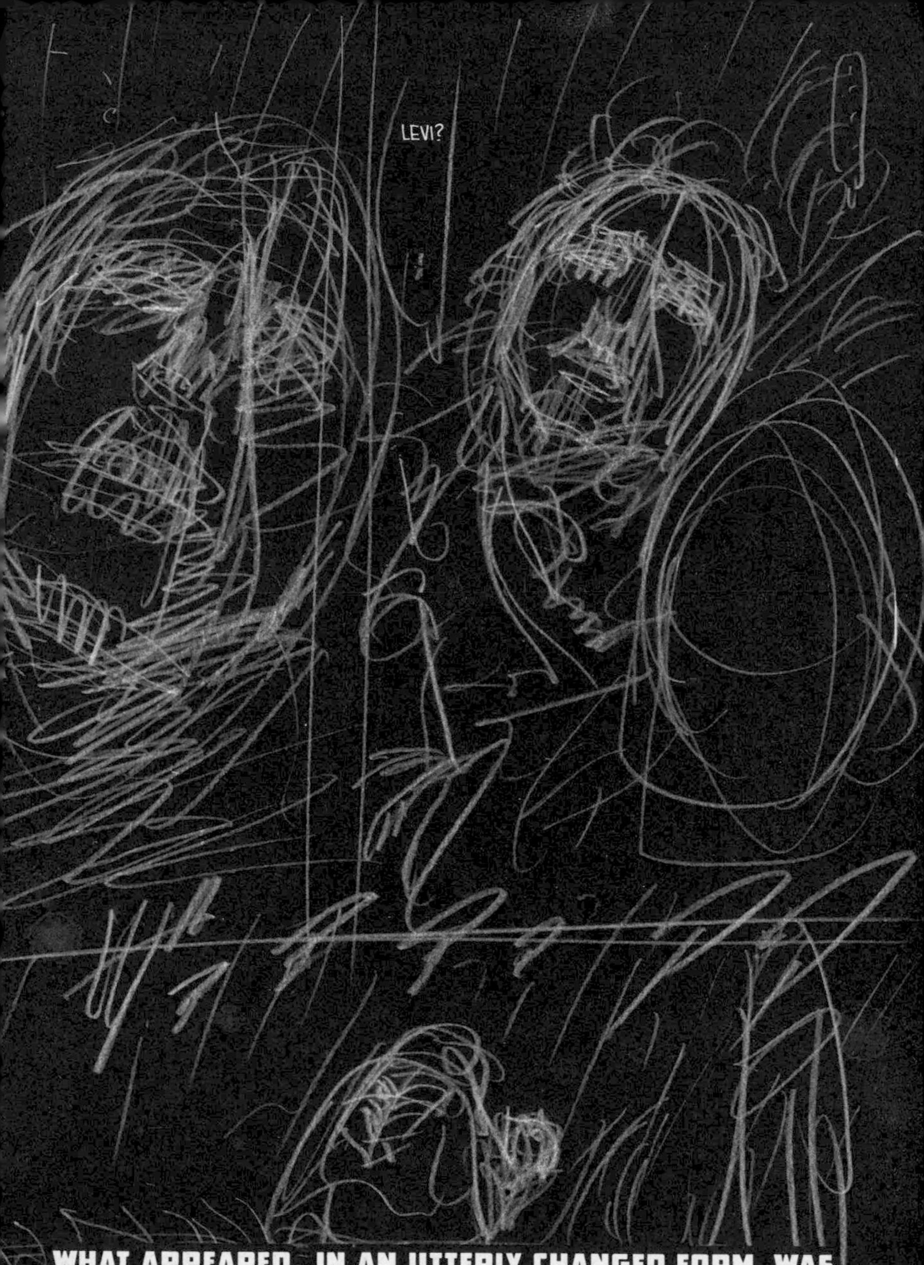
LEVI?

WHAT APPEARED...IN AN UTTERLY CHANGED FORM, WAS "THE STRONGEST." THE DARKNESS WITH NO END IN SIGHT CONTINUES...

VOLUME 29 COMING 2019

A Kodansha Comics Trade Paperback Original
Attack on Titan 28 copyright © 2019 Hajime Isayama
English translation copyright © 2019 Hajime Isayama

Published in the United States by Kodansha Comics, an imprint of
Kodansha USA Publishing, LLC, New York.

Publication rights for this English edition arranged through
Kodansha Ltd, Tokyo.

First published in Japan in 2019 by Kodansha Ltd., Tokyo
as *Shingeki no kyojin*, volume 28.

ISBN 978-1-63236-783-9

Original cover design by Takashi Shimoyama (Red Rooster)

Printed in the United States of America.

www.kodanshacomics.com

9 8 7 6 5 4 3 2 1
Translation: Ko Ransom
Lettering: Dezi Sienty
Editing: Haruko Hashimoto
Kodansha Comics edition cover design by Phil Balsman